After Diana

After Diana

Irreverent Elegies

edited by
MANDY MERCK

VERSO

London • New York

First published by **VERSO** 1998
© the contributors
All rights reserved

Ross McKibbin's piece first appeared in the *London Review of Books*, October 2, 1997
Judith Williamson's in the *Guardian Weekend*, September 13, 1997
Alexander Cockburn's in *The Nation*, September 3, 1997
Peter Ghosh's in the *London Review of Books*, October 16, 1997
Christopher Hitchens' in *Vanity Fair*, December 1997
Jean Baudrillard's lyric in *Diana Crash* (edited by Francoise Gaillard), Descartes et cie, Paris, 1998
Mark Cousin's in the *Harvard Design Magazine*, Winter-Spring 1998
Homi K. Bhabha's in *Artforum*, December 1997
Elizabeth Wilson's in *New Left Review*, November-December 1997
Régis Debray's in *Diana Crash*; Francoise Gaillard's in *Diana Crash*
Christopher Hird's in *Index on Censorship*, November–December 1997
Marc Augé's in *Diana Crash* (edited by Francoise Gaillard), Descartes et cie, Paris, 1998
Francis Wheen's in the *Guardian,* March 11, 1998
Tom Nairn's in the *London Review of Books*, October 30, 1997
Articles translated from the French by John Howe

VERSO
UK: 6 Meard Street, London W1V 3HR
USA: 180 Varick Street, New York, NY 10014-4606

VERSO is the imprint of New Left Books

British Library Cataloguing in Publication Data
A catalogue record for this book is available from the British Library

Library of Congress Cataloging-in-Publication Data
A catalog record for this book is available from the Library of Congress

ISBN 1-85984-265-8

Design by **POLLEN**, New York, New York
Printed and bound by R.R. Donnelley & Sons, Virginia, USA.

CONTENTS

introduction

AFTER DIANA

mandy merck

fter Pillar 13 at Pont de l'Alma; after the People's Princess; after the flowers and the cellophane; after the conspiracy theories on the Net; after the New Compassion; after 'Candles in the Wind' and 'Sandals in the Bin' (for Mother Teresa); after Earl Spencer *contra* the tabloids and the 'tacky' Diana Fund; after Earl Spencer *pro* the Althorp Diana Museum, the Althorp memorial pop concert and the £9.50 gravesite tours; after Dodi's secret love child; after Harry met the Spice Girls; after the Palace advertised for a 'top-class communications director'; after the bodyguard's book deal; after the Diana scratchcards; after the New Disillusion; after the backlash against sentimentality; after the backlash against the backlash . . . comes this collection, whose title is itself 'after'—in citation of—the frequent use of the phrase in the British media in the days since August 31, 1997.

Whatever the meaning of that road accident and its aftermath, one notable reaction has been a rampant sense of futurity. Of course, this penchant for periodization is a major impulse of the press, for whom every anniversary is a story, who endlessly attempt to commemorate years, decades, centuries and now—an interval so vast that it seems oddly underwhelming—the millennium. And where the press keeps time, academia cannot be far behind, posting its designations of past and present, change and significance, across chronology. In Britain in 1997, this sense of transformation was heightened by two events, only four months apart—the election of a Labour government for the first time in 23 years and the response to the death of the Princess of Wales.

If the true extent of public engagement with both occasions was debatable (Labour, despite its large majority of MPs, was only elected with 45 percent of the vote, and many argue that the mourning was far less extensive than originally supposed), that of the pundits was overwhelming. One might doubt the descriptions of the 'mass outpouring of grief', but the mass outpouring of opinion was irrefutable. After the saturation media coverage came an even larger effusion of opinion elsewhere. Throughout the universities, conferences were convened, seminars scheduled and special issues of journals commissioned. At the Freud Museum, analysts gathered to discuss mourning and melancholia in memory of Diana. In the churches, clerics declared the public response to her death 'the most important spiritual event of the past 25 years' and duly summoned the faithful to sundry convocations dedicated to pondering the meaning of it all. As the brochure for one of these ('Death of a Princess—Postmodern Spirituality and the Gospel') asked, 'Was or is God saying anything to us through all this? Is there a new atmosphere among people in this nation?'

The portentousness of this inquiry was characteristic of the general punditry of autumn '97. If a Sunday *Observer* panel of September 14 failed to channel the Almighty in its survey of the state of the nation A.D., it wasn't for want of faith. Under the slogan 'New Britain', the paper's editor, Will Hutton, enthused about the Dianafication of the country with a group ranging from sociologist Stuart Hall through novelist A.L. Kennedy to psychotherapist-by-royal-appointment Susie Orbach. Despite Hall's measured scepticism ('I don't feel the radicalism. I'm uncertain whether it will have any effect.'), his co-discussants hailed the responses to Diana's death as evidence of Britain's newfound 'emotional maturity' (Kennedy); 'freeing ourselves from the reins of the past' (Hutton); 'growing up as a nation' (Orbach).

The *Observer* is Britain's most leftward Sunday, and often quite sensible, but its sort of exaggeration was evident across the liberal-left. A number of feminist commentators fell over themselves to indict other feminists who, in failing to celebrate the Floral Revolution, were not only denying that the personal was political but cosying up to 'those frozen sticks of fossilised shit that are the Court which branded Diana hysterical and mad' (Linda Grant in the *Guardian*) or pandering to 'a patriarchy gone dry-eyed and stiff' (Elaine Showalter in same). Meanwhile in the *New Statesman*, under an 'After Diana' crosshead, Darcus Howe saluted 'this huge movement of British people' which 'removed the veil to expose the new Britain':

> In the recent general election we failed to identify the massive shift in public feeling. We were all left shell-shocked at the uninhibited rejection of the Conservative Party. We swallowed and lived by the myths of how British people were: conservative, gradualistic, instinctively right-wing, the morals of middle England . . . We may add, royalist. And racist to the core. We were monumentally wrong. . . .

Not quite all the press responded to the *évenements* of autumn in this spirit. The satirical magazine *Private Eye* had a field day with the hacks' hypocrisy, quoting the most hilarious encomia to the Princess under subheadings labelled 'Clichés Galore' and 'Statements of the Obvious'. Among the most telling of these citations was another from the *Observer*, this item from 'Mrs. Blair's Diary' (which is, I should stress in case she is tempted to sue, a wholly fictional column):

> Diana has said publicly that the Tories were hopeless . . .
> It always slightly amazes me how the press picks up on stuff like this as if it were compelling genius insight of Aristotelian wisdom and Shavian wit, as opposed to the witterings of a woman who, if her IQ were five points lower, would have to be watered daily.

Unfortunately for the *Observer*, this indictment appeared on August 31, the morning after, among a large number of pre-crash press remarks on the unseemliness of the Dodi-Di affair that *Private Eye* also reprinted. (Strangely, this edition of the *Eye* disappeared on the first day of publication, withdrawn by censorious distributors in a fit of fealty to the deceased Princess and their customers, who were dutifully displaying their newfound maturity in the New Britain.)

But was there a New Britain, unveiled, incited or otherwise manifested by the responses to Diana's death? By the end of the year, many of the soothsayers who'd four months earlier revived Raymond Williams to hail the country's new 'structure of feeling' were rather less optimistic. As the government used its enormous majority to crush resistance to its cuts in single-parent benefits, the hopes which had greeted its unprecedented victory in May disappeared. Indeed, that majority looked likely to consign parliamentary opposition on the left to samizdat protests or the occasional resignation. While Labour appeared more and more susceptible to the blandishments of big business in regard to tobacco advertising, media monopolies, trade union rights and the minimum wage, as it installed a number of sullied entrepreneurs in the upper echelons of its government, the newly compassionate nation speedily saw off a group of East European refugees unwise enough to turn up at Dover in pursuit of political asylum.

To be fair, a minority, in the press and elsewhere, predicted this from the start. As occasional warning notes were sounded about the bouquet-bearing mourners treating panhandlers in the tube just like they had in the Old Britain, Desmond Christy observed in the September 12 *Guardian* that Diana's

> funeral becomes a part of a dialectic between tradi-
> tion and modernisation, between the old and numi-
> nously New, between old Conservatism and New
> Conservatism (ie, Labour), between those who think
> (don't trust them!) and those who feel (vote for
> them!). Diana's funeral becomes part of the Blair

project— even as he is seen to protect the monarchy,
he simultaneously undermines it.

The last point proved the only error in Christy's prediction. From the moment the Prime Minister (with a little help from his spin doctors) declared Diana the 'People's Princess', he did less to undermine the monarchy than to renew its legitimacy. As commentators (notably the conservative Melanie Phillips) immediately observed, Blair—despite his stagey declamation of St. Paul in the Abbey—turned the tragedy to huge personal account, offering the catch in his voice, his Christian beliefs, and his own choirboy countenance as claim on the virtue represented by the deceased. But, instead of applying this as a counterweight to the crown, Labour sponsored a backstage rapprochement between the Windsors and the Spencers, and a public one between the Queen and her subjects, which restored crucial equilibrium to the principle of constitutional monarchy. On the Sunday after the funeral, Blair made the PM's annual pilgrimage to Balmoral and held four hours of talks with the Queen after predicting that the monarchy would 'change and modernise'. 'Ask not for whom the bell tolls,' wrote Hugo Young in the next day's *Guardian*, 'it tolls for the Republic.'

By November 20 and the Queen's golden wedding anniversary, the *Independent* headed its front page, 'New Labour sells a New Monarchy', quoting Blair's praise for Her Majesty ('She is an extraordinarily shrewd and perceptive observer of the world. Hers is advice worth having. . . . ') and the royal reply, which very shrewdly described hereditary monarchy and elected government as 'complementary institutions, each with its own role to play, and each in its different way exists only with the support and consent of the people.' As for the people, were they behaving—in the description of Liberal Democrat leader Paddy Ashdown—'more like citizens than subjects'? Indeed, who *were* the people for whom Diana was the People's Princess? Despite the impression of the mourners' social heterogeneity given in the media (notably by those chosen for TV interviews), an *Observer* scratch poll of 500 on the Mall discovered a rich vein of Tory tabloid readers. Others have remarked on the metropolitan character of the crowds around Buckingham and Kensington Palaces in the fortnight after the accident, notably their combination of Londoners and tourists.

This uncertainty, counterposed to Labour's opportunist appropriation of Diana's popularity, did not go unremarked. By the end of the second week A.D., 'the people' had begun to appear in quotation marks. Even earlier, on the day before the funeral, John Lloyd warned in the *Times*:

> It had been one of the received wisdoms of anti-communism that whenever one met the People capitalised, one knew something undemocratic was afoot. A People's Princess is not a People's Democracy to be sure; but in recasting the people as the People we move into dangerous territory.

And if there was no agreement about who 'the people' were, there was even less about what they wanted. Amid the celebrations of a new (non-racist, non-homophobic) republicanism, others questioned the motives of the mourners. At one extreme were fears of fascism, if not the Stalinist spectre raised by Lloyd; at the other complex diagnoses of group psychology. In response to the widespread argument that the New Britain had at last loosened its upper lip and learned to express public grief, *Guardian* columnist Decca Aitkenhead insisted that most of those who lined up overnight in the rain to sign the condolence books were not 'mourning for a woman they never knew, but from a desire to locate themselves in a spot where history will for once reach out to them, as they huddle in their ones and twos, pluck them up, and bring them inside, gathered together in a collective historic experience'. The whiff of condescension in her rhetoric (the reverse side of the utopianism so often espoused after Diana, and almost as common among its left opponents) reminded a friend of Virginia Woolf's rather more disdainful remarks on the funeral procession of King George in 1936:

> We stood in the Sqre to see the hearse: all London in an access of loyalty and democracy jumped the Sqre railings . . . and though some stalwarts held the gates,

the mob was on us, and Leonard who is a democrat
was squashed between 5 fat grocers. . . .

Nevertheless, Aitkenhead's image of people lining up for a place in
history is suggestive. The Mall was a massive stage for thousands of individuals eager, if her description was correct, 'to play a part in a momen-
tous occasion' (eager, we might say, to enter the spectacle their own
spectatorship had created). It's not unusual for a crowd to constitute a
significant element of a large public event, but in London, until the
royal family arrived on the Friday before the funeral, the on-lookers
and their tributes were the whole show. In the void left by an exceptionally spectacular woman (her body now invisible, yet represented
over and over again in the the photographs carried by crowds) or, in the
judgment of the tabloids, by the Windsors' late arrival from Balmoral,
the spectators became the spectacle. And in a culture where visibility is
power, is it any wonder that this congregation was assumed to have
agency—indeed, assumed it of itself—often on behalf of 'the people'
writ large? Thus followed the histrionic grief of some mourners (literally making a spectacle of themselves) as well as the claims that 'we' killed
Diana (our public avarice for spectacle spurring on the paparazzi). Thus,
too, the elated belief that the Queen had deferred to the power of the
people in broadcasting her statement to the nation, expanding the route
of the funeral procession and flying the national flag over Buckingham
Palace at half mast.

The apparent responsiveness of the monarch to those who stood
beneath her balcony taps into another fantasy, one with its own peculiar
history in the annals of psychoanalysis. When the young Jacques Lacan
was a student of psychiatry, he trained in forensic medicine under Gaetan
Gatian de Clérambault, head of the Special Infirmary of the Paris
Préfecture de Police. Among Clérambault's patients was one Madame X,
a 53-year-old woman who claimed that King George V was in love with
her. From 1918 onwards, Clérambault later wrote, she often travelled to
England and waited for the King outside Buckingham Palace. On one

occasion she saw a curtain move in the palace window and interpreted this as a royal signal.

Clérambault gave his name to the psychiatric term for the erotomania, the delusion that one is loved by a person of high rank. Later his student wrote his medical dissertation about another psychiatric patient who believed herself to be loved by notable individuals, including the Prince of Wales. This patient, a self-educated countrywoman whom Lacan called Aimée after a character in one of her own unpublished novels, dedicated a work of historical fiction defending the monarchy to the Prince, and mailed it to Buckingham Palace. Its lines include a prescient psychological explanation for the powers we attribute to our idols, religious and otherwise:

> You probably approach your particular idol with so much emotion it makes you forget your sufferings and endows you with fresh strength. . . . No doubt you have at some time been cured of a headache by a friend telling an amusing story; similarly, when the emotion involved is in proportion to a much loftier kind of feeling, you are in the presence of a miracle.

On April 17, 1931, a private secretary at the Palace returned the typescript of this novel to Aimée with a curt message explaining that it was 'contrary to Their Majesties' rule to accept presents from those with whom they are not personally acquainted'. By the time it arrived she was in the women's prison at Saint-Lazare for stabbing a prominent Parisian actress she accused of persecuting her.

Aimée's *ressentiment* led her not to republicanism but to its opposite, a devotion to her social superiors with a deadly underside. Such homage is a fate more familiar to American celebrities, although both the Queen and Princess Anne have been subject to violent attacks from strangers. But this curious lineage of royal fantasies does seem to prefigure what the London *Evening Standard* columnist Allison Pearson has described as the widespread 'delusions of intimacy' with Diana. However powerfully the Princess's personal sorrows had engaged the public, however great her compassion for the afflicted, the posthumous presumptions of royal requittal, the belief that Diana loved us all back, bore a bizarre resemblance to the syndrome whose medical history has enjoyed such an uncanny connection to the British crown. And in September, instead of the discreet rustling of the royal curtains, the flag was lowered, the funeral route changed, and the monarch marched out of the palace to bow before the passing bier—all at the command of the people. In this respect, and that of the communal longings of the mourners huddled in the rain, Lacan's conclusion to the Aimée case is instructive:

> Modern society leaves the individual in a cruel state of moral isolation, one especially painful in regard to occupations so indeterminate and ambiguous that they themselves may be a source of permanent internal conflict. Others besides myself have emphasized the extent to which the ranks of paranoia are swelled by those unjustly denigrated as inferior or limited—schoolmasters and schoolmistresses, governesses, women employed in minor intellectual activities, self-educated people of all kinds. . . . That's why it seems to me this type of subject should greatly benefit from being incorporated, according to his individual abilities, into some kind of religious community. Here, in addition to other advantages, he would experience a disciplined satisfaction of his own self-punishing tendencies. If this ideal solution is not available, any community would serve the purpose so long as to some extent it fulfilled the same conditions: the army, for instance; any militant political grouping; or some association devoted to good works, philosophy, or moral uplift.

• • •

Four months after the death of Diana, the *Guardian* noted that the royal family had commissioned the MORI polling organisation to question focus groups on their attitudes to the monarchy. The Blairification of the House of Windsor (like the Dianafication of New Labour) was still news, but the poll's results were not made public. In their stead, the paper asked another research firm to assemble its own focus group to air its views of the crown since autumn. The six members of social classes B, C1 and D from the conservative London suburb of West Wickham were unlikely representatives of anything much, but their discussion amplified the quantitative data which a post-funeral Gallup poll had gleaned from a thousand telephone interviews across the UK in September. 'Middle England' (as the *Guardian* characterised their panel in the usual casual metonymy) was still pro-monarchy, but not uncritically so. Despite the Queen's agreement to pay tax, open Buckingham Palace to the paying public, decommission the royal yacht and separate (some of) her relatives from the public purse, the group regarded the royals with hostility. In contrast to Diana (who one respondent thought had died at just the right moment) the Windsors were variously criticised as remote (the Queen), lazy (Prince Andrew and Princess Margaret), self-opinionated (the Princes Charles and Philip) and out of touch (*tout court*). While the crown worriedly consulted Blair's advisors for PR tips, its subjects discussed 'the nation's longest running soap' (a description by then current in the House of Lords) with a certain amount of contempt.

And yet, as the *Guardian* concluded, there was 'no great clamour for a republic'. Indeed, in the week after Diana's funeral, Gallup recorded a rise—from 65 to 71 percent since 1994—in the proportion of respondents who believed that the monarchy would exist in the next century. Moreover, the poll indicated a desire for the crown's continuance, although in a 'more democratic and approachable' form (71 percent)— the same desire (or lack of desire for greater change) expressed in West Wickham four months later.

In a rapidly written addition to his new book on 'our constitutional revolution', *This Time,* Anthony Barnett argues that the events of autumn '97 synthesised the monarchist/republican opposition by weakening both sides. The mass assembly for Diana's funeral 'acted out the two measures needed for the inauguration of a President: a *non-royal* was selected and then *endorsed by the people*'. Even more promising, he maintains, was the fact that this 'president' was already dead, and thus 'symbolic' and 'decorative'. Barnett makes much of the possibilities suggested by a decorative head of state. The popular support for a referendum on the continuation of the monarchy (69 percent in early 1997) is adduced to a crucial rise in the electorate's claim to sovereignty. And if Britain's citizens should choose to 'have a hereditary Head of State as decoration', this needn't rule out a republic. So taken with this motif is Barnett that he develops it into a metaphor for the redecoration of Britain's nineteenth-century constitution, comparing the contemporary electorate to servants 'intent on taking over the Victorian house for themselves'. And with all the taste of their class, they rip out every fireplace except the big one in the lounge, whose grandeur is retained to represent 'not their subordination but their ownership'.

Again, it is difficult to ignore the snobbery in this familiar evocation of tenants buying their council houses and proudly installing carriage lamps at their doors, or in its echo of Barnett's earlier *Iron Britannia*—where he characterised the petit bourgeois Margaret Thatcher as the nanny taking over the Conservative's country house. In any case, it is doubtful that the principle of hereditary rule, however endorsed by referendum, could be reduced to a mere detail. While some nations whose heads of state enjoy substantial powers might prefer a decorative—or, even better, posthumous—executive, the fantasised replacement of the British monarch by a dead president fails to address two key issues of constitutional reform: (1) What institution might best counterbalance the extensive powers currently vested in Parliament (even given the move to regional assemblies and a non-hereditary second chamber)? and (2) how could any such institution be staffed through inheritance in a government of citizens with remotely formal equality? Moreover, the fact that New Labour (despite its discourses of decentralization and one-member-one-vote) is notoriously ruthless with its

own dissenters, while gallantly indifferent to the inequalities perpetu-
ated by wealth, offers little reason to hope that its increasing co-operation with the crown is designed to enthrone the people—with or
without quotation marks, capital letters or fireplaces.

Two themes emerge from this volume's survey of the commentaries
after Diana, and neither of them new. The first is the authoritarian populism which Stuart Hall identified in Thatcherism. In the optimism of
early autumn 1997, the *lèse majesté* of the mourners and the presence of
Elton (and male partner) in the Abbey were often compared to the government's stylistic informality (first names in Cabinet meetings, lounge
suits at City dinners, Oasis at Downing Street) as well as to its more substantial commitments to devolution and the European Convention on
Human Rights. While it is far too early to dismiss any of these initiatives,
they stand in curious contrast to the compulsory re-education of single
mothers, state curfews for their children and (should all else fail) the
revival of prison ships. What we may be faced with is the incoherence of
a new administration more internally divided than it wants to seem (and
thus even more anxious to suppress dissent among its own).
Unfortunately, the contradictions of this regime may match those per-
ceivable in the discourses after Diana, the desire for a kindlier, less stuffy
society combined with a new deference, albeit to a figure of authority so
abstract that she has to be dead.

This brings me to the other old theme still current in the New
Britian, conservative modernisation. Like 'the people', 'modernisation'
has become a key term in the aftermath of the Princess's death, and its
usage has been similarly oxymoronic. In conjunction with the crown it
now implies what Hugo Young has described as 'a better monarchy, a
monarchy that can come down to [the people's] level without depriving
them of residual awe, a monarchy whose passing might reliably command a display of national grief half-matching that accorded to Diana.
Adaptation, that Blairite watchword for almost everything, is the name
of the royalist game as well. It's the quality that has kept this country, for
better or worse, conservative.'

For worse, that conservative modernisation could entail not only the renewal of royal authority—accessible yet awesome and reglamourised in the next generation by its descent from Diana—but also the larger reduction of rights in regard to work, welfare and education begun in the '70s. Here, the retention of the monarchy in the trophy form envisaged by Barnett has an ideal avatar in Britain's latest monument to modernisation, the Millennium Dome project inherited from the government's Conservative predecessors and now being built at Greenwich for an estimated cost of £758 million. As critics on all sides complained that such a sum could have built four major hospitals, wired up every school to the Internet or financed the threatened arts budget for the next four years—or, one might add, paid for the monarchy for the next nine—the minister responsible replied,

> People feel atomised, fragmented and set apart from one another. They feel that the community spirit of the country has gone, diminished in recent years. The celebrations will enable people to come together to share something; something people felt in the wake of Diana's death. . . . I'm not suggesting the Dome will start us on a more upward course—but it might help.

Fittingly, the Dome (a large canopy supported by cables suspended from upright struts) has a strikingly coronal design. As a vaguely 'futurist' edifice erected to commemorate a mythological history on the site of an invented (and imperial) chronology, it is the perfect figure for conservative modernisation. And, as with the monarchy, the people are made to pay for it in the name of national unity.

By June 1998, ten months after that Paris car crash, discussions of its consequences continued unabated. In Britain, a new collection from the right-wing Social Affairs Unit, *Faking It: the Sentimentalisation of Society*, used the responses to Diana's death to attack all the old usual suspects (feminism, psychotherapy, comprehensive schools, etc.) under the heading of 'emotional correctness'. Predictably, the ensuing discussion eschewed these issues (and the monarchy, endorsed by *Faking It*'s authors) to defend the Princess herself, unwisely accused by one contributor of 'childlike self-centredness'. 'Carry On Mourning', Britain's biggest-selling tabloid cheerfully bade its readers, as summer, and a spate of Diana hagiographies, loomed.

Whether or not she, like the legendary American activist Joe Hill, would have suggested organising instead, the contributors to this book are of that mind. If they dispute the imminence of a profound transfer of power, they never doubt its desirability. What remains is *how*. The worldwide reactions to the death of an extremely famous aristocrat may have been seismic, but the consequences, if any, are yet to be determined. What happens to our politics—be they that of the state, ethnicity, sex or class—depends on those who live on, after Diana.

one

MASS-OBSERVATION IN THE MALL

ross mckibbin

t he week before Princess Diana's funeral and the funeral itself were, by agreement, a remarkable moment in the history of modern Britain, but most of us, despite broadsheet press commentary which was frequently sensible and thoughtful, have found it difficult to understand or even to know what happened. And this, of course, is due to the fact that the dominant intellectual categories of the twentieth century are secular and rational: we are in a sense taught not to be able to understand such 'irrational' phenomena as the reaction to Diana's death, or indeed anything to do with public attitudes to royalty, and are frequently embarrassed if asked to do so. Historians of the twentieth century are particularly disabled—historians of medieval religion or Byzantinists at least know what questions to ask. Futhermore, we are compelled to measure things which are almost immeasurable. The great majority of the population, after all, did not leave flowers in front of the palaces or anywhere else. Over one-quarter of the adult population did not even watch the funeral on television. Most of those who were there were not weeping. Does that mean they were emotionally unaffected? On the other hand, many more watched the funeral on television than watched the Euro 96 England-Germany match, hitherto the record-breaker. Does that mean we feel more intensely about Diana than about the national game—or simply that more women watched the funeral than watch soccer? And, in any case, can people articulate what they feel in ways we can understand? In due course we might know these things but at the moment we do not.

This is why historians and sociologists of the 20th century have approached the subject of royalty and its audience gingerly, and few have done so at all. However, by coincidence, the first and still the most sustained attempt to understand our reactions to royalty was published exactly 60 years ago; and it was, also by coincidence, a study of a single royal event. This was Mass-Observation's study of King George VI's coronation in 1937—*May 12*. Two hundred 'observers' were posted about the country and instructed to note what they observed; with the exception of those who kept a record of what they themselves felt, they were not to intrude or act as mediators—simply to observe. There are all sorts of problems with Mass-Observation's techniques, as any historian knows, and they have not been universally admired—the sociologist T.H. Marshall thought these contemporary reprints of British life by members of the public at least in part 'moonshine'. It is also true that observers, though instructed merely to record the ordinary and everyday, tended to record the extraordinary on grounds of interest and inevitably 'edited' what they saw (since 'facts' do not speak for themselves), but it is unlikely, given that they were trying to measure degrees of emotions and sentiment, that anybody will ever do much better.

The possibilities and limitations of Mass-Observation were apparent to anyone who was in London the week that Diana died, particularly in the Mall or outside the palaces. I recorded my own impressions in as mass-observant a way as I could and tried to come to conclusions consonant with what I 'saw'. In the end, my regard for Mass-Observation and what they achieved was enhanced, since I found it difficult to reach conclusions which were anything more than tentative in face of evidence that was quite intractable. And it is the case that one tends to notice the extraordinary or unexpected: I expected, for instance, the great banks of flowers but failed to anticipate that they would produce a very pungent, sweet smell which will affect, I am sure, how everyone remembers the scene. One of my strongest memories of the Mall was of something absolutely untypical: an elderly black woman singing hymns in a cracked voice without regard for anyone else. She was singing for Diana alone. More typically, almost every bouquet was accompanied by a card, letter or poem. There was some surprise that the flowers were left in paper or cellophane. But these were individual presentations and the paper kept them individual. Not everyone gave flowers: there were many posters and manifestos attached to trees or railings—with people happy to identify themselves, in one case as 'Freddie Mercury's cousin'. A very large proportion of the bouquets and messages prob ably a majority—came from children, often collectively; from playgroups, kindergartens, primary schools. Some classes sent whole books in which, presumably, every child contributed something. How far there were parental guiding hands in all this is hard to say. The language (and spelling) suggests not much. From what I saw, parents left their children to write what they wanted. At a rough guess, I would say there were an unrepresentative number of cards and letters from Asian children, though that could be wrong. What was characteristic of the letters and poems as a whole is how highly-charged and emotionally uninhibited they were. Some exceptionally so. The most common words appeared to be 'angel', 'heaven', 'soul', 'paradise', 'smile', 'cared', 'love', 'grace', 'peace' and 'at peace'. Many of the letters hoped that Diana would have the peace and happiness in heaven which she failed to find on earth: hoped that she was now 'free from her troubles'. Most, directly or indirectly, expressed a sense of personal loss. A significant number (which surprised me) were to both Diana and Dodi, and I doubt this was merely gratitude to Harrods, who were dispensing free Evian and coffee in the Mall. Many were in fractured English and I saw several in French. Very few mentioned the royal family. Some of the posters were 'political': 'Diana—the only jewel in the crown'; 'Charles, you've lost the best thing you ever had. Good luck to Wills and Harry,' said one poster stuck to the railings of Buckingham Palace.

As many people noted, the whole atmosphere was very 'democratic': rarely can the railings of our royal palaces have been treated with such disrespect. Posters, cards, letters, even rosaries were stuck in and stuck on them any old way. There were also many forms of demotic art—drawings, sketches, paintings and photo-montages. And there were gifts, mostly from children—huge numbers of teddy-bears and related comforters. But not all from children. Outside Buckingham Palace, for instance, was prominently displayed a bottle of Bailey's Irish Cream—perhaps a more effective comforter. There were innumerable candles, many intended to be votive, and some so large they could only have been bought at an ecclesiastical supplier.

As to the people, a steady day-long stream became a flood after six. Many were parents (frequently both parents) with children, but the population as a whole seemed fairly well represented. The majority were women, but only just. There were many 'businessmen' (for want of a better word), with dark suits and briefcases, who were bringing flowers—and this again was a surprise. Most striking, and something confirmed on the day of the funeral, were the large numbers of young couples, with as many men as women holding flowers. The queues of those waiting to sign the books of condolence increased throughout the week until Friday, when 43 books became available. On Thursday the sign said 'waiting time 7 hours', but the police said eight. (The police were helpful and good-humoured.) The queue, again, was pretty representative, though understandably biased towards the hale and hearty. Once more the majority were women, but not a large majority. I think the queue was disproportionately non-white, but that is said without much conviction. There seemed to be a considerable number of tourists both in the queue Americans particularly, and in the crowd, where a great many Italians and Spaniards were taking photographs. There is a view that the reaction to Diana's death represents a 'Mediterraneanisation' of our culture, but the slightly stunned look many of these Italians and Spaniards wore suggests not. The number of photo-seekers around Buckingham Palace was so large that the police had created photography-only queues.

Making sense of this is not easy. The tendency has been to read into these events a profound change in British life, but the evidence points in different directions. Most of the letters and poems, for example, were written in an instantly recognisable, though very heightened, graveyard style of the mid-nineteenth century. The twentieth century has been bad at devising a language of grief and mourning: the result is that the feeling for Diana has resorted to rhetorical conventions which in other circumstances we would regard as out-dated. On the other hand, there is a timelessness, too, about our responses: we are surprised that so many people seemed to have a quasi-religious view of Diana. But throughout the twentieth century observers have been 'surprised'. In 1935, 1936 and 1937, years of many royal events, Kingsley Martin, the editor of the *New Statesman*, was astonished at the 'recrudescence of sheer superstition' surrounding the monarchy. People endlessly spoke of 'royal weather'; there was much publicity given to a crippled Scottish boy who learned to walk 'after' having met George V; in 1939 it was alleged that the inhabitants of Southwold crowded around George VI to 'touch' him for his magical curative powers. These stories are very similar to those which have appeared about Diana and the effect she had on the ill. Their recovery, it is said, has been 'like a miracle': what is twentieth-century about that is the care people take not to say: 'it's a miracle.' But there is no reason, even allowing for twentieth-century caution, to think that the enormous fund of popular 'religion' which surprised Geoffrey Gorer in the early Fifties has much diminished. He noted the widespread belief in astrology, spiritualism, an afterlife, in the power of prayer, charms and good luck, which he attributed to the feeling of helplessness which (he thought) so many people had about their own lives. I do not think this has much changed.

The memorial literature also underlines the extent to which people believe, as Diana herself believed, that the social good depends on individual goodness, kindness, understanding and, above all, love. Some have argued that this belief stands for progress, for the emergence of a new and gentle Britain. Certainly, humane sentiments of that kind represent a repudiation of the hard-faced values dominant over the past twenty years. That this is progress, however, is more doubtful: it is highly traditional to believe that the social good is dependent on individual goodness. Moreover this way of thinking gives Diana semi-magical qualities, thereby reinforcing the age-old notion that royalty is magical. In fact, Diana's social authority depended on political powerlessness. As Freud's biographer, Ernest Jones, argued of George V (and the argument holds for Diana), once the monarch becomes divorced from the discharge of political power, once government 'decomposes' into two persons, one 'untouchable, irremovable and sacrosanct' (the king), and the other 'vulnerable in such a degree that sooner or later he will surely be destroyed' (the prime minister), the king is held to be 'above criticism'. As such, it becomes difficult for him to be unpopular. Hence the paradox of Diana's hold on our emotions: its strength was in direct relation to her political powerlessness. It is unlikely that flowers will be strewn in the path of Lady Thatcher's coffin, and she was certainly 'destroyed', but, unlike Diana, she wielded power and achieved what she wanted.

It has been widely argued that Diana's enormous popularity is a result (perhaps even a cause of) the 'feminisation' of our values, which are now though to be softer and less aggressive, a process accompanied by the 'Catholicisation' of our public ceremonies. There may be some truth to this and it could be related to the fact that such a small proportion of the male population has had any experience of the Armed Forces. One thing which does seem to be new is the willingness of young men to grieve publicly in a 'feminine' way. This was very apparent both before Diana's funeral and at the funeral itself, but was first manifested after the soccer crowd deaths at Hillsborough, when Liverpool's Anfield Stadium was thick with bouquets and gifts (usually supporters' club scarves). And there was nothing very Protestant about the mourning or the funeral: not merely the lack of restraint but the fact that both Earl

Spencer and Prince Charles crossed themselves—an act which would have brought the monarchy down a generation ago. I doubt however, that this is as new as it appears: the mid-Victorians, for instance, would have found it all much more familiar than we do. My guess is that the stoicism thought to be typical of the British character is a product of the later nineteenth century and reached its apogee in the first fifty years of the twentieth. And even this is perhaps a fiction. Mass-Observation of *May 12*, describes very unbuttoned crowds whose behaviour, if not extravagant, was not restrained. In a couple of cases the lack of restraint is almost suspicious. Outsiders had two stereotypes of the British: there was the famous discipline and constraint, but there were the excitable, partisan crowds, even more excitable than the Italians, especially at sporting matches. Arguably, what is exceptional in British history is not the extravagance but the stiff upper lip.

And we should remember who was being buried. The three great public funerals within living memory—George VI, Churchill and Mountbatten—were all heroic males intimately associated with war and empire. Diana was the reverse of this, and the kind of mourning associated with them would have been wholly inappropriate for her. Diana stood for the most traditional image of woman. The first to leave flowers, cards and letters were children and they made the running. This reinforced the picture of her, not as heroic but as a loving mother and a mother who cared for the outcast—her 'constituency of the rejected', as Earl Spencer rather craftily put it. More difficult to explain, as with the whole phenomenon, was the intensity with which these traditional attitudes were expressed. It was clear from the beginning that in many people's minds the Queen of Hearts was close to the Queen of Heaven. And since this Queen was wounded and vulnerable the identifications became stronger. Nor is there much doubt that Diana's physical appearance, like Eva Perón's in her last days, was what many thought the Queen of Heaven's should be: blonde, beautiful and soulful. This should not be underrated.

Although Diana's appeal is largely traditional, it is also eclectic. Who else could bring the Queen Mother, Tom Cruise and Ruby Wax to the same ceremony? Her friendship with many of the heavyweights of popular culture, and their attendance at the funeral, evoked a world of strong pleasures and emotional stimulation very attractive to young adults. Again, this is not as new as it appears: the future Edward VIII, as Prince of Wales, carefully cultivated his relationships with the stars of prewar popular culture and that—what in the interwar years was always called 'glamour'—was undoubtedly an element in his enormous popularity. Then, too, the media were problematic in his life as they were in Diana's. What role they played in the days after Diana's death is, like so much else, almost unknowable, since the relationship between the media and the audience is usually reciprocal. In this case, the first steps were taken spontaneously and it is the first steps which count. The original decision to bring flowers and cards to the palaces was not the media's, although the extent of media reporting might well have made those who had not thought of doing so feel they should. Equally, the behaviour of the huge numbers who watched the hearse on its way north might have been influenced by what they had seen on television of the behaviour of the crowds in Central London, but the applauding of the hearse and the throwing of flowers at it were also clearly spontaneous—an instinctive and moving awareness of the funeral service as a rite of passage. Although it was said that to complain of the media's excessive attention to Diana in death was risky, in practice many people did complain. A guess is that large numbers thought the press was overdoing it, but were 'drawn in despite themselves', as Mass-Observation said of George VI's coronation. Such ambivalence is what we would expect; but it would be wrong to imagine that public emotion was merely worked up by the media.

In 1953, in a famous article, Edward Shils and Michael Young argued that popular celebration of the present Queen's coronation marked a 'degree of moral unity equalled by no other large national state'. Can we say the same of Diana's death? In Shils and Young's terms almost certainly not. In the first place, the popular reaction to her death was international—more intense in Britain perhaps, but definitely not confined to it. Diana really was the most famous woman in the world in life and the most famous person in death. If the reaction does mark 'moral unity' it cannot be British alone. Does it mean that Britain is now more 'democratic', less deferential; that in mourning her we were, as the *Observer* put it 'united against tradition'? There was certainly a strong whiff of 1789 in the royal family's return from Balmoral and they had a beleaguered look throughout; while the whole tone of the funeral was a long way from the House of Windsor. Our traditional élites are now held in much less respect than they were a generation ago, and that is no loss. The country's democratic potential is greater than ever: but that potential has not been realised, and the reaction to Diana's death demonstrates the limitations as well as the strengths of modern British democracy.

When Shils and Young wrote of Britain's almost unique moral unity they meant primarily that the industrial working class was more successfully integrated in Britain than in any other major country. That class now hardly exists and the political system which integrated it has not adjusted to its political and social decay. The result is that the economically and socially deprived are relatively more deprived today than they have been for over half a century, if not longer. The decline of a particular sense of the nation which Shils and Young (rightly or wrongly) identified in 1953 has left many out in the cold and no one (including the present government) is inviting them back in. The exclusion of the poor has been accompanied by the triumph of individualist ideologies and the defeat of the idea of social solidarity. This bears on Diana: those two countries where Diana worship is most intense, Britain and the United States, are not simply the two where celebrity and glamour are most admired, but where social solidarity is now weakest and individualism strongest. In them the remedy for social failure, poverty or homelessness is to be found in individual virtue. Love, care, goodness are no less valued, indeed are perhaps even more valued, but they are not thought to be found in the social sphere. The remedy for social exclusion or distress is individual action and individual virtue; the more the possessor of such virtue is associated with women's traditional qualities the more she is cherished.

When in the nineteenth century the Roman Catholic Church raised the Virgin in the battle against materialist or collectivist ideologies it knew what it was about. Diana, for many of the same reasons, in her turn became 'saviour of the world', as one of the posters outside Kensington Palace put it. Much that happened after Diana's death involved powerful and generous emotions; but a democracy which admired her with such intensity is both incomplete and immature and will always exclude those who apparently made up her 'constituency'.

two

A GLIMPSE OF THE VOID

judith williamson

We have a powerful need to make sense of things, to find stories that explain and connect what happens in our world. The more unaccountable an event, the harder our sense-making mechanisms whirr into action, weaving a fabric of meaning to clothe naked experience. Sometimes, however, that fabric itself rips, precipitating a crisis—psychic or social—until it can be mended, reformed or rewoven even more tightly.

The death of Princess Diana was an accident, a completely senseless occurrence. And it was, at first, hard to believe not only because of its suddenness, but because the absence of someone whose image had been so present in our culture seemed a contradiction in terms. Freud once said that the imagination does not know the word 'no', and Diana was so omnipresent in our cultural imagination that the concept of 'no Diana' was literally impossible to grasp. Even as the television brought us endless 'further developments' on her death, it also brought us endless further pictures—including, strangely, the image of a sad, funereal Diana presiding over it all, like a reaction shot to her own fate.

Like millions of other people, I found myself weeping as I took in the news. The death of this young woman who was already so vulnerable seemed like the deliberate blow of a cruel world. The thought of two children with no mother and a lifetime of public duty was—and is—bleakly poignant. It would be a hard-hearted person who could remain untouched by that card on her coffin that read, simply, 'Mummy'.

But then, it was a good few weeks for the heart—only the head has had bad press. However, one of the useful things about having a head is that it can help us understand our hearts—to look at our feelings truthfully.

And the truth is, we live a lot of our emotional lives by proxy. Life is messy and confusing, but many of our feelings are caught up in media stories—real and fictional—whose meanings are clear and well-secured. Diana's death destabilised familiar meanings, both because of its unpredictability (it was not a plot move we had seen coming) and because it removed the real person behind the images, so that they were suddenly, simply images—as if paper money was suddenly revealed as just paper. The drive to go physically to the Palace and other landmarks has perhaps been an attempt to grasp something more solid—a run on the bank of the Real.

But into this breach of meaning rolled the great sense-making machines of our society. Strikingly, as if to compensate for its briefly-revealed inadequacy, The Image bounced back in full force as more and more pictures accumulated in the newspapers, culminating in huge memorial editions, packed with photos as if their very quantity could somehow make up for the living presence they lacked.

Written copy, too, moved into overdrive: while the tabloids sought to make sense of it by trying to explain the event—finding endless angles on who to blame (paparazzi; driver; Al Fayeds; royals)—the broadsheets and weeklies performed exactly the same operation, but more grandly, by trying to explain everyone else's reaction to the event, finding endless angles on what it Says about Us. So we learned from the *New Statesman* that we are now modern: from the *Observer* that we are now more 'feminine'; from just about everyone that we are now an unrepressed, emotionally frank nation able to express ourselves freely. As the tabloids cannonised Diana, so the broadsheets cannonised 'the people' whose response had been so modern, so frank, even so radical.

But just as the accident probably had no single cause and very likely no culprit, so the emotional events of the succeding few weeks may have had no single overriding meaning. What they did have, however, was a structure, and that structure has barely been mentioned.

When I walked around Kensington Palace, reading some of the thousands of notes and poems to Diana, I was moved to tears. But the notes made me think about not the Princess, but the people who wrote them. There was an unprecedented outpouring of self-expression, of writing—both in the condolence books and in the often lengthy verses and cries from the heart which, protected by polythene bags, floated on the sea of flowers like so many messages in bottles.

What struck me (obvious as it is) was this: that, just like a message in a bottle, they were outpourings of emotion to someone *who wasn't there*. I have no doubt that the feelings expressed were real, just as I know my own tears on August 31 were real. But how much easier it was to pour out all that intensity to someone we didn't know, *who was not there* and, in a sense, never was—how much easier than to express those feelings to people we *do* know, who *are* present to us. It was like writing those emotional letters you never send—except this time it was safe to, because there was no one to embarrass us by receiving them. I remember once hearing the Bishop of London say that this world would be a paradise in 30 seconds if we truly loved one another. All that feeling in the park wasn't directed by us at one another, either personally or socially, but at a figure once remote and now completely absent. It is a structure of feeling perceptively described by Shelley as 'not what men call love . . . but . . . The desire of the moth for the star/Of the night for the morrow/The devotion to something afar/From the sphere of our sorrow'.

And that sorrow was there before the Princess's untimely death. One man, interviewed by the BBC, said he cried more at Diana's funeral than at his father's, eight years earlier. This doesn't mean that he is emotionally deficient; rather, that he must have had eight years of feelings waiting for an outlet. Feelings can be simultaneously real and displaced, and far from showing what an unrepressed nation we are, the outpouring over Diana's death suggests how much we fail to express in our actual day-to-day lives.

So for most of us, if we are honest, the greatest shock of Diana's death was the sudden pulling of a central thread from the dense weave of cultural life, which left raw edges and unravelling holes. These holes exposed some of our own underlying feelings, usually well-wrapped: a sense of the world's sadness, remorse, perhaps, at Britain's past few sorry decades; sadness of loss in our own lives, and, simply, of ourselves.

But these real and painful feelings were knitted back almost at once into that a great web of stories, meanings and explanations: as quickly as possible we made sense of it all again. If death tells us anything, it is how little, really, we know about what it all means—and how low our tolerance is for facing that unknowing.

three

THE PLUMAGE AND THE DYING BIRD

alexander cockburn

t he short century of the common man begins and ends with a royal passing: in 1914, the murder of Archduke Franz Ferdinand at Sarajevo, and now, the death of Princess Di. The Diana cult— what else can we call it?—offers her as 'the People's Princess', but this is merely the sleight-of-hand of old fairy tales, where the prince most admirably displayed his royal essence by moving among his subjects as a commoner.

Diana now hovers near sainthood, a status to which she was not insensitive during her lifetime, gliding through the AIDS wards as a Madonna of the Damned. To the English kings was attributed the gift of healing scrofula by simple touch. The infant Samuel Johnson was touched thus by Queen Anne in 1712. With Diana this asset was re-created, often at the level of kitsch—as in André Durand's painting *Votive Offering*, depicting the Princess placing her hands on a gaunt AIDS victim amid a troupe of saints.

On the one hand, the AIDS patients; on the other, Gianni Versace, at whose memorial the Princess was so conspicuously present the summer before her own death comforting Elton John. Diana's involvement with the fashion industry, affirmed by an auction that same summer that brought in $3.25 million for seventy-nine of her castoffs, was often cited as an example of her modernity, her blending of royalty with show business, in an equation Versace was perfectly equipped to exploit, to their mutual advantage.

Yet we can say with equal justice that the conflations of power with fashion are late-medieval. Johan Huizinga wrote in *The Waning of the Middle Ages*: 'In the domain of costume, art and fashion were still inextricably blended, style in dress stood nearer to artistic style than later, and the function of costume in social life, that of accentuating the strict order of society itself, almost partook of the liturgic.' Fifteenth-century men, Huizinga observed, 'persisted in regarding the nobility as the foremost of social forces and attributed a very exaggerated importance to it, undervaluing altogether the social significance of the lower classes.'

Today, when concentrations of wealth and power make the fifteenth century look like a playpen, men have understood very well that the saintlike mien of a Jackie O (whose own relics were auctioned off not so long ago) or a Princess Di is a most useful cover for corruption, whether of Aristotle Onassis or of the appalling Al Fayed family, about whose practices the British Department of Trade and Industry compiled a damning report in 1988, made public two years later. Apropos the Al Fayeds' takeover of Harrods, the report stated: 'The Fayeds produced to us birth certificates which were false and which they knew to be false. They repeatedly lied to us about their family background, their early business life and their wealth. . . . The evidence that they were telling lies to us was quite overwhelming. . . . After watching and hearing them give evidence for two days we considered that Mohammed and Ali Fayed were witnesses on whose word it would be unsafe to rely on any issue of any importance.' This is why Dodi's father has never been able to win British citizenship, and no doubt why he and Dodi, whose own financial dealings were insalubrious, were ecstatic to have the Princess aboard.

Her style gave them allure, and their money gave her comfort, as it had her awful father and her step-mother before her. Di's ascent after 1981 coincided with a huge leap forward in speculative accumulation on both sides of the Atlantic. The adoration now poured on her is reminiscent of the groveling of Edmund Burke in 1790 toward that adornment to the feudal corruption of the French Bourbons, Marie Antoinette: 'Surely never lighted on this orb, which she hardly seemed to touch, a more delightful vision. I saw her just above the horizon, decorating and cheering the elevated sphere she had just begun to move in—glittering like the morning star, full of life and splendour and joy.'

These were the lines, in Burke's *Reflections on the Revolution in France*, that stirred Tom Paine to such piercing sarcasms in *The Rights of Man*. Burke, wrote Paine, had never expressed a moment's joy that the Bastille had been pulled down: 'He pities the plumage, but forgets the dying bird. . . . His hero or his heroine must be a tragedy-victim expiring in show, and not the real prisoner of misery, sliding into death in the silence of a dungeon.'

And so, now that flowers heaped outside Kensington Palace have long since turned to dust, what weight should Diana carry in the economy of mourning? The best answer was offered by Percy Bysshe Shelley in his 'Address to the People on the Death of the Princess Charlotte,' written in November of 1817, after the passing, in childbirth, of this daughter of George IV. Shelley juxtaposed Charlotte's end to the almost simultaneous execution of three Luddites, framed by the government of the day:

> We cannot truly grieve for every one who dies beyond the circle of those especially dear to us; yet in the extinction of the objects of public love and admiration, and gratitude, there is something, if we enjoy a liberal mind, which has departed from within that circle. . . . But this appeal to the feelings of men should not be made lightly, or in any manner that tends to waste, on inadequate objects, those fertilizing streams of sympathy, which a public mourning should be the occasion of pouring forth. This solemnity should be used only to express a wide and intelligible calamity, and one which is felt to be such by those who feel for their country and for mankind; its character ought to be universal, not particular.

The death of Charlotte, Shelley concluded, was 'a private grief'. As for the barbarous execution, by hanging and quartering, of the three laborers, Jeremiah Brandreth, Isaac Ludlam and William Turner: 'Let us follow the corpse of British Liberty slowly and reverentially to its tomb: and if some glorious phantom should appear, and make its throne of broken swords and sceptres and royal crowns trampled in the dust, let us say that the Spirit of Liberty has arisen from its grave and left all that was gross and mortal there, and kneel down and worship it as our Queen.'

MOURNING FOR A BETTER MONARCHY

dorothy thompson

t he end-of-year surveys with which the British press filled up the newsless days after Christmas spoke almost universally of a change in 'the nation' brought about by the violent death of Princess Diana. 'We' are supposed to have dropped 'our' traditional stiff upper lip and become a feeling, caring nation (like, one supposes, other countries). A populist prime minister who elevated the dead lady to the role of 'People's Princess' won the universal acclaim of the tabloid press.

Yet, the picture of 'a nation in mourning' is a considerable oversimplification. It seems clear that nearly everyone in the country was to some degree shocked, even shaken by the death of the Princess and the violent circumstances in which it happened. This is hardly an uncommon response to the sudden death of a young and glamorous celbrity. Alistair Cooke in an interesting 'Letter from America' compared the British reaction to the death of Diana with the American, particularly the New York, reaction to the death of Rudolph Valentino, when the city went into shock. The icons of youth and beauty are not supposed to be taken violently from us. The way in which the sentimental response was in the case of Princess Diana indulged and prolonged does, however, represent something significant. The piles of flowers in their plastic wrappings, the gathering of crowds in the streets, the writing of messages of condolence in public books is not customary in Britain even for the funerals of the royal or the famous. There seems no doubt that this public manifestation of grief gave some people who feel excluded from the major currents of public and political life an opportunity to join in a national manifestation which was earning the applause of the establishment and the media. It offered a sense of belonging, of being a part of the nation. Diana's status as the mother of the future monarch gave her death a national significance; as a manifestation of Englishness the demonstrations over her death may indicate emotional needs which contemporary politics do not sufficiently recognise.

But perhaps the most controversial question among the commentators about the events of 1997 is the nature of the attitude to the monarchy expressed in these large demonstrations.

We know little of the social composition of the mourning crowds. No one I know bought flowers, wrote a condolence message or joined the crowds in the streets; few watched the televised funeral. Most people I know blessed *Private Eye*, kept out of the way and marvelled at the hypocrisy of the tabloid newspapers and the political demagogues. Former Conservative MP George Walden described on the air the popular response as a mixture of deference and popular sentimentalism, and this was a widely supported verdict. But what is involved in this idea of 'deference'? There are historical precedents which help us to analyse the extent to which Diana's royal status informed and deepened the popular response to her death.

Some commentators have seen elements of republicanism in the mass mourning for Princess Diana. She was, after all, out of favour with the Royal Family and involved in an apparent conflict with the heir to the throne. There is a natural tendency to see any criticism of the incumbent royals as being 'republican', but the attitudes to the monarchy which were demonstrated in the course of the popular response never appear to have involved hostility to the crown as such. Had the crowd been republican it would surely have cared very little for the behaviour of a group of people who were due for removal anyway. The response comes closer to what Craig Calhoun, in his discussion of the Queen Caroline affair, called the concept of good kingship. Where the crowd takes sides in royal squabbles there are likely to be a number of elements involved, only one of which is any kind of republicanism.

Of the historical precedents which do exist for popular movements of the type which we have been experiencing none is an exact parallel, but there are one or two cases in which comparisons could perhaps help a contemporary analysis. The two that come to mind in particular are the death of Princess Charlotte in 1817 and the Queen Caroline affair of 1819–20, events echoed in the circumstances of Victoria's accession in 1837. The widespread demonstration of public grief at the death of Princess Charlotte and even more the convulsions which accompanied the attempt of George IV to exclude his estranged wife from a place at his side when he was crowned have raised questions and continuing controversy among historians.

Princess Charlotte was the only legitimate member of her genera-tion of the royal family in the early years of the nineteenth century. The nine sons of George III were restricted by law from marrying without the permission of the reigning monarch and had mostly settled for non-legitimate relationships, many of them in fact much like conventional marriages. The need for a legitimate heir had forced the Prince of Wales, later George IV, into a marriage with his cousin Caroline of Brunswick which had resulted in the birth of a daughter, Charlotte, in 1796. After the birth the parents went their separate and far from monogamous ways. Charlotte made a popular marriage in 1816, soon became pregnant and was confidently expected to succeed when her aged and insane grandfather and her unhealthy and unpopular father died.

In 1817, however, Charlotte and her baby died during what had apparently been expected to be a normal healthy birth. With their deaths there was suddenly a huge gap in succession to the throne, but the massive public response was not provoked simply by dynastic con-cerns. Byron, a convinced republican, wrote

> *. . . .in the dust*
> *The fair-haired daughter of the Isles is laid*
> *The love of millions*

and

> *Those who weep not for kings shall weep for thee*

George Eliot recalled in one of her letters that a French musician coming to London in search of work during the days immediately after the death of the Princess could get no employment because he was wearing a coloured coat and the whole capital was in mourning. Clearly there was an element of universal feeling here. Death in childbirth was a fear among all classes in the nineteenth century, just as fear of death in a violent road accident is in ours. The sudden death of the young, rich and beautiful is particularly shocking at any time. But there is also the cluster of feelings that surrounds the throne which helps to explain the response in this case.

The need for a good monarch is an essential element of monarchism, and the British people have for centuries been profoundly monarchist in sentiment. Criticism of the throne has been, even among republicans, nearly always based on the expense and inefficiency of the monarchy or the bad behaviour of a particular ruler rather than on the assertion that a republic is a better form of government. The monarchy has tended to seem most insecure when the incumbent is immoral or unpopular for other reasons. The young Princess and her baby son had represented the possibility of a new, young and pure figure to replace the old and corrupt heirs. The mourning following her death was in part mourning for the hope of a better monarchy.

The question of gender also comes in here. In folk memory England has always been at her best under queens. From Boadicea through Elizabeth and Anne female rulers have developed mythic qualities. The reign of Victoria in the later nineteenth century was to reinforce this idea, so that by our own time it is the female members of the Royal Family who seem to embody the monarchical principle. George

IV was to discover his subject's respect for royal females when he attempted to prevent Charlotte's mother from becoming his consort when he inherited his father's throne. George IV came to the throne three years after the death of his daughter. He had no legitimate heir nor the likelihood of any and his brothers had only infant progeny, brought into being by the need to fill the gap left by Charlotte and her son.

George's various attempts to rid himself of his spouse, Caroline, by charging her (in some cases quite justifiably) with immoral and undignified behaviour came to a head in his attempt to exclude her from his coronation in 1820. A 'delicate investigation' into her behaviour led to the attempt, through an unusual constitutional device, a Bill of Pains and Penalties, to gain for the future monarch a divorce which would not involve any public investigation of his own unsavoury private life. The public support for the Queen in the course of the examination and the enormous celebration which greeted her victory has been described fairly by Nicholas Rogers as 'a spectacular popular mobilisation, arguably the greatest in the whole Hanoverian era'. At a popular level the support for Caroline—described incidentally, by the young Macaulay, then a Cambridge undergraduate and a strong supporter of the Queen, as 'the Daughter of the People'—amazed politicians and the establishment in general. Republicans jumped on the bandwagon and defended the Queen against her spouse, but again the popular response was more against immorality and bad behaviour by the King than against the monarchy as such. The British monarch must observe the familial values of his people as well as the laws governing matrimony. The crowds who flocked into the streets and signed petitions in support of the Queen had little or no personal knowledge of her, but saw the need to protest against a monarch who was trying to be above the law.

The Caroline agitation was, in fact, one of the first popular movements in which women took a separate part—there were at least seventeen purely female petitions sent in to Parliament in support of the Queen, including one signed by 17,652 'married ladies of the metropolis'. It would be interesting to have a gender analysis of the Diana demonstrations—there certainly seemed, on random viewing of news reports, to be a strongly female bias to the crowds. There can be little doubt that the support for Queen Caroline was a revival of that evoked by the death of Charlotte, though whereas Charlotte had indeed been a young wife of unblemished reputation, the description of her mother as an innocent woman wronged is better ascribed to the desire for a mythical figure of a pure character as head of the state than to any accommodation with the realities of the Queen's private life. Nevertheless, this was an assertion of the moral and customary right, whatever the legal position, of a wife and mother to the protection of her legitimate spouse, and in addition the simple demand for good behaviour from the King. The call was for reform of the monarchy, not for its abolition.

Seventeen years later George's niece Victoria, who had been a baby at the time of his coronation, came to the throne. The memory of her aunt and her cousin were undoubtedly factors which helped her claim against that of her Hanoverian uncles for which there was some High Tory support. Radicals and republicans and it would seem many women, particularly younger ones, rallied to her support against her reactionary and authoritarian uncle. One member of the aristocracy had earlier written that she looked to Victoria to 'save us from Democracy, for it is impossible that she should not be popular when she is older and more seen'. At the time of her coronation the Duke of Buckingham and Chandos noted that 'the bitter disappointment caused by the untimely fate of the last female heiress presumptive gave deeper feelings to the interest with which she was regarded'.

Victoria's reign, the longest in English history, saw a strong reinforcement of the familial and domestic in the public image of the Royal Family, the development of rule by example as she herself expressed it. By its end her political actions had for a long time been masked by the image of a mother of the nation and the empire. An examination of the history of twentieth century British monarchs demonstrates the extent to which moral and familial rather than political language and values are clustered around them. It was after all an entirely familial matter which led to the only abdication in this century, and the press, broadsheet as well as tabloid, has given far more space to family disputes among the royals than to the activities, charitable or quasi-political, which occupy much of the time of those whose incomes derive from their royal status. The contemporary demand that the Royal Family mourn in a way that the tabloid press and television viewers deem to be the correct one is a part of this definition of the essential character of the monarchy. These are not demands though, however critically they are framed, that would be made by a populace which was anxious to do away with the monarchy, and the extent to which politicians of all parties have played along with the demands indicates a desire to accommodate the 'popular sentimentalism' which was let loose by the death of Princess Diana in such a way as to strengthen the monarchy by the cure-all of 'modernisation'.

MEDIATE AND IMMEDIATE MOURNING

peter ghosh

a t the beginning of September 1997 the Oxford historian, Ross McKibbin, decided to go down to London—three times in fact—to try to understand what was going on there following the death of Princess Diana. Writing (as I do) in full consciousness of the burdens of the past, he had some ulterior motives: he wished to celebrate the 60th anniversary of Mass-Observation's striking study of the coronation of George VI, *May 12*, and he also sought to make some amends for the stupefying lack of curiosity displayed by the national media. The result was an essay in the *London Review of Books* (October 2, 1997) on the mourning and funeral of Princess Diana which was one of the best judged and most thoughtful pieces to have appeared amidst an immense coverage. And yet, being written from the Mass-Observer's perspective—that is to say, virtually as a participant—it placed a premium on *immediacy* of experience and analysis at the expense of other angles of approach. However, in one form or another, all the public's mourning of Diana was vicarious and *mediated*—even those who went down to London did so only as a result of messages conveyed to them by newspaper, TV and radio; while for most people (but for how many? and for how long?) mourning was not done in person, by going down to London where it would be open to the eye of the Mass-Observer, but at home, principally by sitting in front of the TV. Ross McKibbin has triumphantly vindicated M-O as a technique and has produced a unique record of his own—something given to very few academic historians; but he also came close to omitting the mediated quality of the events which lay at their heart. Might I then offer another view?

The assumption has been widespread that the act of mourning was a public hiatus, 'a remarkable moment in the history of modern Britain', but it is not so. The death and mourning of Diana occurred within the context of a pre-existing media audience of enormous dimensions, established over a number of years, and everyone knew this. Tony Blair knew it, when he made his statement at 10:28 A.M. on the Sunday morning of Diana's death—a time when half the 'British people' had not even woken up—and left the Tories invisible, without hope of redress. The BBC knew it, and pre-empted *its* rivals just as effectively.

The Gross Hypocrisy Prize—and this in a week where the shade of Tartuffe was as much in evidence as that of Diana—must go to television. By putting a microphone in front of distressed mourners and asking them to emote on cue, they claimed that they were giving the ordinary inarticulate citizen 'a voice'. In fact the BBC, reasoning from Diana's known vulnerability, both of emotion and of situation, had planned for the event of her death in advance—as indeed was announced in the following week's *Radio Times* by John Morrison, Editor, TV news programmes: 'we had worked to a fictional scenario involving the death of a leading royal in a car crash in a foreign country recently. It proved amazingly prescient.' (Connoisseurs of the contemporary debasement of language and feeling will note that this was labelled 'The BBC Way', and appeared as part of a special 'Tribute' to Diana.) But the pre-arranged nature of the response was always obvious given its machine-like precision and uniformity: as early as 6:40 A.M. on that first Sunday morning, 'the news operation [was] at full stretch, serving ten BBC national and international networks'. Manipulation was also registered by the mass protest of viewers against it—they finally secured the restoration of ordinary programmes on BBC2 in the afternoon—just as it was by the subsequent condemnation of BBC coverage voiced by 98 percent of those contacting Radio 4's *Feedback* programme and also by the rather different response of ITV and ITN. It is a truism to consider the commercial stations as the more 'popular' networks, yet they were much slower off the mark and their ordinary programmes received (as is well-known) very good ratings on that same Sunday night. They are, however, decentralized: ITN cannot impose itself on the regional stations, which are thus less liable to dictation. Perhaps, then, the 'people' did not want what BBC Director General John Birt was so efficient in providing for them?—at least, not in such draconian fashion and without any alternative.

All the same, when we consider both the size of the media audience and the extraordinarily powerful kickstart given by Blair and Birt; when we consider, too, that Diana's death occurred at the end of the school and summer holidays—a time when 'real' news stories are at a discount, and one of the latest periods in the year when an open-air carnival in London is still feasible—the mourning seems almost overdetermined: it would have been extraordinary if it had *not* happened. It's true that the BBC did not give instructions about the laying of flowers, although undoubtedly lessons in state primary schools were devoted to the production of memorial pictures and booklets which then appeared on the railings; but anyone who had watched the coverage of the death of the murdered black teenager Stephen Lawrence, or the Liverpool toddler James Bulger, or of the Scottish schoolchildren massacred in Dunblane, knew exactly what the conventions were regarding cellophane and messages, and why the association of death with children—at first sight so curious—was automatic and apparently unquestioned. In saying this, I do not mean to question the sincerity of the public grief, but I do wish to see it for what it was—the product of a specific and analysable context. 'Irrational' feeling may not be 'rationally' analysable in its essential nature, but its historical occurrence certainly is.

The analysis Ross McKibbin offered us was largely socio-political. But while I am convinced that there is an important element of truth in what he said, it remains implausible to state that 'individual virtue', 'love, care, goodness', were the whole or even the primary cause behind what happened. If they had been, the remarkable coincidence of Mother Teresa's death at the same time would hardly have been passed over as it was—for whatever our view of Diana, noone will contest which of the two women had the greater, indeed the only, claim to have *sacrificed* some part of her life on the altar of loving care. No, in its content as in its scale, the mourning can only be explained by the nature of the pre-existing interest in Diana. I do not depreciate her real-life interests, but what she personified was not landmines and AIDS. It was a cocktail of sex, glitz and royalty, which seemed (like many forms of virtuosity) so self-evident in her lifetime, but which will in fact be hard to repeat. Combining the attributes of a Princess Margaret and a Marilyn Monroe really was quite unusual. Though the analogies between Diana's media life and that of the fantasy soap opera are embarrassingly obvious, her near-perfect fulfillment of the formula remains extraordinary: degrees of wealth, leisure, and physical preening 'we' can only dream about; a 'plot' of essential simplicity and (in its settings) predictability; and then an added garnish of moral commitment with a much broader slug of emotional upset that anyone could identify with—something which, in the teeth of all the evidence, seemed to make her 'one of us'.

Once we accept that the mourning was the ritual of a previously formed media community, then all the contradictions that were noticed in the social composition of the crowds fall away. A media community *can* embrace the men in suits (although evidence of the participation of middle-class male professionals is almost non-existent), the Home Counties women who pointedly refused to buy copies of the homeless people's magazine the *Big Issue*, the tourists and the picture-takers (on the one hand)—as well as the Asians, the poor and the rejected (on the other). One can see why, rationally, Tony Blair should take up the theme of national unity at this time: as some Labour politicians stated, the funeral rites were for many of them a re-enactment of that precedent moment of national unity, the general election. But though the election was remarkable in its way, the analogy will not hold: elections are not simply media events (though they are that as well): again, emotional abstention was barely tolerated in Diana's case, let alone different parties of opinion with balanced access to our screens. A media community is at once the most extensive and the thinnest community of all, where any kind of solidarity may be imagined; but this tells us nothing about social solidarity in 'real life'.

What we, rather than those really affected, should make of what happened is in one sense simple: where media are significant, these events should be weighed carefully; where not, not. How this works out concretely is more problematic. The royal family, who depend so much on the media, may well be disturbed. The old prop supplied by a Reithian BBC has gone, as has been progressively clear since the monarchy's *annus horribilis*, and if it does not build bridges to that world where ratings and finance are the real king and queen, they may be in difficulty. On the other hand, although the Windsors have had a hard time, the logic of any sort of personality worship, let alone worship of the mother of the princes in direct line of succession, continues to place them at an enormous advantage. (It was no doubt typical of Earl Spencer, an aristocrat, to think that an appeal to 'blood' ties would work against the royal family; but since their blood is even better than his, he was palpably mistaken.) But whatever the future chances of the monarchy, I doubt that for the ordinary viewer this was a remarkable moment in our history. Princess Diana's funeral may have beaten the Euro 96 soccer championships in the ratings but the vicarious catharsis which comes through *other* soaps or sports is something which happens every day of the week. Her ratings were so high because they were occasional, and her elegies belonged to a much, much rarer class of event—the celebrity death.

For this reason the dangers that some descried in the public grief are at worst remote, and at best illusory. In the illusory category comes the idea that the mourning was a kind of mass hysteria, 'of the sort that let the Nazis in'. This is unjust to the mourners whom Ross McKibbin so sensitively portrayed, and displays ignorance not merely of German history but (once more) of the difference between real and media events. More real was the mindless, uniformitarian conformism induced first by the BBC, but spreading to almost anyone who had it in their power to pay some public or semi-public 'mark of respect', without even the barest attempt to consult the public thus affected. Second prize in the Tartuffe Stakes, with a special mention for self-awareness and propriety, must go to the anonymous Oxford University official who thought it relevant to close the Bodleian Library in honour of that notoriously bookish alumna of the university, Princess Di, with a Highly Commended to the ITV programmer who thought that Jane Austen's *Emma*—which hinges, after all, on the profound fulfillment experienced by someone Diana's age marrying someone Charles' age—-was appropriate viewing for the evening of her funeral. But though picking up on the absurdities displayed by a form of censorship yields a certain 'behind the Iron Curtain' *frisson,* the foundations of this censorship were always voluntary and commercial despite its bureaucratic and malodorous superstructure.

Still, let us not forget those people who put up with forms of media restraint all the time. Thus it is only the London media and inhabitants of the Home Counties who think that the Queen is necessarily 'with her people' (as even broadsheets had it) when she is at Buckingham Palace. Scots did not take such a dim view of her residence at Balmoral, while the way the emotional temperature dropped as one moved outside a 100-mile radius from London was palpable. And was it not noticeable that the only sports event that came to grief was Scottish? (As I say, sports events are media events, too, and hence the extraordinary enthusiasm displayed by experienced media/sports stars in wearing black armbands, seeking to impose funerary rituals on Italian motor races, etc.) Most productions by the 'national' media have a pronounced metropolitan bias, and the mourning of Diana was no exception.

If there be any more profound cultural shift at work, it relates to the way we choose to celebrate death socially, something which has been progressively at a discount since 1918. But whatever happens in the future, it will not be a reversion to a so-called Victorian (but really pre-modern) type. Through either war, disease or poverty, failure to live out one's biological life-span used to be commonplace; the experience of the aged had the highest of all imprimaturs attached to it, long life, just as it does in large parts of Asia and Africa today; while dying in old age really was a cause for celebration. But in the developed world this has all changed, and the aging of populations up to and slightly beyond that span is a financial and ethical *problem*. It is for this reason that today the only deaths which really engage us socially are the deaths of the young and very young. Diana's own relative youth and her associations with children and motherhood were thus crucial to her mourning: had she been five years older, it would have been a different story.

This, then, was a set of events which were absolutely explicable in their media presentation and reception, and yet they were still exceptionally unlikely as events. It was statistically extraordinarily unlikely that a woman of such fame, of such social advantages, and with such specific attractions, should have died at such a particular age—and so it is almost unthinkable that anyone alive today will see anything like the first week of September 1997 again. Even a near-repetition will inevitably appear routine. In this sense, quite different historical analogies suggest themselves. Consider, for example, the extraordinary media obsequies surrounding the sinking of the Titanic—an event which so mesmerised the nine-year-old George Orwell that it meant more to him than the entire reportage of the Great War. Did anything like it ever happen again?

six

PRINCESS DI, MOTHER T., AND ME

christopher hitchens

S aturday, August 30. By tradition, the waning of summer. Returning latish from a beach picnic to find the telephone trilling away, I pick it up and discover CNN on the line. Will I comment on 'a breaking news story'? 'We have a report from Paris. Dodi Fayed has been killed in a car accident and there's no word on Princess Diana. She's in the hospital.'

Well, no, *of course* I won't comment. I wasn't born yesterday. I don't even know what's happened. And the only reason I am on the CNN Rolodex, for a call like this, is that I sometimes fill the anti-monarchist chair in roundtables on the subject. From 'Mr. Republican' to 'royal-watcher' is a ludicrous move, and in this case a potentially sickening one. *Well, yes, Bernie, the news of Princess Diana's double amputation—unconfirmed at this time—reminds us all once again of the need for Britain to have a written constitution.* No thank you. They entreat from Atlanta. I am firm.

Sunday, August 31. Wake up and hear the news. When I pick up the telephone, it seems somehow *heavier.* And the telltale tone warns of messages left since I bleeped the previous night. It takes almost an hour to spool through the calls from television stations. There are more than 30 of them. I call back the *Today* show.

Why am I doing this, or do I do this? Well, I can never forget Gore Vidal's advice—not originally addressed to me personally, I need hardly add—that one should never pass up a chance either to have sex or to appear on the small screen. As a bloated husband and father, I am now free to reflect that this remark was obviously made well before the advent of . . . cable TV.

There's another reason. If you drone on as I do about the use of television to created a bogus 'consensus' that is miles wide and a millimeter deep, then you ought not to be 'out' when they ring and say, O.K., fair's fair—it's your turn. They'll only say, Well, we tried to be 'inclusive,' but he squirmed free of our outreach program. (You really don't think they really talk like that? They really do.)

Monday, September 1. Washington is deserted for Labor Day, if you except the knot of mourners already gathering outside Her Majesty's Embassy. A 20-year-old boy, interviewed as he leaves flowers there, is asked what She meant to him. 'Role model,' he replies at once. 'A very strong role model.' Say *what*? But the interviewer acts as if this makes sense to him. At the studio, I find that Katie Couric is already in London and sitting outside the palace, where a crowd is seriously worked up against the press. I can only hear America's sweetheart through a crackling earpiece. Those interviewed before me, including Katherine Graham, are all agreed. The Princess has been slain by the paparazzi. Michael Cole, smarmy spokesman for the Fayed family, is interviewed by Miss Couric and is allowed too much of his own way for my taste.

From the perfectly fluted lips of Miss Couric I hear the detested words 'Christopher Hitchens . . . royal-watcher'. It's my turn, along with Andrew Roberts of the *Sunday Times*. He blames the paparazzi also. I say, Look here, steady on, chaps. This driver was going so fast that he got the radiator of a big Mercedes shoved into its front seat. (*Imagine* the damage.) A danger to everyone on the road as well as to his passengers. Perhaps not all the Fayed 'security' team are such fragrant characters. A sneering, drawling voice comes from London. 'It's a disgrace for

Mr. Hitchens to effectively blame Princess Diana for her own death. . . . You are a left-wing republican journalist.' This—at least the first bit— is a low blow, as well as a split infinitive, and I squeak in protest, unsettling Miss Couric. We are soon out of time. I seethe uselessly at Roberts, who generally takes a pro-Charles and anti-Diana line and looks down on mob emotions, but is today playing the crowd-pleaser. I must arrange to cross swords with him properly one day.

Still, at least this was traction: something said against the mounting tide of drool and its sinister accompaniment—the hoarse cry for blame and punishment. Get home to find the answering machine filled up again. Begin to learn the first rule of 'media rush', which is that if you say something on one network, all the others want to book you at once so you can come on and say precisely the same thing. No wonder politicians look like zombies when they are campaigning. The *Los Angeles Times*, which asked me for a quick op-ed comment on the death, has run it under the headline WHICH WAS THE REAL DIANA? MOTHER TERESA OR MRS. SIMPSON. How irritating. When I am not arguing that Britain should be a constitutional republic, I am trying to point out that Mother Teresa is no synonym for innocence and humanity. Yet that's exactly how headline and caption writers always use her. I must complain when I get a spare minute. Meanwhile, it's about 10 radio interviews from the kitchen and then off to MSNBC. I repeat the point about the Ray-Ban-wearing, probably drug-sodden cowboy in the Fayed entourage. But a lot of people don't want to hear this. It's a combination of masochism in the press—crying before they can be hurt—and 'denial' in the crowd, who can't bear anything that might taint the canonization in progress. This is yet another time when everything depends on how people 'feel' and not at all on what, if anything, anyone thinks.

A bizarre discussion has begun. It's all about the British national labia. Are the *upper* ones of this unit, people desire to know, sufficiently rigid? Or as rigid as they once were? Has flaccidity set in? Why are they asking *me*? Suddenly this ghastly question is—you must forgive the expression—on every lip. I can't wait till it isn't.

Tuesday and Wednesday, September 2 and 3. Another beatification is taking place before our eyes. It's that of Prince William. Grief-striken people want to make him King at once, elbowing aside his grandma and his dad. See me, feel me, touch me, heal me. Don't people have any pity for this boy they so adore? Can they hear themselves, when they urge him toward a throne that ruined the lives of both of his parents? Is he to be some kind of blood bank? I refer to 'the House of Dracula' on MSNBC and get into 'quote of the week' in the next day's *New York Post.* Oh dear.

Kathie Lee Gifford—I'm learning a lot about the TV wasteland this week—goes before her studio audience to say that the U.S. Constitution guarantees the pursuit of happiness, also the free press. What to do when the first is challenged by the second? Why, change the Constitution! There are cretinous studio cheers, undoubtedly expressing a certain 'mood'. Where to begin? I could write a letter, pointing out that the 'pursuit' stuff isn't in the Constitution but in quite another document which declares American independence from the British monarchy. But . . . nah. This wouldn't be the week to bring *that* up.

Thursday and Friday, September 4 and 5. Things are beginning to blur, also to clarify. One or two voices are being raised, of the 'enough already' sort. Maureen Dowd writes scathingly of celebrity martyrdom. The great Brian Lamb asks me onto his Friday-morning C-SPAN journo hour, paired with Wes Pruden of the *Washington Times.* It's clear we've both been asked because we are not votaries of the cult-in-formation. The calls and faxes run in our favor, from audience members who are in despair at the wall-to-wall effect. But we still only discuss one other topic. It's the absurd photograph of the fundraising Buddhist nuns, testifying on the Hill against the luckless Al Gore (or is it the lucky Al Gore, since his week of shame has been buried in the flowers of a far-off field?). Brian Lamb prods me and I say, half asleep, that if those could only be Mother Teresa nuns caught on the take it would make my week. By the time this show has been repeated later in the day, that remark looks like poor taste. And my telephone has approached melting point, as people ring to tell me that M.T., that ghoulish fourteenth-century vixen, has finally dropped from her Calcutta perch. Once again, I am offered slivers of 'equal time' to be disobliging about the idea of someone who has just died. And, once again, all the coverage is predicated and organized on the assumption that everybody thinks and feels the same way—indeed, that there is only one conceivable or available response. I also notice something about blanket coverage. More Means Worse! One excuse for doing only one subject from early morn to dewy eve might be that you can visit and revisit each aspect of the situation, inform people very fully, and bring in every point of view. But the networks and the newspapers are doing none of these things. They are creating an echo-chamber atmosphere, based on complete uniformity and regular repetition. I would find this rather chilling even if I agreed with what was being said, or rather, sobbed.

Tom Brokaw's people call. They assure me that there are those at NBC who feel things have gotten out of hand and out of proportion. Will I come on a *Nightly News* segment that says so? This involves almost a whole afternoon of waiting about, in the pleasant company of Ben Bradlee, among others, to say so. The promised 'segment' is a nanosecond blip in a torrent of inexpensive, unanimous sentimentality.

Saturday, September 6. The Spencer girl's funeral live on all channels. Having been suddenly moved, to my own slight surprise, by the last, wraithlike pictures of her on the Fayed 'surveillance tape', I am unmanned again to find that I have the same taste in hymns ('I Vow to Thee My Country' in the Cecil Spring-Rice version, 'Cwm Rhondda'—'Bread of Heaven', from the Welsh—and the 'Londonderry Air', known to some as 'Danny Boy' and to us republicans, I suppose, as the 'Derry Air'). I have long regarded her brother, Earl Spencer, as a posturing lordling with shady friends and a grudge against a press which printed unpleasant truths about him several years ago, so I tune out his speech. A mistake. Anthony Holden, the best of the week's many real 'royal-watchers', points out that the address contained a brilliant Wars of the Roses ingredient that more than matched Elton John's rose. So I have to watch the whole thing again. Worth it. The weekend edition of the *Financial Times* contains an obit for M.T., written by her official hagiographer, Navin Chawla. With the compassion and humility of his sort, Mr. Chawla uses the shelter of the obit for an underhand attack on your humble servant. Mentioning my pamphlet *The Missionary Position: Mother Teresa in Theory and Practice*, he says that 'in the west, the book was largely dismissed as the rantings of a conspiracy theorist'. Oh no it wasn't. It was dismissed—widely ignored might be a better phrase—as the dronings of a poor wretch who had no invisible means of support.

My *Vanity Fair* piece on the monarchy ('Tarnished Crown', September 1997) is still on the newsstands, and I have to resist the temptation to check it for prescience in view of the awful and unexpected news. But let's have a peek, Hmmm. Out-of-touch monarchy being upstaged by clever young Tony Blair. Diana the only popular and charismatic one. The other royals dowdy and exhausted, except for the handsome boy Prince who ought to be spared the gruesome succession. Charles terminally stiff and awkward. Kitty Kelley's book about to burst on the scene. . . . Hey, this isn't bad. But could I honestly say I guessed that people could feel this way about *Diana*? Forget it, Hitchens. There are depths of the soul that are hidden from your sort. On impulse I call Kitty Kelley. I hope she's not weakening. Her answering machine no longer plays the national anthem and no longer invites you to 'leave your royal message'. (Before that, it was Ol' Blue Eyes crooning 'My Way'.) Perhaps she *is* weakening.

Sunday, September 7. I'm asked to appear on *Meet the Press*. (By now, the people in my building are used to seeing camera crews in the lobby and limos at the door.) Sally Quinn and I face the usual suspects in London, including Andrew Roberts again. I can see him this time: a rather faded blond with a sickly grin. He doesn't have the grace to climb down about the drunken driver, but he no longer poses as a defender of the Princess, and suggests that Prince Charles was the real injured party in that frightful marriage. Tim Russert gives me plenty of time to make a bad boy of myself, while smilingly assuring me in the break that I can forget about the next segment which deals with matters Calcuttan. I have already met a priest in the greenroom, who demands to know if I have ever experienced an act of God's grace. (Isn't he supposed to be in church at this time of the morning?) My answer, which is in the negative, appears to offend him personally. When can we expect a separation of Church and Network? Not this week.

Monday, September 8. An interesting finding, but one that is difficult to record without sounding like a Nixonian politician or a spin doctor. My personal voice mail is running 10 to 1 in my own favor. As a general thing, complainers write and ring much more than those who approve. But those who call me up (I'm in the book) or write to me are overwhelmingly positive. Some people prefer to telephone the magazine in the hope of getting me fired, but in the course of the week—so I am assured—that tone changed in my favour also. I get so many Mother Teresa calls that I put a message on my answering machine, telling of her many services to the richest of the rich and the tawdriest of the tawdry, and of her many lectures on sexual continence to 'the poorest of the poor' (as it seems compulsory, for some reason, to refer to them). The *Washington Post* 'Style' section reprints the gist of this, as does the *New York Post*, referring to me as Christopher 'Hellbound' Hitchens. The number of 'hits' on my answering-machine multiplies. All are enthusiastic except for a Father Daly in Maryland who nearly suffers a clerical thrombosis while leaving his foam-flecked message, in which I am contrasted to my disadvantage with the noble and pure example of the young Earl Spencer: a rare instance of fawning Anglophilia from a Hibernian windbag. He is good enough to include his number, which rude communicants almost never do, so I send him a fax advising him that someone is using his name to leave insulting inarticulate noises on the voice mail of strangers. I promise all my cooperation in the unmasking of the culprit.

Tuesday, September 9. As Diana Week becomes Teresa Week, a difference of emphasis emerges. Whereas the Princess was promoted from human to martyr all in one go, and proposed for metaphorical or media canonization at warp speed, Mother Teresa has been drowning in 100 percent adoring and favorable publicity for 25 years. And now that she is a candidate for literal canonization, the media can't find anything to say that it hasn't said many times already. (This ought to, but doesn't put people on their guard.) When I am accused of attacking the old girl just after she died, my strategy is to say that I always attacked her when she was alive.

Wednesday, September 10. Peter Jennings calls. Will I come on a *Nightline* special that covers M.T.'s funeral in Calcutta? Yes. After he hangs up, I think: Good man. He also tried to inject a sceptical note into the Diana discussion. Then I think: Another chance for a bit of grave-dancing. Who am I to be calling people ghouls? I'm the authorized, official pissser-on of people's funerals. This goes to show that we live in a pluralist culture and society where all shades of opinion are canvassed and indeed broadcast. I take another gulp from the poisoned chalice of publicity.

A breakthrough. The Calcutta *Telegraph*, one of the best newspapers in Bengal, has published an essay about M.T. which says, 'It was the misery of Calcutta that built up and continued to sustain her reputation, that induced the rich and powerful to give her money and patronage. But Calcutta has little reason to be grateful. It was she who owed a tremendous debt to Calcutta. No other city in the world would offer up its poor and dying to be stepping stones in a relentless ascent to sainthood.' The piece is by Sunanda Datta-Ray, one of India's most reputable writers. And the London *Times* has reported it prominently. This gives 'permission' for other media outlets to report that there is dislike of M.T. in her home base. Still, it's amazing to see how hesitantly most TV and radio and print people approach the very idea that there could be another side to a question. Nonetheless, however tentatively, more of them are calling me for comment. I get 10 minutes to myself on a Murdoch-owned TV channel in Australia. Junkies need their daily fix.

I am starting to look permanently made-up, which is one of the signs of the micro-celeb. Also, I half knot a tie in the mornings, on the assumption that I'll need it in the course of the day. When this is over, will there be withdrawal symptoms?

Friday, September 12. Up to the big city for *Nightline*. The whole ABC set is arranged as if we lived in a one-party monotheist state. 'Mother Teresa: A Mission of Mercy'. 'A Tribute'. Etc. I was always taught that the news should not editorialize. (Call me old-fashioned if you will.) Still, I know from conversations with researchers that every network is under the same pressure. You did live coverage for the Princess and not for the Saint? For shame! So here we all are, staying up to an impossible hour in order to give live coverage to something that almost nobody wants to watch. Want to know the ratings for the M.T. funeral? Four point one was the highest, and that (if I do say so myself) was for ABC, CBS and Fox posted 1.5 and 1.4 respectively. But the earlier wall-to-wall meant we were stuck, no doubt for reasons of 'balance', with another wall-to-wall.

And there was nothing to watch. Whether held back or not by the Indian troops, the poor of Calcutta stayed away in droves. Vast tracts of open pavement were on view behind Jennings's head, and there were huge vacant spaces inside the stadium. Nonetheless, a script is a script, and must be adhered to. 'Astonishing outpouring' was a standby left over from the previous week. Best moment—the attempt to go to a reporter who was in the thick of it. 'I'm standing in the street, Peter,' he yelled, hand pressed to his earpiece. 'A totally empty street, as it happens.' That did not make the air. But since there was no American TV audience to watch the absence of a Calcutta audience, there must be some doubt as to whether this non-audience ever really transpired at all. The newspapers reported the 'surprisingly' low turnout, and some claimed to find a paradox in the sponsorship of the obsequies by the might and pomp of the Indian state. Actually, it was back in 1972 that Indira Gandhi adopted Mother Teresa and gave her India's highest decoration. (Yes, the same Indira Gandhi who went on to suspend India's constitution, lock up the press and the opposition, and impose a policy of compulsory sterilization.) Mother Teresa was no stranger to might and pomp—it was the press that was a stranger to the evidence of it.

•   •   •

I get my chance to say some of this, but at the precise moment when I am invited to do so, unseen by me, the camera lingers on the open coffin, the upturned old face, and the sprinkled incense. My wife, watching at home, has lately, what with one thing and another, become quite hardened. But she told me it gave her quite a turn even so. Watching a tape, I whistle at the amazing timing. Fifteen years I've waited for *Nightline* to ask my opinion of M.T. And now this. But ABC can now claim to have canvassed, and transmitted, all shades of opinion.

The Greek tycoon scribbler 'Taki', in *The Spectator*, writes a courageous and outspoken column, going against the stream once more by praising M.T. for her charity work. He adds that I personally 'must be enjoying her death. After all, his mendacious book might sell a copy or two among those who don't know what a snake he is.' And, presumably, even among those who *do* know. A vaguely consoling reflection.

Sunday and Monday, September 14 and 15. I am denounced, in the same news cycle, by a columnist in the *New York Post*, by Cardinal O'Connor, and by Rosie O'Donnell. Every time I put down the phone, it rings again. Brent Bozell in the *Post* has heard the fragment of an M.T. obit that I recorded for National Public Radio about a year ago, when it looked as though she might check out. *All Things Considered* is denounced for including me. 'There you have it', fumes Bozell, 'the life of an angel, reduced to dirt by a reprehensible Marxist guttersnipe.' I had no idea it was that easy. Mr. Bozell is proud of his loyalty to his

namesake and father, who was a speechwriter and biographer to Senator
Joe McCarthy. They share a tendency to flattering exaggeration.

Ms. O'Donnell kicks off her diatribe with the usual description of
M.T. as 'pretty much a living saint', and denounces ABC for featuring a
puke-making Brit (whose foul accent she lampoons). 'What kind of a
cynical person? . . . I wanna get this guy on!' I telephone her booker and
publicist. First, I loved the 'pretty much'. Second, I'll come on any time.
Third, I was the guy who wrote a *Vanity Fair* Spotlight on her in
September '93. The accompanying pic had her grinding her high heel
into some man's underwear. I always thought Betty Rubble was a bad
career move for her. So it's come to this. I have to become the sort of person who rings up daytime TV shows.

The *New York Post* reports Cardinal O'Connor, 'leader of New
York's three million Catholics', deploring 'the almost unbelievably tasteless manner in which some of the television and radio stations reported
on the life and death of Mother Teresa'. His spokesman, Joseph Zwilling,
is reported by Karen Lee Phillips as having identified me as the target of
this homily. I call Zwilling. What is it in my book or my critique to
which he objects? Zwilling denies saying any of this to the reporter, and
says he's never read my book. I call the reporter and tell her that Zwilling
is calling her a liar. Let God sort it out. In the last interview I read with
the cardinal, he regretted having denounced *The Satanic Verses* without
going to the bother of reading it. A useful late-blooming insight, probably too quickly forgotten.

Words to avoid this week, or perhaps any week from now on: 'idol'
and 'icon'. These once meant only the show-biz versions of graven-image
worship, or the cult of mortal beings. Now they mean the real thing. And
spiritual and secular leaderships compete to prostrate themselves. By the
way, what have we 'chosen' for our idols and icons? A simpering Bambi
narcissist and a thieving, fanatical Albanian dwarf. Nice going.

Tuesday and Wednesday, September 16 and 17. Kitty Kelley launches. I
send a samizdat copy to a friend in London. There's a skirmish on both

flanks of the Atlantic. Was her timing in bad taste? Is there anything new in her book? Does she make anything up? By now I'm back on the everyday turf of Pacifica Radio, BBC World Service and CNBC's *Equal Time*. I go through the motions (no, it wasn't; yes, there is; no, she doesn't). I learn something from going on a chat show on Irish radio with antique British satirist Richard Ingrams, former editor of *Private Eye*. Apparently, Evelyn Waugh always maintained that the Queen Mother could get pregnant only if suspended by her legs from a chandelier. So perhaps the artificial insemination story is well founded. But it's not the same somehow. I don't get the chance to say that M.T., having campaigned in Ireland in 1995 to keep the Irish constitutional ban on divorce, then instantly gave an interview to *Ladies' Home Journal*, approving the divorce of her friend Princess Di on the grounds that her marriage had been so unhappy!

The *New York Times* runs an article comparing the fate of Kitty's book to mine. The wistful, therapy-sodden headline: BEING CRITICAL WHEN BELOVED FIGURES DIE. Kitty is quoted as being suitably sad and restrained, and turning down requests for interviews 'immediately following Diana's death'. The reporter goes on: 'That kind of reticence was not shared by Christopher Hitchens, who quickly agreed to interviews in the aftermath of Mother Teresa's death'. Including, indeed, the one that led to this stab-in-the-front article. And it's O.K. to rush before the cameras if you are going to say the same thing as everybody else. Still, being underbid by K.K. in the brazen stakes is a trophy of a kind.

• • •

What I learned from my brief excursion into the rarefied media layer is this: Michael Frayn was right, in his novel *The Tin Men*. There really is a department somewhere which asks consumers of news whether, on learning of a train crash, they want 'children's toys still lying pathetically among the wreckage' or, on learning of a plane crash, they want it 'backed up with a story about a middle-aged housewife who had been booked to fly aboard the plane but who had changed her mind at the last moment'. If ever you criticize the prevailing news values, whether to a booker or a researcher or a pre-interviewer or a presenter, you will always be told that the public wants it this way, and is only being given what it wants, and indeed likes what it gets. So that's all right then. Of course, the public can have it any way it likes with entertainment, or sports, or chat shows, or movies (though I think that people in focus groups who demand moist and happy endings should be compelled to view the 'product' produced in their name). But news can't be made to fit a profile, because news by definition involves telling people what they don't know, and may not even 'like'. That in turn is why so much trouble is taken, in designing news coverage, to put the emphasis on what people know, or think they know, already. That's why a fringe republican, this past September, achieved brief notoriety as a 'royal-watcher', and that's how miners in West Virginia happened to be shaken awake and polled about whether a certain Charles could now decently wed Camilla Parker Bowles. If the miners had not desired this treatment, surely they would not have been given it.

seven

THE SECULAR SAINT

sara maitland

'It was just like Lourdes,' said several of my friends and acquaintances who had actually been to the Mall during the week after Her death to look at the crowds looking at each other and sharing their grief. (None of the people I know admitted that they went because they wanted to share *their* grief.) 'It was just like Lourdes.'

At Lourdes—the premier shrine of the Virgin Mary in Europe—there are crowds of people. Between the performance of elaborately choreographed ritual activities, people tend to drift about, seeking emotional or spiritual experiences or the loss of ego in the place's collective spirituality. The crowds are dense, highly charged, and susceptible. Pride of place is given to the suffering, particularly the sick, since Lourdes is famous for its miraculous healing spring. Those normally among the most marginalised become the centre of attention, and are also seen to represent the healthy, the fit and the secure. The very ill are wheeled through and among the crowds by enthusiastic carers, who gain merit both from their demonstrated compassion and from their close association with suffering. Around the shrine there is a marketplace of vulgarity. In the centre of the shrine is a huge church, a small grotto and a complicated queuing system for both the secular toilets and the miraculous baths.

Everywhere there is religion. The iconography of Western Christianity is blatant and dominates the mood and forms the expression of feeling. The externals of religious faith are flagrantly displayed. The candles flicker. Each evening there is an enormous procession—the air is warm and thousands of flecks of fire dance in the dark. A long trite song with a frequently repeated refrain winds on and on. This the iconography not of religion in general (though flowers and candles are symbolic across faiths and geographies), but quite specifically of Roman Catholicism. Throughout the world there are special shrines in honour of Mary: Lourdes, Fatima, Guadeloupe, Knock, Medjagore, Monserrat. And one of the reasons why they are so successful is because Marian devotions give Roman Catholics a strong sense of identity, of difference and specialness. Even other Christians can't really share her. *Our* Lady, not yours.

At a superficial level then the scenes in the Mall were quite like Lourdes. There were an awful lot of people, in dense and highly emotionally charged crowds, who had a large purpose but very little concrete activity. A remarkable amount of attention was given by the self-appointed acolytes of this occasion, the journalists, to anyone who could display 'suffering'. In the absence of many very sick people, any outsider would do: the very young, the very old, ethnic or sexual minorities. By paying attention to them specifically, media professionals could both identify with the whole crowd and gain merit from their own visible association with such suffering.

There was, too, a marketplace of vulgarity. Among the bestsellers (apart from the flowers and the candles which I will come to) were loops of black ribbon, icons of the Princess and union jacks. Not a bad transfer from crosses, icons of Mary and portraits of the Pope. And towering over the whole scene was the high cathedral of monarchy, Buckingham Palace, which provided a focus of (disgruntled) attention.

There was a grotto—in the shape of the room in St. James' palace where the sacred books were laid out for signing. There were long patient lines of people. There was a strong feeling of ownership, and hence identity: our Princess, ours, not yours, our *English Rose*. A mysterious *we* emerged: just as the sick at Lourdes are an affirmation of a shared identity, so the carefully selected interviewees in the Mall became representatives of the grief of 'ordinary folk.' (In light of this, the number of black people chosen for vox pops was quite extrordinary in a country where, *pace* New Labour, old racism still thrives.)

And a great many of the central images from religion, specifically from Catholic religious traditions, were displayed. In particular, flowers and candles. Flowers heaped up anywhere that could possibly function as a shrine—expensive and useless flowers, not to be displayed for beauty but simply to generate volume. In Catholicism flowers have long been a sign of popular devotion. In the crypt of St. Peter's in Rome, for example, I have seen someone move a bunch of flowers from the very meagre display around the tomb of Pope Paul VI to that of John XXIII, despite the fact that it was already piled high. This was not an aesthetic but a political act: one of the requirements for canonisation (for being declared an official saint) is that there be demonstrable popular devotion to a deceased candidate. Thus laity can influence such decisions by making clear that there is a popular cult; an obvious way to do that is to heap a tomb with flowers.

Candles are the next step down this line. Although it is perfectly acceptable to light candles at people's graves, or in their memory, they are more sacralised than flowers are, more explicitly devotional. More flowers than candles lie on the graves of the beloved departed; more candles than flowers are offered in exchange for prayers at the shrines of saints. If there is a statistical correlation you could say that the Diana cult in the Mall was at an earlier stage than Marian cult in Lourdes even though there is clearly some overlap: the flowers may have died, but the Elton John candles are still selling world-wide.

If there was indeed some real parallel, both in emotion and in iconography, between the Mall and Lourdes, it is at least as interesting to look at how they were different.

The first difference was the clear absence in the Mall of anything that parallelled the liturgical function of the priesthood. One of the most marked presences at Lourdes is that of the clergy (and the sub-clergy, in the shape of nuns)—people in easily recognisable uniforms who represent the forces of order, who will take all the emotion and channel it properly. If Buckingham Palace represented the Basilica, there was no one at the altar. (Both high altar and balcony compel a crowd below to look upwards, they are elevated via their own gaze, they are given a specific performance, a job to do.) Did the anger expressed towards the Royal Family by the crowd stem from their lack of someone to lead their emotions, to provide a focus, a place to look? Unlike more optimistic left-wingers I am unable to see this anger as a sign of the end of monarchy. On the contrary the crowd's passionate demand for the physical presence of members of an institution whom they believed to have driven their beloved to the grave seems to me to speak for a need for royalty that is alarmingly strong.

The second, and to me more interesting, difference was the complete absence of any contribution to the activities in the Mall, or more widely to the memorialization of Diana, from the Roman Catholic Church. It was quite conspicuous—though on the whole the media chose not to notice it—and apparently took place at every level of Roman Catholicism. Almost every head of state around the world sent unctuous messages of sympathy. Who was the exception? The head of the Vatican, His Holiness Pope John Paul II. At the other end of the ecclesiastical scale, Anglican Churches went into overdrive with extra opening-hours and waves of enthusiasm for the new wellspring of 'spirituality' that they were 'failing to meet' (according to the Archbishop of Canterbury), while Catholic parishes stood aloof. In my parish church—in a small sub-industrial town in the East Midlands—we prayed for Diana Princess of Wales somewhere in the middle of the list of the dead for that week— her demise marked no more nor less than that of the local deceased. That was it. We prayed for the repose of her soul and went on to the next business (which, for the liturgically ignorant, is the taking of the collection—doubtless *far* more important). I do not know if this was policy—national or diocesan—or an individual decision of our parish priest. I do know anecdotally that it was repeated in a number of other parishes with different demographics. To me, indifferent to the drama of the occasion, this seemed both entirely appropriate and something of a relief, and I never heard any complaints about it from other lay members of the congregation. Either Catholics managed to be unmoved as a community or they did not feel that it was a Church event.

The *Tablet*, the British weekly magazine of progressive Catholicism, had a leader article when it came out the Thursday following Diana's death, but by the time I proposed a small feature for the edition of the week of the funeral, the editorial decision was that they had already covered all the bases. The *Catholic Herald*, the weekly Catholic newspaper with a more conservative and nationalist stance than the *Tablet*, covered the event and the funeral, but without any religious hoo-hah. They were quite taken up by the death of Mother Teresa, which was clearly judged to be of more importance to their readers than Diana's.

From the point of view of traditional Catholicism this is not at first enormously surprising. Roman Catholicism probably rightly sees itself as more international than other mainstream UK Christian denominations. It is less concerned with English Roses, or indeed English princesses of Wales, who, according to the law, cannot ever be Catholics. From an official RC position Diana was an adulterous and heretical divorcée, who was carrying on with a Moslem. Moreover she was a woman whose standing in the world derived directly from her connection with a Royal Family unique in Europe in that it makes religious claims dangerously close to the papacy's own. The Church of England (and incidentally the Presbyterian Church of Scotland) is Established. The monarch is 'Head of the Church,' 'defender of the faith' and still appoints Church of England Bishops and authorises Anglican doctrine and liturgy. Diana, it might seem, is absolutely no concern of the Catholic hierarchy—whether in terms of personal or institutional morality.

Nonetheless the uninterested posture of English Catholicism (it is important to remember that Scottish Catholicism is not quite the same animal) towards the death of Diana has some curious elements to it.

English Roman Catholicism has been distinctly bullish of late. It almost appears to be going into partnership with sharing, caring, emoting and *non-socialist* New Labour. The religious flavour, fervour and sometimes rhetoric of Blairism suits Catholicism rather well. You can care for the poor and the oppressed without giving an inch on ideology, without even being asked to give an inch. This has been a problem for European Catholicism since the French Revolution. How can you seem to love the poor if the people who are loving them most effectively are doing so within an ideological or political framework which you must necessarily repudiate in order to maintain your own sense of identity? All liberation theology is inevitably suspect from the Vatican's point of view precisely because it draws on discourses which undermine the Church's more worldly ambitions.

But New Labour has got it just right. It even uses the vocabulary of most social action Catholicism: goodness rather than structural change, community rather than communism, partnership rather than unionism, fairness rather than justice, sharing rather than redistribution, self-reliance rather than state hand-outs. Before the May '97 general election the Roman Catholics Bishops' Conference of England and Wales produced a booklet of guidance to its members on the theological concerns that they should consider when preparing to vote. It was as near as it decently could be to an endorsement of Blairism. Most interestingly it fudged the one political issue which is supposed to be nearest to the heart of Catholic laity. It refused to allow Labour's continued support of legal abortion as a reason for not voting for its candidates and this despite the fact that the present Pope publicly describes abortion as the premier symbol of human rights abuse. The bishops did not condone Labour's position on abortion, but they made conspicuous efforts to place it within the context of other issues. Despite stringent denials this was a pro-Labour document. On the Prime Minister's side, there is the little 'scandal' of Blair personally receiving communion in his wife's Catholic parish. (It is difficult to believe that his parish priest did not know who he was, nor that he was not a Catholic). There is Blair's decision to remove his children from standard state education to send them to a grant-maintained premier Catholic school. Of course he can't actually be a Roman Catholic— neither the electorate nor the spin doctors would fancy it—but he would be if he could, was his message. An alliance both personal and political was being forged.

Meanwhile, the Roman Catholic Church has been profiting in a number of ways from the troubles of the Church of England. It has gained an enormous ethical authority from the difficulties that the Church of England has had in articulating a united front on issues such as sexuality, gender discrimination and the family. Judaism has gained likewise. The Chief Rabbi and the Roman Catholic Archbishop of Westminster now speak on 'moral' subjects to at least as much media attention and considerably more media respect than the Archbishop of Canterbury does. Why authoritarianism has so much credibility is a different question, but the Church of England, like the old Labour Party and the Conservative Party, is seen to be weakened and discredited by its inability to eliminate dissension.

Roman Catholicism has also picked up some high profile converts, including members of the Royal Family (the Duchess of Kent) and of Her Majesty's last government (Ann Widdecombe). There have been persistent rumours that Diana herself was receiving instruction (Catholic-speak for getting ready to convert) from, or at least baring her soul to, the Jesuits at Farm Street, socially the most up-market London Catholic Church.

The hierarchy also went to peculiar lengths, even waiving its hard-held insistence on celibacy, to admit a group of ex-Anglican clergy to its own priesthood. Some of this was pragmatic: it solved, or at least helped, a serious recruitment problem. Over 25 percent of the priests of the Diocese of East Anglia are now ex-Anglican clergy, and they have not been retrained; this constitutes a major cultural change within the Catholic Church. But the enthusiasm on the part of at least some Catholic bishops, notably Cardinal Basil Hume, to have these priests went well beyond the purely practical. It risked further souring difficult relations with two particularly sensitive groups of Catholics: priests who had left the job in order to get married and Roman Catholic women who wished to be ordained. (It was broadly understood that the clergy who left the Church of England and sought to become Roman Catholic priests did so because of their objections to the ordination of women.) It was considered more important to receive and affirm these married Anglicans than to avoid alienating these two groups, and others. I do not see any conspiracy here, but I do believe that at one level it was a deliberate attempt to shift the Catholic Church up-market and increase its profile among the cultured middle-classes, thus reducing its dependence on Irish Catholicism.

Hume himself is an establishment figure, and he clearly enjoys the intellectual and social sophistication of his grateful new boys. English Catholicism is rife with anti-Irish racism, of a kind that is difficult to describe. Until the last twenty years Catholicism in England was the heritage of eccentric aristocrats and immigrant communities. Since the emancipation of Catholics in the 1820s and even more since the re-establishment of the hierarchy in the 1860s, English Catholicism has wavered between pride in its peculiar social status, attractive but dependent on Ireland, and ambition to become fully integrated into English life. It has always drawn a large section of its leadership from Anglican converts—Manning and Newman being conspicuous among them—but in the past it has seemed to be more interested in drawing these people away from the English establishment than in using them to insert itself into that establishment. Now, however, the English Catholic hierarchy, like New Labour, wants to move its base away from the working classes, the welfare poor and the socially excluded immigrant groups and into middle-England. It wants to join the establishment; it has even hinted that it wants to be the establishment: intellectually viable, attractively traditional, totally respectable but still maintaining its links with the 'poor'. It is doing rather well.

If this is its chosen trajectory, why was the Roman Catholic Church so stand-offish about Diana? Particularly since Diana's mother, Frances

Shand Kydd, although also a divorcée, is herself a Catholic convert, the English hierarchy could have had at least a toe-hold in the funeral arrangements had they wanted. But the requiem mass held at the Cathedral was a private ritual, a million ecclesiastical miles from the weird post-Christian semi-pagan carryings-on just down the road at Westminster Abbey. And preaching at this mass, Cardinal Hume did something that would have been unusual if not extraordinary at any requiem—he launched into a disquisition about the, not very specific 'moral flaws' of the deceased. If it is untraditional for a lay man (even a member of the peerage) to use the pulpit of Westminster Abbey to slag off the royal family and the mass media, it is equally unusual for a member of the clergy to use the pulpit of Westminster Cathedral to remind a congregation of the moral inadequacies of a dead Protestant.

So what was going on? I would suggest that there is an underlying struggle for the ownership of some images and even emotions. The Roman Catholic Church, in Europe at least, has traditionally been the keeper of certain icons. Protestantism's deliberate rejection of conscious religious symbolism and sacrament has left Catholicism 'in charge' of many of the central representations of so-called high culture for the last five centuries. All the best architecture and large swathes of the visual arts and music (less so of literature, for reasons to do with the Protestant ease around concepts of 'word') have been linked to ethical and aesthetic performances and ideals which have been authorised and guaranteed by Roman Catholicism. Simultaneously, Catholicism has used these same symbols to provide a conduit and form of expression for mass emotion (a role taken on in the United States by Christian fundamentalist sects). In consequence, while Protestantism and the Enlightenment have provided creeds for the bourgeoisie, Catholicism has maintained its representational grip on both the poor (agricultural and industrialised) and the aristocracy. The secularisation of society, and the necessarily accompanying individualism and loss of a shared hyper-narrative, seems to have barely begun to challenge this hegemony.

But the need felt within the highest echelons of the Church first to 'modernise', via the extremely unmodern vehicle of the Second Vatican Council, and then to reassert authoritative control over its own members at a level unprecedented in history, suggest that members of the pro-papal, centralising, traditionalist wing of the Catholic church are well aware of their culturally threatened status.

Where Catholicism has been particularly effective is in the management of cultural representations of femininity and the valorisation of acceptable virtues. Catholicism has defined what virtue is, among other means by the canonising—making and patenting—of saints. It has also traditionally defined what women are. The 1996 letter from Pope John Paul II to the women of the world praising our 'special genius' was an opportunist and desperate effort to persuade the Beijing Conference on Women to resist the widespread enthusiasm for linking contraception to aid affirmed at the Cairo Population Conference the year before, but that does not mean that he was not perfectly sincere in his essentialist understanding of women and his belief in his duty to tell women all about it.

It is not just the British Royal Family which was challenged by the invention of 'Diana, Princess of Wales' through the curious cooperation between the desires of the crowd, the needs of the mass media and the ambitious individualism of a female aristocrat. If the Windsors had come to believe that they represented Britishness—reticence, the hereditary principle and Victorian family values (and a bit of income tax is a small price to pay)—the papacy had invested far more deeply, giving up the papal states in the late nineteenth century in order to represent emotional and ethical verities around sacrament, symbol and the function of femininity.

In the Mall Roman Catholicism saw its whole discourse fairly thoroughly colonised. Its iconography, admittedly mediated through Eva Peron and Madonna (note the name), and the emotional frisson which it generated, were shanghaied on behalf of a woman who was not a Roman Catholic and whose life could not ever be co-opted by Catholicism. The enthusiasm of the crowd was claiming a new saint (that language was explicit as well as implicit) which the Church has uniquely reserved the power to do. It was claiming a new patron saint of femininity whose lifestyle was precisely the opposite of that propagated by Catholicism. In the new model the crowd was declaring that beauty is more crucial to virtue than poverty; emotional sincerity more important than truth; self-discovery superior to chastity; love to marriage; fashion to humility; glamour to grace; youth to wisdom.

Roman Catholicism makes saints. Despite energetic attempts to knock her from her pedestal they had a brand new one ready in waiting: Mother Teresa, who was precision-honed for the job—old, chaste, devoted to the Holy Father, spiritually beautiful (a crafty term for ugly or wizened), poor (despite her more dubious patrons she did not die with £25,000,000 salted away while pushing her husband's family for a larger settlement). It was hard luck that she timed her own death so badly, lost in the aftermath of her rival's. The Catholic hierarchy has always been a bit suspicious of mass devotional movements that try to force the pace for canonisation of individuals, but usually there is room for the Church to give in, to applaud popular sentiment and to endorse the sanctity of people if they have to. Rose of Lima, Thérèse of Lisieux, Bernadette of Lourdes and—over a rather different time scale—Joan of Arc are all women whom the Church canonised despite initial doubts or outright condemnation, because popular pressure demanded it. But this time it was different. In the case of Diana the devotees were not asking anything of the Church, they were taking the imagery and doing it themselves. And that is threatening.

After all, a key claim of the Roman Catholic Church is that although we have a male and bearded king we also have a Queen of Hearts. She is virgin and devoted mother, she is humble and obedient and chaste and attentive and adores the clergy and is capable of offering up her children to God while still being totally devoted to them. She suffers a lot but never complains or gives press interviews, and she loves and loves and loves. Catholics do not need another one. No one else should either.

eight

LAMENT FOR LADY DI

jean baudrillard

eh, dis done Dodi,
qu'as tu fait de Lady Di?
Il l'a emmenée au lit
puis de là
sous le Pont de l'Alma.
Sous le Pont de l'Alma
coule le Seine
et roulent les princesses
en Mercedes.
Sur le pilier numéro treize
elle s'est crashée
Diana la Belle,
traquée par ses reporters même.
De ce crash impérial
le Zouave lui-même,
qui n'en espérait pas tant,
le Zouave en bave
et nous aussi,
qui en révions, depuis longtemps.
Choc frontal.
Ecran total.
Punto final.
Ah, Dodi, Dodi,
qu'as tu fait de Lady Di?

hey, look here Dodi,
what have you done with Lady Di?
He lead her to bed
then from there
under the Pont de l'Alma.
Under the Pont de l'Alma
flows the Seine
and glide princesses
in Mercedes.
She smashed
Diana the Beautiful,
followed even there by her reporters.
Over this imperial crash
the Zouave is salivating
into pillar number thirteen
and so are we,
for we'd dreamed of this for ages.
Frontal shock.
Total screen.
Full stop.
Ah, Dodi, Dodi,
What have you done with Lady Di?

(*Translation by John Howe*)

Text: Jean Baudrillard **LA COMPLAINTE DI LADY DI**   © Music: Renaud Gillet

nine

FROM ROYAL LONDON
TO CELEBRITY SPACE

mark cousins

othing is more unsettling for a public figure, insitution or even place than to become an object of popularity. Popularity brings an excess to its object, a superfluity of fantasy. Moreover the love and enthusiasm it bestows today heralds the disillusion and aggression which will follow it tomorrow. Yet while it lasts it sneaks up behind normality with a recklessness which makes it peculiarly resistant to conventional forms of understanding.

Institutions live through assent rather than through popularity, which would derail their settled operations. Popularity has objects but is without objectives. It does not take a form, or rather it can use every form. Sometimes it spills into the organization of space, which becomes a scene for the enactment of love, and when it does it transforms space into a field of affective forces which not only 'represent' or 'symbolize' the popularity of its object, but 'performs' these relations in space. This happened to parts of central London in the week in September between the death of Princess Diana and her entombment at the Spencer estate at Althorp.

Royal London, a space of state occasions governed to the minutist details by pre-ordained codes of protocol of the British establishment, was occupied by crowds who developed their own ways of using and marking the space in a way which challenged and transformed the authorative choreography. The political consequences—the role of the monarchy, the relation between the state and monarchy, and the future of republicanism—are still being digested.

Normally Royal London is buried beneath the traffic of Central London, which has no ancient architectural expression of kingship. The separation of powers is fully realized at an architectual and urban level. Buckingham Palace, a dull aristocratic pile, is isolated as a large traffic island at the end of the Mall. Indeed for most of the time the space of Royal London, the Palace, the Mall, St. James' Palace, Green Park, St. James' Park, Whitehall and Parliament Square is given over to traffic and tourists who fail to find the centre of London.

Only on prescribed royal and state occasions does Royal London become visible, and it does so not as an architecture but as a procession-al route which links church (Westminster Abbey) and state (Parliament) with the monarch (Buckingham Palace). In political terms it can be seen as a form which answered to the needs of a constitutional monarchy domestically, yet needed on occasion to produce the forms of display which communicated imperial power. In this sense Royal London and indeed the monarchy is an invention of the late nineteenth and early twentieth century.

Despite the conviction that the monarchy continues an age-old unbroken tradition, the Hanoverians and the Windsors were brought over from Germany to do a relatively modern job, the symbolization of the British Empire, under the direction of their political masters. Royal and state occasions required an imagery of imperial pomp, and a processional route could accomplish this much more effectively than purely architectural solutions. The route was able to show the world, through photography, the popular support for British power. Coronations, funerals, royal marriages, the royal birthday, the open-ing of Parliament, state visits all filled the annual calendar with a suf-ficient showing of national unity and imperial strength without disrupting the life of Central London. It was an urbanism of power which existed mostly in the representations of ceremonial circulated throughout the world, yet curiously secondary in the capital itself. This is one reason why tourists cannot find London.

This periodic structure of Royal London, which depends upon the emergence of a route, marked by flags and policemen, buttressed by crowds, belongs to a history of state-sponsored urban choreography which has been neglected, except in its fascist forms, in favour of the more thrilling history of street demonstrations and popular revolt in cities. Yet it is clear that the ideologies of national and imperial dominion were importantly embedded in this elaborate outdoor theatre. Doubtless as other European monarchies were reduced to inexpensive constitutional devices in which ceremonial was cut to a minimum, the reason why the British monarchy was preserved at an expensive distance from the lives of ordinary citizens was due to the continuation of imperial and great power delusions among its political class. The idea that the monarch still needs the anachronism of her own yacht to visit the world is testimony to the slow death of these illusions. The processions and the ceremonial continue, no longer in the service of imperial destiny but cut of a kind of English reluctance to throw anything away, and out of the conviction that the trappings of royalty are a magnet for tourists.

Two things changed this. First, the decision taken by the Queen in the 1960s that the Royal Family needed a new role. In ways that she must now rue, it was felt that rather than focus upon the figure of the monarch, it was the Royal Family which should be the central image of royal representations. Different from us, but also the same, this family could continue to stress domestic unity, as a family. Rarely can Fate have felt herself so tempted. Second, was the decision to have closer links with the media, especially with television. The coronation of 1952 had been crucial in this respect. The BBC had made it the first national event to be covered by outside broadcasting. As an exercise in planning in an unscripted area it was counted as a triumph and led to the close co-operation of television companies and the administration of royal events. Television brought the event to people in a way that inaugurated the mass character of a national TV audience. Royal London was now known no longer through photographs distributed to the furthest reaches of the empire but through family television. The representations were deferential, the commentary sententious. All seemed well. Doubtless in deciding that this television coverage should extend *into* Buckingham Palace, into the domestic lives of the family, their spouses and their pets, it was assumed that the coverage would remain deferential and willing to censor, just as it was assumed that the family life in question would continue to demonstrate that the family was the cement between church and state. Interest in the Royal Family would be rekindled, an interest which would benefit from the televised presence of an exemplary happy family. Royal space retreated somewhat from the formal and the ceremonial to the private (if rather extensive) domains of the monarchy. They were shown walking their dogs, fishing, riding, chatting to tenants, all the normal things that an urban population characterised by increasingly high levels of unemployment loves to do.

Rarely can a decision which was so disastrous have been taken so lightly. The Queen seems not to have noticed that she presided over the dysfunctional family from hell. The rest of the story is well known. By the mid-1990s the monarchy was wobbling. Diana was establishing herself as an independent celebrity and had refused, in the embattled language of the Palace, 'to go quietly'. The Duchess of York brought a touch of farce to the proceedings. Even politicians began to worry in public that something 'had to be done'. But every time a 'something' was attempted the situation become more comic. The only card up the sleeve of the monarchy was the coming funeral of the Queen Mother (for she is 97) which it was assumed would unleash a tide of recovered memories from the age of innocence, and remind the British public of their debt to the Royal Family as a symbol of resilience throughout the war. But the death of Diana cheated them even of this. They were forced to consider and plan a ceremonial on their own turf, Royal London, which if mishandled could throw the monarchy into a manifest crisis. This was a problem without precedents set for people who reason only by precedents.

Already by the morning of August 31, after news of the death of the Princess, small crowds began to appear at Buckingham Palace and Kensington Palace. Some brought flowers which, for lack of anywhere else to leave them, since no one received them, were left outside the gates. Media coverage began to notice this. By lunchtime there was a new element to the story. While everyone in Britain with a flagpole seemed to have made great effort to fly their flag at half mast, the mast at Buckingham Palace was shown to millions—quite flagless. An official explained quite correctly but in a manner worthy of Marie Antoinette's publicity agent, that the flag only flew when the monarch was in residence, and since the Queen was still in Balmoral, her Scottish castle, no flag was appropriate. Many who were interviewed on TV alluded to this as evidence of the Royal Family's 'coldness' or indifference. Indeed as the week wore on the media began to demand the monarch return from the glens and that she 'speak' to us. It began to look like the demand that the King and Queen return from Versailles to Paris two hundred years ago.

Each day the crowds got larger and it was clear that something was happening even if it was not clear what. Three things were evident. A large number of people wanted to be in the space of Royal London as an expression of their feelings about the death. They also seemed eager to talk: talk with others, talk to TV interviewers, talk not just about the death but about themselves and the relation they had with the Princess at the level of fantasy. And they wanted to leave something there. This started as flowers, but continued with a vast abandoned host of teddy bears and also writing, miles of writing from scrawled phrases to lengthy considered letters, all hung out for public consumption. Talking and walking. The congregation (for it was not a crowd) walked around itself and talked to itself. As if this was the place from which it wanted to speak—the space which is normally Royal London. Outside the Royal Palaces, and in the Royal Parks, St. James', Hyde Park, there was an outpouring of narrative. Partly this was because the narrative which had captivated so many, the story of Diana had now ended. Already. earlier in the summer, as she was reported to be in love with Dodi Fayed, public interest turned to the speculative question of what would happen next. Now people knew, but this merely resulted in more stories, of who people were and what Diana meant to them. Modern memory often takes this self-referential form, for when asked what you were doing when Kennedy died, you are not so much being asked to perform a feat of memory as to authenticate the fantasy that the two things are linked.

Obviously flowers are a conventional tribute paid at death, but as bunch was piled upon bunch that week they also become building materials, floral bricks which banked up into great terraces which began to clad the perimeters of the palaces with an installation of popular sentiment. It is interesting that officials did nothing to try to remove them, but restricted themselves to tidying up. The flowers were not just a tribute, they were in some sense a challenge to the powers that be, that there was a popular if utterly pacific occupation of Royal London that contained an implicit assertion of the validity of its intervention. Together with the teddy bears and the messages the whole area became the founding of a kind of cult of Diana. Everyone seemed impressed by what was happening but at a loss to account for it. Editorials speculated that the British were learning to become emotional. But what was the emotion, and what was its relation to space?

Perhaps a defining difference between this and any previous contemporary public reaction to royal death is that Diana (for that is her mythical title) was a celebrity. This was confused because she was, or had been, royalty. But she died as a celebrity having completed (as no one else has) the transition from royalty to celebrity. Some like Grace Kelly have moved the other way. But no one has made her trip. Being a celebrity is very different from royalty—it involves a different relation to people, and a consequent difference in the use each makes of space. The celebrity is more like a saint than a royal figure, especially the diluted figures of constitutional monarchies. The royal figure is divided between the monarch and the private person, a division expressed in the traditional doctrine of the king's two bodies. There is a clear distinction between the public, distant and mysterious body and the homely off duty pensioner who merely lends the monarchy a body. The mysterious body is invested not in the person but in the institution's claim to continuity (*Le Roi est mort: Vive le Roi*). A photograph of Elizabeth Windsor swimming would belong entirely to the realm of the comic, while that of Chairman Mao swimming had political and symbolic meaning.

The celebrity and the saint have an entirely different relation to the body, for the body is fundamental. The saint monstrates him or herself through the body. Both saint and celebrity are always recovering and their recovery is marked in the body. The saint is recovering from original sin, the celebrity usually from something more recent. But the Betty Ford Clinic has become the equivalent of the desert father's pillar. Both enable them to 'take control' of their lives. The saint and the celebrity have abjured 'denial'; their bodies are both trained, if to different effects. If the comparison seems stretched, it is enough to remember that saints are an odd lot, and they were not canonised simply for their devotion and example, but for their miracles. But 'working miracles' is simply a tautological statement that something has rubbed off them. This 'something' is their celebrity. Levi-Strauss's term for this is the 'floating signifier'. He argued that in any language there are always more things to signify than there are available signs. So some signs have the function of absorbing and making their own all the excess meaning in a culture. They attract the power and prestige which attaches to those excess unnamed things. He was intrigued when living in New York that some people were referred to as having 'it'. The 'it' did not have a stable fixed meaning. It was exactly this 'floating signifier'. This is the 'it' of the saint and the celebrity; we are invited to think through them and with them in order to think.

This difference between royalty on the one hand and the saint and the celebrity on the other involves a difference in our relation to them, a difference in the forms of our identification, and a difference in our spatial relations to them. The monarch is an object of the middle distance. To be close to the monarch would be to usurp the aristocrat or courtier. The subject is set at a respectful distance and the space between monarch and subject becomes the zone where the institution of monarchy works its way into the fabric of normality. The relation can be expressed as well in time: monarchs have often been calendars of popular memory, a dating machine for recalling events. School children learn the *dates* of monarchs, as if this were adequate descriptions of periods in history. Royal death calls out not so much grief and mourning, but a doleful solemnity. It tends to demand a certain reserve as if death were experienced as a military defeat, the monarch's subjection. As such the corpse of the monarch is of no further significance: it merely announces another coronation. By contrast the identification with saints and celebrities is of a different order. It is hungry, restless with love, full of demands. If the conscious formula is 'I love Diana' the unconscious fantasy is Diana loves/will love/should love me. This narcissistic identification reveals the stalker who is at the heart of adoration. It weeps for the suffering celebrity with tears of self-pity; her sufferings keep reminding me of my sufferings and how similar they are. The wish to consume the celebrity determines the space between us.

At first that space is the wish to see her. The paparazzi rightly insist they are our creatures however much we disavow them. The wish to see her is propelled by a logic of increasing intimacy: her, all of her, inside her. This scopic bulimia resonates through her death. The fantasy, widely reported, that the image of her damaged body was already on the Internet brings the logic to its virtual end. For the initial sight of the celebrity breeds a strange contradictory wish 'to be there', there where the celebrity is, a 'there' where if you were there, the celebrity could not be. Narcissistic identification demands the presence of two people but only one place. A narcissistic crowd is not any crowd, and it is not a collective thing. It is the scarcity of place in pursuit of the smallest place, there where the celebrity is. You are much more likely to fall and be trampled in a narcissistic crowd, for it lacks the dumb animal co-ordination of the true crowd. It generates a lethal hunger, an excitement that has no term for satisfaction. In terms of 'being there' there are only the resisters of expectation and the aftermath. The question of where the celebrity is, or what is the space of the celebrity, is answered by an impossible fantasy: 'closer', but closer to what, closer to where? Not that the crowds in Royal London exhibited this logic, for this was the aftermath. Long patient lines formed to sign and write in books of remembrance. But by the Thursday the unconscious guilt which follows on such identification showed itself by the beginnings of collective hallucination. In the room at Kensington Palace set aside for the memorial books, in an old portrait with a large black background, many mourners began to see the image of Diana's face.

Finally, the service at Westminster Abbey. At a political level the service, and the organisation of the cortege to the Abbey, and finally from the Abbey to the country seat of the Spencers, constituted a complex compromise, a hybrid event which set aside protocol, liturgy and precedence while masking itself as traditional. The Palace, Downing Street, the Church, Diana's family negotiated a kind of truce which seemed to incarnate the spiritual dimension of New Labour. It was a state occasion but not a state occasion, royal but not royal, funeral but not funeral, televised but censored. Two oddities characterized its performance: first, the form of the televisation and, second, a completely novel relation between the inside and outside of the Abbey. The event was not just televised for the home audience but relayed to crowds outside the Abbey, a relation which underlined the theme of being and not being there. The televised form was novel; it had been agreed that the royal family and other mourners would not be in shot, as if television had to repress the insatiable visual demand which was denounced as the cause of Diana's death, as though there had to be a collective retreat of lenses. During most of the ceremony the camera was compelled to discover a renewed interest in the architectural details of the Abbey, of the pattern of the floor. But what came as a shock to the bearers of convention was the clapping, for Elton John and especially Diana's brother, Earl Spencer, whose address in any case would have at earlier historical periods been thought of as treasonable. In fact this clapping did not originate in the

Abbey but from the crowds watching relayed TV. It arose outside and drifted into the Abbey where it rippled from the back of the West end up the nave towards the choir. Doubtless it was quite inappropriate, but it obeyed the deeper mimicry which characterizes congregations in church. In one way it symbolised the presence, outside, of the crowd whose constitution the service was trying to appease, the people. They intervened not in the historic mode of breaking in, but through a loop, as feedback made possible by television. It was in this sense that the television was important, no longer in producing a split between the event and viewers as in a spectacle, but in mediating the very space of the event.

Ultimately the reaction to Diana's death had been contained by the procession of the cortege and by the service, but royal space had probably been sacrificed as the price. Something of the confusion about what it all meant was expressed journalistically. Some commentators were swept along by the strong convictions that the crowds represented something new—the first national demonstration of a public openness surprising in a nation renowned for biting its lip. For others it evidenced a lamentable example of the media's capacity to engineer hysteria. Staunch royalists were critical of the Queen while old Marxists felt their first shaft of sympathy for the Duke of Edinburgh and his stiff pained exasperation. Underneath it all was a decisive shift in the representation of public life, from the protocols of royal space to the logic of celebrity. Finally, the cortege set off out of central London, out to the suburbs and the motorway, where it seemed swallowed up by the unremarkable landscape.

ten

THE PRINCESS, THE PEOPLE AND PARANOIA

sarah benton

day one

● did not grieve for Diana. When I woke at four in the morning and
1 heard the news in the night darkness, it horrified me. It was such
a huge event. I had not realized how large a part Diana had played
in my life and times. The effects of death are idiosyncratic: there are no
oughts and shoulds in how one reacts, and anyway how one reacts is
beyond one's control. Someone's death may pass over you, rocking and
scraping a bit. but over. Or it can smash you to pieces, plunge you into
a bottomless abyss, hurl you into outer darkness. How you react is not
a testament to how much you loved the person, how intimate you were:
it marks only how their life latched onto something in yours. Diana's
death didn't latch onto anything in mine, so I didn't grieve, but it did
into the lives of millions who are usually beyond the reach of politics.

The momentousness of it was reinforced and shaped by the BBC:
from four in the morning, while England slept, the BBC launched a no-
holds-barred onslaught on my attention, rushing into every crevice of
memory and imagination. It hurtled past the biggest gap: who was this
Dodi, whose name twined round her injured body? Son of Al Fayed,
unaccountably denied British citizenship, corrupter of the English
Parliament. How bizarre. The components of this tragedy were unfamiliar, could not all fit into one simple myth. Was it the fall of the

House of Windsor? The curse that the old Windsors would inflict on the new (Muslim, first generation) family? The fates' punishment for an embrace with Islam? The doom that awaits such a dangerous liaison as Diana and Dodi's?

After several hours of listening in the dark, I went out. My neighborhood in north London is a poor, unsettled area and home to many refugees, asylum seekers, exiles. Once Jewish, Irish and white working class, now all those plus Algerians, Iraqis, Kurds, Turks, Somalis, Nigerians, Pakistanis, Bangladeshis, Indians from India, Africa, the Caribbean. . . . When these were up and about, I went out for the Sunday papers, which were largely empty of the news of Diana. I went to a cafe run by Algerian immigrants. The day before I had showed one of them, Mouloud, a newspaper report of a particularly gruesome massacre in Algeria, wanting to share my dismay, put some real life into this stark horror. He peered politely and shrugged. This morning, the morning of Diana's death, when there was nothing in the papers, he greeted me with 'Isn't it terrible!' There was nothing I could tell him that he didn't know already. He was gripped and shaken: he saw that Diana's death was an unhindered, un-owned common ground between him and his customers, British and Arab, in a way that news from his home country was not. Diana is the first Brit whose name was better known in soccer-playing nations than Bobby Charlton's.

Perhaps this was just Mouloud fending off my intrusive clumsiness. It is likely that Diana's death was the first national event which he felt eligible to join: death, unlike birth or marriage, is leveling, deprives the family of their ownership of the person to the point that anyone can belong to the funeral party. In death, the person's moorings are cut and we can all rush in to claim the heritage. In fact, if we don't claim it now, at this moment of death, we may never have another chance. Funerals cause more family rifts and bitterness than weddings. As I meandered home, person after person—faces I recognised of people whose names I didn't know, neighbors, who usually at most said 'Chilly today'— stopped, nodded at my armful of papers and said 'Terrible isn't it?'

day two

By the next day, Diana's death had saturated the entire public world, and this common ground had stretched out and covered the whole area. It had not only replaced the weather as a general 'Chilly, isn't it' sort of greeting, but strangers who would not even comment on the weather were giving each other their view of Diana's death. It was the medium of exchange, and without introduction they volunteered remarks about their own state of grief, heartbreak, anger or, quite often, irritated indifference. Two neighbouring shop workers were chatting on the street, one Turkish cypriot, one Afro-Caribbean. He said 'They killed her', and she replied 'Course they did' and he said 'Jealous'. I knew what they were talking about.

day three

By the third day, one newstand had pasted a home-made photomontage of Diana in the window. Its maker—a very reserved Pakistani—had selected about 20 photos in which she sat with black children on her lap, kissed black people and walked beside Muslim men. Imran Khan as well as Dodi. I realised then that photos of Diana constitute a vast resource from which one can construct any image one likes of her—Mum; shy ingenue; jet-setting Glam Queen; weeping, therapised anorexic; heroic campaigner against land-mines; neurotic narcissist. . . .

But two images were not available. One was of Diana with animals. Now this is odd, because the royals dote on animals: they share their photographs with horses and ponies, corgis, Jack Russell, Labradors, not to mention the corpses of deer, tigers, pheasants. The royals keep their gloves on when touching people, but take them off to touch animals. Only Diana spurned beasts, dead or alive. The royal relation to animals speaks of land ownership, of permanence and stability, of nonchalance about hygiene, of food abundance and large rooms, of lives where others will clean away hair and muddy footprints, of relationships which are safely asexual, that shouldn't consume time better spent roistering with animals. Unpartnered women keep cats as a mark that they have a proper home and have accepted their solitude. Diana didn't and hadn't.

But animals, too, as we know from films and children's literature, are the true test of human goodness (the dog is the only one who snarls at the con man). They smell the authentic person in a way that looks-fixated, self-deluding humans can't. This is why royals, surrounded by false speech, take off their gloves for them—smell, lick, trust me. I'm human underneath this tiara and glazed smile. The most insistent animal lovers are the most distrustful of other humans, the most distrustful of the tricks of visual appearance. This lack of pets and horses was the most un-English thing about Diana; the quality that she shared with much of the Muslim and the Third Worlds, where furry creatures carry rabies and take the food from babies' mouths. It would have been harder for her to pass as a commoner if she'd had a pedigree dog at her heel.

The other unavailable image was of Diana as plain. This is also odd because when she first became famous she was not at all beautiful. At that time I worked on the editorial side of a weekly magazine and almost every day hopefuls came in hawking their cartoons. They were technically very proficient. But not one captured a recognisable likeness of Diana. She looked too horsy, her nose was invariably huge, the make-up was gaudy, she looked silly. But that's what she does look like, they would protest. We never used them. No one would have recognised her. Her charisma lay in this: her body was rendered ordinary by pen or paintbrush, but made radiant by the camera. The camera allowed each of us to possess her in any way we wanted. And, as newspapers discovered to their immense profit—and immense initial surprise—there was no such thing as Diana fatigue. Not another picture of starving babies—we've had two in the last month. Oh good, another picture of Diana—we need three a day to keep up. Every publication, for every type of reader, found this out.

They discovered there was always a mass market for any *photos* (not cartoons, drawings or paintings) of Diana, so insatiable was this appetite for her. Or rather appetite for photos of her, for it was the photo which was the commodity, not Diana herself, and it was *to get the photo* that men would go to any lengths, criminal lengths, risking-their-lives lengths.

So as the Thatcher/Major years dragged on, had an image of Diana become as essential to our lives as commodities with daily use value? Was this the only life-giving part of our public culture? Was there such endlessly renewable energy for Diana-consumption precisely because she operated outside the political dimension of equality and justice, or because the need for her image was as powerful as the believer's need for the icon hanging beside the front door? Did we all position ourselves in relation to her, hostile and loving, contemptuous and needy, and need to see her every day in order to know our own ground?

Diana marketed the myth of transformation—not collective, political transformation, but personal transfiguration. She had (in the myth) been an ordinary girl transformed by marriage and designer frocks. If she could be why not me—and would I do it better? If Charles had made her so unhappy, could not I have saved her? Famously, millions of people dream of having tea with the Queen; perhaps Diana gave even more millions dreams of power, of being a prince or princess. She was an unfenced blank into which our energetic imaginations could leap, transforming ourselves as she had transformed herself, and transforming her outcome in better ways than she transformed her own. Girls' comics are still filled with stories of ugly ducklings who turn themselves into swans, either when their authentic quality is perceived beneath the dowdiness, or through hard work and sacrifice. The essence of this ambition is not authenticity, it is performance. We may not know how hard Diana trained and rehearsed to speak on the level with the crippled and dying. We do know the story of the plump girl who starves herself and cripples her feet in order to create the perfect illusion of the balletic swan. No wonder the English National Ballet was one of the select organisations which Diana patronised. Behind the illusion of every perfect woman there is, we know, the story of suffering that the transformation has demanded: she is a martyr to the cause of her own performance, which her audience demands she gives, and gives, and gives again. This is what Diana could not forgive: how *hard* she worked to give that performance, which so enhanced the Royal show: how much the Royals benefited; how little they appreciated what she had done.

Transfigured, transforming, giving, open to all—how unlike Camilla. The public can not take to Camilla, who is too self-possessed: with her does and horses, she is authentically what she seems to be (including intransigently English). We cannot put ourselves in her place, or in her suitor's. She gives us nothing. She keeps us out.

day four

By the fourth day, almost every local shop had a commercial commemorative picture of Diana in the window, invariably a solitary portrait. It was then then that we began to hear vituperative comments—not in my neighborhood, but in the central parades where the journalists clustered—about the Queen's absence, her failure to act like the unifying head of the people. The desertion of a leader in a crisis, as analysts from Freud to military commanders have pointed out, is the factor most likely to induce panic in a group. Were those who demanded, in venomous voices, 'Where is our Queen?' actually battling to quell their own incipient panic. Did it spread across the palace parks because panic is hysterical? Or were they voicing their own disappointment that what should have been a great, communal, selfless occasion could not be without the blessing of the Queen's presence? This puts the feeling close to that most commonplace of political emotions—anger at the absence of the parent who is pledged to protect and solace you. We have been abandoned! We have been betrayed! Our leader has failed to live up to our hopes!

The central flaw in this demand was that Diana was the Queen's ex-daughter-in-law. As the mother of the treacherous husband, the Queen was so implicated in this rift that she could not possibly unify without betraying someone or something. Did those who demanded her presence believe that if she appeared in the gardens, the desertion, divorce, fornication would disappear in a puff of smokes? The demand was for a casting back to the fairy-tale beginning, the marriage, all present and correct. The happy tale had been brutally sundered by Charles's perfidy, compounded by the Queen's incompetence as a parent. But the presence of the Queen in her capital city, heart of the nation, would have revived and given a proper ending to the tale. All one again.

It would also have meant that royalists did not have to acknowledge the rift, and take account of the other stories. It was the rift, of course, which had created the space for the Muslim and Arab appropriation of the death: if Diana had died in Dodi's arms, an engagement ring possibly in her possession, then that was because Diana was divorced and in a position to marry him. One up on you, all you Islamophobes—but what lengths they will go to keep their English blood from being sullied by an Egyptian Muslim. The mother of the future King of England dies in the arms of an African Arab. How does the imagination deal with that image?

day five

On Thursday, I got a copy of a Japanese paper for which I had written an article on her death, and was astonished to see it on the op-ed page, along with a leading article on Diana. In Japan? What was the common denominator that made her a universal symbol as well as a global commodity? How had the English rose transformed herself into a universal symbol? Was it her looks, her supra-political mystique or her causes: AIDS and land-mines?

Now, I heard an echo of 1980s CND and the campaign against the poll-tax. Then, I had thought that those campaigns marked the end of the old socialist/communist era, when people were marshaled as armies, and the uniformity of their militancy constituted their impressive strength. The change, I had thought, began with the Anti-Nazi League of the late '70s (when, despite the uniformity of the Socialist Workers' Party placards, a myriad groups manifested their identity in home-made signs). Ever since English mass movements have depended on assimilating and honoring the home-grown impulse to demonstrate defiance.

The withering of authoritative texts and historic models for proper protest allowed the old seeds of popular protest to flower. And flower they did, in 'events' that often looked more like colourful carnivals than stern, disciplined militias, more seizing the time, as carnivals do, than marching against time to a single goal.

Perhaps uniformity and military purpose had never smothered popular protest: Doris Lessing recalls that the Communist Party marches of the 1950s, loved by the children, reminded her of old church picnics. The festive multi-formity of the 1950s bubbled up despite the military uniformity of the leadership, which always had the last word. Today, anarchic, self-made politics is the rule and dour disciplinarians are the deviants. What is known today is that the more any claim aspires to universality, the more it must honour the very diverse motives, hopes, reasons that different people adduce for their support. This is the defining contradiction of any contemporary mass movement. To be universal it must be diverse. In contrast, a universal appeal will fall on deaf ears, as made only in the voice of a self-important elite. How can it be otherwise in this giving age of self-knowledge and individual counselling? Only in brief and specific instances can a common line be imposed.

At first it seemed as though Diana's death was one of those moments. The uniformity of the press coverage, the single focus on the cluster of London palaces, the common tribute of flowers, and the unifying power of the familiar symbols of monarch and death made it seem as though an invisible hand were directing all citizens to feel and think and act the same way. But over the days it became clear that this was not so. The crowd split, and those ugly voices were heard questioning the Queen's sovereignty. The Queen's only route to a universal language was to jettison public dignity and speak the hegemonic language of personal feelings.

day six

On the sixth day, my care-worker, who is ghanaian, a widow and mother of two, came to my house. We are not intimate, but as she came through door she stood and held her arms open wide for me, and said, 'Isn't it terrible?' For her, the momentousness of Diana's death should have swept away English reserve, and I should have fallen into her arms where we would have wept and embraced in shared mourning. This despite the fact that she, an evangelical Christian, disapproved terribly of Diana's intimacy with a Muslim. Such intimacy suggested either a flightiness with the fundamentals of life, or a preparation for the most profound, incomprehensible abjuring of Britain and Family.

day seven

And on the seventh day, there was the funeral. (In my neighborhood only orthodox Jews keeping a strict Sabbath, unrepresented in that pile-up of French Catholics, English Protestants and African Muslims, were left out.) I watched with an Irish single mother, a widow, who didn't really give a fig about Diana, yet could not be wrested from the communal mourning, and knew more about Camilla's shenanigans than does MI5. She thought young Earl Spencer a bit of a ponce. People have often relayed to me extraordinary detail about the lives of Diana, the Queen, Fergie, Camilla, Louise Woodward and Matthew Eappen's home lives—that I have never gleamed from the news sources I read and listen to. It is this combing of the media for small details that fit one's case that creates the different bodies of 'knowledge' about Diana, and the bodies of knowledge in turn define different constituencies of interest in her. Over that week, so very much was said and written about her, from numberless different viewpoints, each adding something new, that we now have a vast tapestry of knowledge, a Dianology. This is now part of Britain's public culture. Some of the new knowledge has been quickly assimilated: the importance of touch, the vitality of tears. Some, which Diana's death allowed through the gates, has now been pushed back outside again, in particular the common perception of women and outcast males: they had done her in. They had exiled her, scorned her, let her be hounded to death.

the nature of power

But by the end of the first week. It was not grief, but anger and shared paranoia which I noted. I found absurd the journalists droning on about the 'national outpouring of grief' in the face of the evident anger so many expressed. The journalistic focus on central London picked up on anger about the failure of the head of state to unify, to protect and provide, to do for us what we can't do for ourselves. There's nothing new about that; a politics which *doesn't* assume that somewhere there should be a powerful body who protects and provides (but usually fails) is rare.

The other anger springs from paranoia, a manifestation of a popular belief in the nature of power. The immediate assumption that 'they' killed her, particularly strong among black and Asian people, follows Elias Canetti's analysis of paranoia in *Crowd and Power*: that the persecutor has the form of a crowd. It is the faceless multiplicity of the persecutor which makes it threatening. This is far from the West's notation of a single Dr. No figure who, by stealing some secret or nuclear warhead, threatens the destruction of the people, or even of a Mr. Soros who can single-handedly scupper the West's currency dealings. The idea of the lone arch-villain was rooted in the bourgeois fiction of the thirties, the age of dictators; in modern popular fiction, the threat is more likely to be a group of conspirators, cover-up merchants, or an army of alien invaders.

In home-made paranoia, the enemy is faceless crowed. A lone Lee Harvey Oswald or Sirhan Sirhan has no public meaning: a faceless army of CIA or FBI agents. mafiosi or Cuban exiles, MI5 phone-tappers or Palace bureaucrats, does. And even when a single killer hits, say, a John Lennon, the fear is magnified because we know there is a horde of mad fans out there, stalking, hunting. . . . In the field of power, numbers are always magnified and, stripped of individuality, dehumanised. 'The Assyrian came down like the wolf on the fold, and his cohorts were gleaming in purple and gold . . .' Byron's vivid imagery slithers easily into childhood nightmares of wolves and demons. Powerful men have a legion of mistresses and servants: warlords command thousands. Any minority making a political claim will find a way to compute the statistic to assert that it is, in this one respect, in a world majority. Single mothers, the disabled, Afro-Caribbeans can translate themselves into the majority of non-nuclear family members, those without perfect bodies, the non-white majority. In the public domain, size always trumps quality. That's why Charles was jealous of Diana. Her crowds were always bigger.

The persecuted individual also becomes much larger than one individual. A public murder does not have to be of a famous person for it to be public, but the victim has to stand for many, to be a symbol. (Thus, women killed by husbands, children by parents, become public figures when political concern focuses on these hitherto most private of killings.) Killing a symbolic person represents a desire to kill the same quality in many: femaleness, blackness, childhood or in Diana's case, goodness, or perhaps the embrace of Islam or Al Fayed, or defiance of the British royal establishment.

Like many paranoias, this one attributes not just unusual powers to the persecutors, but great significance to the persecuted. A fear of persecution may not be well-founded: it may be a fantasy of importance. It may be a desperate desire to dub the humdrum with meaning and significance, to find value in what is treated with indifference or disregard. Diana was a rich and powerful woman, and clearly it was not a shared access to power that allowed so many to identify with her. Rather it was a shared fear of the power of others, and anger at being subject to their power. But this passive 'we' crowd was not a revolutionary crowd. It was not mobile, it had no common purpose. Indeed, the very immobility of the mass, prepared to stand in line for hour upon silent hour, was its most striking feature. The immobile crowd, standing so patiently, each person in it looking inwards to their own history and feelings, waiting to bend, with lowered head, at a small table and make a mark of condolence. Active, moving crowds, keep their heads up, look around, and pick up clues for what to do next. (Canetti asserted the readiness to stand was a peculiarly English trait, indicating how highly personal independence, the individual dislike of belonging to a crowd, is prized.)

Among the mass of people, though given no voice by the press, were those who saw Diana as representing their own martyrdom and exile. Among them are outcasts who in the past have appealed to the Queen for rescue from their persecutors: those being men in uniform or dark glasses, state agents who lurk unseen down every telephone line, in social security, housing and immigration offices and at every border crossing. But only those with a British status have made this appeal to their head of state. The Queen's dominion shrunk with the British Empire: now the Queen of Hearts has more potency than the Queen of lands and boundaries.

For those with a 'well-founded fear of persecution' Diana's death was terrifying evidence of 'their' power. This power includes the ability to identify a target, to track it across boundaries, execute the action (often, but not invariably death) and to leave no trace but an inescapable fact from which everything else must be inferred.

In the world of the poor and the exile, the identity of this overarching power may well be obscure. 'Remote control', one Arab refugee said to me, imitating a TV zapper; he sees it at work wherever there's a mound of money, a mine of gold, a well of oil. And it's not hard to find a connection between Diana and big money. A conscious centre of power gives shape and meaning to the otherwise meaningless feelings of being betrayed. unloved, unwanted, unintended.

So though the persecuting agents may just chunter along, doing what they're paid to do without giving it much thought, its fits better to see them as a conspiracy, or as the tool of a directing power. Even those at the apparent centres of political power always protest that they don't know where power lies. The further away you are from the exercise of political or economic power, the more absolute, cohesive and conspiratorial that power seems. (In contrast, men who exercise economic power, in legal or illegal activities, are often puffed up by the sense of their own power. But this is because they can limit their field of vision; if all you want to do is arrange a shipment of heroin and you absolutely will not be accountable for its consequences, you can feel very powerful.) Where tremendous power is attributed to an opaque, secretive agency, extraordinary efficiency is also attributed to it. While the actual agents of MI5 or the CIA complain of its bureaucratic ineptness, those who fear and envy their power believe these agencies can execute just about any action, however improbable, that they wish. The existence of a conscious directing power is the foundation stone of both the political and the religious imagination.

The policies and actions of these are based on the assumption that they are engaged in ceaseless strife against a numberless, faceless horde. 'There's always more where they came from: they all look alike to me: there's only one language they understand: force' say immigration officials sourly scanning the applications of immigrants; say security forces hauling away tree protesters; police cracking the heads of pickets; the army pulling in Irish Catholics—the IRA sniping at the army. Diana fleeing paparazzi. So if Diana spoke the public language of love and suffering, her body spoke the language of persecution and martyrdom. But when this body language is put into words, the sentiments sound mad. Few white English people speak this language in political life, and most will only tolerate its emotive cadences in religion as long as it is immured in high church English. But it makes up the stuff of public speech in much Arab, Islamic, and black poetry and rhetoric.

Diana's present to Muslims was to pick one Muslim, to proclaim that he was a unique individual and therefore that all Muslims, like everyone else, are unique individuals. I have no idea where she placed his Muslimness, only that her choice of a Muslim as her true love was a tribute to all Muslims in the Islam-hating West. She wasn't stating an Islamic case, merely affirming the humanity of people who see all white Westerners as irredeemably dehumanising them.

This was part of Diana's gift, as she moved around, embracing individuals from the untouchable, numberless hordes of lepers, people with AIDS, mutilated black children, homeless youth. Depending on the individual, the potency of her touch was either to redeem the individuality (and thus humanity) of the outcast, or to hint to the outcast mass that there was a way of belonging to the main community. Paranoia, the

fantasy that one is surrounded, pursued, thwarted by implacable ene-
mies, is a fundament of politics. If it is a defining feature of the politics
of any outcast group, then, to follow Freud's etiology, its origin is in the
homoerotic desire to be joined with others like oneself. The political ideology and consciousness of one's outcast group here plays the role of the
superego or conscience. It insists that you do not want to join the oppres-
sors, who self-evidently hate you and want to exterminate you. To identify with the oppressor is false consciousness and a betrayal of one's own
identity, which must be that of hating the oppressor. In this analysis, then,
the frustrated desire to be embraced becomes a feeling that you hate them,
becomes a feeling that they hate you, becomes a feeling that they want to
exterminate you. The alternative to this politics of bitter spurning is a bitter nationalism. In nationalism, the excluded and oppressed remake themselves as subjects on an equal basis.

day 120

They had done her in. They had exiled her, scorned her, let her be
hounded to death. That perception has not been built into the Diana
memorial. It was the common voice of women and outcast males, but
as quickly as it shimmied up on the first days it has subsided. Now to
have this viewpoint is to prove yourself marginal. When Diana said it,
in her *Panorama* interview, she was dismissed as paranoid. Did her death
prove her right—or merely bury her fear in that mountain of gentle
flowers. Her angry, accusing brother has been revealed as an unfit
memorialist and guardian. But if Diana has a posthumous sanity, those
who believe in the deadly powers of 'them' have been returned to the
margins of the mad. By now, Diana has been returned to the embrace
of the Royal Family and only those who celebrate her good works now
speak of her. That claimed interview with her, published in France, in
which she spoke if her love for Dodi, sank quickly into oblivion. Diana's
memorial is constituted both of new knowledge about emotions, and of
mass forgetting and not knowing.

There are many problems with taking Freud's etiology of individual paranoia and treating it as a metaphor for mass politics. The most obvious is that it suggests that the exclusion, maltreatment and rejection of the outcast is imaginary. Diana's actual death, and her language of feelings, briefly allowed into the public domain the forbidden experience of being outcast, abandoned, orphaned. The media, dependent on coverage of royalty and Diana for their profits, and the establishment, dependent on public loyalty, were forced to treat this with respect. Diana's life and death did not just mark popular change in what public discourse should be about, it also helped to bring it into being. She made it legitimate in a way that no Rumanian orphan or Algerian exile or Rasta outcast ever could have done. Public culture has not been able to assimilate that act, because public life cannot assimilate those who are outcast, whose experience has been made illegitimate. That would upend the patterns of power.

eleven

DESIGNER CREATIONS

homi k. bhabha

a phone call from a friend in Milan brought the news that Gianni Versace had been shot in Miami. On Lake Como, where we spent some weeks that summer, an hour away from the Versace estate near Cernobbio and the resting place for his ashes, his tragic death was at once an incessant and evanescent item in the international news, and at the same time, a very local affair.

'Gay boom-boom,' said Franca, the perfumed and petite woman who cuts my hair, the next day, acting out the curbside assassination, horrified and hungry to talk.

'A beautiful son of the lakes,' I said piously and provocatively, testing the waters in this vacation idyll where the Lega Nord propagates the secession of the North from what it considers the degenerate and impoverished South.

'Yes, *si, una sensibilita italiana* . . . but he liked a different kind of life, *una vita americana*, all mixed together . . . gay, drugs, black, white, who knows what else?'

'But the family? He was very much a family man, surrounded by his sister, and—'

'And Naomi and Kate . . . and Elton John,' she interjected. 'A kind of family life, I suppose . . . and Princess Diana . . . and that woman from Monaco. But is that family life . . . one day Milan, one day Miami . . .

catwalks and gay bars, never *really* knowing the people you meet, where they come from, who they *really* are; and then this killer. Who was *he?* Half Filipino-half American.'

'You think Versace knew the guy, Cunaa—'

'*Who knows!* Does *he* know who he meets in a bar, can he remember? Can you believe what somebody tells you about themselves in such places, such shifting people, here one day, gone the next . . . you lose hold of *yourself* when you live like that. You lose your footing, your soil. Then one day, *boom boom!* like a bad movie and everybody asks questions . . . questions . . . questions . . . just like a film.'

Behind me, Franca's rapid reflections competing with the agitation of her clippers; in front of me, a bank of magazine images, courtesy of *Oggi,* a garbled gallery of Gianni's life, lived in the fast lane, the fellowship of the Fabergé bauble—Gianni glittering, Gianni with Sting and Madonna— and then, finally, Gianni prostrate before the high escutcheoned gates, in the shadow of the sandstone mansion, his head oozing a profuse, misshapen profile of blood. In the days that followed, we drove through France and Switzerland on our way back to Britain, chased by an image trail of Versace vérité. One image of mourning—one that would remain indelibly present in a year marked by images of mourning—was doomed to a prophetic afterlife: Princess Diana, sheltering a tearful Elton John in a warm embrace, both of them dressed in Versace black.

Later that summer, in Westminster Abbey, Elton John sang *Candle in the Wind,* with the refrain changed to 'Goodbye England's rose'. Diana's untimely death overshadowed Mother Teresa's, and established the Princess in the role of the universal carer and sharer, which had over the years become the Mother's prerogative. Have any other deaths ever gripped a global audience with as much tenacity and tenderness as those of the controversial 'passed over' Princess and her rather passé playboy boyfriend? The figure of the dead Princess united the divided opinions that trailed her when she was alive. For instance, her taste for the indulgence and opulence of an Al Fayed existence (courtesy of Harrods) was interpreted as her refuge from the coldness and narrowness of British family life. And once she transcended the very narrow and singular circle of the British monarchy, her cosmopolitan philanthropy became the mark of her appeal.

With the celebrated demise of communism and the global adoption of the free-market model, we have come, some say, to the 'end of ideology'. The familiar use of this phrase suggests that the triumph of Western liberalism is quite uncontested, and the values of individualism have been universally affirmed. Accompanying such assertions is a narrative of global transformation that no longer sees change as part of the struggle between different systems of government embedded in conditions of historical and philosophical specificity. The 'end of ideology' argument has resulted in a peculiarly ahistorical and decontextualized approach to political 'turning points' seen as emanating from the emancipatory temperaments of great leaders—Gorbachev, Mandela, Blair—rather than emerging from the sustained struggles and strategies that form the collective will of a people. In this moment, at the limits of history as we have known it (the much vaunted moment of the postnational, the transnational, the 'glocal'), we are witnessing the dawning of the philanthropic 'transindividual'—George Soros, Ted Turner, Princess Diana. *Colossi* bestriding nations and cultures, these 'moral' authorities of the free world stand for the power of almost unmediated direct action. Where once the 'image' of international governance was dominated by faceless bureaucrats pacing the corridors of power in aseptic Geneva, or presidential figureheads lip-synching crafted communiqués through clenched teeth, we have now become used to a currency dealer opening windows of democracy behind the Iron Curtain, a media mogul from Atlanta lecturing governments on love, faith, and charity, a late glitterati Princess bravely striding by a field sprouting landmines.

But there is another side to such gestures of public virtue. The effulgent sentimentality that turned the Princess at one moment into the savior of a people made frigid by Tory rule, and at another, the guardian angel of a people set free by the 'social marketeers' of New Labour, does little justice to the complexities involved in constructing such an image. In the orgiastic baring of the British soul that followed her death, Diana has been symbolized and sentimentalized out of existence. Her greatest achievement was to craft an 'image' for herself; against the longest personal and political odds she established her own *style* of agency: a public presence signifying survival and *ressentiment*, frailty and feistiness, anorexia and an enormous appetite for life. The People's Princess' and her friend the couturier were linked in their shared concern to change the 'look' of their times and the public gaze that goes with it. Diana was no less concerned with her 'market' than Versace was with his, as *New Yorker* editor Tina Brown immediately picked up during her June 1997 *téte à téte* with the Princess (relayed in the September 15 issue):

> She understands that in marketing terms the Windsors are a decaying brand, one that requires repositioning by a media genius . . . 'I tried again and again to get them to hire someone . . . to give them proper advice, but they didn't want to hear it,' she says. 'They kept saying I was manipulative. But what's the alternative? To just sit there and have them make your image for you?

Diana's interest in the (re)presentation of herself *as image* is not to be read merely as a narcissistic act of self-projection. (Of course, one man's progress to power is another woman's crafty manipulation.) Salman Rushdie, in the *New Yorker*, saw through the empty charges of manipulation to the intelligence that lay behind the mythmaking, when he wrote: 'Diana was not given to using words like "semiotics" but she was a capable semiotician of herself.' In defining a role for herself, Diana had to create a constituency and appeal to a sector of the nation's 'imagined community'—a people—who, like her, were struggling to find a representative and *representational* image for themselves, a 'sign' of public belonging, as well as an insignia of authority. Elton John got it just right in attributing Diana's saving grace to her gift for ministering to 'those whose lives were torn apart'. A tawdry advertisement in the *New York Times Magazine*—she is depicted wearing her auctioned-off gowns in a set of commemorative stamps, official postage in the republic of Togo—said much the same thing. The 'essence' of Diana's virtue, the ad reads, was seen in her 'embracing the plight of society's so-called "untouchables", such as: sick and handicapped children; the homeless; battered women; victims of terminal disease; victims of anti-personnel landmines'. Jogging mythical memory reveals, of course, that the Roman cult of Diana—goddess of the chase—was explicitly connected with the lower classes, plebians and slaves, who were responsible for her elevation into the pantheon. (Such a distant echo between the Dianas develops a macabre significance when we realize that the goddess's festival is traditionally held on the Ides of August, and it was at the end of that very month that the Princess's death led to her adoring apotheosis.) Her own sovereignty somewhat sullied, the Princess of Wales chose as her 'people' those who had an attenuated, even marginal, relation to the well-established lobbies of the (declining) welfare state. Her affiliative community, in the realms of public concern and communication, was not limited to the victims of social inequity traditionally contained within the platform and prerogative of national politics—the unemployed, the working classes. Her concern for AIDS victims, and those who were threatened, life and limb, by the presence of landmines, gave her an international demesne and a cosmopolitan appeal that the royal family had stoutly resisted.

Diana's categories of care certainly overlapped with those of established interest groups, both national and international, but her idiom of involvement was more intimate, less influenced by the rhetoric of 'state' or the pious proverbs of public philanthropy. Her voice was as socially mediated (and media oriented) as any other; her 'image' as much a piece of statecraft as any public persona. The difference, as I discern it, is this: Diana's language of identification never equated the amelioration of suffering with its annihilation. Her utterances sought to 'stay with' the pain, to keep visible the terror rather than transcend it, to signify survival as an ongoing negotiation between the pathologies of the private and the public, celebrity and sufferance, in unequal parts. If my own description has been slowly turning Diana into a 'figure of speech' while assessing her more public configuration, I am only following her lead. Her iconic presence is, of course, intimately connected with her beauty and demeanor—'more than just an acute natural beauty . . . a strange overbred plant, a far-fetched experimental rose', in Tina Brown's phrase—but looks aside, Diana was also considered to be something of a 'mouth'. She was both celebrated and castigated for her confessional mode, her infamous media revelations that were read, in ways that recalled cold-war *nomenklatura,* either as signs of royal disloyalty or personal desperation. What undid her, remember, was the leaking of her cuddly, touchy-feely conversations with a beau to whom she complained about the frigid horrors of living among the Hanoverians.

Making her image, forging a constituency, was as much a verbal art as a visual one, and I am not merely referring to the reams of newsprint and miles of videotape lavished on her. My emphasis on Diana as a kind of *representation* of herself is to credit her public 'instinct' with something more complex than natural sincerity and something less venal than self-serving strategy. It is by weaving an affective, ambivalent presence out of those two warring imperatives that makes Diana as *image* different from other comparable public figures and their figurations. Her celebrated 'touching' of an AIDS patient, and visits to the hospice accompanied by her children, helped to shift a public's reluctant gaze from homophobic fear to a measure of human empathy. In Diana's presence, whether image or event, there was something more palpable and tangible than the customary still-life (*nature morte*) of the deadpan Queen Elizabeth with grenadier guard at hand, or at arm's length, exchanging endearments with a brace of corgis.

Why has Diana's life and death, and to a lesser extent, that of Versace, left us with moving images that dwarf others from this year? Franca's energetic observation, made months ago on Lake Como, comes to mind: 'Then one day, *boom boom*! like a bad movie.' Rushdie's *New*

Yorker essay has already likened Diana's crash to David Cronenberg's movie, in an extended allegory on contemporary star-doom. There is certainly a filmic quality to these events—one a *Miami Vice*-style assassination, the other a car chase and crash that gave new meaning to the phrase 'the accident of history'—that has overshadowed other incidents this year. What is fascinating about the movielike narratives of these celebrity lives, however, is not simply the commodification of wealth, rank, and beauty or the fetishism of style and power. Such frames of reference are too conceptually distant, too Film Studies 101. To understand the efficacy of popular images in such terms tends to normalize the extravagances and excesses, the passions and interests, provoked by public fantasies staged around the spectacle of unreachable figures who turn into iconic 'intimates'. How do we grasp the nearness of these events, the proximity that lurks in their very presence?

In *The Political Forms of Modern Society*, the French political philosopher Claude Lefort attributes this intimacy effect to a mechanism of the modern media that he calls the 'constant illusion of a *between-us*, an *entre-nous*'. The media of late modernity—visual or inscriptive—represent, for Lefort, the template for how ideology functions in our time. The 'talk show', for instance, which produces a hallucinatory moment of reciprocity between the interviewee's celebrity and the audience's anonymity, is a case in point. For the gap of social division—between self and other—is concealed not by the illusion of homogeneity or totality but by an incitement to participate, to dialogue, to talk, to question: the 'subject' is invited to 'incorporate the terms of every opposition. . . . At the same time he is lodged in the group—an imaginary group in the sense that individuals are deprived of the power to grasp the actual movement of the institution *by taking part in it* (italics mine). . . . It installs within mass society the limits of a "little world" where everything happens as if each person were already turned towards the other. It provokes a hallucination of *nearness* which abolishes a sense of distance, strangeness, imperceptibility . . . of otherness.' The 'little world' of the *entre-nous*, then, is the stage on which the transindividual becomes both a familiar presence and a phantasmic icon—at one moment, as common as the grainy picture in the daily papers, at another, as strange as the same face caught in the bleached, harsh light of the tragic news flash . . . one day, suddenly, *boom boom, just like in the movies* . . . and all of us are left only with questions . . . questions . . . questions . . .

twelve

THE UNBEARABLE
LIGHTNESS OF DIANA

elizabeth wilson

myth

I n the week after Princess Diana's death I was baffled and deeply alienated by the public response to the horrifying accident, and its amplification by the mass media. I could neither understand nor share the apparent outpouring of grief nor the explanations for the flowers, the poems, the queues and the candles thought up by media commentators. Of course, I thought it was terribly sad—the death of a young woman and mother when on the threshold, it seemed, of a happier period in her life—but I did not feel I had lost a friend or a member of my family. On the contrary, since a neighbour of mine had just died, I was painfully aware of the difference between the death of someone who actually was a friend and the more ethereal loss of someone known only as a media figure.

Nor did I believe that the tragic event had in any real or permanent sense 'united the nation' as we were being told. I did not believe that this marked the beginning of a transformation of the British personality as we shed our stiff upper lips and openly expressed our emotions; I did not believe this meant that the nation had become 'feminised', nor that henceforth we would become a different, more 'caring' society.

In the first week after the accident the only public expression of dissent from these prevailing views appeared in the *Guardian*. Its columnist Mark Lawson reported that the BBC had been inundated with demands from television viewers for less coverage of Diana's death and its aftermath, and the readers' letters column in the *Guardian* newspaper expressed anger and scepticism in varying degrees. 'Broadcasters . . . seemed determined to create rather than reflect the mood of "a nation in mourning",' wrote CJR Abbott, on September 2. 'Don't they realise that the strange mixture of hedonism, self-pity, media manipulation and noblesse oblige displayed by the former Princess of Wales in recent years mattered little in most people's lives?' While Mike Pokorny admitted that 'I never realised that Diana had single-handedly led the campaigns for the eradication of AIDS, leprosy, landmines and youth homelessness. And to think I had always assumed that this selfless and saintly woman only ever used the media to manipulate her own image.' But the very next day the heretics were slapped down in no uncertain manner by Andrew Heath as: 'curmudgeonly; clever-clever; slightly nasty minded; and above all wholly contemptuous of what ordinary people think and care about. Your letters page yesterday was a useful and pretty representative sample of the attitudes of the British intellectual left.' The following week *Guardian* journalist Linda Grant devoted the whole of her column to a similar attack on the 'sneering, Puritanical distaste' of 'the Left' (whatever that is—we weren't told). 'The Left', she pontificated, can't cope with beauty, is terrified of feelings and guilty of 'sneering, elitist condescension'.

Between the death of Princess Diana and Dodi Fayed and the funeral of the Princess, I felt desperate to write something, to try to mount a serious challenge to the apparent general consensus. Then, gradually, several journalists wrote thoughtful articles that went against the general grain. Nicci Gerrard in the *Observer* in particular wrote 'Let's hear it for stoicism', and questioned whether the unfettered outpouring of vicarious grief was as wholly virtuous as everyone seemed to have assumed. She and Mark Lawson in the *Guardian* voiced my doubts and my resentment, and expressed my disquiet with the whole way in which the aftermath of the princess's death had played. So perhaps there was nothing further to be said after all.

In the following weeks, however, the ongoing media discourse on Diana continued to evolve. Despite all the protestations of guilt, despite the regrets of those who admitted they had bought the tabloids which had—perhaps—contributed to the Princess's death, the revised version of Andrew Morton's *Diana: Her True Story* headed the bestseller lists the moment it appeared. There was intense debate on the Internet as to the cause of her death, and there and in newspapers in Egypt and other Arab states a conspiracy theory developed that she had been murdered by MI5 in order to prevent her marriage to a Muslim. At the same time the continuing investigation into the causes of the crash shifted the focus of blame from the paparazzi and the media to the chauffeur and drunken driving.

Yet despite the flood of daily coverage and comment (including more rubbish than I have ever read in my life before) certain silences were maintained. This was a classic case of the way Roland Barthes argued that a 'myth' is created. In his *Mythologies*. Barthes developed the idea that a myth is a representation which, in articulating one set of meanings, silences possible alternatives. His best known example was of the photograph of a black soldier in a French army uniform saluting the tricolour in the 1950s, in the context of the Algerian troubles. Barthes interpreted this as a statement that there are (good) black men who are loyal to France. Thus, the image he deconstructed silently buried the arguments in favour of decolonisation, substituting a subliminal message reassuring to conservative opinion and white racism.

In investigating the 'myth' of 'Diana', which is, of course, much more complex than any single photograph, it is just as necessary to look for what is not said. The exploration of this myth of our times is a search for the cracks in credibility that fissure our society.

opera: romantic tragedy

Surprisingly little was made of the operatic nature of the love story between Princess Diana and Dodi Fayed. Yet this had every ingredient of what the French romantic novelist Théophile Gautier called 'modern love.' 'The fallen woman and the fatal man', were, for Gautier in the 1860s, the essential components of 'modern love' and 'modern love' was the staple of the narratives upon which many of the great nineteenth-century operas were based.

Diana fitted to perfection the twentieth-century idea of a 'fallen woman', in spite of the fact that we have consciously rejected the very idea. We no longer have 'fallen women', instead we have confused women, women finding themselves, women breaking free from restricting relationships. Yet underneath it all the image of the fallen woman remains, the woman, that is, who from love or desperation, breaks her marriage vows and accordingly finds herself in a no-(wo)man's land of social ambiguity. Of course, since this was the 1990s, Princess Diana was not cast out of polite society and condemned to a demi-monde of kept women, as Violetta in Verdi's *La traviata* was. Yet her fate was not so dissimilar, since once she left the Royal Family there was no clear social group or caste to which she belonged, no clear social role for her. Tina Brown, of *Vanity Fair*, described a luncheon she had with the Princess and the editor of American *Vogue*, at which Diana told them she thought it unlikely she would marry again: 'Who would take me on? I have so much baggage,' she reportedly said. Her social situation was unique and she was as much in uncharted waters as the *demi-mondaines* of Edith Wharton's 1905 novel *The House of Mirth*, whose heroine, Lily, fatally descending the social scale to eventual destitution finds herself at the midpoint of her downward spiral in a strange half-world of unanchored women living in unexplained ease in luxury hotels:

> Through this atmosphere of torrid splendour moved wan beings as richly upholstered as the furniture, beings without definite pursuits or permanent relations, who drifted on a languid tide. . . . High stepping horses or elaborately equipped motors waited to carry these ladies into vague metropolitan distances, when they returned . . . to be sucked back into the stifling inertia of the hotel routine . . . [They]

seemed to float together outside the bounds of time
and space [and]. . . . through this jumble of futile
activities came and went a strange throng of hangers-
on: manicurists, beauty-doctors, hair-dressers, teachers of bridge, of French, of 'physical development'.

The life of the Princess was not pointless nor exclusively dedicated to
self-indulgent luxury in this way—the difference a hundred years has
made is that women have more opportunities for independence and
self-development, and Diana was making use of such opportunities.
Nevertheless, her independence was ambiguous. In one way Diana had
fewer choices than most of us, owing to her attachment to the world of
international royalty where, it seems, women are still defined overwhelmingly in terms of marriage and their relationship to men. Diana's
predicament after her divorce illustrated the ambiguity of all women's
lives, was a paradigm of contemporary confusions. There is really no
consensus whether women should concentrate on being mothers or go
out to work, whether they are still oppressed by men, or have overtak-
en them and now threaten masculine identity.

So while Diana's situation was not defined in the moralistic terms
of nineteenth-century social rules, she did to some degree play the fascinating role of 'fallen woman'. The media permitted and even encouraged acts of excess and a lifestyle that, like Violetta's, seemed both
glamorous and slightly out of control, the waltz always threatening to
become a *danse macabre*, while Edith Wharton's cloud of 'strange hangers-on' were certainly reincarnated in some of the psychics, trainers and
gurus to whom Diana turned for help.

And then the fatal man appeared in the form of Dodi Fayed.
Whether he was really suited to this role we shall never know, and we can
tantalisingly play out forever different alternative scenarios of what
Diana's life with him might forever have been. She might have, as she
was rumoured to have said she intended, retired from public life to live
in idyllic, albeit jet-setting happiness and become simply a wife and
mother once more (a pronouncement that does cast a rather ambiguous

light on the strength of her commitment to the causes she had made her own). On the other hand it all might have gone horribly wrong, so that, ten years down the line, we might have known that she had embarked on a series of less and less 'suitable' relationships, seeking, like aging film stars before her, a series of ever more bizarre consorts, gigolos and toy boys. Dodi Fayed, who was older than she, was, of course, no toy boy. Neither did he seem quite to match the Byronic ideal of doomed romantic hero, although his lifestyle did, as it turned out, transform him, however unintentionally, all too completely into the 'fatal man'.

Yet precisely because the love of Princess Diana and Dodi Al-Fayed was extinguished seemingly at the very moment of its consummation, it becomes forever operatic. It fits with a long Western tradition of doomed love, of romantic passion as inextricably linked to death; it is a reworking of *Romeo and Juliet*, of *Tristan and Isolde*, of *Wuthering Heights, Anna Karenina* and Daphne du Maurier's *Rebecca*. For this reason it touched a deep, unconscious chord. Like the real life drama of the suicides of *Mayerling*, this tragedy will surely be the raw material for films, for theater, for whatever art forms there are in a hundred years time. Unfortunately, it is musically more likely to be Andrew Lloyd-Webber than Verdi.

This aspect of the Diana myth effectively occludes any concerns or doubts that could be labelled 'feminist'. Glamorised, tragic, operatic love is so potent that, caught up in it, we no longer worry about whether Diana really was, after all, a feminist icon, a woman reaching for independence and refusing the humiliating traditional role of virtuous but betrayed wife (a role still seemingly much in fashion in the Conservative Party).

soap opera

So we had 'Candle in the Wind' rather than *La traviata* (the title of which, translated, means 'The one led astray'). This was opera, but it was also soap opera. If opera is very often melodrama dignified and made sublime by music, then soap opera is melodrama domesticated. We have long grown used to the idea that the whole of the Royal Family has become a soap opera, and there can be little more to say about this, other than that Diana played the familiar role of the heroine who becomes the evil woman, only to then undergo further transformations into the strong woman, the survivor, a heroine of a different kind.

Soap opera characters must invite the identification of an audience if they are to be truly successful, and Diana was perfect for this, since she embodied in her person a number of contradictory, even incompatible roles. To begin with she was simply the ingenue, the fairy princess, but she rapidly became mother, crazy neurotic, wife betrayed, self-obsessed narcissist, glamour star, woman-struggling-for-independence, survivor and, latterly, saint, strong woman, and even political interventionist. This excess, this surfeit, amplified by the media, meant that she became a living simulacrum, that is to say, a copy without an original, a multiple personality with no 'real' Diana to which her public could return. But that did not matter; on the contrary, it made her more than ever an object of fascination and multiple identifications. It is hardly surprising that so many women expressed grief at her passing, lined up to sign books of condolence and left flowers, prayers, candles and poems, for she was anything and everything. Or at least her image was. And yet what does it say about our ideas of beauty if so many women of all creeds and colours identified with a woman who was white, blonde, beautiful and thin, the most traditional style of beauty?

This image was a massive wish fulfilment. For it had two completely contradictory messages for the public. To the unhappy divorcée, to the bulimic wracked with guilt, to the betrayed lover, to the woman of a certain age, it seemed to say, on the one hand, to be rich and beautiful does not make you happy, and on the other, if you suffer maybe you can be like her. There was consolation of a conservative kind in her at times obvious misery; yet her looks and wealth cast a veil of glamour over even the dreariest chapters of her life—which is also the role of soap opera. It is about 'ordinary people', but the very fact that they are actually television stars or personalities removes their 'ordinary'—life and death—problems from the very realm of ordinariness they were supposed to represent. Thus the Diana myth, while appearing to address the contradictory nature of women's lives today undermined its own potential radicalism by burying it in glamour and melodrama. What was even worse was the way in which some commentators (feminists, if you can believe it) hailed the outpouring of emotion as the 'feminisation' of British culture. This was surely the greatest insult of all. It reaffirmed a reactionary stereotype of women as the only sex with feelings, the only ones with tear ducts, the only ones who 'care'.

don't cry for me, cry for gran britannia

One aspect of 'Diana's death was the way in which a cloud of 'pundits' of various kinds tried to make sense of the apparent 'outpouring' of grief. In a particularly unenlightening round table discussion for the *Observer,* for example, Stuart Hall said it meant something complicated, while Simon Jenkins said it didn't mean anything much at all.

It certainly seems to have been the case that many individuals felt able to revisit and work through tragedies and losses of their own in the context of this shocking public event. Perhaps, as some cynics suggested at the time, it also revealed an emptiness in the lives of those who had felt so bound up with Diana's life without having ever met her. (For those who *had* met and been charmed by her, the situation was clearly different.)

The Church of England seemed to take heart from the unexpected and at least partly spontaneous creation of a kind of secular religion, or religiosity, but surely it revealed rather the extent to which official Christianity in Britain has become almost entirely bankrupt, unable to connect with the lives of most people in any meaningful way. For me, one of the most profoundly depressing aspects of the event was just this empty religiosity. It may seem unfair, or in Linda Grant's term 'elitist,' to dismiss as empty the way in which millions of individuals sought to express genuine grief. Yet it was rather indulgent, for if it was 'compassion' it had no hard edge. I always thought that religion—or any decent secular philosophy, for that matter—involved rules, precepts and beliefs that were bound sometimes to be hard to follow, hard to live up to. Mourning for Diana, by contrast, was soft-centered in the extreme. It seemed simply to be, if we are to believe the media, an outpouring of 'caring', an expression of 'emotion' (what emotion?) without an accompanying clear morality or set of spiritual beliefs. What was really so great about all this vague and formless emotion? Far from rejoicing at the way in which this ectoplasm enveloped the land, I am appalled by the idea that the expression of emotion—any emotion—is necessarily always good.

One of the hidden agendas may have been—as some suggested—a generalised regret for eighteen years of Thatcherism. I suspect that many people in Britain do now regard those eighteen years as being ones of missed opportunity and a decline in public values; but, as opinion polls show, the British seem to want goodness and 'caring' without hard choices: the NHS, but low—or preferably *no*—taxes; better working conditions, but no trades unions; fair shares and better times for all, but no redistribution of wealth; a society stripped of deference, but wall-to-wall *Hello!* magazine. Grief for Diana expressed that perfectly. You could emote all you wanted without having to think hard about anything.

The media, as Mark Lawson pointed out, put a brilliant spin on things. At first, the media was the villain: paparazzi had hounded the Princess to her death, and they had done so because the tabloids, like the insatiable plant in *Little Shop of Horrors*, demanded ever more food in the shape of human lives to satisfy their hunger. For a moment it even seemed as if the grieving public was itself to blame for having read the tabloids in the first place. Soon, however, the spotlight was turned on the hateful, out-of-date royals.

This was the expression of 'feeling' at its worst. There was something very unpleasant about the way in which the Royal Family was bullied and hounded for not displaying emotion in the way in which the tabloids approved (and I say that as a convinced republican). It made some people feel better and gave them someone other than themselves to blame; but how did it make Diana's sons feel? It was shoddy and cheap to condemn the Queen for refusing to express a depth of grief she surely could not have felt, and I felt embarrassed by her little bob as the Princess's coffin passed.

The big blame story became their inability to move with the times, and one of the more permanent 'lessons' to be drawn from Diana's death was that the House of Windsor must be reformed. This was possibly the most depressing aspects of the whole affair: that an opportunity for finally getting rid of the whole fake pageantry and undemocratic claptrap of the monarchy was seemingly missed; instead Diana may have saved the monarchy. Indeed it has since become clear that this was always Tony Blair's intention, and the curtailment of royal budgets coupled with Blair's eulogy to the Queen on the occasion of her golden wedding has skilfully worked to this end. Thus the myth performed the further task of *appearing* to address outworn privilege while actually strengthening it.

the politics of diana's death

The Prime Minister, Tony Blair, played an important role in encouraging the expression of emotion by his own reaction to the death of the 'People's Princess', and managed to create the impression that there was a link between the nation's mourning of Diana and the victory of the Labour Party in the May '97 election. The rejoicing on election night seemed to be an outpouring of relief that the country had finally got rid of those embarrassing, seedy, unpleasant, clapped-out Tories, and the election night 'myth' obscured the fact that—wonderful to relate—we had done it without ditching any of their policies! A brilliant squaring of the circle had been magically achieved, but what this really meant in terms of unchanged monetarist policies is only now beginning to sink in.

The Labour Party seems to assume that they won the election *because* they ditched anything resembling a 'left-wing' policy, but no one knows how many of their supporters voted Labour not just for the 'middle England' reason that they no longer felt scared of the unions or another winter of discontent, and not just to get rid of a hated government, but because they hoped that the Labour Party would prove more radical in government than in opposition. Such hopes have so far been disappointed. There have been some encouraging initiatives—promises of an ethical foreign policy, the relaxation of immigration rules, an enlightened attitude toward lesbians and gay men, a more positive view of Europe—but these have been outweighed by what seems like an alarming tendency to bow to pressures from a right-wing direction, and the seamless continuation of far-right economic policies such as privatisation and 'flexible' labour markets.

The link to Princess Diana is in the domination of emotion over content, and in the individualisation of collective issues. Tony Blair appealed, and continues to appeal, to formless, vague yearnings for an undefined good. The Labour Party is identified as the person of Blair himself: in his 'On the Record' television 'apology' in November '97 for the events surrounding Formula One motor racing and tobacco advertising, he said 'trust me', never 'trust the Labour Party': '*I* am a pretty straight guy'—'*I* didn't get it all wrong'—'In the end the country has got to look at *me* and decide whether the *person* they believed in is the same person they have got now' [italics mine]. His evangelical style has been noted, and the Evita/Diana/Blair axis mobilises the emotions of the crowd in the service of what Stuart Hall named as 'authoritarian populism'. By this Hall meant the way in which a populist leader (he was writing of Margaret Thatcher) could ventriloquise popular feelings as a springboard for undemocratic moves. Whereas Mrs. Thatcher tended towards the confrontational, Tony Blair appeared more consensual, at least to begin with, and attempted, with considerable success at first, to clothe the continuation of Thatcherist policies in more 'caring' language. The grief over Diana's death was supposed to create the impression that the 'caring', 'unified' nation was the same one that voted Tony Blair into power, and that in showing its feelings, the nation somehow endorsed Blair's 'vision'—whatever that really is.

For me, therefore, the hidden, oblique politics of Diana's death were profoundly conservative. They masqueraded as progressive, but they were populist. They claimed to be modern, reforming, a call for change, but they were undemocratic and intolerant. The last and most serious aspect of all was the way in which her own best acts and interests were mobilised in the interests of charity.

The eighteen years of Tory rule has seen a concerted and continuous onslaught on the very notion of the public sphere. All collective, state provision was rubbished; the idea that progressive taxes constituted a fair and rational method of redistributing wealth was denounced: the thought that anyone had a responsibility to do anything for anyone other than their 'family' was sidelined. The way in which, for example, Tony Blair defended Harriet Harman's decision to send her son to a selective school was to say that, of course, she would do her best for 'her children'. The idea that doing 'your best' for your own children might involve damaging the prospects of *other people's* children was right outside the frame. The reality—that universal free education (without any of the fudges of opte-out schools and so on) only works if everyone signs up to it—was never mentioned. For Tony Blair as for Mrs. Thatcher, it seems as if there is no such thing as society—we have a duty only to our own families; a narrow creed if ever there was one.

This is a good example of the way in which debate has narrowed as the public sphere has declined, and, sadly, the good Princess Diana has acted to reinforce these assumptions. No one would wish to belittle the importance of her gesture in shaking hands with a patient with HIV. That did enormous good. No one would deny that her patronage of Centre Point, the charity for the young homeless, her campaign for the abolition of landmines and the other causes to which she devoted herself were beneficial and often brave.

Yet it would seem that her work also acted to reinforce the idea that charity can substitute for the public sphere. The shortfall in public spending in all the important areas of life that affect us so much is to continue. The only way—and the only *correct* way, it seems—in which

MEMORIAL EDITION

NEWS OF THE WORLD

SUNDAY, SEPTEMBER 7, 1997   55p   *ALWAYS IN OUR HEARTS*

Princess
Diana
1961 - 1997

Now you belong to Heaven

Angel on high. Diana's coffin enters Westminster Abbey followed by William, Harry, Charles, Philip and Earl Spencer

Immortal invisible: a famous aristocrat becomes an 'angel on high' in the words of a popular British newspaper.

(News of the World, September 7, 1997)

A Floral Revolution? The gates of Kensington Palace are barricaded with bouquets

(Adrian Dennis, Rex Features London)

SHE WAS THE QUEEN OF MY HEART

A ten-year-old's tribute continues the British association of death and children which resonated at the Dunblane massacre.

(Mirror Syndication International)

Royal gamble: can the monarchy survive by tying Diana's memory to William's reign?
(Mirror Syndication International)

Messages in bottles: a mass outpouring of affection to someone who wasn't there.
(FSP/Gamma)

Catholicism is colonised for the canonisation of a secular saint.

(Sidali-Djenidi/FSP/Gamma)

The spectators become the spectacle: mourners keep vigil near Buckingham Palace.

(Dave Cheskin, "PA" News)

Princess Diana Logo: celebrity, symbol, icon.

(Ian Jones/FSP/Gamma)

A cover for corruption? The Princess is pictured with Dodi Fayed in a tribute displayed at his father's emporium, Harrods.

(Nils Jorgensen, Rex Features London)

In New York's East Village, a local delicatessen commemorates Di and Dodi.

(Photo by Skùta Helgason)

A postmodern Princess and a New Labour prophet. Above, cartoonist Steve Bell on Tony Blair's modernising gospel in the *Guardian*.

(September 15, 1997)

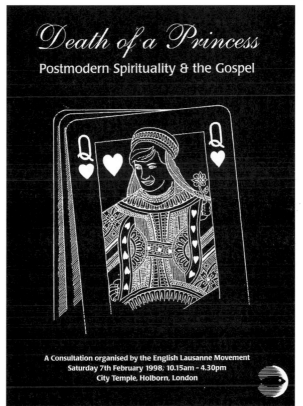

Above, leaflet for a conference on Spirituality after Diana.

(English Lausanne Movement)

Views on the Royal Family

What kind of monarchy	1994	No
The monarchy and the Royal Family should stay pretty much as they are now	29%	15%
The monarchy and the Royal Family should continue to exist but should become more democratic and approachable, rather like the monarchy and Royal Family in Holland	54%	71%
The monarchy should be abolished and replaced by a non-executive figurehead president like the ones they have in some continental countries	12%	11%
Don't know	6%	2%

Taking everything into account, do you think the events of the past ten days have increased the public standing or done damage to the public standing of the Queen and the Royal Family?

Increased public standing	30%
Done damage to public standing	53%
Neither / No impact	10%
Don't know / Refused	8%

Thinking of the Sunday of Diana's death, do you think the Royal Family was right or wrong to take the two young Princes to church that morning?

Right	62%
Wrong	28%
Neither right nor wrong	3%
Don't know / Refused	8%

If you heard it, how would you describe your personal response to the Queen's broadcast to the nation on Friday evening? Would you describe it as very favourable, somewhat favourable, somewhat unfavourable, or very unfavourable?

Very favourable	27
Somewhat favourable	40
Somewhat unfavourable	12
Very unfavourable	7
Neither favourable nor unfavourable	1
Did not hear it	11
Don't know / Refused	3

If you heard the address of Earl Spencer, Diana's brother, at the funeral on Saturday, did you think he was or was not being critical of the Royal Family? If "he was": Do you think he was right or wrong to be critical?

Right to be critical	55%
Wrong to be critical	10%
Neither right nor wrong	2%
Was not critical	25%
Did not hear	3%
Don't know / Refused	4%

Taking everything into account, has your opinion of tabloid newspapers like the Sun, the Mirror and the Mail gone up or gone down as a result of the events of the past ten days?

Gone up	12%
Gone down	59%
No difference	22%
Don't know / Refused	6%

From what you know, would you be in favour of or against a law making it more difficult for the media to report on the private lives of the Royal Family and other people in public life?

In favour of a law	83%
Against a law	14%
Don't know / Refused	3%

Daily Mail

Death crash driver was criminally drunk | Could Diana yet destroy the monarchy? | James H I love so very

CHARLES WEEPS BITTER TEARS OF GUILT

Modernising the monarchy: a Gallup poll taken after Diana's death shows 71 percent in favour of a more 'approachable' Royal Family.

(Daily Telegraph, September 11, 199

the gaping void can be filled is charity, because in charitable giving the individual chooses how to spend her or his money. It is not taken away by the state; the giver makes the choice.

Unfortunately the giver too often does not make that choice, and charitable giving has declined even if the Princess Diana Memorial Fund is awash with lucre and the National Lottery mounts up. Of course, the obscene manner in which the arts are to be funded by what has often been termed a voluntary tax on the poor, shows how much, or rather how little, this government, like the last, really cares about the arts. But in the context of Princess Diana, the message of the myth is that charity is good, the state bad. We are good, and we feel good if we give to charity; but the state is greedy and authoritarian if it takes these matters out of our hands. Yet surely, it would be more rational, honest and adult, if, in voting for a better health and education system, we also recognise that we have thereby signed up for a financial contribution to these public goods.

The emphasis on charity ignores one of the hardest-learned lessons of the nineteenth century, that charity simply does not work. Throughout the whole of the Victorian epoch successive governments, reformers and moralists clung desperately to the idea that state intervention was an evil and that philanthropy was and must be the only route for the amelioration of poverty and misery. The utter failure of charity to do this job pushed Parliament slowly and painfully towards the state intervention that is now, one hundred years later, being destroyed. Read Dickens if you want an accurate picture of the charitable society.

One of the media gurus who had a field day in the wake of Diana's death was the psychologist Oliver James. On an edition of the *Moral Maze* radio programme he was moved to yelp rather desperately that Tony Blair had got it all wrong; it wasn't that we needed to get back to traditional morality, or rather we couldn't because this was what late capitalism did—it created atomised societies, it split up families and destroyed communities in its search for profit. The only solution, he suggested in an article in the *Guardian,* was a more caring form of neocapitalism, which to some of us may seem like a contradiction in terms.

Lastly, there is the riddle of why feminist columnists such as Linda Grant believed that anyone who didn't sign up to the grief-for-Diana syndrome was an elitist member of a 'Left' that couldn't cope with feeling. It seemed particularly strange that this grossly reactionary stereotype should be mobilised at a time when 'the Left' is in utter disarray.

This was possible because the rump of the Left—and it is hard even to define who or what this is—has been marginalised so completely that today it plays the hopeless role of Cassandra, the prophetess who was doomed never to be believed. So thoroughly has the very idea of anything resembling socialism been delegitimated that those who attempt to speak in and/or renew its discourse cannot be heard: it is the babblings of madness. The disintegration of the Soviet Union and its evident corruption has been the excuse for the rise of a doctrine that nothing other than what is can ever be: the end of history. There is no alternative to monetarism even if as a doctrine it is far emptier than socialism and spawns regimes every bit as corrupt as the USSR.

In the case of Diana's death 'the Left' could be attacked also because socialism was a product of the Enlightenment that it is now fashionable to demonise as a terroristic project: there was never 'reason', there was only a different form of domination masquerading as rational. Thus grief for Diana privileges the values of feeling over reason and is therefore a good, whereas ideas associated with socialism, such as justice and equality, make a fatal claim to rationality and are therefore bad.

Into this massive political vacuum of thought step the twin figures of Tony Blair and Princess Diana. And, just as 'Candle in the Wind' reduces the whole complex story of Diana to one single, easy sob, so the myth of the 'People's Princess' condenses the whole complex political challenge of our times into one poignant moment of regret without real change.

In his novel, *The Unbearable Lightness of Being*, Milan Kundera explored the idea of how bearable, how 'light', the sorrows and tragedies of the affluent society at one level seem. Likewise, in *Watching Dallas,* her analysis of soap opera, Ien Ang saw the genre as expressive above all of the sorrow that has no name, of the vague griefs and discontents of the welfare societies of the West. In the week after the car crash that killed Princess Diana and Dodi Fayed, it was surely just this unbearable lightness of being that poured out, our grief that the consumer society, which claims to offer us everything we could ever want, actually gives us so little. Princess Diana embodied that unbearable lightness, the suppressed consciousness of an emptiness at the heart of our coarse and philistine society.

As we wept for Diana we forgot how we kicked the homeless and loathed the poor. We forgot that the other side of the coin of Diana worship is the bullying of the Royal Family, just as emotional support for Louise Woodward went hand in hand with intolerance and even violence towards individuals who failed to express 'adequate' support for her, and coincided with the renewed demonisation of the two disturbed ten-year olds who killed the toddler James Bulger.

Instead we were wafted to the heavens, and Diana smiled upon us, as in one of those Catholic oleographs in which rays of light surround the saint like bolts of lightning. Diana's halo was our halo. Indeed, Diana *was* our halo, and we wore her with pride.

thirteen

ADMIRABLE ENGLAND

régis debray

1 have to admit I got pretty scared in front of my television that morning, Saturday, September 6, 1997; London was the throbbing heart of the planet. I can recall no mediological suspense to match it. The funeral procession had been cleaving the crowds for an hour when the royals suddenly appeared from somewhere, on foot, like commoners. The Queen in person, escorted only by her family, came to the gates of Buckingham Palace and waited there, one among millions of citizens, her subjects, to watch the coffin pass. Not in front of them, but as it were with them. The world rocked on its foundations: the Queen of England, *waiting*! It was a long, long time before the cortege arrived. It is extremely rare to see a sovereign just hanging about. No one had ever seen the Queen kicking her heels before.

And for whom was she waiting? Her absolute opposite. A queen of hearts, a diva of glamour, a heroine of photo-novellas. Her worst enemy. The old England stood humbly in the open air awaiting the new. Old Europe, walled up in its rites and its palaces, was emerging a little way from its distance and invisibility to pay homage to America. The culture of public duty was as it were stepping down to meet the culture of intimacy thrust into the center of our lives by the camera and satellite. Was it—was *she*—going to vault the footlights? Step down from the stage (the Palace) into the stalls (the West End)? Abolish the semiotic break? *Surrender?*

No. The Queen placed a foot on the top step, but descended no further. She held back from the fateful frontier. The irreparable was not committed. The TV commentator kept a climate of doubt going for several long minutes: was she going to join the procession, to pace the roadway in mufti? Was she going to melt into the crowd, into that flux of collective and carnal emotion? To lay the ultimate symbolic transcendency of this democracy—the crown held by divine right—at the feet of postmodernity?

That step too far would have meant the symbolic collapse of the United Kingdom; the end of a dynastic legitimacy; and on a deeper level, a victory for the law of the heart over the Law, full stop; for the horizontal over the vertical, and for what Peirce calls the Index—the sign attached to the thing itself by a direct bond, like a photo—over the Symbol—a conventional sign cut off from the thing it represents, like a word.

The Palace divided the pudding: half the family, the Princes, were in the flux, a few paces ahead of civilian society; still a little isolated, but a homogeneous part of the emotive procession behind the gun carriage. The keystone, the Queen (with her mother and sister: sacrality is in women's hands) went back on stage to resume her role of composition: not carnal, embracing, instinctive presence, but cold representation at a distance. At the finish, symbolic hauteur carried it by a nose over the fusional indexicality of live contact. The vital monarchical minimum was protected, saving the institution's symbolic transcendency from collapse. Hollywood did not sweep all before it; Laurence Olivier had upstaged the Actors Studio.

How does a new technological device shift a whole domain of tradition? Walter Benjamin, one of the founding fathers of mediology, asked himself not whether photography was an art, but what it had done to change our idea and practice of art. The collision between two heterogeneous sequences—technology and culture—is what ought to absorb our attention: Catholic Church meets cathode-ray tube, college meets computer.

What parts of themselves must these institutions rearrange, to avoid being undone by the meteorite that has landed in the garden? The

British monarchy, and the Windsors in particular, are not made for the 'live' technologies with their sociological effects of sensory and tactile culture, humanitarian compassion, idolatry of the body and of closeness. Royals belong body and soul to the old school of show business, wholly pivoted on the semiotic break: the map is not the terrain, the actor is not his character, the queen is not her femininity, the symbol is not the thing. They live by the rule of separation: of the pit from the stage (by the footlights in a theatre, by the Palace railings in London); separation of the author from his text, of the flesh from the Word. There is the same relationship between the queen and her physical body as between a prerecorded broadcast and a live quote, or a theatre play and a happening. Or between a painting and a photograph (when it is taken live and not posed or official).

Diana, the world's most photographed woman, was a photo; Elizabeth II of England is a painting. The ascendancy of the Queen requires that everything directly experienced should be far removed from the center of the representation; Diana's magic assumes that all that was far from the center of the (monarchical, ritualized, protocol-bound) representation should be experienced live. And how communicative that magic is, since it is the very motor of our communicating mechanisms. The monarchy is cold by duty and by profession; the jet set is warm because it lives on live images. Diana died of the 'indexical' paradigm that brought her to life in people's hearts: palpitating uncoded emotion, immediate resurrection of the body by live TV. Once she had put herself in the frame the shooting never stopped. A victim of photographic fire.

Diana, it is said, did not read books; she looked, listened and danced. Live Charles reads books and lives a scripted life. He is said to be distant, cold. He hides behind his function, his body is not him. Diana wanted the map to be the terrain, the private the public, the sign the thing it represents; she thought a princess could be 'all woman'. Like the videosphere itself she could not bear the idea of a separation, which she thought hypocritical, between an individual and her public character, between feeling and conduct. She touched souls because she touched bodies, and yielded herself up to be touched, in hospitals, gymnasiums and bedrooms.

The indexical universe is tactile. It caresses and hugs. The symbolic universe, Charles's universe, stifles impulses and switches off. It disincarnates the concrete and asks the spectators to suspend disbelief and meet it halfway.

A millionaire aristocrat became 'the People's Princess' not through populism but because she espoused the people's values and references, its mediological environment. She reigned in and with the street because the person in the street, you or I, lives not a scripted life but a live one; not by looking at written pages but at the small screen; not with devices for projection at a distance (cinema, theater) but in immersion devices (rock concerts, live TV, video games). The laid-back attitude of America itself—but the jet set's America, not the establishment's.

Diana's funeral was a double miracle, an astonishing marriage of ancient and modern, like an outdoor Apollinaire poem. The first miracle, a sparkling one, of mass mourning: the ethnic vitality of a great people inventing a world legend on live TV by gathering around a central sign (the British are at their best when they foregather, unlike the French). A second miracle, of protocol this time, in Westminster Abbey: the raw faced down by the cooked, cries of dissent drowned out by Anglican hymns, Elton John bracketed between two religious canticles, Earl Spencer's deeply 'heartfelt' and 'civilian' outburst allowed, but the seditious integrated into the solemn. The marvel of gothic pop, that British creation: the symbolic order of ritual having to capture the indexical order of sound-image, as the only way to avoid being pulled apart by it. The union flag was flown at half-mast over Buckingham Palace. The crown accommodated; it did not abdicate. The old world suffered a severe jolt, but stood firm.

And once again the continent is in Great Britain's debt.

(Translation by John Howe)

fourteen

THE COMMON TOUCH

naomi segal

● n her interview with Martin Bashir for BBC's *Panorama* programme on
1 November 20, 1995, Princess Diana described bulimia thus: 'You fill
your stomach up, four or five times a day—some do it more—and it
gives you a feeling of comfort, it's like having a pair of arms around you.'
What this image suggests is the curious feeling of the body being embraced
from the inside. She added immediately 'But it's temporary' —and indeed
it must be. This point of balance, achieved momentarily and regularly with
bulimia; is impossible with anorexia. Anorexia's rhythm is that of a gradual,
inch-by-inch continuum towards an ideal end a point of emptiness, each
stage being a slightly increased ratio of refusal. Bulimia — and this is what
makes it an easily kept secret, a structure of visibility that remains strictly
invisible —is not a continuum but a circuit. The circle it describes has four
outer points: the excessive ingestion of binging →fullness (negatively, 'the
bloated stomach'; positively, 'the embracing arms') →the excessive expulsion
of vomiting →and emptiness, which, unlike the emptiness of anorexia, is a
version of stasis equal and opposite to the moment of comfort in that it
brings a pleasure close to orgasm. To borrow Diana's own words again—this
time from Andrew Morton's *Diana: Her True Story* 'I remember the first
time I made myself sick. I was so thrilled because I thought this was the
release of tension.' If the moment of being emptied is pleasure, the point of

greatest fullness is one where the skin 'fits' exactly so that the sense of being held is a snug relation of content to surface, balanced on that fine line between satisfaction and disgust. Then the limit point is reached, the internal meniscus breaks and guilt brings it all up again. Referring to a time, much later, when she had gotten over her bulimia and become able to believe the adulation of a grateful crowd, Diana commented to Morton: 'I can now digest that sort of thing whereas I used to throw it back.'

That the skin is not a single object but a surface facing two ways is shown by its dual function: it holds in and it keeps out, invites sensation and protects against it. This is the basis of the circuit of bulimia— a circle around, into and out of the surface-point of the skin. Radiance, surprisingly perhaps, works in a very similar way. How frequently and with what fascination commentators use the term, along with a plethora of cognate images, to describe the 'Diana effect' we shall see in a moment. Radiance ought to mean a system of light (or sound or heat) emerging from the interior of the person: thus we speak of the secret radiance of pregnant women or of eyes shining as the 'windows of the soul'. But really we are thinking of a circular system in which what comes out has first been put in. Only our gaze made Diana look radiant. She was, as Martin Amis put it, 'a mirror, not a lamp'. Rilke describes this exactly in the second Duino Elegy when he likens angels to mirrors that 'draw their own streamed-forth beauty back into their own countenance'. 'She's so beautiful', breathed the crowds in Australia during that first tour. That skin! Those eyes! Ever after, people who met her in person remarked on her radiance. It was as if, they said, she was lit from within; or again, in the words of a doctor in a Moscow hospital, 'she was a wonderful person; it was written on her face.'

'An instant radiance' is said to have emanated from Princess Diana 'when she walked into the room'. Put another way, 'she glittered, and the glittering sucked you in'. She had a 'stellar luminescence', was 'shining' and 'golden', 'illuminated our lives', was both 'gentle' and 'flamboyant', 'flashed those sapphire eyes' and radiated warmth'. Commentators from all political sides have compared her to a light source: a 'beacon'

(Margaret Thatcher), a 'comet' (Simon Jenkins), a 'shining light' or a 'bright star' (Lords Archer and Hurd), a 'crescent moon' (Simon Hoggart), a 'paper lamp' and the 'sunshine' (Maya Angelou, Donatelle Versace and the *Bury Free Press*). Most accurately—the mirror effect again—Nicci Gerrard has her presenting to us the 'dazzling surface of our accumulated desires'.

All this light seems to have circulated around that 'fabulous' skin which bulimia remarkably did not affect—'My skin never suffered from it . . . When you think of all the acid!' she marvels in Morton—but the camera always did. In addition to lighting up the space in which she moved, she is also a reflector whose exceptional ability was to throw back (throw up) beams from artificial sources. If she was 'the unusually multi-faceted reflector of a fragmented and fractious time', it is because her beauty, once she had 'stepped gingerly into the spotlight' and then 'got to the footlights', turned from something theatrical to an accessory of the camera: it 'leapt through the lenses' in an 'effect of bursting flashbulbs and the dazzle of halogen'.

Such mechanised reflexivity might be understood in two main ways. Commonly, but mistakenly I believe in this context, we find the notion that Diana was so apt a mirror because she was herself—at first, at least—a blank or empty reflector. Thus to Hugo Young, unlike John Kennedy who was 'the leader of the western world', Diana 'was an empty vessel', or, to Nicci Gerrard, she was 'the perfect vessel for our desires' because during the years of her lonely marriage, 'her cosseted surface bloomed and her abandoned inner life dwindled'. By this reasoning the surface was all there is: 'like a fur coat, a beautiful but empty skin' waiting to '[grow] some insides'. This is the image of an ideal anorexia, the body as a sheer surface, containing nothing. I want to argue, on the contrary, that we have to understand Diana's skin in terms of the bulimic circuit, an image of exchange in which fluid is the key. What flows into and out of the dazzling surface of a beautiful woman is gender.

Observe the following four accounts by two men and two women:

It's funny but when I met her I could swear I could
tell she had come into the room even though my

back was turned. The first thing that struck me was her glamour. She had the most beautiful skin. The other thing was that she seemed genuinely interested. She said different things to different people. She wasn't one of those important people who goes around saying the same thing to everyone. She tailored the conversation to suit. She was introduced to ambassadors, authors and journalists and every man in the place was turned to jelly. But she was also very funny —using humour against herself.

Sarah Lincoln, the *Observer* (September 7, 1997)

In spite of the glamour, she exuded a vulnerability which was puzzling, if compelling. And those who saw her in the flesh fell for her charisma as I did after hearing her address—controversially—a Catholic, pro-family rally shortly after her separation [. . .] Diana astonished everybody by giving a gentle but extremely liberal speech.

Ros Coward, the *Guardian* (September 2, 1997)

And I could see easily how people could fall for her, She was a tremendous natural flirt, and once [. . .] I was able to imagine myself becoming her victim. She was presenting the Literary Review's annual poetry prize at the Cafe Royal. I was seated at a table about as far away from her as it was possible to be, but I had the spooky impression that she was looking at me all the time. She wasn't, obviously. But she had that quality which the subjects of old-fashioned oil paintings often have: of seeming to be following you with their eyes, wherever you happen to be.

Alexander Chancellor, the *Guardian Weekend* (September 6, 1997)

I wasn't the first person in my family to encounter Diana. My mother shook her hand many years ago, back in the days when she was still Shy Di. Long before she began grooming herself to become the Queen of Hearts, Diana came to my home town in South Wales to open a new children's wing at the hospital where my mother works. I remember my mother arriving home, gushing about how lovely and sweet and kind and caring Princess Di really was. And I remember my reaction—totally unimpressed. How times change. In my own defence I have to say that the Diana I encountered at the London Lighthouse last year was a different model. [. . .] I remember thinking how thin her legs were, and how clipped her voice was. It was only when she finished speaking, and got down to shaking hands, that the real value of her visit became apparent. The Di effect was remarkable to behold. Faces flushed with excitement. Eyes lit up. And, corny as it sounds, a feeling of genuine love pervaded the room. For the next three days, I went around telling everyone how lovely and sweet and kind and caring Princess Di really was.

Paul Burston, *Time Out* (September 3–10, 1997)

All these spooky impressions by all these surprised converts share one thing: they were seduced. 'She was one of the half-dozen most seductive people I have ever met announced one memoirist in the *Guardian*. '"Seductive, yes. Not sexual", said a former equerry. "She flirted with men, women, children"'. And men, women and children, gay and straight, black and white, old and young—as they say—found in her what they wanted a woman to be: beautiful without being sexual, beautiful and sexual, funny, gentle but liberal, looking at me all the time, shy, groomed, in control, lovely, sweet, kind and caring. This is the effect not of an empty vessel but of a surface in and out of which gender courses with perfect fluidity.

The fluidity of gender is, if we examine it, more precisely a fluidity of the feminine. The varying valency of body fluids, from the 'pure' to the viscous, from idealised sperm to dangerous blood, relies on the greater or lesser coefficient of femininity in and out of place. Most feared, of course, is its circuit through bodies marked as male. Conversely, it has its sanctioned movement around the female body in such forms as bulimia and radiance. We cannot be surprised to see its politics enshrined in a circularity of the gaze.

All that light—in, out of, around and through this woman's body. In the early days, everyone noted that 'shy'—or was it 'coy'—upward glance,' as the cameras slid through her diaphanous skirt or as, more peculiarly, she gazed up adoringly at her royal beau. Peculiarly because everyone knew that she was tall and he was short. We 'don't do it Di' feminists made much of those absurdly posed shots of her carefully placed a step or two below him, or seated while he leaned avuncularly down. The relation of power to the gaze is analysed by Foucault in *Discipline and Punish*, where he describes the people looking up to the monarch: 'Traditionally, power was what was seen, what was shown and what was manifested [. . .]. Hitherto the role of the political ceremony had been to give rise to the excessive, yet regulated manifestation of power.' At such moments royalty was on display and the people were allowed to look, not on the face of power, certainly not into its eyes, but at a proper distance and logically from below. Genet's *The Balcony* satirises this relation of mass to icon when the denizens of his brothel present themselves as the Queen, the Judge, the Bishop and the General on the balcony that marks the liminal point between two worlds. The balcony and the television screen are such transmitting skins, two-sided in their function of presenting and protecting. We gazed up and, by a certain distortion, we saw her gazing up, too.

In fact Diana had an 'upward glance' because she was, as conventional gender arrangements have it, too tall. This characteristic took some time to be 'grown' to her advantage—'she was very wise, very tall and very beautiful. She loved me,' said Arnaud Wambo, aged 8, of

Cameroon—not only because it conflicted with the sincere objective of being a good wife, but also because it upset the micro-image of monarch and subject that her marriage represented. When she accepted her height—what she called in Morton's book, 'getting comfortable in this skin', vertically as it were—she came to embody a strange simultaneity of the dual verticality of power.

Power is vertical first, as we have just seen, because the few are on display to the many. Foucault explains how the individualization that follows from being gazed upon made a major shift in the late eighteenth century. Typically in feudal regimes (of which the British monarchy is a late version writ small), rituals and ceremonies ensured that those with power and privilege become known to their public by an 'ascending' individualization. Over the last two centuries, on the other hand, the downward gaze of a punitive surveillance or discipline individualizes the common man or woman.

It is in this sense that Princess Diana was, as endless accounts from all quarters marvel, 'one of us'. She was stared down by the royal family, who judged her unstable, and more complicatedly by us, who wanted to see 'the part that wasn't the Princess' exposed through the part that was. We also—as we discovered with contrition after she died—must have wanted the discipline by which photographers persecuted her, hounded her out of doors and forced her indoors, with the threat of 'face rape', 'hosing her down', 'whacking her' or 'blitzing her'.

Individualized by the disciplining gaze as a 'basket case' (her own phrase, to Bashir) or simply a pretty woman, but also by the ceremonial positioning of her triumphal public role, Diana was a double-facing skin between the feudal and the modern modes of the exercise of power. Thus she was presented for both our gazing and our gaping, in that 'gilded cage with a mirror but no bell—and no mate', to quote the feminist journalist Beatrix Campbell. At the same time, used as we had become to zoos in which the screen is constituted by our car window rather than the ball-and-chain cages, we were getting in closer. What is skin for, fabulous, comfortable or tortured, if not for touching?

The skin connects and contains all the senses, but its prime faculty is, of course, the sense of touch. However far back we look, the sense of touch, with its characteristic taboo, came first. It precedes the oedipal taboo and makes it possible. It prohibits pleasure in the name of danger or disrespect. We learn not to touch fire and not to touch our own or others' bodies by the acquisition of common sense and modesty; we replace the skin by the supplementary surfaces of clothes, gestures and the rest; we 'grow' femininity or masculinity while longing for an idyllic pre-gendered state when we believed we were—and, earlier, actually were, with our mother—living in a common skin. Actually, of course, touching never gets us back inside that skin, but as sexual pleasure and curative miracles tend to suggest, it gets us as near as possible.

And so, for every image of light paraded in the literature of the Diana effect, we have two or three images of touch. Liminal again in its value, these images seems to offer some deft combination of the royal touch and the common touch—two notions that are not very different after all, since only the great and mighty can have them.

With the 'common touch' (the term is most often quoted from Kipling's 'If') go all the protestations of her 'ordinariness'. Of course she was ordinary—we all are. Of course she was unique and extraordinary—we are all that too. (We are even all radiant, probably, in the eyes of someone or other.) But she was extraordinarily ordinary, 'one and a million', in a way only the great and mighty get to be: God first, and so on down. This explains the ubiquity of her smiling and glowing gaze, perceptible across a crowded room or even through the back of Sarah Lincoln's head, and it also explains the imagery of the miraculous that is typical of 'the royal touch'.

It began with Henry II in England and Guntram, a sixth-century king, in France. At first, apparently, their miraculous healing was exercised on any disease, but gradually it focused on scrofula, a name for a range of disfiguring skin conditions. It is amazing how often—considering how rarely she must actually have encountered it—leprosy, that archetypal object of disciplinary examination, is represented among those conditions that Princess Diana was prepared to touch. At its most grotesque, here is a caption in the celebrity weekly *Hello!*: 'She made a point of reaching out to those whom others were loathe to touch, including AIDS sufferers, lepers, and these Indian Untouchables (above).'

Of course it could not be literally as much of a 'two-way thing' as it seemed and, more importantly, felt. A close friend of Diana's in her last weeks, Rosa Monckton, reveals that though the Princess 'had a unique ability to spot the brokenhearted and could zero in on them, excluding all hangers-on and spectators', she regretted the loss of the HRH title because it 'did present a barrier, an invisible one, but a barrier nevertheless, which made people stand back a little and enabled her to get on with what she was doing'. The skin that glowed and 'pressed the flesh'—as she, presumably, would never have put it—'ungloved' was also trying to become, like Madonna's, 'as thick as an armadillo'. So— did she 'break through the carapace of fame [by tearing] at her own scar tissue'? Or was she, like a countess in *War and Peace* sourly described by Pierre Bezukhov, 'varnished by all the looks that have passed over her?' Or something between the two, held together by a finally cohered skin in which she could feel, as the French say, *bien dans sa peau?*

Certain hints suggest that Diana could only begin the work of touching after she had finished with her eating disorder. In the Morton confessions, she says both 'I think the bulimia actually woke me up' and 'it's like being born again' since she managed to keep her food down. Thereafter she controlled what she brought up—'seven years of pent-up anger' expended in an outburst to Camilla creating a state in which 'the old jealousy and anger [was] still swilling around, but it wasn't so deathly as before'—and what she kept back—'digesting' the public praises that she had earlier vomited out. Other accounts, both the more guarded narrative of the 1995 *Panorama* interview and Rosa Monckton's story of her experiences in 1997, suggest that, on the contrary, the strain of servicing her public's emotional demands tended to drain her and led directly to eating binges. Bashir asked her how often did she fill herself with food in a bulimic bout:

It depends on the pressures. If I'd been on what I call an 'away-day', I'd come home feeling pretty empty, because my engagements at that time were to do with people dying, people who were very sick, people with marriage problems, and I'd come home and it would be very difficult to think how to comfort myself, having been comforting lots of other people, so it would be a regular pattern to jump into the fridge. It was a symptom of what was going on in my marriage. I was crying out for help, but giving the wrong signals, and people were using my bulimia as a coat on a hanger, they decided that was the problem. Diana was unstable . . .

'Anxiety between the four walls' of her marriage and the two of them trying to 'keep everything together' in creating a coherent face for the public prevented the woman, in this scenario, from exploiting an ideal circuit of intimate attention between herself and her husband; instead, a much larger circuit of income and expenditure was set up with the anonymous multitudes who 'cried out' to her. The almost comic comparison between two forms of comfort, one embodied in merciful acts, the other found in the fridge to be ingested with hysterical haste, shows just how unreliable such hydraulics may be. Diana was 'drained and exhausted' by those who found that in the 'essence of herself [she] handed round' a source of 'nourishment' or 'sweets' that they could 'never get enough of'. Put like this, the picture seems to be of a public in love with her, in the sense that we may all be in love with and endlessly demanding of the good mother. But remember Virgina Woolf's Mrs. Ramsay, another source of radiant nurturance, who is a lighthouse for everyone else but, left alone, shrinks into internal darkness?

Because behind the logic of the circulation of gendered fluids around a woman's skin there is not only the positive (bulimic) corollary of liquid excess flowing out of control but also the negative (anorexic) one of dryness, petrification, in which all that remains under the garment is a skeletal coat hanger.

If this did not happen to Diana—and cannot now happen to her, as all those images of a future Norma Desmond or Brigitte Bardot fall away—it appeared nevertheless with some frequency as the shadowed underside of all that glowing light. This fluid light was occasionally set up as a contrast with the rest of us—for journalist Jan Morris, the more she 'floated' as a sort of ideal child the more our ordinary lives were 'drab and everlastingly flinty'—but much more often used to characterise the rest of the royal family as that dinosaur dynasty which could not swallow Diana. Almost all the portrayals of them at this sorry hour parade the adjectives 'stuffy' and 'stiff'; where she is fluent, pliable or tactile, or turning 'her huge mascara etched blue eyes soulfully upwards to the camera's lens'. They are caricatured as the figure she is not, 'standing bolt upright with her handbag on her arm, extending a stiff gloved hand'. Her ready tears make Prince Charles 'dry-eyed and stiff', 'the body held together, the hands that don't touch. Her light exposes the monarchy 'to withering scrutiny' from which they emerge, at the worst, as a 'dumb, numb dinosaur, lumbering along in a world of its own, gorged sick on arrogance and ignorance', or even 'frozen sticks of fossilised shit'.

Why such vituperation, couched in such aggressively desiccating terms? The overriding image seems to be of a dead tree, all armature and no sap. It is less than thirty years, however, since the Queen started this whole process by inviting the cameras onto her estates to film a set of nicely posed domestic groups, giving rise to the 'knit yourself a royal family' metaphor through which one of my teachers expressed a righteous republicanism. These were rationally (and quite sensibly rationed) breaches of the enclosure of invisibility, and followed logically upon the upward gaze by which we children bought savings stamps in the 1950s with the head of Prince Charles or Princess Anne on them: five Annes equaled one Charles, if I remember correctly. Any dynastic system, however rigid and closed, must open up some entry points for the absorption of daughters-in-law. Some digestive juices are needed if the latter are not to be spewed out almost as fast as they are ingested. But can the tall and graceful be consumed by the short and charmless? This seems to be what Diana's beauty is asking.

There are, I would like to suggest, four versions of female beauty that were embodied in succession by Princess Diana and which traced another cycle of emptinesses and fullnesses. The first is the virgin. Of course she had to be a virgin, as Sarah Ferguson, for instance, did not. As she herself puts it in Morton: 'I knew somehow that I had to keep myself very tidy for whatever was coming my way'. Who among the rest of us did not watch with embarrassed fascination as the last of the pure maidens was offered up to what we recognised as a merciless machine? Because the idea of an ideally unbreached female body was already thoroughly anachronistic—in other words, a fairy tale—and because it seemed as if everybody but she knew the system wanted her as its reproductive conduit: needed her to be simultaneously closed, open and empty.

The anachronism of the royal family, into which the absurd virgin is inserted as its inner tube, thus appears to have no lubrication and no real point of entry. It has to take in but cannot absorb anything not of its own matter; it is immune. Either we did not yet realize that in the 1980s or, if we did, we somehow thought we would not see the process of chewing and spitting-out enacted with the same logical visibility as that weird balcony kiss. What also developed at this time, and increased exponentially later, was our not very logical wish to believe her undigestible because she was too much like us—*pace* the fact that the Spencers are an even older dynasty than the Windsors and offer consistent recent evidence of throwing up and out their incoming women.

The second version of female beauty is the waif. Goodbye Norma Jean, farewell Emma Bovary. What we did not yet recognize as a saint in the making started visibly suffering on the bourgeois-realist scale: the fucked-up marriage, the woman frizzled by halogen, wasting away under our gaze. She confessed adultery and bulimia and audiences were at once touched by her eagerness to expose herself and repelled by her apparent skill at manipulation. For she wasn't ever only a waif—whether because she was a poor little rich girl or because she was also a wronged wife (whoever thinks of Monroe as a wife?) or because she showed steely anger or simply because she was always better to look at than the rest of the family, she always seemed to bend rather than break. At this point we ceased to be amazed by their ordinariness any more, sensing that they couldn't do it like she could. Wasn't it interesting how much less shocked we were in *Spitting Image* by the voice of the Thatcher puppet (that of a man) than by the Queen Mother's (the accent of a Northern biddy)? But we no longer derived pleasure from their much less impressive ordinariness, because hers had glamour.

Her charitable and even flamboyant charisma gave us the exhibition we wanted. We radiated back the pleasure her glowing surface offered us. She had stopped being bulimic by this stage and was dazzlingly transmitting our desires back to us in the form of love. Charm is, according to Camus's Clamence, the ability to make people say yes to you when you have not even asked a question. What she represented—like a present-day therapist, scornful of the couch—was a listening gaze.

Even before she was dead, her daily beauty set about making the others in the story ugly. Most specifically we were both horrified and pleased that Camilla, who had been preferred to her by a man incapable of seeing what we saw, lacked everything she so splendidly had. Diana provided the body that dynasty demanded but the system could not contain her for the peculiar reason that Charles did not desire her and everybody else did. Her skin implied the family's shell, her glowing surface their dry unmirroring surface. As if the public realized suddenly that what it required of royalty was not simply to be allowed to look at something either paraded or veiled, but to go on staring at something beautiful, something that gazed back beautifully. For this, of course, she soon had to be dead.

'Just before she died,' said my mother, 'you could see in the photographs that she was happy—no, that's not the right word: fulfilled.' My mother was not the only one to notice a difference. The fulfilled woman is my third version of female beauty. At last her healthy skin was full of good material, not gorged but loved just right, no more nor less than a person needs. Never mind if he was a foreigner, a notorious playboy, the son of an intruder; Dodi made our girl feel good. Curiously the two of them, in the only whispers to have reached us before disaster struck, each used the opposite of the expected metaphor. While Diana reportedly phoned Cindy Crawford to say, 'For the first time in my life I can say that I'm truly happy. Dodi is a fantastic man. He covers me with attention and care,' Dodi confided in Max Clifford, 'She fills up my senses', quoting a song by John Denver. And these metaphors may be why we believed them. 'Whatever love is'—to quote Prince Charles when he almost certainly knew very well—it is probably a state in which each party feels full of the other's good fluids.

The last version of female beauty starts to come out the other side of gender—immortal invisible. Dead, she has no body. The only one who can be with this body is not the king but the king of kings. Her beauty becomes that of the angel. In awe of this new status, Bernie Taupin excised all the lines of 'Candle in the Wind' that might offensively remind us of the waif she used to be, 'Never knowing who to cling to when the rain set in' making way for the completely senseless 'Never fading with the sunset when the rain set in'. Diana did not instantly become a saint, for all the selectiveness of memory. She first transubstantiated into that impossible being, a woman with no body. Not just collector and carrier of our sins and martyr somewhere between Jesus and the scapegoat—but also the dustless space on the Louvre wall that people went to stare at when the Mona Lisa was taken down for cleaning. The essential point about that massive funeral pilgrimage (whether spontaneous or choreographed) is that for the first time they knew they were going to see— nothing. That is surely why the grief was both bewildered and free, and why, also, it is not unjust to call it 'virtual grief' or the culmination of a relationship with an 'imaginary friend', because surely that is what bereavement is. Letting it all out in that excessive way signified that the circuit was broken and there was nowhere for the stuff to go except into and through the streets of London. The common touch got translated into the co-presence of people in one place at one time who were will-ing, in the absence of any other function, to represent commonality in their own massed bodies. After the funeral and cortege had passed, they hardly knew what to do. 'I hope we'll keep in touch every September 6,' said two women touched by the whole experience.

NOTE

I am grateful to Bette Kane, Anna Motz. Jeffrey Newman. Stella Rosenoff and Leah Segal for the loan of material used in this article, and to Dawn Clarke for discussions on bulimia.

fifteen

DIARRHOEA

glen newey

'God's wounds!' I will pull down my breeches and they shall also see my arse,' James I, author of the self-deifying *Basilikon Doron*, once said of the early Stuart paparazzi as they thronged forward for a glimpse of the royal mug. It's unlikely that the present incumbent will ever respond in like manner to the demands of her subjects, though she doubtless finds their importunities no less irksome than the most high and mighty prince. James, whose tongue was too big for his mouth, was given to slobbering around Westminster, fingering his codpiece with all the steely composure of a Captain Queeg; in historical lore, his delicate disposition was due to the shock, during gestation, of his father's being blown to dogmeat in the Kirk o'Fields at the hands of the deranged James Bothwell. He was fortunate in being able to dignify the prerogative with a custom-made ideology, whereas the Electress of Hanover has to square hers with lip service to democracy. This calls for a trickier thaumaturgy than anything essayed by James. Modern-style monarchy demands not bared hindquarters, but public privacy.

Things get harder when the distance that lends enchantment cedes to the contempt bred of familiarity. And now the glitziest bauble in the royal diadem—which worked as a charm to direct attention onto Diana and away from her dismal in-laws—has gone. Diana-babble seminars continue to proliferate in institutes of higher chat, where such non-questions as the effect of her death on the 'national psyche', or the ludicrous idea that Diana was 'a role model for women' (all you need is global celebrity, an ex who's heir to the throne, two dozen or so million, the odd palace . . .) are earnestly debated. The meconium, which spurted in torrents from the media's organs in the first few weeks after her death, maintains a steady flow yet. *Private Eye* was censored merely for printing, without comment, the astounding journalistic humbug which followed her death alongside the same hacks' hatchet-jobs of a few days earlier. *De mortuis nil nisi bonum*, and all that, but in the present case the sheer nullity of the nil goes well beyond standard obit-page unction. The only precedent known to recent memory, at least in the west, was the martyrdom on Dealey Plaza.

Loopy fanzine drool and schoolgirl crush-gush became the order of the day. Suzanne Moore's effusion on the day after the death in the *Independent,* which in the old days gave royal coverage a wide berth, was by no means the most gut-wrenching example.

> Icons do not die. Diana's afterlife is only just starting. Forever frozen at the height of her beauty, Diana, like Marilyn, that other troubled goddess, will not age. She will continue to glow, forever young, forever vital, in the hearts of those she touched. For the pop princess, the people's princess, the media princess understood the power of touch, the language of intimacy, of a hug, a gesture that was always more eloquent than mere words.

As it stands this is, admittedly, hard to improve on. Most of the ambient contradictions of the subsequent press coverage are bodied forth in this dribble. It opened the way for such profound meditations as 'her footsteps will always fall here, along England's greenest hills', in the words Elton—then about to be elevated to the knighthood as unofficial troubadour of the velvet revolution—was to warble in the Abbey a few days later. Its mangled match of Binyon and Bard ('her beauty . . . will not age') slotted the dead princess firmly into the traditions of old England. Note the pastiche hymnal feel of 'forever young, forever vital', the artless bathos of 'the pop princess, the people's princess, the media princess'— as if Diana's knack for PR somehow confirmed a talent for 'intimacy'. Beneath it lurks that hallmark question of duff journalism: *How does it feel?* This in its way would be apt enough as an epitaph for a fleecy under-blanket. As for the greater eloquence of gestures than 'mere words', one is inclined to say: it depends whose words.

It still seems necessary to add a corrective to these outpourings. Diana, Princess of Wales was, indeed, one of the tragically misunder-stood figures of our time. As the furore over her *Le Monde* interview shortly before her death showed, her motives have been whitewashed by the press, the public and, most of all, by herself. Towards this end, the photo Diana chose for *Le Monde* as her snap of the year—of herself clutching the ultimate designer accessory, a dying third-world infant— was good for a few air miles. It was wholly in keeping that Diana's end should so decisively eclipse the croaking of Mother Teresa in the same week. Beside a dead princess, what price a leathery Albanian virgin?

Diana came a long way since she posed gawkily with Prince Charles for the royal engagement mugshots in her blue two-piece, looking like a stewardess for Air Bulgaria. Marriage, bulimia, divorce—it all came and went as if history were a waking dream. There were the charity balls, the furtive humps with James Hewitt, the tiff with Tiggy. There were the nui-sance phone calls, Will Carling, and more balls. None of it helped her emotional development. As Harold Wilson famously said of Tony Benn, she immatured with age. Latterly Diana blossomed into a world-class air-head, an intimate of that self-selected international elite who boast a phenomenally low brains to cash ratio. As with the old Miss World inter-viewees, her most fervent wish was to help all the suffering people. And so it came to pass. Her lemon-sucking *Panorama* fess-up showed that in her last years Diana husbanded her energies for the greatest good cause of all: Diana, Princess of Wales. In the old days, AIDS sufferers furnished the compassion-fodder, though she confided to one well-known homo-

sexual activist that she did it for the families of the dying, rather than
'your lot'. Latterly were land-mine amputees, and there was barely time
to catch breath for another photo-op with footless peasants in Somalia
or Bosnia—children for preference—before jetting off to New York to
flog surplus frocks to the Manhattan charity-feast set. It all kept her on
the front page.

The press orthodoxy when Diana was still alive was that trashing
one party to the Windsor-Spencer misalliance necessitates trumpeting
the other's virtues. In many ways, though, the problem was that they
were too alike. Tabloid wisdom has it that Charles was too 'intellectual' for
his goofy consort. But time and again the prince of the blood royal has
also revealed himself, beyond all possibility of statistical error, as a man
of stupendous vacuity—whether it's by dopy pronouncements about
architecture, or passing the time of day with a cauliflower. The ear-tug-
ging inarticulacy, as the dauphin strives vainly to string half a dozen
coherent words together, fairly jams the craw. The rival camps' media
offensives during the break-up and divorce unwittingly drew the parallel: neither too bright, both cosmically self-pitying.

Another whim the Waleses shared was for off-the-peg spirituality.
Shortly before the fatal crash, while clocking up just four vacations
over five weeks, Diana hoped to grant an audience during a request stop
at Chios to Bartholomew I, the Greek Orthodox Church's top beard.
The record doesn't state whether the patriarch showed up. No matter:
there was always another God-botherer or cod guru just round the corner. So, down in Chios, there was just time to regurgitate the tzatziki
before helicoptering off to Chesterfield, England, to sit goggle-eyed as
the local Madame Sosostris burbled on about Romany lore, dark
strangers from across the sea, Harrods gold cards. You can't keep a good
ectoplasm down.

One of the numerous incongruities which Diana's head had to contain was the regular commuter-run between dying children and society
rag-men like Gianni Versace. At his funeral service in Milan Cathedral
a few weeks before her own wipe-out, she achieved her apotheosis.

Choking back her own inconsolable grief, she reached out. Out to Elton alongside her in the pew, to tousle his wig and stanch the flow of rheum from the one-time coke-nose. Jonathan Swift himself would have been hard-pressed to pen anything half so emetic.

In all this the wailing Princess compared unfavourably with the Duchess of York who, to give her her due, never pretended to be more than a good-time-girl on the make; latterly the Duchess confided to a US magazine that she eats 'as a way of getting over Diana's death'. Polls taken just after the smash suggested that public 'support for the monarchy' had dipped below fifty per cent, though the royals' standing apparently rallied later on. For this the colostomised dotards, tobacco-chewing dipsos and Mediterranean beachcombers currently loafing in Kensington have only themselves to blame. In the circumstances the barfly existence of Princess Margaret, with her booze, fags, endless Caribbean vacations, and her *declassée* insistence on being styled 'Ma'am' ('Ma'am darling' to intimates), is almost admirable. Beneficiaries of a system which exalted the feckless at the expense of the worthy, they now find themselves brought low by one of their own.

What's notable about this, of course, is the *agreement* between the Firm diehards and flower-wielding Dianistas that she was not of their ilk—a point concurred on by the message-scribblers and by Charles's 'confidant', sylphid ex-Food Minister Nicholas Soames. The latter's post-*Panorama* bid to brand Diana as a rogue elephant in the herd stood little scrutiny beside the royals' illustrious record of incest, delirium and crypto-fascism. It was nonetheless from this false premiss of difference that much of the ensuing blarney flowed. Before she was cold Diana was enthroned as an unroyal royal, a fruitcake who was 'just like us'. This double-think was to play itself out first one way, then the other, as we'll see.

The Versace funeral marked the nadir. Commentators at the time didn't fail to register the ghastliness of it all, before her stock rocketed into the ionosphere a few weeks later. What had begun, creditably enough, as as an exercise in nob-clobbering turned, without a beat, into an act of ritual prostration before the 'icon'. One of the stranger myths of the cult of Diana is that she was a great beauty. In the pre-nuptial days, as the family snaps show, she was no more than a blonde, rather vacant dumpling. Some time in the mid-eighties—no doubt a side-effect of the old binge-and-barf—she started looking like Medusa on crack, and it stayed that way. Maybe the trauma induced by repeated irrigation of the royal bowel played its part. But critical judgment musters no lustre beside the sheen of global celebrity, and royal celebrity at that. Imagine Diana's life as a comparably talentless prole—a single mother in Gateshead, say—and you get the picture. Enthroned, she might had done untold damage. Republican hopes were dashed when the Merc bashed the pillar.

Despite the brief upsurge of *simpatico* sans-cullotism after the Pont de l'Alma, the Banana Monarchy lives on. Bagehot's 'dignified' part of the Constitution is, in hack lore as in that of academic poli-scifi, a mere figurehead. It is seldom acknowledged that this, the Madame Tussaud's view of the constitution, fails to justify the status quo. If it were merely a matter of creating a figurehead, the job could equally well be performed by someone who isn't human, alive, or even animate. One of the corgis would for example make a passable head of state, or a waxwork of the Queen Mother. Of course, noone charged with the task of casting her likeness need mould the effigy too closely on the snaggle-toothed hag of real life; serial prosthesis has in any case made the line between sitter and simulacrum hard to draw. But noone today who's not out on day release believes that Her Majesty, or Her Majesty's progeny, ought to wield real political power. The truth nonetheless is of course that she does.

In Nigel Dennis's brilliant, now lamentably neglected 1955 satire *Cards of Identity*, attention is paid to the fabricated tradition of the Royal Co-wardenship of the Badgeries. This involves pulling a stuffed badger from the now-gone Forest of Hertfordshire on a trolley through the public thoroughfares. Dennis was perhaps inspired by the not dissimilar real-life ceremonial which marks the turn of each century at All Souls. 'There is a token badger, but according to tradition it is maintained by the Yeomen of Hertford Forest. It is a stuffed one, of course.' When the character Vinson asks what form the ceremonies take, he is told that they don't feature 'the actual, token badger . . . Normally, you get a clip of artificial fur set in an osier staff. This is an emblem of the token.' Later Vinson is confronted with the stuffed rodent, which seems 'to hold in its mounted paws the fate and destiny of the whole nation'.

During the 1980s of blessed memory the only two nationalized industries not subjected to the contagious blastments of Thatcherism were the Church of England and the monarchy. Even the New Government has no plans to privatize God—though or perhaps because the Old Left, aberrantly, want it. Tony Benn has waged a campaign these thirty-odd years to disestablish the state religion. Those who feel the need for a living human figurehead could, however, consider the following modest proposal. What is the present-day monarchy but a feather-bedded public-sector monopoly? There's no reason why the royals shouldn't go the way of coal, railways or sewage. Market doctrine demands that this bloated Triton be called to account. Rival families could tender for the contract; few are liable to prove as devoid of aptitude for the job as the House of Saxe-Coburg. Tenderers would aim to offer the state the most competitive deal, offering a rental on the palaces and funding their own Civil List. Alternatively, the successful consortium could be granted a patent to raise capital to buy the freeholds via a share flotation. Income could be generated by charging admission to visitors, farming out exclusive 'By Royal Appointment' product endorsements, and that fine old royal tradition, the sale of knighthoods (back to James I again)—a move which would also help to depoliticise the current gongs-for-bungs baksheesh by shifting the honours system firmly into the private sphere.

A public screening body would of course be required to vet candidates for suitability; after all, noone wants to see a wog on the throne. What's needed to keep it warm are English, or failing that Protestant, or failing that caucasian, glutei maximi. More radically, the mullahs of Millbank might consider opening a market in monarchy, with several families competing freely for custom. The palaces could be owned or rented on a time-share basis. Supernumeraries such as the beau-monde snappers, the Osrics and scion-branch trinket hucksters, could be ruthlessly downsized, and pointless capers in the Cairngorms put to the axe—following through with full rigour the Princess Royal's suggestion that the hulk of the *Britannia* be scuttled. What would be left would be a leaner and meaner royal house. It may be said that a stuffed badger would be cheaper, and would comport better with the dignity of the office. It's hard to disagree. Much is made by royalists of the 'drabness' or worse of a republican constitution. The proposition of a queenless Britain is sometimes darkened in op-ed discussions by the gizzard-freezing thought that a Jeffrey Archer or Richard Branson might assume the consular dignity. But no matter. The heads of figureheads are wood, and need be nothing else.

All this was belied by the figure of Earl Spencer, who like Blair but unlike the surviving royals, was generally judged to have fought a good death. The ginger Earl's halo slipped soon afterwards through wrangling over property in a divorce suit caused by his own prodigious fornication, but before the tabloids got stuck into him he enjoyed a few weeks in the sun. So, improbably, the poor dumb mouths' tribune appeared, in the form of a South African-resident, multi-millionaire aristo. The royals duly found themselves caught in a bizarre version of the noblesse oblige pincers. Seventeenth-century placemen like the Spencers are apt, in any case, to dismiss the Graeco-Germans in Kensington as irredeemably bourgeois, and who can blame them? Charlie Althorp's pulpit slot offered an unmissable chance to kick his heartily detested in-laws. Meanwhile, from the other flank, the tabloids and telly orchestrated 'national grieving' on behalf of the great unwashed. The masses responded by creating a wilderness of flowers. In death, the toff totty of yore mutated effortlessly into classless beatitude.

This sounds, of course, the death-knell of old-style deference, but the in-itself has yet to become the for-itself. Much has been made since the Paris prang of the monarchy's 'need' to 'modernise'. The royals, in the grunting idiom, should try to get 'in touch' with 'ordinary people' (one of the many curdling features of the first day's TV coverage was the ro-and-fro between studio-bound patricians and what anchor-speak dubbed 'ordinary' folk, ululating outside Kensington Palace). For the royals, populism is a dead end. It's hard to see the Queen shopping for tripe in Tesco's or popping down to the local for a pint of light boiler, let alone splitting a splifferooney or three after dinner with her bekaftaned hubby. In the end what this means is that we want these people to be set above us and we want them not to be set above us. In becoming more 'like us' the question soon follows: so you're more like us; why are you up there while we're down here? Rather than pulling the fat out of the fire, the Dutch model of 'modernised' monarchy is liable to collapse into its Romanov or Bourbon counterpart. Canard distinctions between current personnel and institution falls to the obvious thought that it's in the nature of the institution to exalt mediocrity. The argument which the Government applies to hereditary peerage applies with added force to that of hereditary monarchy: those who would get on by merit anyway, can. The sole beneficiaries of the present arrangements are those who wouldn't. This reasoning, is to be sure, brutal. It also prompts the obvious charge facing meritocracy: why should the birth-accident of innate talent get rewarded, when a mere entry in Burke's isn't? But the point is rather drastically missed when this reasoning is applied from the top of the heap downwards rather than from the bottom up.

Admittedly, the dominant impression the Windsors convey—by design rather than by accident—is of a clan of stolid zombies, barren of feeling and clenched of brain. The monarch herself, at least in her public persona, has all the mercurial spontaneity of a speech-synthesiser. Nowadays only the royals, and especially Her Majesty, display the mogadon quality which once characterised the whole of British public life. Given this, it can seem that any 'feelings' are better than none, even the pinchbeck sentimentality of those September Days. These patent failings—not indulged, of course, like Diana's—gratified those for whom a mass emote is better than a mass debate. But for those of us whose interest burned out long before her candle ever did, the blubathon at least provided anthropological diversion. To this extent the Prime Minister's performance recalled the Thatcher years, when following some high-death-toll disaster like the Marchioness or Hillsborough, the Leaderene would pop up in hospital, fastening on maimed victims, or relatives of the dead, with the alacrity of a vulture on offal. This time round the Prime Minister was ready with a second-hand oxymoron, apt in its very inaptness, which the papers picked up and ran with through the week: 'the People's Princess'. Those who commented, with unconscious irony, on the Leader's knack for 'capturing' the popular mood had it about right. You couldn't have staged it—an on-cue sound-McNugget, delivered en route to morning worship, by the earnest wingnut, in sober suit and black tie. Little Willie Hague chipped in, proposing that the late Princess should bequeath her monicker, JFK-style, to Heathrow Airport (why not the Channel Tunnel?). Unsurprisingly, Blair won this contest by a good furlong. Having set public opinion on its way, the PM's 'approval rating' went platinum.

In the fervid pre-funeral atmosphere public aspiration fastened onto the blondly blank figure of Prince William, whom benevolent nature has spared the toby-jug features of his papa. Young William was the nearest surviving remnant of the dead Princess, and importantly reincarnated her vanilla looks. He thus became the standard-bearer for a brighter royal future (Blair's death-day sermon duly bestowed a reference to the 'boys', absolving them of blame for the late events). Perhaps the succession should leap-frog over Wills's hapless father from Queen to grandson? Instead of a Direpublic, we could allow ourselves to hope once more for a new model monarchy. This move was clearest in the Althorp oration, where 'these two exceptional young men' became Princes in the Tower, members of Diana's 'blood family', to be guarded from the snarling predation of St. James'. This executed to a full Hegelian cycle: from positing its own contradiction, the monarchy moved on to the negation of the negation. In life, Diana had been a royal outcast, who needed no royal title to confirm her apotheosis. But in death, her posterity would prove to be reason's cunning way of ensuring the royals' survival. Her pariadom signalled not the death of the institution but its transfiguration, helped along the way by her mediatorial sacrifice. Hence the curious double-edged quality to Diana's isolation from 'the Firm', mentioned earlier. Her mummified image, so different from the emotional deep-freeze of the in-laws, showed them what they needed to become to keep their grip on the throne. This penny seems to have dropped with the Queen on the Thursday after the death, with the hasty cutting short of her annual Balmoral beano in favour of a walkabout among 'her people' in Kensington.

There remains the fantasy that monarchy can hunker down happily with ochlocracy. But it's equally fantastic to think that the manifestations of 'popular grieving' afford reassuring signs of democracy's rude health. Post-political Blairian rhetoric is prone to subvert the language of democracy for its purposes. This is not only witnessed by Diana's smooth passage from princess to honorary prole, in a form of inverse Peronism; the subversion works deeper, turning the very idea of popular legitimacy on its head. Self-styled tribunes give tongue to popular 'feeling' on its own behalf, which thus confers legitimacy on a containing operation to rescue the status quo. This ventriloquizes the general will, passing off a desire for 'greater openness' in the monarchy as the authentic vox populi. The PM's Party Conference speech a few weeks later hitched a ride on the bandwagon, with an undisguised appeal to its audience's amour-propre ('we are a giving people') which, as Blair continued, 'says nothing about our politics'. Nothing, and everything.

It is a moot point whether many people gave a toss about the absence of the union jack from the mast over Buckingham Palace, or that the royals were still vacationing in Balmoral while Diana turned cold. Noone confronted with the roll-call of *connerie* recited above could seriously represent Diana as a woman of exceptional qualities, or quality. Yet this is exactly what was claimed. Utterly humdrum deeds became the stuff of eulogy. Breathless sophomorish columnists continue to pant over her ability to walk and talk at once. Diana's postmortem canonization didn't occur *despite* her faults, but because of them. For this reason, there's little bounty in asking why she should now be touted as a role model for our times. Flailing around in search of the adult within, Diana immeritously rose to her bad eminence. In its more besotted manifestations, Diolatry drags mediocrity before the public gaze, and shows it reflected there in gilded splendour. Who could fail to be captivated?

sixteen

DIANA, POSTMODERN MADONNA

françoise gaillard

Perhaps nothing happened on August 31, 1997. The Nikkei gave no sign of nervousness, the CAC 40 did not slip, the Dow Jones was free from jitters. The planet had awoken in a state of shock, but the pulse of its economy beat strong and steady. The econoworld that squats behind our stock-market dictatorship long ago abandoned the management of emotion to the rest of us, without having to suffer a cut in dividends. The economy is kept judiciously apart from horror, a simple emotional value with which it is not concerned. We live in this schizophrenia. Perhaps that is what drives us to overinvest emotionally in news items that make no ripples in the universe of the market, like helpless bystanders with a confused feeling that the events possess a meaning whose wider significance escapes us. It seems that through this emotional investment we use these occurrences to interpret the state of our society.

In any case, when people learned of the death of the Princess of Wales they looked at passers-by in the street to see whether they knew, whether or not they looked sad, hurt, devastated. Words were exchanged in a stunned, phatic mode, the same words repeated over and over, filled with the pained incredulity that generally accompanies news of misfortune. The same words, uttered on every street corner of our global village. Something in the air had changed. From early morning when the news broke, it was apparent that the main event was not the crash itself but the thing that was happening now, that was going to get steadily bigger over the ensuing hours and days: books and more books of condolence, lines outside palaces and consulates, oceans of bouquets laid before the symbolic places, the people's tears shed everywhere, the exceptional world-media coverage (causing a British newsprint shortage).

After four months, the emotion had not yet subsided. Flowers still appeared at the end of the place de l'Alma underpass. The British awaited the Queen's Christmas broadcast with unusual interest. Magazine editors got ready to recycle the Princess's photos in their New Year spreads. Conferences were organized here and there; seminars took place; austere newspapers brought out special supplements on the event. People everywhere were still looking for a meaning in this unprecedented collective phenomenon.

Is it possible that we were witnessing the birth of a myth, through the declension and recombination of all the mythemes on which our society feeds: celebrity, great wealth, beauty, youth, car crashes; but also fragility, anxiety, depression, the other side of the Hollywood star stereotype? No one was surprised when Elton John's contribution to Diana's funeral turned out to be the warmed-over remains of a song written for Marilyn.

But two considerations oppose this theory. First, mythemes are still short of meaning even when they are identifiable. They are really only usable in advertising. Second, the ethos of postmodern societies is inimical to grand narratives. These societies do not make heroes, just celebrities; and the Princess of Wales was a prime example of a celebrity.

Her story is like a novel by a second-rate writer who could only imagine a future of dull domesticity for the amorous relationship between Di and Dodi, and came up with a cop-out ending: the car carrying the two turtle doves crashes in a senseless accident. It may just be feasible to use modern obscenity to save the situation, stopping the fairy tale short on a big close-up of crumpled metal enclosing unseen shattered bodies. But it is a very clumsy solution, closer to photo-novella than Balzacian drama. Appropriate too, because from beginning to end the whole affair was about nothing but photos. It is suggested that Diana died because she wanted to escape from the photo. If there had been a 'happy ending', though, it would have been the photo that moved away from her. There would have been nothing left for the paparazzi to reveal. For kisses only 'sell' when they are stolen, dragged out of clandestinity by a voyeuristic lens. Love only gets onto the tabloids' front pages if it is just beginning ('romance') or if it is illegitimate. In the first case it is the stuff of dreams, especially when the idyll takes place in a setting of wealth and celebrity; in the second it is swathed in a perfume of scandal which helps slum-dwellers forget the pervasive stench of cabbage soup. Conjugal embraces, the comforting arm round the shoulder, the tender complicity of an established couple, would only bore people and might even generate feelings of rancour: ' . . . and on top of all the rest, they look as if they might be (durably) happy!' That would be doubly frustrating for us, their benevolent public. First we would be deprived not only of the dramas people of that sort owe us in exchange for the celebrity we confer on them; and then of the consolation we get from the idea that there is some form of immanent justice: they too have their troubles! Because, let's admit it, with their insolently luxurious lives, they are only bearable if we can feel sorry for them. Just as we only forgive them their happiness if we can have it and make it the stuff of dreams . . . and because we know how fragile it is. So there they are, doomed to supply us with dreams or tragedy: fairytale wedding in a golden coach at Westminster Abbey or death in a black Mercedes wrecked in a Paris underpass.

We are inhabited by persistent traces of the popular culture so well embodied in Proust's Françoise, who is blind to the sufferings of the kitchenmaid working at her side but sheds torrents of tears over remote catastrophes reported in the newspaper. These random eddies of abstract susceptibility, punctuating a brutal indifference to the ordinary miseries of those close to us, have always been one of the popular forms of kindness. Press journalists have long exploited this primary psychology; TV has made it a main stock in trade, with the 'telethon' its practical application. There is something very postmodern about the way this advanced technology reactivates us on forgotten, archaic levels.

Diana gave us everything, everything we had a right to ask of her, dream and misfortune both; but even those offerings are not sufficient to explain the worldwide reaction to her death. We have to look elsewhere for that, starting with the perfect accord that had been forged between her and our time; our time that was so completely hers.

· · ·

The death of the Princess of Wales could have appeared scandalous. It was seen as a tragic destiny because Diana was a celebrity. For that alone she owed us the tragedy. It was the repayment of her debt to us for making her celebrated; after that, she could hardly just empty the till and retire to live happily ever after on its contents. Part of the implicit contract between these celebrated people and ourselves, their devoted admirers, is that they give us our money's worth of passion, intrigue and drama. The price can be heavy; but celebrity has become a consumer product, so it is paid.

Did Diana give us more than we paid her for? No amount of looking into this sacrificial economics, more blatantly mercantile every day, can really explain the 'Diana effect'. It is more useful to examine the reasons for her celebrity. What had she really done to deserve her glory? Nothing at all really. She was simply the product of an evolution in the social demand for uncommon characters, the same development that lies behind the passage from hero to celebrity. The hero was distinguished from other mortals by what he had accomplished; his renown was earned by his extraordinary actions. This model changed with the generalization of the videosphere: what counts most towards celebrity now is not the *exploit*—lending itself to narrative and appropriate to an age of oral or written culture—so much as the *image*. Another difference is that unlike the hero, who is preceded by the rumour of his or her exploits, the celebrity starts as a face broadcast by satellite, like a universally recognisable logo or brand. Mother Teresa, who has been (wholly idiotically) compared to Lady Di, was a character left over from the age of heroes transported into the age of celebrities. That is why, despite everything, the small stooped silhouette and the thin, worn face, even when forced to live the lifeless life of pure image, still come across as symbols: you cannot see them without being reminded of devotion, charity and Third-Worldism. But these days the symbol is regarded as parasitic on the image, which tries to eject it altogether so as to exist in purely iconic mode. In this way, through endless repetition in the imagination, through the wearing away of induced meaning, even in Mother Teresa's case, the symbol ends by being absorbed into the icon. A sign of the times. Diana did not have to experience this obligatory passage through the symbolic. Nor in fact did she have to live a heroic or heroizable life, like Eva Peron for example. For she was born at the same time as the uncontested reign of the image. And what she gave us was not an 'inspiring' or 'beautiful' story but a sheaf of photos to leaf through. . . . Features and news editions had a very easy time when she died. Can we even remember her voice? Her sayings? In fact we never listened to them. All we wanted was to see her.

Mother Teresa made a gift of herself, Diana made a gift of her image. It is highly significant that people should confuse these two types of offering and see them as representing the same form of holiness.

To return to the question of celebrity: Diana was its ultimate embodiment precisely because, being associated with no memorable deed or exploit, her image could serve as a universal referent.

She understood instinctively—doubtless because she was a child of the videosphere—that image capital had taken over from symbolic capital, and she made use of this knowledge against the royal family. But the folder of action shots she put together was unique of its kind, because it was graced by the prestige of the monarchy, something based on secrecy and reserve, functioning in an altogether different mode of representation from the one she practised herself. Through a sort of spontaneous adhesion to her time she made the mystery of royalty serve to constitute its opposite: the postmodern cult of celebrity. That was her touch of genius; think of the Monégasque princesses who stupidly allowed celebrity to damage the mystery. Diana knew that this aura of another age distinguished her from other celebrities who these days appear from nowhere and usually go back there quite quickly, fulfilling Andy Warhol's promise of fifteen minutes of fame for everyone.

By naively shuffling levels of meaning in the representation, by discounting the full to the price of the empty, could Diana have been proposing to transcend the opposition between hero and celebrity, symbol and icon . . . perhaps by reanimating the image with an idolatrous charge? Was that the regression in which we were involved with her? As she never existed except as an image—both her strength and her weakness—there is no guarantee now that we will ever be without her. She will be with us as she always was, on paper, glossy or otherwise, on teeshirts, mugs, baseball caps, ashtrays and all the other 'souvenirs' that combine piety and tourism in one inexpensive artefact. A cult always brings the merchants running, and they are legion. So much so that Lady Di's image has had to be registered as a trademark. Diana Princess Logo: now *there's* a title for a postmodern fairy tale!

For its heroine, though, it seems her destiny is not to become a myth or legend but to remain an icon forever. It was before the icon, in any case, that the crowds laid their flowers and candles and bowed their heads in contemplation. And their pious gestures, spontaneously undertaken, had the unforeseen result of reinflating an empty icon from the age of image with something more like the religious content of earlier times. Of course the mass activity was only going to last as long as the emotion. But all the same, could that be what Diana had been preparing for us in secret: a promise to re-enchant image with the emotion that stands in for the sacred in our society? Is that her true legacy? Is that why we adored her?

Diana had been working to turn herself into an icon throughout her life as a 'celebrity', in much the same way as Pharaoh worked on his mummification. She had strong assets: a slightly dumb beauty, a sweet, half-childish eye, a ready smile kind and vacuous by turns. It was her smoothness—her sleek surface, the slick delivery of her image—that made her so photogenic, so much the stuff of icons. The condensation that took place in the collective imagination after her death, in which her royal person was somehow confounded with that of a saint, result-ed at least as much from her iconographic style as from her goodness. One is reminded of some Spanish virgin saint, more doll than fetish, whose image is dressed and undressed for different festivals or proces-sions. But showbiz sumptuery has replaced religions sumpuousness, so what this postmodern icon really suggests is something on the lines of a Barbie doll. When the whole world's television news rummaged through its archive footage, what it produced was something very like a supermodel's press book. No need to add that Diana dolls are already on the market.

Diana provided us with a place to lodge our affects.

We live in a time when suffering is no longer politically regulated. The chain of causality— historical, political or religious—having bro-ken, knowledge of horror and barbarity no longer tells us anything except that evil is obvious. As a result a reservoir of pain accumulates inside us, an excess of unemployed grief.

Our state is very similar to the passive resignation to misfortune we imagine characterises women in traditional societies, forever weeping and wailing, except that we no longer know how to cry as they do. The sight of a tiny Rwandan orphan or an Algerian farmer butchered with his fam-ily leaves us dry-eyed; we no longer know how or why to weep. For although these days all that happens is experienced in the fatalist spirit proper to natural catastrophes, most of the scenes of horror that come to us through our small screens are still, despite everything, haunted by the spectre of politics. And although we no longer know what to make of this spectre, it pollutes our suffering with vague feelings of guilt. But Diana's death served as an overflow conduit for all the unshed tears. It was a case of calamity striking for no reason, a pure misfortune; pure because clear of all implications; pure as the Princess's Pietá face. This was misfortune in its tragic dimension, beyond human understanding, therefore not so much something to identify with as an invitation to let go, to overflow, to pour out a suffering too long contained. Isn't that what the ancient Greeks meant by catharsis? If Diana really is a sort of saint, it can only be in the post-modern context of an ecology of misfortune that found a loud echo among the people of the global village. The world wept over the scandal of an affliction that no signifying chain can integrate into a narrative (in other words, supply with a meaning). But we were also weeping over our own bereavements, our own dead not properly honoured in the passing, and showing by our tears that we wanted death to get its ritual back and our societies to resume the collective work of mourning. A death like that— without physical decay, without a bridging period in hospital—fit the role to perfection.

Doubtless this has something to do with the fact that the British people did not allow itself to be dispossessed of its mourning, despite the media which tried to appropriate a moment of national emotion either by stoking up conflict between the people and the Royal Family (the tabloids) or by openly questioning the future of the monarchy (the 'quality' press).

But even if the British got a certain malicious pleasure out of making the royals leave their pedestal and stand about in front of the palace with everyone else, no one should see this as betraying a republican itch or a desire to modernize the behaviour of the crown.

Nothing like that was in the cards at any time. It was a much simpler matter, touching on the most archaic level of relations between monarch and subjects: the people, on becoming aware that they weregenuinely grieving, required the Royal Family to make an appropriate display of their own participation in the popular grief. For is it not part of a monarch's role to stand with the people when they are suffering?

So all the English were really asking of their royalty was that they resume their royal function. It therefore seems a pretty good bet that the monarchy will come out of this test strengthened, especially as it had the intelligence to let the people manage their own grief and put on a decent public display of royal sorrow.

Elizabeth II unbolted and thrown down? Certainly not. Disliked perhaps in the role of wicked mother-in-law, but restored as guardian of the crown. Even if some, still gripped by uncontrollable emotion, entertained fantasies of seeing the crown on the head of a young orphan prince still associated with another crown: one made of white flowers and bearing the word *Mummy*.

Diana's death recalled the monarchy to its main duty, that of proximity to its people. This is often, and wrongly, taken to imply that the monarchy's own approach has to be simplified. The royals are not required to bring their mode of life even slightly closer to that of ordinary people; they just have to stay in touch with their subjects in moments of distress, anxiety or affliction.

Here too the regression was full-blooded, to the greater profit of royalty. Diana belonged to us so completely that we were not even surprised by a paradoxical situation in which, instead of the people being invited to take part in the mourning of the great, the Royal Family was (as it were) summoned to share the suffering of the people. Is that what a 'People's Princess' is, a Highness capable of bringing about an upheaval on that scale?

Because 'the people' is, in practice, an ill-defined and unstable sociological and political entity, the lesson to be drawn from this story—a worrying one for our democracies—is that since it is easier to weep together than to live together, emotion of this sort may come increasingly to stand in for the social bond.

(Translation by John Howe)

seventeen

FEELIN'S

richard coles

Fee-eelin's . . . woah woah woah, fee-eelin's . . .
woah, woah, woah, fee-eelin's . . .

n the aftermath of the death of Diana, Princess of Wales, one of the herd of sacred cows sent lowing on its way to the abattoir was *God Save the Queen.* Too stuffy for new caring, sharing Britain, said the newspapers, who called for suggestions for a replacement national anthem. A clear favourite emerged early—*I Vow to Thee My Country*—on the grounds of its associations with both Princess Diana and sport. A better choice, in my view, would be *Feelings.* That plangent, all but wordless, chorus from Morris Albert and Mauricio Kaiserman's international hit of 1975, seems to me to capture perfectly the governing mood and spirit of Britain today, no longer haunted by an imperial past, no longer deferential, no longer emotionally constipated, no longer formal. More than that, it is a Britain which judges authenticity by a test of sincerity. Show me not what you think (or believe, even) but what you feel; that which is true is that which is most deeply felt.

To a sterner generation it would all seem pretty embarrassing, the kind of weedy silliness to be written off as a lapse of taste. That generation, however, now finds itself the object of contempt, for 1997 was an annus mirabilis for Sincerity Cultists. They are now in the ascendancy, carried along on the back of a new government, caring and sharing, open and friendly, tender and compassionate in everything but policy. The real victory, however, was achieved not through the offices of politicians, but by a traffic accident.

The key events unfolded in the immediate aftermath of the death of Princess Diana in an underpass in Paris. It began, as royal dramas do, utterly predictably. The princes Charles, William and Harry emerged from the baronial frumpiness of Balmoral, the morning after the accident, led by the Queen in a small fleet of closed, glossy-black cars. They swept past the media at the gate, went to church unflinchingly, and returned to the castle, without a tremor passing across those famously stiff upper lips. The mood was sombre, restrained, formal and public, an impeccable display of the classic royal reaction to triumph or disaster: *business as usual.*

The reaction was extraordinary. Court correspondents on the television and radio did their usual thing— black-tied, vicar-voiced, respectful—but the tabloid newspapers the next day completely changed the mood. In that awful, familiar mixture of deference and threat the headlines demanded *Show Some Heart, Ma'am! Your People Are Grieving! What About the Boys, Ma'am?*, as if the family's decision to take the bereaved sons to, of all places, a *church* on the morning after the death of their mother was an act of cruelty. To me it looked sensitive, thoughtful and compassionate, simultaneously an attempt to achieve some sort of normalisation of utterly abnormal circumstances, and to allow the family, in their varying degrees of grief, to begin to come to terms with what had happened. Not only was it entirely appropriate for the immediate needs of the family, it also quite properly acknowledged the public need for an appearance.

Nevertheless, streams of maudlin imperatives poured forth. Caught unawares, the tabloids (and the 'quality' press, too) were frantically trying to get the tone of their coverage right. Great rhetorical confusion followed, as if a page half made up for the death of the Queen Mum had been jumbled up with a page half made up for the next Diana scandal.

But the really interesting story was the reaction of the royals. Normally, in these situations, the line is held, the hectoring demands of the newspapers die down, and life gets back to whatever the royal equivalent of normal might be. In this case, however, it was different. After a day and a half of sang-froid, the line gave, and the days leading up to the funeral saw the spectacle of precedent after precedent tumbling. The Queen gave a special broadcast to the nation, uprooting herself and her bemused family from Balmoral and returning to *her people*, as if the people of Scotland were not quite as much *her people* as the people of sw1. Flags fluttered at half-mast in the most unlikely places—BandQ, MacDonald's, Tesco—and from time to time one or another palace disgorged uncomfortable-looking royals to stoop over mouldy piles of chrysanthemums and teddies and childish drawings. *Aaaaah*, we all went, *they're just like us, really*. I went to Kensington Palace and St. James' Palace to talk to people about what they made of the tragedy, to look at the flowers and the cards and the books of condolence (for work, not pleasure, by the way). Most moving were the books. In a palace corridor, table after table was occupied by what the media call *ordinary people,* moved perhaps for the first time, to prose and poetry. Some people wrote pages and pages, mini-pot boilers of regret and remorse; but this time they were all about *their* grief and regret and remorse. These writers were attaching their own lives, and their own disappointments to this one huge event; by entering into the Grand Tragedy of Di, what we belive to be our littler ones were amplified. The sheer weight and force of the emotion was quite phenomenal. An American friend of mine in town for the week said he'd never realised how unhappy the British were until he saw the lines of the lachrymose, stretching from Buckingham Palace to Admiralty Arch. This was not merely a death: this was a paradigm shift.

But why should *this* death, the death of *this* person, be so significant? Why should it have caused the institution which most resolutely symbolises constancy, tradition, certainty, to stumble? The key image is not the piles of flowers at the barred aristocratic gates of palaces and mansions, nor Elton John's incomprehensible song, nor those stiff, suited men walking behind the hearse *en route* to eternity: it is the Union flag at half-mast over Buckingham Palace, in the place where the Royal Stangaro has always flown whenever the monarch is At Home. The latter symbolises the continuing rule of God's Anointed, unfailing, unflagging, despite what fortune may hold; the former symbolises the identification of being British with having the correct feeling. It was the Standard of National Emotion. Di's death sacralised feeling, elevating her from high priestess to Goddess of the Cult of the Sincere.

Princess Diana was halfway there in life, destined for this greatness as surely as the Dalai Lama for his. Prettier than a film star, richer than a nabob, luckier than a gypsy, as . . . er . . . *unacademic* . . . as a Sloane, and as cunning as a stoat. Diana was possessed of formidable natural advantages. From the very beginning of her public life, when she transformed herself from a fresh-faced young thing working in a kindergarten (*aaaah*) to the heir's betrothed (*ooooh*), she began to accumulate extraodinary and mysterious powers. First, she was the fairy-tale Princess: blonde, nineteen, shy, the English Rose, thrust by love of a Prince of the Blood Royal into the center of National Life. This was nothing new. For hundreds of years male royals have recruited wives from the dull ranks of the English aristocracy, inventing a whole new genre of discomfort in the process (there's something quintessentially English about a horsey woman in a tiara). But Diana was different. She was a child of different generation, who imagined herself not only as a promoted English aristocrat, but also as the rags-to-riches heroine of a far more contemporary story. The latter came to the forefront as her career advanced. In her famous BBC interview she revealed a kind of wholly unreconstructed royal hauteur—*battered this, battered that*—simultaneously with the faux naiveté of the pop star—*you can't imagine what it was like for an ordinary person to be suddenly thrust into this extraordinary life* . . . An Earl's daughter, who grew up on one of the Royal estates? So two mysterious and powerful narratives were at work simultaneously, the traditional fairy tale, and the modern fairy tale, the Princess and the pop star.

These twin frequencies throbbed throughout the early years, when all was rosy (key image, her dancing with John Travolta at a White House state banquet). And then, tragedy. The publication of Andrew Morton's barely disguised ghost-job of the Real Di, *Her True Story*, magnified what was already hers to the power of ten. The accounts of her private anguish married to that cold, unfeeling, two-timing Prince, her reckless leaps down staircases, her wee-hour fridge raids, and the air of nameless, shapeless, colourless misery billowed around her, inflated what had been 'story' into 'legend'. In fact is wasn't inflation, but alchemy. Diana did not merely become a bigger version of herself, she became something else again. One of the consequences of this transformation was the shift in media perception. Editors began to see her and write about her in a different way once they'd worked out that her 'truthfulness', as expressed by the publication of the book, had cost her any deference they may have felt they once owed her by virtue of her position. In finding a way to appeal directly to the public, without going through the channels of a doubtless hostile palace, she massively increased her public profile. But she didn't win control of it. On the contrary, control passed from officials to editors. The most obvious consequence of this was her pursuit by the media, which changed from dogged to ruthless. And that pursuit in turn changed her. She began to behave and appear not as a royal—a sort of glamorous vicar—but as a star. Not a film star, which had overlapped with royalty already in the person of Princess Grace of Monaco, but a pop star. Pop stardom was much better suited to her needs than film stardom, for she wanted not to be someone else, but to be *herself.*

The BBC interview was fascinating because she finally went whole hog and *came out.* I remember watching it, completely transfixed, realising that she wasn't Diana Wales, but Diana Ross. In that interview she exchanged her royalty for celebrity. In the place of duty, reserve, mystery she claimed honesty, openness, transparency. The narrative of her life radically departed from the traditionaly royal example of somber frumpy virtue and keyed into the full-blooded celebrity exemplar of believe-in-yourself, dream-come-true fulfillment. This is what pop stars are tuned to, licensed by us to live out in full view the dreams of everyone else.

For we live in an age of dreams. In spite of the success of science, politics, capital, business—all highly pragmatic activities—when we examine what we actually believe, modernity is far dreamier, far more fanciful than the medieval world of Scholasticism. Consider the forces which have shaped it: Romanticism, which views the world as an aesthetic project and turns life into art; the ideas associated with Freud, more poet than scientist; the great and dreadful political ideologies of left and right both of which bent the world to their beliefs about what the world *should* be rather than what it actually *might* be; and popular culture, more than anything else a culture of dreams. Two tiny examples: Steven Spielberg, one of the most powerful and important film-makers in the world today calls his production company *Dreamworks;* Manchester United Football Club, the most powerful and important soccer brand in the world today, describes itself as the *theatre of dreams.* In the United States, in particular, everyone talks about their dreams, about dreams as goals—*if you don't have a dream, how you gonna make your dream come true*? Pop music, football, art, opera, film, television, sex—all have become vehicles of dreams, glimpses of other worlds in which we are better, happier, richer, more desirable, more successful, each one of us a hero or heroine living in the happy ever after. Pop stars are the aristocrats of this dream culture, both embodying the dreams of their fans and feeding them at the same time. In the 1980s I was for four or five years a sort of minor pop star in Britain; it was hardly on the level of Diana, but it was an instructive experience for anyone interested in the culture of dreams. If there was one thing I learned from it, it is that the essential point about dreams is that they're *not real*; and of course, if you live your life in unreality then you'll pay a price for doing so. More to the point, if your life has public currency, and if, as in the case of Princess Diana, it expresses aspects at the heart of the political, social and economic arrangements a society lives by, then the confusion of the real and the unreal has consequences that reach further than the merely personal.

The most significant of these consequences is the notion that sincerity—a pleasing but private value—should be mistaken for truth. Being sincere does not mean being true, it means expressing what you feel. This is fine if you're on Oprah exposing your various pains and discomforts for the entertainment of your peers; it is a positive virtue in one's personal relationships; but it is no way to run a monarchy, in which personal relationships express public and political values. This is antiquarian, absurd even, in a culture which has largely lost sight of the notion of public dimensions to personal actions. Even the Queen herself seems to have thrown in the towel on this one in New Britain's People's Monarchy, as Downing Street and the palace are promoting it, the Queen and her philandering husband recently chalked-up their golden wedding, a ridiculously cosy, middle-class marker for a most uncosy and un-middle-class union. Nevertheless, the opportunty was taken to thaw them out a bit publicly, so they hosted a banquet where a handful of *ordinary people*, looking exquisitely uncomfortable surrounded by the relics of European monarchy, advertised the classless nature of New Britain to the world's media. A classless Britain expressed by a Royal Banquet? It's a Britain as classless as the one expressed by Prime Minister Blair's Downing Street cocktail parties, open to any famous, successful, important ordinary person his private office can think of. Classless Britain means Oasis eating canapés with the First Lord of the Admiralty.

In the week of her Golden Wedding the Queen was reported to have said how much she dislikes people being deferential. Well, abdication would solve the problem, but why should the monarch, God's Anointed, the Head of State, the Supreme Governor of the Church of England, the Defender of the Faith etc. etc. so suddenly speak of her dislike of deference? Out of deference to poor dead Di (did you note the Queen's bow as the cortege passed Buckingham Palace?), who changed the nature of deference along with everything else. I met Diana on a few occasions —we both supported the same AIDS charity—and it was fascinating to see how she functioned, particularly the way in which she managed to be both royal and un-royal at the same time. As is normal on these occasions the punters were lined up and briefed on how to behave. The first time I met her she was still married to Charles, so we were told to bow, address her as Your Royal Highness and generally mind our Ps and Qs. Of course, when she actually turned up, we did none of those things. It would have seemed far too stiff and formal as she breezed in, charmed our pants off, and gossiped most improperly about her relations. You went straight to informal without passing go, and after your half-a-minute with her, before she was moved on to the next group, you were left thinking (1) how charming, (2) how informal, (3) I want to be her friend. But none of those would have been possible had she not been a royal in the first place. That trick of embodying royalness and subverting it in your favour simultaneously is impressive, one the surviving royals would do well to master.

On another occasion, not long before her death, I was at a function at a center for people affected by HIV, about to be graced by her presence. We had been given name badges, as per, but my friend exchanged his for the Princess of Prussia's, who'd left early. Diana approached, saw his badge, and said, quick as a flash, 'There's only one Princess around here, honey . . . ' or words to that effect. It wasn't much of a joke, but it was made by *her*, so it got a laugh, was repeated in three gossip columns the following day, and left us all charmed. Again, an example of how she managed to be both royal and un-royal simultaneously, but it also hints at another mysterious truth, another key element in her extraordinary make-up. Diana was a gay man.

If there is a model for Diana's transformation into New Diana, it is coming out, the defining event of modern homosexuality. Royalty and gay men have always got along: the Queen Mother and Princess Margaret, in particular, are famous fag hags, and below-stairs at royal residences has traditionally been as gay as the merchant marine. On the one side there is the royal, placing a high value on loyalty, discretion, attention to domestic detail and devotion to the appearance of things; on the other side, the male homosexual, placing a high value on glamour, the feminine, degree and mystique. Diana, however, was more than a fag hag. She had all the right reflexes, but with her sensitivity to trends she evolved in addition a complex identification with the narratives which shape contemporary gay identity. In a nutshell, that amounts to a cross between *Somewhere Over the Rainbow* and *We Shall Overcome*. Some of the key ingredients are a sense of a blessed life lying just over the horizon, for which we long; a lively and imaginative sense of the magical; a sense of internal and external oppression; the elevation of heart over head and its subsequent deployment as a rhetorical and political battering-ram. It is also an aesthetic project. It takes an imaginative feat to replot your life not according to the pathological definition of homosexuality we inherited from the fields of medicine and psychology, but according to a redemptive, triumphant act of liberation. The Gay Pride March and Festival, which Diana would have loved, is the chorus of Hebrew slaves from Verdi's *Nabucco* remixed by Giorgio Moroder, and while I would much rather have gay pride than gay shame, there are drawbacks to choosing so Hollywood a model for one's liberation. As a narrative, it is something of a blunt instrument, a simple moral fade with a rather peremptory and unsubtle denouement, in which all dreams come true and everyone lives happily ever after. In fact, coming out is not living happily ever after, as happens in stories; it is a change in circumstances, as happens in life. It is work-in-progress, not the showstopper.

Coming out, as the defining gay narrative, has been overtaken by AIDS in the past decade or so, which is a much darker and grimmer tale. Nevertheless, coming out rhetoric has helped shape AIDS rhetoric, too, one which again had powerful appeal for Diana. Indeed, one explanation for Diana's devotion to AIDS charities is that they produced a highly successful rhetorical model to fit her own experience. It is difficult now, fifteen years later, to imagine how different gay life in Britain was before AIDS arrived. For those of us affected by the first wave, it changed everything. Our lives were turned upside down and our expectations utterly transformed. The first reaction was shock and grief, but when we settled down for the long grind, some pressing needs emerged. How were we to ensure that people were made aware of the risks of getting infected with HIV? And how were we to ensure that those infected received proper care and attention? The atmosphere at first was a mixture of ninety per cent indifference and ten per cent hostility—I remember a leader article in the *Daily Telegraph* which chillingly pontificated, *The problem with* AIDS *is that it is not confined to homosexuals*—so clearly we had a major public relations job on our hands. The strategy which evolved had two main thrusts. One was to scaremonger, as a means of getting people's attention and passing on life-saving messages; the other was to spin the image of the gay man. This second thrust was the more difficult one, particularly as the reality of AIDS seemed to support popular myths; indeed, it wasn't long before the wrath of God was invoked as a cause of this new plague. We realised—and this wasn't a cold, Machiavellian decision—that if the public could be presented with images of gay men with AIDS not as monsters reaping the dread harvest of what they'd sown, but as sons, brothers, uncles, fathers suffering the appalling symptoms of a viral infection, then that would be a move towards breaking down that widespread resistence. At the time, 1 was involved in Red Wedge, an organisation set up by a group of loosely allied pop stars to present political ideas to pop concert audiences, and to seek to mobilise first-time voters as the 1987 general election approached. Education, housing and employment were the issues that dominated our agenda, but I found— unlike others who were not directly affected as I was—that AIDS was a different matter altogether. Success or failure was not simply a theoretical matter, or a matter containable within a familiar political discourse. It was life or death. The public response to Michael Buerk's reports for BBC News on the East African famine and the success of Live Aid convinced us that if we could only enlist sympathy, then support would follow. It proved to be an enormously effective strategy. By enlisting the support of media, arts, show business—all industries with a high proportion of gay and gay-friendly workers—the images we wanted to present began to be seen and heard fairly widely. The death of Rock Hudson had a powerful effect in widening and deepening public sympathy, but we still needed something extra to effect the change. We found it in Princess Diana.

As soon as Diana became aware of the epidemic she lent her support, tentatively and privately at first, and gradually more and more publicly. Then came the famous footage of her touching someone with HIV, an image of incalculable value to an entire generation of gay men, who will be eternally grateful to her for it. It was an *aaah* image, which was exactly what was required. Two things happened: first, it made caring about people with AIDS respectable, and second, it reflected back to the Princess the image she had been searching for. She had been kind to sick children from the beginning of her public life, but then so had every other royal, and it's hardly controversial to do so. Sick homosexuals, though, were another thing entirely. She was out on her own on this one (oddly, a place where she always seemed at home) and thus distanced herself from the stiffly conventional charity of the other royals through annexing new territory for herself. She became caringly countercultural, and I think she also found an enormous rapport with gay men, particularly gay men coping with the horrors of the epidemic. The common experience of many, growing up misunderstood, disliked, miserable and thereby prone to self-hatred, feelings of worthlessness and all the rest of it, clearly chimed with her. The fabulousness of gay men, involved in the arts, theatre, television, dance, design—the world of glamour—excited her; and, most powerfully, the myths of gay redemption provided her with a model for her own. AIDS added another important dimension. As we found out when we were trying to raise awareness and funds in the 1980s, there is a certain rhetorical strength to be found in terminal disease. To most people, unused to that prospect, it acts as a logic-beating imperative. A decade down the road and I'm more sceptical about that. Gay men with AIDS are not the only people facing the prospect of an early death—there are other equally deserving, but less well campaigned-for sick people—but you lose sight of that hard fact when it is your friend, lover, self you're fighting for. That logic-beating imperative, however, is a useful weapon to have at your disposal, tactically extremely effective. Diana became highly skilled in its use.

It can be seen put to great effect in the *Panarama* interview, in which she spilled the beans about her marriage. We saw the Princess sober and alone, smartly composed in a widowish Kensington Palace salon. The lighting was subdued, she was dressed impeccably, it had a Sunday evening feel. The significant exchange came when the interviewer, Martin Bashir, asked an awkward question—agreed in advance, of course—about her adulterous relationship with James Hewitt. He asked her if she'd been unfaithful, and she replied 'Yes. I adored him. Yes, I was in love with him.' So in answer to a very straight question, a forensic question about whether she had or hadn't committed adultery. instead of a simple yes or no, she replied with a yes-plus. This was not an answer but a justification. She finessed the forensic matter of her guilt or innocence of infidelity by turning a cross-examination into a romantic soliloquy. She presented herself not as an adulteress, but as a romantic heroine, compelled by true love to finally throw off the shackles of a loveless marriage to a cruel and unfeeling (and, by implication, far more culpable) adulterer and seek what solace she could in the arms of a dashing major. That he turned out to be not so dashing after all was a point neither she nor Bashir chose to develop at any length.

Another telling moment occurred at one of her last public appearances, the memorial service for her friend, the designer Gianni Versace. She sat there in the front row cuddling a tearful Elton John during the funerary pomp, an image which was shown around the world. A friend of mine was sitting behind them and saw a rather different image. While we saw the Princess and the pop star caught up in the emotion of the occasion on the *Nine O'Clock News*, what he saw was the Princess and the pop star facing not an altar but a camera crew. Diana and Elton had been seated—of course they had—in prime position for the benefit of the media, and were staring not at a dozen wreaths but a dozen lenses. I don't doubt their grief was genuine, but let us not lose sight of the reality that it was not private.

A similar moment appears in the film she made about landmines. The press had been invited along to show her emoting appropriately with unfortunate people with blown-up this and blown-up that, thereby adding saintly gloss to her and promotional high octane to the campaign to ban landmines. At one point one of the press pack had the temerity to ask her if she felt it was appropriate for her to be publicly involved in so political a campaign, whereupon she winced, turned away from the camera. and muttered, '*I'm not a political animal.*' You could have fooled me. Again, a serious and quite proper challenge on an agenda of her making was deflected and spun back as a cynical besmirching of her kindness.

This is the heart of the matter. I don't doubt that Princess Diana felt deeply for the miserable—indeed, I've seen her feeling deeply for them with my own eyes—but feelings are private things, to be expressed privately, and not arguments testable in public debate. As long as she confined them to her private life then there could no public problem. But her life became a soap opera and then something more (and less) than a soap opera and those private feelings acquired public force. This dynamic reminds me of a concert I went to in the 1980s, when Diana Ross sang to a crowd of several hundred thousand in New York's Central Park. There was a priceless moment between numbers, when Ms. Ross noticed that some among the hundreds of thousands were talking to each other from time to time rather than giving her their undivided attention. She broke off to chide us for our rudeness. What kind of person would mistake a huge concert in a park in front of several hundred thousand strangers for a family gathering? Someone for whom the distinctions between public and private have become blurred to the point of meaninglessness.

In a pop star this is not so bad, unless you are dependent on one, but in Diana's case it was, because her life was not her own. She was a public figure whose actions had political implications for the constitution of the United Kingdom. Now we can get rid of princesses and monarchies—it is technically and politically possible to do so, and many other more enlightened nations have done it—but it will be far more difficult to rid ourselves of the influence of Diana the Legend. She was probably the most famous woman of the '90s, admired by hundreds of millions of people all over the world who followed every twist and turn in the drama of her life as it unfolded. But the drama—or melodrama—proved so irresistible that we've lost sight of, or lost the will to look for, its darker aspects: for example, the moral blindness which results from exalting heart over head; the unquestioning belief in the rightness of acting in accordance with one's feelings, which, in her case, left a trail of romantic and marital casualties in its wake; the smothering of cold, hard responsibilities with a fluffy pillow of sentimentality. And now, with Diana dead, those darker aspects slip further from sight—or, worse, appear no longer dark in the gilding brilliance of canonisation. Her claim to be our Queen of Hearts was staked in life (I wonder if she'd ever read Lewis Carroll, by the way, the creator of the original capricious royal who believed six impossible things before breakfast?), but in death, one wonders if she wasn't a little unambitious. In the sleeve notes to the album made to celebrate her life and work, and to raise money for the memorial fund, she is quoted thus: *Nothing brings me more happiness than trying to help the most vulnerable people in society. It is a goal and an essential part of my life, a kind of destiny. Whoever is in distress can call on me, I will come running, wherever they are.* This is closer to the Queen of Heaven than the Queen of Hearts.

eighteen

DIANA AND THE BACKLASH

linda holt

'   he most important fact about the Princess was also the most
     obvious. She was a woman.' Perhaps ironically this observation
     comes from the right-wing philosopher and notorious anti-
feminist Roger Scruton. It begins the answer to his question why Diana's
'death, by removing her imperfections, permitted the myth of her goodness, generosity, and devotion to mankind to take hold of the popular
imagination.' What Scruton calls the rapid 'feminization' of society, and
'the inevitable consequence of the breakdown of marriage and the family' has, she argues, produced a rising generation, which, lacking trust-
worthy fathers, will always favour feminine values over masculine ones.
Scruton's two other most important observations about Diana—that she
was divorced, and divorced from Charles—amplify the argument. We
see in Diana 'the quintessential modern mother, the holy single-parent
family, the family without the father, in which the male is never more
than a child'; and her divorce is not just from 'any old man, but from
the heir to the throne, the one who represents the traditional authority
from our kingdom, the symbol of the patriarchal order.'

Scruton, of course, bewails the Diana cult because it offers yet more
evidence of the degeneracy of modern society, which feminism, and
democratization, have fostered: 'The matrilineal Britain of our popular

culture was beatified in her, and henceforth the icon will be inextinguishable.' Like almost all other commentators at the time of Diana's death, Scruton equates Diana with modernity. Her life, death and the responses to it—from Tony Blair to the Royal Family to the 'people'— were heralded as new and progressive, so that Diana herself became 'the moderniser,' as a *New Statesman* editorial titled her. In retrospect it is not hard to see why media commentators jumped to this conclusion in September '97. Untimely deaths are easier to bear (and write about) if they promise a better future. The talk of modernizing and newness which had helped Labour to victory in May still seemed fresh and credible. The association of Diana with New Labour and New Britain was inevitable within hours of her death when the original modernizer, Tony Blair, told the world's media she was the People's Princess. Finally, the contrast with an increasingly unpopular Royal Family, the ultimate symbol of all that is anti-modern, was irresistible for scapegoat-hunters such as Earl Spencer, the media themselves and their consumers. Like politicians, the media depend on talk of the new to sell themselves. Rarely, though, have politicians, journalists and public figures been so united and (apparently) unquestioning in identifying themselves with a new or modern phenomenon as with Diana and her mourners. This peaked in murmurings of revolution. September's heady rhetoric obscured the ways in which Diana's death reinvigorated a patriarchal monarchy. It also released an atavistic genie in the form of 'the people', bent on quasi-religious devotion.

Few commentators apart from Scruton were troubled by the modernity of the Diana phenomenon. Where it acquired a political spin, it was anti-conservative. According to a *New Statesman* editorial, 'the response to Diana's death . . . has shown, even celebrated, the end of the age of deference, the triumphant confirmation that Britain is not, and need not be a conservative country (where the Conservative Party is "the natural party of government"), but a dynamic, liberal place, where our hearts warm to those who take risks, where the first test of a nation's quality is its authenticity and the most vile of workaday sins that of hypocrisy. Diana could be both rich and deeply committed to the outcast, so long as she was authentic and open in both: hardly an unchallengeable stance, but it is the country's mood. As such, she was a moderniser. The spirit of modernity insists upon equality of respect and rights for everyone and upon a passionate search to place political trust in the people, not elites.'

Diana's success as New Labour heroine *par excellence* should surprise no one. To make itself electable, Labour notoriously expunged socialism from its vocabulary and thinking. With Diana's death, 'republicanism' became the word to be avoided at all costs. So in its place the leading magazine of the British Left gives us touchy-feely morality ('where our hearts warm . . .'), appeals to populism ('it is the country's mood') and vague liberal assertions. It is of course a formula familiar from New Labour's pitch for power: the editorial itself notes Diana's funeral was 'rich in paradox. In her relations with the media, in the redesigning of her public life after the failure of her marriage, in her commitment to good works, Diana's conduct was both deeply sincere yet calculating; not unlike Tony Blair's brief performance before the cameras when he mourned the loss of "the people's princess"'. Like all the mainstream British media, however, the *New Statesman* remains complicit with the American culture of celebrity, to which both democratic politics and the monarchy in Britain have fallen prey in the last decade. Blair and Diana emerge as the chief figureheads and instigators of this new politics of personality. Its vacuous double-speak, as in the *New Statesman* extract, opposes celebrity to conservatism, or Conservatism. The point about the response to Diana's death, it insists, is that it *isn't* deference. But not only was the age of deference overtaken by Thatcherism long before Labour's victory in May '97 but the actual response to Diana's death is left vague and unquestioned. Why is mass fan-dom better than deference? How is it anti-conservative? Blocking such questions by invoking *authentic popular feeling* leaves open the wish-list about its political significance. New Labour rhetoric functions similarly, obscuring Labour's conversion to neo-conservatism.

Again it is hardly surprising that the modernizing princess should be claimed a feminist heroine. While no one stated Diana's feminist significance as baldly as Scruton, the *authentic popular feeling* which her death occasioned and which she herself came to stand for was almost universally praised as emancipatory, an essentially feminine and feminist corrective to 'a patriarchy gone dry-eyed and stiff' in Elaine Showalter's phrase. Celebrating 'Diana the Destroyer' whose 'inquisitive crusading sentience . . . showed the House of Windsor up for what it was: a dumb, numb, dinosaur', the polemicist Julie Burchill noted 'Diana's was not the republicanism of economics and pie charts; it was, like all her politics, based on emotion and none the worse for it'. Showalter admired Diana's 'strength, and determination to make her life count', seeing her as 'one of the great success stories of contemporary psychotherapy'. Feminist writer and psychotherapist Susie Orbach described the response to Diana's death as 'the expression of some kind of emotional literacy'. The feminist columnist Suzanne Moore expatiated on Diana as 'a saint, supermodel, international superstar and a sex symbol all in one deliciously toned body'. Again, Diana's achievement was her emotionality— she 'validated personal experience' by speaking 'from the heart'. Moore commends her for bringing 'into public life an intensely personal language of pain and distress and love and affection' because 'such language, coded as feminine, is too often dismissed as inappropriate, as somehow inferior, as far too emotional to be worth taking seriously'. Indeed her death transformed this into 'a new structure of feeling'. Although Moore concedes that Diana was not a feminist, she implies she was a feminist role model because she was 'a product of the raising of female expectations brought about by feminism'.

Another feminist commentator, Linda Grant, was provoked to defend Diana and popular reactions to her death against the 'cynical Left' (even though this only amounted to private acquaintances who avoided her funeral, a handful of critical letters to the *Guardian*, and a single commentary by the journalist Euan Ferguson in the *Observer*). Accusing Diana's detractors of class bias and misogyny, Grant praised her for raising public consciousness about land-mines, AIDS and homelessness. Similarly guilty of 'sneering elitist condescension' were those who thought 'the grief displayed by the general public was vicarious or even phoney'. Like Moore, Grant avoids actually calling her intervention feminist, although its assumptions are unmistakably signalled as such. She refers approvingly to two female commentators on the response to Diana while Ferguson is left to represent the (male) Left, whose difficulty, she claims, 'in confronting the truth about the emotions' expressed by Diana's mourners 'is that it has always been terrified of feelings'. Broadcasters, too, 'trained in the gathering of facts', were condemned for having 'no idea how to express emotions'—Grant's evidence for this being the BBC's (male) Head of News, who said that the people on the streets were 'more articulate about what the Princess meant to them than the journalists and pundits in the studio', Like Moore, Grant recites the feminist mantra that the personal is political. Moore uses it to imply that Diana exhibited a feminist consciousness by refusing to suppress her personal feelings in public ('She understood instinctively that the personal was political, for she lived a life in which she was expected to suppress her personal feelings because of political duty'). Grant, on the other hand, uses it to insist on the validity and political significance of 'ordinary' people's personal emotion about Diana's death. Moore assumes the same when she compares the 'triteness' of 'so many intellectuals . . . from Gore Vidal downwards' with 'the self-awareness and thoughtfulness of the "ordinary people"'. She glosses the contrast as one between popular culture, which 'has for years been moving in the direction of the subjective, the confessional, the unashamedly emotional', and 'official public culture', which 'has yet to catch up'. Indeed a sign of this was 'the mutinous ripple of applause that spread from outside the cathedral to the inside' at the end of Earl Spencer's speech.

The feminist writer Beatrix Campbell also went on the offensive, pronouncing Diana a feminist saint who espoused 'radical causes'. In a vitriolic review of feminist writer Joan Smith's book *Different for Girls: How Culture Creates Women*, she attacks Smith for an essay written before Diana's death which likens her to Miss Havisham. Campbell's grounds seem to be that Smith lacks empathy and so 'cannot speculate about what Diana's story tells us about pain, power and protest'. Against Smith's counsel that Diana needed to get a job, Campbell retorts she did 'rather more than that, of course. She got a self. And a little self-respect.' For Campbell Diana is nothing short of a feminist warrior. 'Lest newspaper columnists forget,' she thunders, 'the foundling princess fished from the shires and Sloane Square to secure an ageing prince's great expectations mounted a life-and-death struggle with the most powerful, determined and dangerous cult in Britain, the Establishment.'

Diana's status as feminist saint may look assured. On British national radio, Elaine Showalter has called her a feminist heroine of epic stature. For some months after Diana's death the only explicitly feminist criticism of this in the mainstream press came from the journalist Nicci Gerrard. Elsewhere, however, as Elizabeth Wilson's article in *New Left Review* (reprinted in this collection) and other contributions in this book show, feminist writers and academics are also dissenting from the Moore-Campbell line. When Showalter asserted Diana's and Mrs Thatcher's exemplary role mole status at a women's studies conference in London in January 1998, her audience booed. But in other academic circles, reverent, sympathetic identification with Diana remains the order of the day. As June Purvis, a British professor of history, wrote in an extraordinary editorial for the academic journal *Women's History Review*:

> Diana was a modern, vulnerable, sensitive, and insecure woman who married into a traditional, autocratic family. . . . That she found the strength to fight back, to analyse her illnesses and to build up her self esteem in ways that she thought appropriate (and which some of us would shun) reveals that streak of steely independence that women have found through the ages when they attempt to define their lives on their own terms. For us today, her life laid painfully bare many of these contradictions and complexities that women face in the late twentieth

century. . . . Rest in peace, Diana. We remember you,
each in our own different way.

All this heralds a new mythology in certain feminist quarters. It was
not so much caused as triggered by Diana and the media coverage of
'ordinary people' mourning her death. From giving cause for feminist
analysis, Diana and her mourners have instead become *feminist causes.*
The pieces quoted above are devoid of argument. While this may be a
characteristic of punditry in general, the lack of explicitly feminist chal-
lenges in the mainstream British media suggests that mythology may be
hardening into orthodoxy. As Gerrard observed of Campbell's attack on
Smith, such feminism no longer means 'believing in equality, but believing in Diana'.

It would be nice to share Showalter's faith that Diana 'was one of the
great success stories of contemporary psychotherapy', that 'she had
achieved independence against enormous odds, and seemed to be on the
brink of realising Freud's formula for adult psychological health: love and
work'. But how do we know? Diana's life in recent years was that of an
international jet-setting celebrity. 'Love' consisted of holidays with an
aging playboy still dependent on his roguish father, and 'work' a series of
photo-opportunities with victims of land-mines, leprosy, AIDS, etc. Diana's
espousal of 'radical causes' was doubtless useful, but needs to be seen in a
context of 'good works' by other celebrities and royals, such as Elizabeth
Taylor's AIDS work and Princess Anne's much fuller but less publicized programme. Similarly, Purvis's conception of Diana as 'a modern, vulnerable,
sensitive, and insecure woman who married into a traditional, autocratic
family' ignores the fact that Diana was herself from a traditional, autocratic
family, an Earl's daughter born on the Sandringham Estate, with a very
old-fashioned and privileged education (girls' public school and finishing
school in Switzerland), and a considerable fortune of her own. Nor did
Diana develop into a closet republican; instead, as Christopher Hirchens
noted, she 'fought tigerishly to keep hereditary royal titles and fortunes for
herself and annex them for her children'.

Such talk is tantamount to heresy. Facts about Diana's life, and especially her actions, which challenge the myth of her goodness, generosity and devotion to mankind, seem irrelevant: being, not doing, is what counts. Diana's public and private identity depended on her royal marriage. Of course, feminist columnists didn't say outright that Diana's halidom relied on her marital status—instead, the myth's ostensible justification was Diana's sincerity, or emotional authenticity. This cleared a blank space where myriad fantasies could be projected and ring-fenced against reason. Those who refused to share them were vilified for being unfeeling, for not *being* the very thing Diana was. Fuelling the fantasies, of course, was a very powerful identification with Diana as 'one of us', which brands anyone less identified as 'one of them.'

This reinforces the binary oppositions—tradition, conservatism, and the elite, versus modernity, progress, and the people—which dominated commentary about Diana's death. So far, feminist writers have merely extrapolated further oppositions from this list: reason and emotion, masculine and feminine, anti- and pro-women. All these oppositions, as we have seen, are then boiled down to an anti-feminist/feminist politics.

What do these feminist politics amount to? Not a useful or coherent political position, but an instinctive stance recalling Burchill's unwittingly self-parodic claim—'Diana's was not the republicanism of economics and pie charts; it was, like all her politics, based on emotion and none the worse for it'. The problem, as much for Diana and the 'ordinary people' who shed tears over her death as for the feminists cited above, is that feelings are not politics. When femininists coined the slogan, *the personal is the political*, it was to insist that women's experience was not purely contingent, that it resulted from a specific set of political circumstances—patriarchy—and that, in this sense, it had a political significance. This never meant that women's—or anybody else's—feelings were simply equivalent to, or sufficient for, a political programme. The expressing of feelings—by Diana, by her mourners, by Tony Blair—which Moore and Grant defend as revolutionary is so much hot air unless it is followed by *political* analysis and action. In fact, labelling emotional expressiveness as 'feminine' merely upholds traditional gender stereotypes, in which men have monopoly on reason while women are creatures of emotion. When feminists champion the personal and emotional against the political and rational, they deny women, and 'ordinary people', the possibility of real political autonomy. The only winners are the professionals who purvey emotion for political or commercial ends.

What, then, does the Diana phenomenon say about contemporary feminism? Those cited above who championed Diana did not mention the preponderance of women among Diana's public mourners. Four out of five were women, according to one estimate, and they were remarkable for not consisting of the usual middle-aged and older royalists, but younger women (and men), closer to Diana's generation than the Queen's. As the journalist Simon Jenkins put it, Diana 'was a spokeswoman for those with impossible husbands, worried about their appearance, wrestling with divorce, careers, children, trying to match impossible expectations. And all the while searching for love and security'. Feminist writer Joan Smith observed how divorce had turned Diana's story into 'a paradigm of women's experience in the late twentieth-century century'. Far from demonstrating the victory of feminism, which Scruton fears and feminists such as Showalter, Campbell and Moore proclaim, Diana indicates some of its failings. Much of the response to her death made feminism look irrelevant and impotent. In identifying with Diana's plight, thousands of 'ordinary women' were showing how feminism had failed to improve their lot, at least on a subjective level. In canonizing Diana as a virtuous victim, they were showing how feminism had failed even on an imaginative level: no more empowered or empowering role model could be envisaged. And by promoting this identification, by refusing to think about it within the context of female emancipation, popular feminist writers like Grant, Moore and Campbell illustrate the decline of rational, political feminism. Indeed, to apply Campbell's criticism of Smith's book, their writing 'mobilizes feminism for unmanaged fury'. Let down by feminism, they embrace victim-power in its name. Like Scruton, they discount how Diana embodied traditional anti-feminist, anti-republican values and how her cult has enshrined them.

Both popular and academic feminist literature were silent on the subject of Diana until the fairy tale began to fracture publicly. Naomi Wolf omits her in *The Beauty Myth* (1990) although her treatment surely offered a classic illustration of the backlash tendency to conjoin beauty with brainlessness. The 'unawakened virgin bride . . . the Cinderella of the pre-feminist imagination, whose life depended on a prince's kiss' was not yet deemed typical. Perhaps she seemed too remote and unreal to merit serious consideration, perhaps she was simply written off as an embarrassing throwback in feminist terms. Yet the world-wide media coverage which her wedding attracted and Diana's own personal popularity, not least as a model for young women who turned the 'Di-cut' into a craze, showed the enduring power of the age-old story about the beautiful virgin who captures the heart of a prince. Women still believed in Prince Charming, even if they didn't like to admit it.

Naomi Wolf's 1993 work *Fire with Fire* includes Diana because 'upon her separation in 1993, she rose up in a fanfare of adoration in the women's media, cherished in her new incarnation as cool, powerful avenger, an entrepreneur of her own persona who has handled her 'product' so 'skilfully' that she is strong enough to take on, on her own terms, the corporate board of one of the richest and most influential conglomerates in Europe—the royal family.' This began with the appearance of Andrew Morton's biography in 1992, and culminated in her interview on BBC *Panorama* in November 1995, which led to her divorce the following year. Following the unprecedented commercial success of Morton's book, Camille Paglia produced the first serious examination of Diana as 'a case study in the modern cult of celebrity, and the way it stimulates atavistic religious emotions'. With characteristic provocation, Paglia located Diana's appeal in 'ancient archetypes of conventional womanhood' and celebrated her beauty, glamour and sexuality, and especially her ability to flirt with the world's media—'a Madonna-Dietrich level of manipulation' as she later termed it. Her implicit target was the kind of feminism which 'sexually redefined woman as simply the white upper middle-class professional with an attaché case'. However, the multiple personae Paglia described in Diana's image were soon reduced to the triumphant glamour-queen who finally gets her own back on her faithless husband, feckless lovers, absent parents and disapproving in-laws. This fantasy of visceral, vengeful woman-power was memorably articulated by Julie Burchill in 1992, when it prompted her to christen Diana 'the People's Princess'. That it could be adopted by Blair, and become Diana's universal epithet after her death, shows how illusory its radical potential was.

Even greater in impact than the biography was Diana's television interview for it both described and enacted her conflict with Charles and the Palace. Acutely personal, revelatory and emotional, it clashed spectacularly with the blank formality and predictablity of royal communications such as the Queen's Christmas broadcast. Mixing the language of traditional romance with the clichés of psychotherapy and popular feminism—Diana was a long-time patient of the feminist psychotherapist Susie Orbach—it replicated the intimacy and therapeutic promise of women's talkshows. In an influential piece for the *Guardian* at the time, much quoted after Diana's death, Suzanne Moore called her a 'a nineties woman with nineties conflicts', hailing her as a heroine of the women's movement, with Gloria Gaynor's 'I will survive' as her anthem. This is all the more striking when set against an extremely vituperative piece ('Diana—Her true colours') Moore wrote in 1993 when Diana announced her intention to reduce her official engagements. What secured the undying admiration of Moore and many others two years later in her television interview was Diana's courage in asserting *publicly* the pain and suffering caused by her failed marriage.

That personal disclosure on international television is a therapeutic, even feminist, act may be axiomatic in the age of Oprah, but there are good reasons to doubt it. As feminist writer and psychologist Jane Ussher has argued, talk shows are a ritualized forum which elevate personal testimony into truth and provide their confessors with fifteen minutes of fame and sympathy. Beyond fleeting emotional catharsis, they offer participants and viewers little: women's woes remain their own, to be sorted out at home, rather than the public domain. Diana's *Panorama* appearance was also 'an archetypally feminine act—disclosure of romantic hurt and pain, presented with doe eyes, flirtatious eyes and downtrodden demeanor'. On one level Diana was presenting a new variation on the Cinderella theme: like Cinderella, she had to be strong and beautiful to overcome her pain, but now what she wanted was not a man, but her work and her boys. On a different level this looked like 'another example of archetypal feminine subterfuge, a misleading state-ment to focus attention on the other villain of the piece, the 'other woman' who had stolen the prince from the poor maiden's arms'. Easily stereotyped in the press as old, ugly, and lascivious, Camilla Parker Bowles makes the perfect late-twentieth-century witch.

The real problem was Diana's tendency to play the victim card. By presenting herself as the rejected, abused woman, she underwrote a range of traditionally oppressive feminine stereoptypes: passivity, inno-cence, virtue, mother-love, suffering and self-sacrifice. In her speeches and charity work, she aligned herself with victims, apparently sharing their pain and suffering; pictures of her tearfully touching or holding them silently drove home the point. The Morton biography, which Diana authorized, drew an almost absurdly lachrymous portrait of a fragile, pitiable girl. Joan Smith and Camille Paglia have shown how Diana's image recalled feminine archetypes such as the *donna abbando-nata* and the *mater dolorosa*. A striking example is the sombre dark blue suit, washed out hair and smudgy kohl-rimmed eye-make-up Diana chose for the *Panorama* interview: she looked as drained as she sound-ed, 'like a crime victim who had been persuaded by the police to meet the press and talk about her ordeal'.

In her 1992 study *Our Treacherous Hearts: Why Women Let Men Get Their Way*, Rosalind Coward argued against the widespread assump-tion that the days of female subordination were over, by showing how many of the 'bad old things' about women continued to exist—'female passivity tending towards victimization, female anxiety for male approval, female readiness to bury their own needs in others (usually unsuccessfully) and female vulnerability when men's support and approval is absent', Diana, of course, manifested precisely these traits in extreme behaviours symptomatic of contemporary female victimhood—eating disorders, obsession with appearance, obsessive dependent behaviour (such as nuisance phone calls), suicide and self-harm attempts.

Diana's solutions, like those of the women Coward documents, remained personal, individual and traditional. Notably absent from her *Panorama* interview was any *political* questioning of the ideologies and social structures underlying her role and treatment as a woman (although her analysis did draw on feminist-inspired psychotherapy, and was certainly read politically by many viewers and commentators). Indeed the futures she envisaged both for her children and herself were entirely within a conventional patriarchal framework in which her son would be King, and she was first and foremost mother of the future King, and then Queen of Hearts—or, as Joan Smith has glossed it, queen of broken hearts. By laying claim to feeling, nurturing, loving, she appealed to the age-old association of femininity with emotion. The responses the interview provoked—people felt for her, women agreed with her, men wanted to protect her or wrote her off as mad—were no less conventional.

That Diana's therapized victim-speak could turn her into a feminist role model seems like a bad joke. But it is the result of the way feminism—as a movement and ideology—has fragmented and become bound up in a cultural backlash against its original political project. Much of what has been called 'victim feminism' has been absorbed into mainstream culture, shorn of its political context, no more than a licence for rampant subjectivity. As Lynne Segal's critique of 'difference feminism' shows, 'traditional gender ideology' has become the new common sense of much recent feminism. In this 'new feminism' even flamboyant consumerism, as exemplified by Diana's pursuit of fashion and beauty, can be celebrated as an emancipatory choice.

Indeed, Diana's commodification of herself as a series of iconic images is likely to be her lasting achievement. Again it is hard to find a positive feminist significance in this, however much Camille Paglia, and others, may have enjoyed looking at her. For it seemed as if Diana's very identity consisted of being photographed and looked at, as if it depended entirely on the (male) gaze, where her own gaze was, typically, averted. She was the absolute archetype of the silent 'looked at' woman, the idealized object of man's desire, and nothing she did altered this or suggested she seriously wanted to. It is precisely because she projected the epitome of artificial femininity so professionally that she could be adopted as a gay (male) icon, but her 'femininity' was not a masquerade she was in control of. Instead it seemed appropriate when the paparazzi appeared literally to kill her. As her death and funeral recalled images from two of the year's most memorable films, *Crash* and *Evita,* her life came to seem like a celluloid fiction in which an untimely, glamorous and grandiose end for its female star was inevitable. More than that, her death seemed immolatory, a completion of ancient narratives about abandoned women, female transgression and self-styled female victims. Both Joan Smith and Camille Paglia had noticed this narrative structure in Diana's life some years before and warned that its conclusion would be fatal. To qualify Roger Scruton, the most important fact about Diana is not that she was a woman, but that she is a dead woman, forever silent, forever frozen in her images. Her death stopped her developing any real emancipation, confirmed ancient misogynist prejudice and made her feminine qualities objects of veneration.

Just as Diana's suffering had no political consequences (however much it temporarily affected polls on the monarchy's popularity), so that of 'the nation' in the wake of her death proved to have little lasting political significance. The high excitement of the funeral week, in which commentators liked to discern popular hostility to Charles and the Windsors and speculate about its republican potential, evaporated as soon as the mourners went home. Beyond a propaganda coup for the people's Prime Minister and a knighthood for Elton, all that remained was the chance of some some feel-good charity and the pilgrimage to Althorp. Diana's own 'good works' have become the unquestionable depoliticized model for a renewed emphasis on charity and private philanthropy, and have helped to legitimize Labour's lack of commitment to providing adequate state welfare provision.

So far, the sole political effect of Diana's death has been to give the Tory Peer Lord Archer the opportunity to propose the repeal of royal male primogeniture so that females would have equal rights to succeed to the throne. Unabashedly designed to promote Archer's bid to be the first Mayor of London, any effects of the proposal, if passed, would not be felt until well into the twenty-first century—even if William V sires female heirs before male ones. The measure was used as a sop to modernization by a Conservative politician for conservative effect, pre-empting republican or feminist responses to the death. This was already obvious at the obsequies, where the royal sons (main focus of concern for commentators and 'ordinary people' alike) were phalanxed by men in suits—real or fictive guardians such as Charles, Spencer, Blair and Major—with no comparable female authority figure to be seen. The youthful figure of Prince William provided a convenient repository for everyone's fantasies. Though the Archer proposal may seem to engender equality in the royal succession, it in fact marks Diana's absorption by patriarchal tradition. Of her blood, and bearing her a close physical likeness (very important for the appearance-obsessed politics of emotion), Wills was serviceable to the status quo: we get the same old monarchy, but with added Diana. As her son, but usefully male, Wills both is and is not the dead Princess. *Pace* Scruton, the most enduring fact about Diana may prove to be that she brought forth not a feminist warrior, but a true Prince Charming

nineteen

MYTHS, LIES AND THE ROYALS

christopher hird

*b*efore the British journal Index on Censorship *published this review of* The Royals, *by Kitty Kelley (Warner Books, 1997), they censored it. The censorship took the form of changes made following advice from lawyers which aimed to reduce the risk of legal action under both the Defamation and Contempt of Court Acts—two of the pieces of legislation listed in the same edition of* Index *as gags on journalists. Fear of a contempt of court action lead the lawyers to suggest that detailed revelations from* The Housekeeper's Diary *be removed from the review. These were not salacious details about the royals' sex lives, but eye-witness testimony of their meanness and wastefulness.*

The changes made on the grounds of a potential libel action were: the removal of the name of Kelley's source about Prince Philip's alleged daughter in Melbourne; the name of the shop to which Princess Margaret returned her unwanted Christmas present and the name of the royal with a cocaine habit. Interestingly, at one stage many more changes were suggested but were successfully resisted by Index's *editor Ursula Owen. Given the extreme improbability of any royal suing over the book, the whole process was a startling illustration of the deference shown the Royal Family in Britain—the very thing which had prevented publication of the book in Britain and which, to some extent, the book was an attack upon.*

One of the criticisms that can be made of this review is that it didn't highlight the weaknesses in Kelley's journalistic method. For example, she repeats the allegation that Lord Porchester is Prince Andrew's father but makes no attempt to find out where Queen Elizabeth and Lord Porchester were nine months before Andrew's birth. But the appeal of Kelley's book is that it is the most complete and uncompromising digest of what has been unearthed about the Royal Family, free of the deference which routinely characterises most books on the subject. It is, however, an open question whether the tone would have been the same if it had not been completed before Diana's death. Even Kelley found it necessary to apologise for the timing of its publication.

• • •

The smart thing is to sneer at Kitty Kelley's *The Royals*, a book which is not available in British book shops. There's Professor Ben Pimlott in the *Guardian:* 'an audacious practical joke . . . as cold as a dead grouse . . . anybody looking for new information should cancel their ticket to the US to purchase a copy . . . historical method is not Ms Kelley's forte.' Or Professor David Cannadine in the *London Review of Books*: 'A book so bad that Britons cannot realise how fortunate they are in being unable to buy it: wholly lacking in historical perspective or context, saying little that is new or interesting, devoid of any coherent argument or overall interpretation, prurient in its obsession with human weakness and written in prose that makes tabloid journalism seem almost fastidious.'

Lets hope there's a touch of irony here. Or does Cannadine really believe that a lack of historical perspective of an interest in human weakness should be grounds for keeping the published word from those of us who are not the authors of books characterised by their concern for historical context and an abundance of footnotes? Perhaps we should be interested in the personal failings of a family promoted to us for most of the postwar period as a paragon of virtue and a model of family life: not because these are their failings as such, but because they expose the gross hypocris of the Royal Family's position.

The tenor of most of the criticisms of the Kelley book has been that of the knowing insider: we all know that they are unfaithful in marriage;

that the Duke of Windsor supported the fascists; that they are boorish and virtually incapable of normal human relationships. In recent years, even the most casual reader of the newspapers couldn't miss some of this. Still, one may be short on the detail. And there is a lot about the Royal Family that *will* only be known to those who have read virtually every book that has been written and have assiduously stored press cuttings from the tabloids. If you haven't done this, then Kelley's book will tell you something you didn't know.

The vast number of books on the Royal Family make it very hard to know how far Kelley's book relies on other people's work and the lack of precise sources is an irritation if you want to hunt them down. But, this apart, it's a wonderful book. You cannot read it without agreeing with the Queen Mother's description of herself: 'You think I am a nice person, I'm not really a nice person.' She is not at all nice—and neither are any of her family. Kitty Kelley, I am sure, is no revolutionary; but she comes from a republican political tradition. What is so appealing about this book is that it displays no sign of being touched by the mystique of royalty— mystique which still infects so much written by British authors about the monarchy and the Royal Family.

One part of this mystique—largely undamaged by anything which has happened in the last 15 years — is the powerful bond between the British people and the Royal Family during World War II. This book paints a rather different picture. 'The King and Queen sidestepped the country's strict food rationing and regularly ate roast beef and drank champagne. Butter pats were monogrammed with the royal coat of arms and dinners served on gold plates.' While London restaurant prices were controlled, the King 'ordered two eggs and six rashers of grilled bacon for breakfast every day and grouse in season for dinner every night.'

And when the war came to an end, while Britain was living off ration books, Princess Elizabeth was living in luxury. 'While her future subjects were still restricted to clothing coupons and wearing skirts made of curtains and trousers cut down from overcoats, she had her own couturier and was ordering strapless satin evening gowns.' The Royal Family received an extra 160 clothing coupons—on top of the 66 which ordinary mortals received; and when they went on a tour of South Africa after World War II, they were issued a staggering extra 4,329 coupons. The Royal Family's privileged treatment during rationing is not, it is true, a Kelley discovery; it is well known to the millions who have read an article by Dr. Ina Zweiniger-Bargielowska in a 1993 edition of *History Today*, a source Kelley acknowledges.

The scale on which the Queen lives is breath-taking, especially when set against the well polished image of her as frugal. In November 1950, at a time when hardly anyone in Britain could afford a foreign holiday, Princess Elizabeth took a three-month trip to Malta. 'Accompanied by her maid, her footman and her detective, she arrived on the island with her sports car, 40 wardrobe trunks and a new polo pony for her husband.' The next year, when she went to Canada, she took 189 wardrobe trunks.

Where the Royal Family are careful with their money is in the pay of their servants. As John Barratt, former secretary to Lord Mounthatten says: 'All the Windsors are as mean as cats' piss.' Christmas presents to servants were blow heaters, bath mats and, from Princess Margaret, a toilet brush. In 1993, as public indignation about the Royal Family's wealth grew, the Queen economised: by making her £5,600 a year chauffeur pay for his shoes and her even less well paid servants pay for their own soap. This notorious meanness is also well chronicled in another book, it too unavailable in Britain, *The Housekeeper's Diary* by Wendy Berry (Barricade Books, NY 1995).

Prince Charles persuaded the British courts to ban the publication of Berry's book in Britain on the grounds that she had breached her contract of employment. It's a pity that we cannot publish information from it in this review, because the book provides fascinating insights into these people's lives and behaviour. It is easy to see why Charles was so keen to keep this book banned: it showed that the contract which was being broken was that between him and his subjects. But the move came from a long tradition in the Royal Family of keeping the public in ignorance of what they are up to. The Queen Mother stopped Princess Margaret's footman publishing a book on some of the more arcane habits of Princess Margaret's former husband; the Queen prevented the *Sun* from publishing the memoirs of an aide which chronicled Prince Andrew's one night stands. And where the royals leave off, the British libel laws take over.

When the courts are not available to the royal family, they lie. As George VI was dying, the Queen Mother rouged his cheeks for public appearances, to disguise his illness. The palace staff were told to deny that this was happening. During the 1950s, the Queen was a great gambler, twice topping the list of money-winning owners. The official palace line was she loved horses, but never gambled. In 1973, they said that Princess Anne and Mark Phillips had never met—in fact, they were just about to get engaged. And, as we now know, they lied again and again about the state of Charles and Diana's marriage. When a police guard at Highgrove truthfully stated that they slept in different rooms, it was categorically denied. When Andrew Morton's *Diana: Her True Story* came out in 1992 it was denounced as 'preposterous'. As the posthumous edition confirms, its account of the Wales' unhappy marriage was based on taped interviews with the Princess herself.

But the palace was not alone in attacking the Morton book: most of the British establishment and its friends in the media—including the Press Complaints Commission—joined in. Today these attacks on the veracity of Morton's work look extremely stupid. But, then, as Kelley chronicles, the British press has a long tradition of complicity in keeping up the image of the royal family.

When Prince Charles visited the Taj Mahal—while engaged to Diana, but continuing an affair with Camilla Parker Bowles—he said, 'I am encouraged by the fact that if I were to become a Muslim I could have lots of wives'. None of the accompanying press corps reported this. When the Queen told reporter James Whittaker to 'Fuck off', he reported it as 'Go away.' When Prince Philip asked the *Independent* to excise a section of an interview, in which he described the former French President, Vincent Auriol, as 'a frightful buggerer', the *Independent* agreed to the cuts.

These may seem small matters; collectively they illustrate how, until recently, the British press did not want to tell the truth about the sort of people who sit on or near the throne. Are people familiar, for example, with some of Princess Margaret's vulgarities? According to Kelley she described *Schindler's List* as 'a tedious film about Jews', and said of the President of Guyana: 'He's everything I despise. He's black; he's married to a Jew; and, furthermore, she's American.' She and her husband asked for a US$30,000 appearance fee for a US charity fundraiser; she returned a friend's Christmas present in exchange for cash.

Then there's Kelley on Diana's homophobia (sacking most of the gay employees because she didn't want them around her sons); her suggestion that Prince Andrew's father is really Lord Porchester; her description of the Duke of Edinburgh hitting a US government driver because he refused to take orders from the Duke rather than the US secret service; and how the royal family's obsessive dislike of divorce meant that the Queen tried to stop Jackie Kennedy asking her sister to dinner because she was divorced?

In view of subsequent events, this particular obsession has some piquancy. But then the royal family's attitude to marriage and sex is, by most people's standards, unusual. Prince Philip had a string of relationships (often with people passed on to him by Lord Mounthatten) before he got married to Princess Elizabeth—an event which proved to be only a temporary hitch in his scheme of things and which was not, on his part, a result of being in love.

Kitty Kelley makes allegations that, during the 1950s, Philip and two other men calling themselves 'the Three Cocketeers,' 'entertained' young actresses; and that he had assignations during a four-month tour on the royal yacht Britannia, one of which left a daughter in Melbourne. If this was the case, it makes Charles's attitude to women more understandable. He also had a marriage of convenience, which did not really interfere with his relationship with Camilla Parker Bowles. According to Kelley she spent nights with him on the royal train during his engagement and within weeks of his marriage he was back with her.

Largely because of the sex stories, this book will not be published in Britain. It's a pity because—as Diana said of Charles: 'He's supposed to be a paragon to people. He's going to be the goddamned Defender of the Faith.' The British monarchy has the most remarkable capacity for self preservation and reinvention and you can be sure that no effort will be spared in the next few years to try and re-establish some of its mystique. The power of this book is that it so comprehensively undermines this and reveals the emptiness of the monarchy's claim to be an upholder of any sort of decent values. If there is only one book you read about the Royal Family, make it this one.

twenty

DIANA, PATRON SAINT
OF THE GLOBAL VILLAGE

marc augé

Lady Di was an image: a press photo or television picture, an image captured without her permission but also controlled by her, like the images that all individuals try to maintain and project of themselves. We all identify with a certain image of ourselves, and other people's perceptions play a part in the construction of that image. But it occurs to me that people who see their own image every day in the press or on the screen — solid, real, a 'perfect likeness'—may come to question the exact nature of these snapshots, these doubles they are constantly shedding; and that they may sometimes become unsure of their own identity.

Multiplied daily, the image would be a little like an unerasable memory: impossible to live with. To outsiders on the other hand these available, disposable images, which can be laid end to end and assembled into a story or legend, constitute strong factors of identification. Images revisited every week for years become as familiar to us as the beings we live with, indeed even closer because, whatever the twists and turns of their lives—the narrative whose episodes we follow—they stay faithful to us. Lady Di left Prince Charles, not the admirers for whom she existed only as an image. It is not surprising that a lot of people felt not just that they knew her, but that part of themselves died with her.

A drama of fifteen years in three acts: radiant bride, betrayed wife, modern woman. Women were able to identify easily with each of these

stereotypes, especially if they were contemporaries, because in the catalogue of princely adventures they found a public and magnified version
of the joys and sorrows of their own existence: episodes of banal intimacy—love, jealousy, betrayal—but also a version of the liberation
movement which was gradually emancipating them from inherited
roles. The Princess of Wales's transformation into a liberated woman,
more beautiful than ever and a global advocate of humanitarian causes,
must have carried a sweet taste of revenge for others as well as herself.

But to everyone, men as well as women, Lady Di's last manifestation,
on a screen rubbing shoulders with John Paul II, Elton John, Bill Clinton,
John Travolta and Mother Teresa, among others, makes her eminently
modern—or postmodern—and by the same token, prestigious.

The worlds of showbiz, business, politics and religion are inter-
mingled. Anyway that is the impression the public is given by the images
it is shown. Royalty has always resorted to stage-management and the
manipulation of images. But in our society, which in principle consists
of free autonomous individuals, image is everywhere: public figures may
be lying low in their villas, palaces and yachts, but we see them every day
in our newspapers and on our screens. In everyone's experience they
exist in image form. Image, then, is not private life or public life but existence itself—a way of existing in the eyes of others—and thus a measure
of intensity of being. A lot of people dream about 'getting on telly': to
be seen, to be sure that they really exist.

Such image games are a product of illusion—or in other words,
Freud would say, a product of desire—but the fact is that these days the
greater part of our relations with others and with the outside world is filtered through this illusion. The paradox of our time—which gives it its
dramatic character—is that only death can 'give body' to an image. But
the sight of the corpse is unbearable and displaying its image unthinkable. This setback or contradiction is what gives the paparazzi their scandalous aspect: when death comes, they go about hawking the image of
the end of an image. But the image cannot just vanish like that, turn
suddenly unfaithful to those who have nurtured it. Of course it has

changed constantly, in the sense of evolving; because it was alive and played the game of substitution, the active principle of all seduction: I am not who you think I am.

Diana's life seemed to unveil a succession of truths represented by different dramatic episodes and changes of outlook: behind the naive young bride a betrayed wife; behind the betrayed wife a seductress; behind the seductress a saint soothing the world's miseries; behind the planetary superstar an exemplary mother. . . . If the game ever ends, if Diana 'finds happiness at last', the story stops too and the image fades. 'A happy person has no history,' Stendhal said. Death is more indulgent; brutal, senseless, cruel death does not always kill the image straight away but may transform it for a time into a holy picture, an effigy. Many were the images of Diana carried by mourners or put up on walls or in windows along the route of the funeral cortege; and it is not out of the question that the Princess of Wales could appear in the pantheon of one of those magical Latin American and Caribbean cults—Candomblé, Umbanda, Santería—that recruit their gods from the past and the present with cheerful impartiality.

In Britain where, at least as much as anywhere else, Lady Di still lives and will live on as an image, people are wondering whether she has also become a symbol. A symbol is only a symbol of something if it symbolizes that thing for a number of individuals who identify with each other and recognize that they have something in common. A symbol is at its users' disposal. Unlike an image, which allows individual identifications, it is an instrument of collective recognition: the body of the deceased, the cadaver, always plays a symbolic role because, if only for the funeral or the mourning period, it remains the mediating object of a relationship between the living who remember, who at least share a memory. The death of one of the world's 'great and good' must possess, *a fortiori,* a symbolic dimension.

In the week that followed the death of Lady Di, star and Princess, what was really startling was not so much the worldwide emotion—linked closely with her image—as the popular feeling in Britain, instantly sensed and put into words by Tony Blair. Commentators wondered whether the death would finish off the British monarchy or save it. One could not escape the feeling that the court might have been a bit slow to grasp the importance of the stakes; that it had been too concerned with Lady Di's image to make a good start in the symbol race the 'People's Princess' had just imposed on it for the last time. The chase between symbol and image, between the people and the Queen, strangely echoed that cavalcade of sinister bikers, like the angels of death in Cocteau's *Orphée*, who chased Lady Di to the gates of eternal night.

Overtaken several times by 'popular pressure', the English court was forced into a mode of *fuite en avant*. As the days passed we learned successively that the Princess of Wales would have a 'semi-state' funeral, that the route for the cortege would be lengthened to allow for the extra million spectators predicted every day, that the British flag would be flown at half-mast over Buckingham Palace; the Queen, Prince Charles and his children were seen shaking hands with people in the crowd and gazing at the mountains of flowers raised by popular fervour.

Eventually the Queen spoke of her feelings, her great esteem for the Princess of Wales. Had the Windsors won, appropriated the runaway Princess's corpse, turned the divorced Prince into a tearful widower and the remote monarchy into a symbol of togetherness and modernity? Perhaps the funeral would provide the answer.

Like a majority of the republican French, I am susceptible to the history of the British monarchy. I am impressed, too, by the strength of a people able to chant in a single voice (and what a voice!), to camp out all night on the lawns of Hyde Park and express its sadness and pain without false bashfulness. The televised spectacle on Saturday morning was a double one, since it conveyed a minutely detailed and disciplined ceremony in shots that were themselves prepared in advance, carefully chosen and framed: a textual commentary in fact, beautiful in itself and effective as well. Great art.

Among the television audience, I imagine, there were few who did not feel some emotion or notice that they were sharing the feelings of a whole people when three generations of men followed the Welsh Guards in the wake of the Princess's coffin; even more so when the notes of *God Save the Queen* echoed from the ceiling of Westminster Abbey as the cortege arrived. The art of adapting ritual, of helping it to evolve, is always and everywhere the essential condition of survival for religions and political régimes. We could rest assured that the old monarchy had managed to adapt.

Then, as the ceremony progressed, I started to have the slightly uneasy feeling that once again, as in the time of its Victorian splendour, England was giving the rest of the world an offhand lesson in politics, showing it the way to go. That behind the ostensible 'repentance' of the Royal Family, the complications of the family drama and the adaptation of ritual, what was being sketched in front of a TV audience of two and a half billion people was the image of a sort of neo-Commonwealth in the exact likeness of the famous global village, the shrunken planet of Internet, economics and rock.

Lady Di could certainly pass for the heroine, symbol or patron saint of a world like that. For had she not travelled the Earth (with Mother Teresa's blessing if the media are to be believed) from Bosnia to Angola, publicizing people's suffering and preaching love? Was she finally anything other than a Contesse de Ségur heroine on a planetary scale? Love: of all the great virtues, the Archbishop reminded us (echoed by Tony Blair, telegenic as the devil himself but quoting St. Paul's epistle to the Corinthians), love is the most important. And Elton John raised the bidding. Of course, St. Paul has only called it 'love' since the authorized version of the Bible got its last facelift. Before that he was still urging 'charity' on the Corinthians, as he still does in the French version; a word that becomes formidably ambiguous when used as a political password.

As the grieving crowds chanted in front of Westminster Abbey, holding their candles in the wind, I could not help wondering—half dreamy, half terrified—if what we had just been watching on worldwide TV was the first masterclass in realist socialism.

(Translation by John Howe)

twenty-one

NEW LABOUR, OLD WINDSOR

francis wheen

I t is, I find, a pretty safe rule in life that any idea supported by Tony Blair, Rupert Murdoch and Jeffrey Archer must be a dud. The campaign by this gruesome threesome to 'modernise' the House of Windsor is no exception.

A modern monarchy is possible, of course—just as it's possible to buy alcohol-free lager or vegetarian sausages that look and smell vaguely like pork. But what's the point? Lord Archer claims that the royal rules of succession, under which male heirs take precedence over females, are an unfair anachronism. Hasn't he noticed that the same can be said of any hereditary sovereign, regardless of gender? Similarly, Tony Blair is putting pressure on Buckingham Palace to do away with 'outdated pomp and ceremony' at the state opening of Parliament. Hasn't he noticed that the Queen will still have all her antique powers and prerogatives, regardless of whether she arrives by Rolls-Royce or horse-drawn carriage?

If Her Majesty had an ounce of gumption, she would tell Blair and his accomplices to bugger off. But, according to the *Mail on Sunday*, she is torn between two conflicting views. 'On one side, she is being advised by her deeply conservative husband, Prince Philip, that Britain's first family is too ancient and steeped in history to be changed.' Quite so: the monarchy cannot be meaningfully reformed—only abolished.

Nevertheless, to appease the modernisers she is considering 'a raft of dramatic reforms which would have been unthinkable only a few years ago. They include a radical suggestion that the title "Royal Highness"—now held by 18 family members—should be restricted to the heir to the throne and his (or her) immediate successor.'

Radical, dramatic, unthinkable. If that is really how Her Majesty sees these trifling adjustments, she must lead a very cloistered life indeed. But then so do her subjects. 'There was another welcome sign of the times yesterday—the Union flag flew proudly over Buckingham Palace,' the *Sun* declared in a triumphant editorial last Saturday. 'The change was not announced, but *Sun* readers quickly noticed, and rejoiced . . . Now a flag will always flutter. The Queen is, as she promised, learning to listen to her people, with wise guidance from Premier Tony Blair.'

More fool her, if she listens to the sort of people who rejoice at such things. And before heeding any more 'wise guidance' from the Dear Leader, she should look up what Blair said about the deficiencies of the British constitution in his John Smith Memorial Lecture two years ago: 'The case for reform is simple and obvious. It is in principle wrong and absurd that people should wield power on the basis of birth, not merit or election. . . . There are no conceivable grounds for maintaining this system.' He was, of course, talking about hereditary peers. When it comes to the hereditary absurdity at the very apex of our constitution, the great moderniser is either too timid or too opportunistic to follow his own logic.

In this, if nothing else, he is very Old Labour indeed. More than a century ago, during Queen Victoria's diamond jubilee, Keir Hardie argued that socialists shouldn't waste their time fretting about the monarchy 'until the system of wealth production be changed'. The subject has been debated at a Labour conference only once—in 1923, when a motion from the Stockton and Thornaby Labour Party daringly ventured 'that the Royal Family is no longer necessary as part of the British Constitution'. George Lansbury, as left-wing a leader as the party has ever had, replied on behalf of the National Executive. 'Why fool about with an issue that has no vital importance?' he asked. 'What was the use of bothering about that just now?' To clinch the argument, Lansbury revealed that he had once 'sat behind two princes at a football match' and, he could assure delegates, 'they were just ordinary common people like themselves'. The resolution was defeated by a large majority.

So the strange love affair between the Windsors and the People's Party has continued. After attending the wedding of Prince Andrew and Sarah Ferguson, Neil Kinnock emerged from Westminster Abbey to inform the press, in best George Lansbury fashion, that Fergie had smiled just like an 'ordinary' person. 'That smile was worth all the rest of it!' he gushed.

The man who deserves most credit for keeping Labour untainted by republicanism is that wily old devil Lord Mountbatten, who realised long ago that it would be a useful precaution for the royal family to woo and beguile influential figures on the Left. During the abdication crisis of 1936, it was he who persuaded Edward VIII that the best outlet for pro-royal stories was the *Week*, a muckraking rag edited by the Communist journalist Claud Cockburn. 'So we're King's men now, are we?' a puzzled colleague of Cockburn's inquired. 'King's men my foot!' Cockburn replied. 'If the King has got around to supporting us against Baldwin, I wish him all the best of British luck.'

Another of his lordship's regular 'conduits' was the left-wing MP and columnist Tom Driberg. In 1946, when Princess Elizabeth was preparing to announce her engagement, Mountbatten asked Driberg to invite a posse of Tribunite backbenchers to lunch with Prince Philip. 'Thank you for being so kind to my nephew Philip,' he wrote afterwards. 'It is most kind of you to say that you will help to give the right line in the press when news of his naturalisation is announced.' Hilariously, Mountbatten even managed to convince Driberg that Philip was himself a bit of a pinko. 'I was agreeably surprised,' he wrote in 1947, 'to find that only the *Daily Worker* appeared to condemn my nephew's engagement on political grounds. Even if they knew the truth about him [i.e. about his socialist sympathies], I feel it would be too good a propaganda point for them to pass up altogether. I am so grateful to you for telling people the truth about him. As you know, I am an ardent believer in constitutional monarchy as a means of producing rapid evolution without actual revolution.'

The picture of the royals as a Trojan horse within the Establishment may seem preposterous but plenty of liberals and socialists have fallen for it—as Prince Charles, Mountbatten's favourite great-nephew, can testify. A left- wing acquaintance of mine who was recruited by the Prince as an informal adviser in the 1980s used to boast that the heir to the throne had done far more than the Labour front bench to discredit the Tories. I suspect that Blair, too, sees Charles as a potentially helpful ally. It is hard to think of any other reason why his antipathy to the 'hereditary priciple' doesn't extend to the principle's most senior beneficiary.

'We know in our hearts that the monarchy is a historical absurdity,' the playwright David Hare argued at a Charter 88 conference five years ago, 'but because we lack the courage to abolish it (as indeed we lack the courage for any radical undertaking), instead we are taking out our anger at our own bad faith by torturing the individuals involved. Newspapers, led by the Murdoch group, have begun the project of putting the royal family in such a state of tension that their lives will become unliveable.'

I see no harm in torturing a few royals now and again, *pour encourager les autres*. But there's nothing to be gained from persecuting the Windsors if those issues that have been so carefully avoided by Labour leaders from Keir Hardie to Tony Blair—the need for a head of state, the purpose of the royal prerogative, the status of the Church of England, the concept of 'the nation'—remain submerged beneath a lot of twaddle about the correct method of addressing Princess Beatrice, or the necessity of curtseying to Princess Michael of Kent. The Duke of Edinburgh may be 'deeply conservative', but he is absolutely right to resist New Labour's blandishments. If he's prepared to take on the combined might of Downing Street and Wapping, I wish him all the best of British luck.

twenty-two

THE DEPARTED SPIRIT

tom nairn

What was it that departed during the first week of September? Much of the country was not convulsed by grief, although we do not know the proportion that stayed unmoved or even critical, and perceived the events as a Southern or heartland spectacle. Yet it appears to he true that even among the more detached, many found themselves touched by unsuspected melancholy, strangely coupled to a sense of liberation and change. An inescapable shift was occurring, displayed in unheard of symptoms like the applause in Westminster Abbey, as well as the mountains of flowers and poems.

But what was the nature of the shift—and what exactly shifted? For all that has now been written around the event, the answer remains obscure. There are nevertheless a number of possibilities, of which the strongest might look something like this: a fairly long-lasting structure of English national identity which, though already in serious trouble, required this sudden blow from an unexpected angle to collapse. Much of the evidence remains circumstantial, but that is often the case when 'identity' is involved. What we are discussing is (or was) a subcutaneous circuit of attitudes and feelings which functioned best when it was unconscious, or taken for granted. Except when called upon, the mechanism invisibly behaved itself. While there and available, few paid it much heed. When it broke down, on the other hand, everyone noticed and looked for an explanation. 'She called out to the country,' Elton John sang at the funeral. But may it not have been the English Rose's country which, in the aftermath of loss, ceased being able to call out in traditional way? If so, a call long responded to—nor really 'down the ages' but for quite a long time, about a century and a half—would not be made or heard again.

I have a corner to defend in this argument, having suggested that the future of the monarchy might have had some relevance to the 1997 general election. It looked like being the first election 'without the Crown', inasmuch as the institution had so shrunk in popular appeal that it would end up being actively despised. Earlier in the year, a TV survey had shown an anti-monarchy majority in Scotland. How long would it be before the same was true in England? The answer was not long coming: six months, if we reckon it between Carlton's televised debate in February and another poll conducted in August, shortly before Diana's death, which showed the first modest anti-royal majority among the English. In April 1997 the royal family had looked like mouldering waxworks: by midsummer it seemed the moving van might be called before too long. May 1 reduced the United Kingdom's 'natural party of government' to a leaderless playground gang. At the time Diana died less than a fortnight remained before the decisive vote for home rule in Scotland, the least royal-minded part of Britain: preparations were advancing rapidly to turn Australia into a republic; the British Empire had formally wound up in Hong Kong; and in Northern Ireland a peace process had resumed. This was bound to imply a more 'neutral' form of government in which the Crown was less prominent.

Then came the accident in the Pont de l'Alma underpass. The monarchy had already been sliding so fast that it was daily harder to measure the fall, Charles Windsor (future sovereign) and his mother were chiefly preoccupied with making life more tolerable for him by navigating Camilla Parker Bowles back into public acceptability. Without offending the wish of two divorcees for a decent life together, one can surely point out that, set against the landslide going on around them, that preoccupation was probably futile. It served to isolate royalty further in a sepulchral world of its own. Even then, the couple's only way was probably out: an Edward VIII-plus solution, with its terminal implications for the future of the institution. After September, can there be any doubt at all? There are still trusties like Verniun Bogdanor and Clive James who feel that 'we' cannot live without the institution, and hence—since this institution is unavoidably genetic—without the well-meaning Charles as a bridge to a brighter future in Prince William's sun. But such keep-it-up monarchism is now far more strained than anti-monarchism used to be.

Like the rest of us, Bogdanor and James saw the last vestiges of life disappear from the wondrous mirror, as the remains were ferried across England. They, too, may have felt the sense of never-more—of a time that had finally expired—yet they could not accept it. Other empires have been shattered on the wheel of military defeat, revolution or economic catastrophe: this one was merely shaken down by an accidental wind into the sweet, wry decomposition of a post-modern September. Though the dying fall still had some grandeur in it, there was an unmistakable relief that it was over. It showed throughout the mourning. What the crowds wanted was enigmatic, but it felt as though they had gathered to witness auguries of a coming time, without knowing what these might he. England is due a future—one that can smartly exorcise the ghosts of Balmoral and Windsor. During the years 1992 to 1997 that wish for a future had become locked onto the figure of Diana. But the fixation was temporary. Her death released it, and since August 1997 it has been walking the streets.

It may be the world of Edmund Burke which lies rotting in the grass: the deeper identity structure founded by Great Britain's defeat of the French Revolution. The scholarship of David Cannadine and Linda Colley has shown how this was done and how vital the monarchy was to the process. The rejigged royal institution was the mechanism for weening an unruly, half-revolutionary people away from its own past.

The defeat of France shored up a potent popular nationalism which, unharnessed, might easily have recoiled on the class-state that had ridden it to victory in 1815. Burke sensed this possibility acutely and devoted his efforts to stabilising the old spirit of tumult and insurrection. As he understood, more was required than success and foreign conquests to fasten it in place. In his own day, during the interminable twilight of George III, conditions did not favour that sort of conservative-domestic *redressement*. When a suitable monarch presented herself 1837, however, the formula of a people's royalism became viable, and was quickly seized on. The tradition invented at that point was a subterranean weld of nationalism and personal regality: the Crown as moral persona, natural and yet nonethnic. Its feigned immemoriality helped cast the English for so long in the moulds of hierarchy, protocol and the stiff upper lip.

This is one of E.P. Thompson's 'peculiarities of the English'—and in its intensity peculiar to England. It echoed and fortified what was to be the true peculiarity of the English throughout this period: Britain. Their imperium was sustainable only by England not being itself. The standard politics of nationalism in the nineteenth-century world were contrived just for that: to enable peoples to become themselves more fully and self-consciously. Anglo-Britain, however, required a more distinctive, tailor-made garment. Neither ethnicity nor Tom Paines republican, civic-territorial nation could have stabilised the vital bond between the English masses and all their alien multinational attachments. The main feature in the making of the Anglo-Brit working class was that it should not appear too crassly to be 'Made in England'. Coat-of-arms Britain represented the hegemony of the English—but also their containment and repression, and the symbolic system of monarchy was a crucial part of that. Its decorous restraint was much more than bourgeois stuffiness. The formula was not infallible, as Ireland would demonstrate. Yet on the whole its efficacy was astonishing: a self-control mechanism for controlling the rest of the world, lubricated by contrived archaism, pageantry, and a sentimental hyper-personalism, all of which preserved the Early Modern, unwritten constitution of England against what Burke perceived as the joint perils of modernity: abstract ideas and liberated ethnic fury.

• • •

It was a one-off world, and it was inside the coffin borne up the motorway to Northhamptonshire on September 6. England was grieving for its former self. All mourners do this to the extent that the shock of death evokes one's mortality. But here the, circumstances do look fairly conclusive. The demise was of, not merely in, the erstwhile national family. During the period of death agony, from 1990 to 1997, popular feeling, as Julie Burchill first pointed out in the *Modern Review* in 1992, had become displaced onto the figure of Diana. She was the royal who wasn't: as everyone said, a 'modern' personality in flight from the waxwork world, yet aristocratic in manner and monarchical in aspiration. An ideal transitional object, therefore, enabling visible change and emotional rebellion without relinquishing nostalgia and the possibility of redemption. As long as this reluctant renegade lived so did the remains of the ancient régime. The jealous goodness-competition between them kept the old national psychodrama going. Spectators could continue to subscribe to one or other version of its hoariest myth: 'modernising the monarchy'. No one knew we were really into the epilogue until the curtain abruptly fell.

But then the entire audience grasped in a microsecond what was up. And they grasped that it was no small thing. The structures of an effective national identity are by definition reproduced in its individual bearers. In that sense it is not an exaggeration to say that on the night of August 30–31 something was killed in each member of the public. In today's computerese, this thing could be imagined as something like a Java-language 'applet' embedded in most Britannic craniums: that is, the micro-code of emotional authentication and orientation through which a community is triggered, maintained, occasionally celebrated—but also controlled. Nor is it so astonishing that they then rushed forward to throw flowers and poems onto the stage. This had been one of the old-est codes around only slightly younger than that of the 1789 French or the 1776 Americans, 'Tradition' is just another way of denoting the fact. Over time it had generated a proportionate amount of national-popu-lar poetics: quasi-familial belonging, idolisation of (and nostalgia for) impossible goodness, the blue remembered hills of here, there and (in the case of London) practically everywhere. Just how powerful the control system had been was clear the day after its annihilation.

A key image incessantly repeated on TV screens that week (usually in slow motion) was of a grinning Diana rushing forward to pick up and hug her sons on the balcony of Buckingham Palace. She did so amid the more kosher-royal effigies, gamely carrying on with the waving and smiling. Queenly matrons probably didn't dispense this kind of warmth (one couldn't help feeling) nor, probably, had Charles known what to do about it. One did not have to be kosher-English to appreciate the scene. Indeed it may even have helped to be black, motherless *and* Welsh, to mention only one subject who effortlessly achieved world media renown at the same time down in the Mall. The prominence of non-Anglos in the pro-ceeding is quite logical—like MP Bernie Grant's defense of monarchy on the Carlton TV debate in February. Once outright colonialism was over, the Windsors' non-ethnic presentation acquired more weight—putative multi-culturalism, as it were—warmer towards minorities than a poten-tially ethnocentric republicanism would be. At the end, Princess Diana herself gave powerful emphasis to that bit of the code. She died in Paris meaning to marry an Egyptian who left poems under her pillow, and was latterly most celebrated for her international campaign against the use of landmines: an increasingly cosmopolitan celebrity, and according to her brother, thinking of quitting England for good.

Yet I doubt if this at all diminishes the event's in-dwelling Englishness. World spectacles require a local origination and vitality. This alone provides the intensity, the dramatic dynamism capable of commanding the widest audience. President Kennedy's assassination was an ultra-American melodrama, and Diana's obsequies had their meaning only under palace walls, among visible relics of feigned time-lessness, fading banners and mildewed hierarchical protocol. The crowds may have been disavowing that 'England' rather than celebrating it; but this may also have been the point.

• • •

All revolutions celebrate one past in order to get rid of another. Here the revolutionaries were demanding a more real, personalised, sincerely lov-ing, etc. monarchy, in order to disembarrass themselves of the Windsors. But the Windsors code is the one they happen to have been governed by for nearly two centuries—'Balmorality'. Such devices have built-in lim-itations: they can't be stretched or re-coded at will, by Princess Diana or anybody else. In one sense post-Hanoverian royalism was an odd instru-ment of adaptation, founded on the response to social change and hence always 'modernising', moving closer to the people (and so on). However, the programme parameters for that were set by many other factors—by a whole environment which, in the summer of 1997, had almost com-pletely vanished. And to think that a Queen of Hearts could change this was real superstition. Unfortunately, Diana herself believed in the magic, as did all too many of the September mourners.

In that case, what can such a tidal current of sentiment portend? Over this point darker suspicions have been aired. Almost from the out-set, the antennae of more critically minded commentators felt some-thing else stirring behind the tears and floral tributes—the air from another country, the distant sound of different drummer.

On September 2, the journalist Isabel Hilton said in her column in the *Guardian* that there was already something oppressive about the ele-giac mood. It was as if the entire population had been spirited into anoth-er straitjacket: obligatory national griefconvulsion, so to speak, intolerant of dissent or qualification. But many people considered her guilty of potentially discreditable heresy. The old establishment taboo on criticis-ing the royal institution had been made inoperative by royal misde-meanor: yet within 48 hours a new one seemed to have sprung up around the monarchy's renegade daughter—as if, however improbably, she had become the repository of the Reithian BBC's nationalised moralism and authority. The following week Joan Smith pursued a similarly dangerous line in the *Independent on Sunday*. 'In recent days. . . those of us who are not willing to pretend emotions we don't feel have been getting an ominous message—that we ought to keep quiet. It's a message which is not easy to defy in the face of repeated assertions about the country being "united in grief".' She had published a book discussing Diana's role as media icon, and a review appeared suggesting the volume ought now to be pulped. Nothing should be permitted to sully the perfection of the departed image. Although 'benign in origin', Smith argued that this process is 'a peculiarly dangerous one' which can also be seen as exhibiting 'alarming manifestations of totalitarianism'. Several other critics have made the same point invariably taking 'fascism' as their point of reference.

The national circumstances, it may be relevant to recall here, are those that prevailed until May 1: a pitiful government which for several years had lurched around in narrowing circles at the mercy of its anti-European, nationalist wing. The election showed how little support 'Euroscepticism' really enjoyed. But at the same time it dramatically reconfigured the political geography of that support. Toryism disappeared from Scotland and Wales. It will never reappear there in its old forms. And the new government moved smartly to promote a liberal (i.e., less Unionist) solution in Northern Ireland. While no longer commanding an automatic heartland majority (as many used to think) Conservatism is unlikely to vanish or break up in England. But it does look as if it has completely lost the British control codes. The crowds might just as well have been mourning 'what united us' in monarchy and imparted a broader radiance of meaning (even if it also cramped our style). For most of those grieving, England is the only possible inheritor: a narrower ground of identity, and one still to be defined.

I suspect it was this lack of definition the critics were responding to. 'Fascism' is inapposite: there was no militarism, and the only flag that counted was the one missing from the Buckingham Palace flagstaff.

Ross McKibbin's account of the events emphasised how diffuse, quirky and quite unhysterical these mostly were. What panic and paranoia there was lay more obviously in the reaction of the authorities, and the media, uncertain how to take in the new mind. And yet, the Cassandras were surely not mistaken in detecting an impatience with insults to mourning which might become intolerance of almost anything this post-British 'we' decided (or was persuaded) was intolerable. There was a vivid sensation of popular authority—but was it really *democracy*? The latter implies a certain impersonality, too, and the legitimation of new institutional rules. There was little sign of this amid the decisive mass emotions. Unfortunately, floral-nostalgic populism is compatible with a deep vein of irrationalism: in the end, the magic won out.

Funerals are also rehearsals. The fact is we do not know what England was rehearsing in its prolonged wake for Diana; but we do know from the history of other identity shifts that no nation simply discards one character and steps unscathed into another. Burke's England-Britain may be dead, but there could be elements in its decomposition which remain toxic. Here, too, it's a matter of guesswork, with reference to the ambient conditions. The old identity syndrome linked to monarchy would probably not have lasted so long without the final boost it got from the Falklands War in 1982. Margaret Thatcher permanently destroyed many of the supports of Britishness, but concealed this damage by Churchillian leadership and her personal ultra-fervent royalism. Once that wore off, the profounder current of disintegration resumed, and gathered momentum beneath the top-layer stagnation of Major's government. It is still accelerating. The drummer may not be all that distant. I mentioned earlier how it took a mere six months for the Crown to fall through the floor, once it had been made openly criticisable. After Diana's interment, it took a mere six weeks for the English Tory Party to reconstruct its historic image comprehensively, in accordance with what were deemed to be the populist lessons of the Mall. The iron man of market law, big-stick sovereignty and sock-it-to-them Windsordom, Michael Portillo himself, went on record at the Party

Conference slobbering over a ghastly Blackpool rock confection of new compassion and multiculturist schmalz.

The nation was in the streets, and her suitors lined up in earnest, The most urgent was of course the new regime carried into office by the May landslide. Has any government of modern times enjoyed such an astonishing opportunity? Only four months after the election Tony Blair ran into a spiritual earth tremor as well; his nation changing its ideological skin. He knew as well as other subjects what was happening and expressed it in his remarks on August 31: the 'People's Princess' was officially sanctioned. But unlike others he had some power to influence what was being buried, and who was to take over from it. There is a sense in which the new constitution of England was in his hands at that moment—a question more important than the devolutionary strategy his government was committed to on Britain's periphery.

In his incisive comments on the event in *Prospect,* Michael Ignatieff underlines the sense of Blair's response. The government 'intervened on the monarchy side'—and repaired what it could of the rupture between past and present:

> In insisting on a large public funeral, in urging the royal family to make a public show of their grief, he loaned them the formidable public relations skills which had won him the election. In the process, he managed the difficult feat of becoming a national rather than a political figure. . . . In managing the monarchy's counter-attack, while simultaneously promoting himself as a national leader, and accomplishing all this without appearing to profit from national distress, Blair may have guaranteed himself the kind of hegemony which Margaret Thatcher enjoyed in the Eighties.

But this means he *has* profited from the distress, and powerfully, by turning himself into the People's Prince. In the '80s to which Ignatieff refers, Thatcher was sometimes mocked for setting herself up in business as an alternative monarch. But at that time Queen Elizabeth and her heir enjoyed much greater prestige: until 1990 the symbolic order remained largely intact, though many of its props had gone. Now, the alternative is a lot more serious. Anthony Barnert puts this argument strongly in *This Time*, a study of constitutional revolution. Keeping the waxworks in business could be a way of concentrating even greater real authority in the prime ministerial function. There is, after all, not likely to be much charismatic competition from an elderly Queen or her eccentric and tarnished heir. So, New Labour has not just inherited the most centralised state in the Atlantic world, the apparatus of quasi-regal sovereignty, and the House of Lords, and a virtual absence of regional contestation within England itself and a preposterous electoral majority—it has been able to elect its own monarch, too. The funeral crowds were in a sense electing their first president, without bothering to set up a republic first. Unfortunately, that candidate was dead. But this didn't matter, since another candidate (the only live one) ended up stage-managing the whole business.

September's funeral-fête showed an England turning away from the British armorial bearings all right, and questing instinctively for a different future. But it may also have displayed a fatal instinct still at work: the one derived from the long historical experience of regality and empire, which is not so easily shed. British popular monarchism established a very powerful fusion of nationality and personality, a channelled identity which worked by separation of the charismatic and the political state. As the latter was battered by Thatcher, and then ruined by Major, the two have shown signs of collapsing into one another. Was this not the sense of plebiscitary Thatcher's quasi-regal autocracy? And has that not become Blair's plebiscitary quasi-dictatorship? In between these phenomena, we now know how the nation nurtured its extraordinary cult of Princess Diana. The heart which burst into the streets in September was as yet far from that of a republic. It remains that of a national romanticism. I would not speak ill of romanticism as such in this context, I doubt whether nations can exist without it. But there is also such a thing as regressive romanticism, one rooted in anteriority even while it feels it is gazing eagerly forward. Burke's world-view promoted that inclination of the heart and September suggested it goes on reproducing itself. Ross McKibbin concluded his observations by remarking how 'a democracy which admired her with such intensity is both incomplete and immature.' Yes, and an unreformed stare will always have some interest in keeping it that way. The Diana spectacle was a kind of splendour in the grass. But republicans perceive the same phenomenon as the essence of the rottenness in the grass. And in the identity battleground we are entering, their instinct ought to be just as peremptory, and asserted just as strongly: *get rid of it*. A Europe-oriented republicanism is the only cure, and the only way of realising the more generous and creative aspirations of the great crowds. Whether or not it has the motivation, this government and its Liberal Democratic allies have the power to do it. Their time has to be now—rather than beyond the great Millennium show, under the government after next.

NOTES ON CONTRIBUTORS

MARC AUGÉ is the author of *Non-Places: Introduction to an Anthropology of Postmodernity.*

JEAN BAUDRILLARD'S recent books include *The Perfect Crime* and *Fragments.*

SARAH BENTON is a freelance writer and editor based in London. She is currently writing a book on civic values.

HOMI K. BHABHA is Chester D. Tripp Professor of the Humanities at the University of Chicago and Visiting Professor in the Humanities at University College, London. His next book is *A Measure of Dwelling: Cosmopolitanism and Cultural Rights.*

ALEXANDER COCKBURN is a columnist in *The Nation* and co-author, with Jeffrey St. Clair, of *White-Out: The CIA, Drugs, and the Press.*

RICHARD COLES, formerly of the '80s pop group The Communards, is a musician, writer, and broadcaster, currently presenting *Nightwaves* for BBC Radio 3.

MARK COUSINS is Director of General Studies and head of the History and Theory Graduate Programme at the Architectural Association in London. His next book is *The Ugly.*

RÉGIS DEBRAY is the author of *DeGaulle: The Future of the Nation and Media Manifestoes.*

FRANÇOISE GAILLARD is the editor of *Diana Crash*.

PETER GHOSH is a Fellow in Modern History at St. Anne's College, Oxford. His next book is a critical edition of Max Weber's *Protestant Ethic*.

CHRISTOPHER HIRD is an independent television producer specializing in factual programmes. Among his current projects is a study of the 300 most powerful people in Britain.

CHRISTOPHER HITCHENS is a Contributing Editor to *Vanity Fair* and a columnist in *The Nation*. His recent books include *The Elgin Marbles: Should They Be Returned to Greece?* and *Hostage to History: Cyprus from the Ottomans to Kissinger*.

LINDA HOLT is a freelance writer currently researching a study of the German occupation of the Channel Islands. She is a regular contributor to the *Times Literary Supplement*, the *Observer* and the *Independent*.

ROSS MCKIBBIN is Fellow and Tutor in Modern History at St. John's College, Oxford. His latest book is *Classes and Cultures: England 1918–51*.

SARA MAITLAND is writer-in-residence in a men's prison in Rutland, England. Her latest book (with Wendy Mulford) is *Virtuous Magic: the Meaning of Female Sanctity*.

MANDY MERCK teaches Media Studies at the University of Sussex. She is co-editor of *Coming Out of Feminism?* and author of the forthcoming *In Your Face: Essays on the Representation of Sex*.

TOM NAIRN is author of *The Enchanted Glass* and *Faces of Nationalism: Janus Revisited*.

GLENN NEWEY lectures in Philosophy at the University of Sussex. His next book is *Virtue, Reason and the Politics of Toleration*.

NAOMI SEGAL is Professor of French Studies at the University of Reading. Among her publications are *The Adulteress's Child* and the forthcoming *Andre Gide: Pederasty and Pedagogy and Coming Out of*

Feminism? (edited with Mandy Merck and Elizabeth Wright).

DOROTHY THOMPSON is author of *The Chartists and Queen Victoria: Gender and Power.* Her next book is *The Chartists in Pictures.*

FRANCIS WHEEN is a columnist for the *Guardian* and the author of *Tom Driberg: His Life and Indiscretions.* His next book is a biography of Karl Marx.

JUDITH WILLIAMSON is a writer and journalist, and Professor of Cultural History at Middlesex University. She is the author of *Decoding Advertisements, Consuming Passions and Deadlines at Dawn.*

ELIZABETH WILSON teaches Cultural Studies at the University of North London. She is author of *The Sphinx in the City and City Streets, City Dreams* (forthcoming).

gracie's
secret

gracie's secret

secret

JILL CHILDS

bookouture

Published by Bookouture in 2018

An imprint of StoryFire Ltd.

Carmelite House
50 Victoria Embankment
London EC4Y 0DZ

www.bookouture.com

ISBN: 978-1-78681-411-1
eBook ISBN: 978-1-78681-410-4

For Ann

CHAPTER 1

Jennifer

London, 2000

I was in the supermarket when the phone rang. The clear plastic bag was heavy with tomatoes and almost ready to tie. When I held my phone against my face, my fingers smelled of them. Ripe and pungent.

'Where are you?'

Richard.

My heart stopped. He was tense. Braced. My stomach chilled. I didn't say a word, waiting.

'Jen?'

'What is it?' It couldn't be you. It couldn't be.

'I'm at Queen Mary's. OK?' He paused and that deathly pause, that hesitation, told me everything. 'You need to come.'

The words hung there. The bag slipped and fell. A tomato rolled free, spilling down the display and coming to a halt against the plastic barrier. A woman pushed roughly past me to reach for spring onions and dropped them into the wire basket in the crook of her arm. Behind her, a baby, hidden inside a buggy with raised hood, started to wail.

'What?' I asked.

The woman tore a plastic bag from the roll and reached for tomatoes.

'Don't freak out, alright.' Richard sounded a long way away. 'Is anyone with you?'

I steadied myself against the bottom of the stand. The woman's grasping fingers plucked tomatoes and filled her bag.

Richard said: 'It's going to be alright.'

I couldn't breathe. 'What is?'

He hesitated and that pause, his fear of telling me, told me how bad it must be.

'There's been an accident. OK? In the car.' Pause. 'Just come.'

'Accident?' My hands tensed with rage. I wanted to throw something, to hit out.

'Call me when you get here. OK?'

'Tell me. For God's sake!'

He sighed. 'Just get here.'

The line went dead. I started to shake. I banged the heel of my hand into the tomatoes. Juice squirted from a split. The young woman jumped back, glared. A couple, passing behind with a trolley, stopped and turned to look, their faces hard with disapproval.

Richard's eyes were heavy. He was waiting for me at the entrance to paediatric intensive care. As I approached, my steps sharp and fast down the corridor, he looked me over, his face strained.

Inside, in the waiting area, his coat lay across a chair. A takeaway cup sat on the table in front of it, coffee stains on the lid. Behind, the wall was decorated with a giant stencil of Minnie Mouse. The tip of Minnie's left ear was peeling off.

I looked round. 'Where is she?'

He pursed his lips. 'Calm down, Jenny. Please.'

I dug my nails into my palms as my hands closed into fists. 'One night. You promised. You promised you'd look after her.'

He'd begged to have you that weekend. I should never have let you go. My voice was strangled as I struggled not to shout at him.

'Tell me right now. *Everything.*'

He sat down and gestured to the chair beside him. I was so brittle I could barely bend my legs.

'A car hit them. Head-on. It was going the other way and skidded and...' He hung his head, spoke into his solid brown lace-ups.

'Hit them?' He'd said *them*, not *us*. I leaned closer, struggling to understand and caught the old, familiar scent of his skin. 'Weren't you there?'

He didn't answer. The heaviness in his cheeks made him suddenly old. My legs, my feet flat on the hard hospital floor, started to judder.

'The airbag went off. Ella's OK. Bruised but OK.' He broke off. 'They sent her home. But the other driver...' He bit down on his lip and looked away.

'What about Gracie?' I pulled away, angry. 'Where is she?'

Richard's eyes found mine. They were red-rimmed. I saw the fear there before they slid back to the floor. He swallowed.

'She's in a coma. They're not sure—'

A sharp pain in my stomach made me lean suddenly forward, doubled over. I opened my mouth, tried to speak, closed it again. My hands pressed against my belt, holding back the pain.

A pause. Behind us, heels clicked down the corridor, turned a corner, faded.

Richard said: 'Keep calm. Please. Everyone's doing their best. OK?'

I struggled to steady myself, lifted my head. I looked past him to the double doors that led further into the ward.

'I need to see her. Now.'

He nodded and got wearily to his feet. At the doors, he made a performance of pressing the flap for a blob of hand sanitizer

and rubbing it over his knuckles, his palms, pointing me to do the same. He tugged out blue wads from a plastic dispenser and handed one to me. I stared at it, then watched him unfold the other one into a mask, slip two elastic loops round his ears and open the flap across his mouth and nose. My stomach contracted. The pain again. *My God. My dear God.*

He gave me a sharp look. 'She may be able to hear.' His voice through the mask was muffled. 'Be careful what you say.'

You don't look like you. You're so pale and fragile, your face still, your eyes closed. Your fringe is brushed back from your forehead and there's a clear plastic mask fastened across your nose and mouth. Your arms are arranged outside the sheet as if you've already been laid out for death to take, and a needle, stuck sideways into the soft skin of your forearm, feeds pale liquid from a bag on a stand. Machines on both sides whirr and click, and, through it all, your breathing makes a soft steady suck in the mask.

I stand and stare. My arms shake at my sides. I fight the urge to leap forward and tear out all their damn wires and tubes and scoop you up in my arms and hold you, run with you, take you home.

A nurse fiddles with the drip. When she turns away from it, she doesn't look me in the eye. Her face is hard and too carefully neutral as if she really wants to say: *so you're the mother, are you? Really? And you let this happen? Where were you, exactly?*

Richard pulls a chair from the bottom of the bed and sets it by your side and I sit down, reach through the metal side bars that form your cage, take your hand and encase it in my own, squeeze it, stroke your small fingers and start to sing to you, my voice so low that only you and I can hear, the songs we sing together in the night, when you're feverish or just can't sleep and need a cuddle, the songs we've sung together ever since you were born and the midwife first put you in my arms, wrapped round in a

snowy white towel, all red and scrunched and beautiful. Such a perfect baby… I thought the other parents on the maternity ward must be mad with jealousy.

My breath makes the inside of the mask hot and moist. I don't know how long we sit there, you and I, joined at the hand, singing together. You can hear me, I know it, you know I'm there, reaching for you, willing you to come back to me.

CHAPTER 2

The doctor wasn't old enough. She looked barely out of medical school and her manner was officious. She spoke to us in a bare consulting room off the corridor. It had squares of rough beige matting on the floor, a cheap settee and several matching armchairs with wooden arms and lightly padded seats. An insipid picture of a vase of flowers hung on one wall. On the other was the stencil of a gawky cartoon dog and cat, grinning.

'We are grateful, Doctor.' Richard sounded lost. He always tried to ingratiate himself with important people in the hope it made a difference. 'Everyone's been so kind.'

We were sitting side by side on the settee. It was low and our knees rose awkwardly. I reached across and squeezed his hand. His fingers were cool and firm and familiar in mine. He pulled away, giving me an absent-minded pat in the process. We made you, this man and I. We were happy once, before our small family broke apart.

'The brain bleed is extensive.' The doctor spoke with exaggerated care, as if we were half-wits. 'That bleeding puts a lot of pressure on brain tissue. It's still unclear how much damage it has caused.'

She sat forward on the edge of her chair with her hands neat in her lap. She gave the impression she didn't plan to stay long.

'Why!' My voice was abrupt. 'She was in a child seat, wasn't she?'

Richard cut in at once. 'She was. I've already—'

I nodded, carrying on. 'That's the point of it, surely? It protects her.'

The doctor hesitated. 'The seat probably saved her life.' She lifted her forearm and demonstrated a rippling motion with her hand. 'But even strapped in, the force of the impact still causes internal trauma to the brain. We call it a coup injury. The soft tissue is thrown forward against the inside of the skull, you see. That causes blood vessels to tear and bleed and the blood has nowhere to go. So it can invade brain tissue and cause damage.'

Richard blinked. 'So what—' he hesitated, groping for the words '—what does that mean?'

The doctor looked at a spot on the wall behind us. She had no softness in her face, just awkwardness.

'The prognosis isn't clear. If there's no change, we'll keep her comatose for as long as twenty-four hours and then review the bleed.' She drew her eyes from the wall and glanced at me, at Richard. 'The coma supports recovery by reducing cranial pressure.' She took a deep breath. 'Her body has been through a significant trauma. You do realise she was resuscitated? She's done well to get this far.' She hesitated. 'There's also the possibility of a contra-coup injury. Bleeding caused by a secondary impact at the rear of the skull. But so far, there's no evidence of that.'

Shouting outside. Voices far below, called from another universe. My car was in the car park, waiting. A space where your seat should be. The footwell strewn with toys and biscuit wrappers and empty juice cartons.

'She's a fighter,' I said. 'She'll be OK.'

The doctor cleared her throat. 'In my experience, in cases like this—'

'How many exactly?'

She paused, gave me a questioning look.

'How many cases have you had? Like this?'

'Jennifer!' Richard, embarrassed.

The doctor's face was impassive. 'In my experience, stability at this stage is crucial. It's the body's best chance of recovery. I suggest you go home and get some rest tonight. We'll call you at once if there's any change.'

'No.' I shook my head. 'No. I'm staying.'

Richard frowned. 'Maybe the doctor's right. If she—'

'I'm not leaving her. I'm her mother.'

He shook his head at the doctor, as if to apologise for me.

I didn't care. All I wanted was to scoop you up into my arms and leave this desperate, sterile place and take you home and draw the curtains and settle in the lumpy armchair in the corner of your bedroom and rock you and hold you close and never let you go.

The doctor rose to her feet. At the door, she turned back and looked at me.

'I can assure you, she's getting the best possible care.'

They didn't let me see you often. In the early afternoon and in the early evening, I was allowed to sit beside you for a short time, to hold your hand in mine and press it to my lips, to stroke your cool, smooth forehead and sing to you. You seemed so far away, my love. Flown from me to an unknown place.

I strained forward to check the slow, steady flutter of your breathing, proving to myself that you were still with me, still in this world. The machines by your bed whirred and pulsed and numbers on monitors climbed and fell and sometimes flashed and on another screen, a line rose and fell in an eternally undulating wave.

A television screen on a mechanical arm was tucked up high against the ceiling. A white enamel sink stood against the far wall with surgeon's taps beside shiny metal dispensers of liquid soap and paper towels and, underneath these, a white metal pedal bin labelled Offensive Material.

No clock in sight. This was a room outside time, where day and night, morning and evening were the same sterile nothingness and the only rhythm was the suck and puff of your breath inside the mask. And I sat there, watching you, aching for you, dreading the footsteps that would come to make me leave.

The hours away from you were heavy. The waiting area was largely deserted. I tried to imagine Richard and Ella at home. She would be resting and he would be fussing over her, awkward and slightly inept but gentle. I wondered how much of him was there with her, and how much was here with us and how anyone could split themselves in two like that.

The ward stilled and quietened. I stood on a side table and pressed Minnie's peeling ear back into place against the wall. I watched the nurse behind her desk, shuffling papers and chatting in a low voice to the young woman who came to relieve her. Resting the side of my head against my hand, I stared at the large clock on the wall behind her as it slowly turned towards night. The light above me emitted a low buzz. The floor shimmered with shifting, cloudy patterns. My mind was numb.

They were wrong. You wouldn't leave me. You were a fighter. I sensed you there, reaching out for me, battling to survive. I closed my eyes, hunched my shoulders and strained to send you all the strength I had, to tell you I was here, willing you well.

'There's a café down the corridor.'

The nurse, a youngster with freckled cheeks, was bending over me. She made an attempt at a smile, pointed to the right, out of the ward doors.

'It's not much but it's better than nothing. You haven't eaten, have you?'

I shook my head. I felt sick.

'It'll close soon. I'll come and get you if anything happens.' She gave my shoulder a pat. 'Go while you can.'

I tensed, ready to fight, then tilted and saw her face. Her eyes were kind. I heaved myself to my feet, swayed and she took my elbow to steady me.

'Try to have something. You've got to keep your strength up.' She paused, considering. 'You might be here all night.'

The café wasn't much, she was right. A sprinkling of a dozen plastic-topped tables with hard chairs and a counter selling tea and coffee, sandwiches and panini, bars of chocolate and crisps. The tables were deserted and the whole place felt forlorn, as desolate as a motorway service station at three in the morning.

I bought a bottle of fizzy water and settled in a corner, rested my head against the cold, whitewashed wall and closed my eyes.

'Are you Gracie's mum?'

A gentle male voice. I opened my eyes, sat up at once.

'What's happened?'

He smiled, put out a hand to calm me. 'Nothing. I'm sorry. I didn't mean to startle you.'

He was tall with floppy dark hair and wore a grey cashmere coat. He was carrying a coffee in a takeaway cup and had a newspaper tucked under his arm. The *Daily Telegraph*.

'May I?' He nodded to the chair opposite mine.

I shrugged. What did it matter? What did anything matter apart from you?

'Matthew Aster. I'm in paediatrics. Just coming off shift.'

I looked more closely. He looked about forty-five, perhaps a little older. His skin had a lined, lived-in look as if his life had been more interesting than easy. His eyes were intelligent and thoughtful and they were searching mine, waiting.

'You're a doctor? Are you treating Gracie?'

'Not exactly but we're a small team here. We talk. I saw you in IC earlier.' He shuffled his feet. They stuck out from under the table. Black lace-ups, neatly polished. 'I'm sorry. Not an easy time.'

He set the newspaper down on the table. There was a picture of the Royals on the front page, a smiling Charles and Camilla on their travels. I'd seen it on the newsstand as I went into the supermarket all that time ago. An image from another lifetime.

He gestured to the water. 'Is that all you're having? Can I buy you something?'

I shook my head. 'I'm fine. Really.'

He pulled a Kit Kat out of his pocket, snapped it in two, set one stick in front of me and unwrapped the other, then ate it, sipping his coffee after each bite.

I peeled off the silver paper and nibbled the chocolate. The sweetness was cloying. I put it down. 'Will she be alright?'

He narrowed his eyes. I wondered what the officious young doctor had told him about me. *The mother's difficult. Rude. No wonder the husband strayed.*

'It's too early to know,' he said carefully. 'But she's doing well. No sign of complications, so far. That's very positive.' He hesitated. 'One step at a time.'

I sipped my water and looked past him into the drab hospital corridor. A stout woman was shuffling down towards the toilets on a walking frame, her head craning forward, her legs swollen.

'This can't be happening.' I spoke almost to myself. 'She's only three. I just want to take her home.'

He reached forward and briefly covered my hand. His fingers were strong and warm with curling black hair above the knuckles. I thought of the way Richard had pulled his hand from mine and how comforting it felt to be touched, even for a moment.

I swallowed, trying not to cry. 'She's everything to me. Gracie. I'd do anything. If she needs, you know, organs, she can have mine.'

He nodded. 'I know. I'm afraid it's not that simple.'

The woman at the counter started to pack away the crisps and chocolate into cardboard boxes. He crossed to her, took one

of the few remaining sandwiches from the fridge and bought it, then came back to me and set it on the table.

'Just in case. It might be a long night.' He reached into his coat pocket and took out a pen, scrawled 'Matt' on the top of the newspaper, along with a mobile phone number, and tore it off. 'If you have any questions. Or if you just need to talk. Any time.'

He picked up his newspaper, nodded to me as if something unspoken had been agreed between us and turned away with a swish of his coat. He had a long, confident stride and a broad back. I stared after him down the corridor long after he had disappeared from sight.

CHAPTER 3

Ella

My body aches. The bed is soft and warm and I long to rest but I'm too afraid to close my eyes. Every time I do, I see her face. Hanging there, a second before the bang. Her eyes are wide, staring into mine. Her eyebrows two neat wedges. Her mouth, the lips painted deep red, parted.

Then the almighty crash, the crack of the airbag exploding in my face, thumping me in the chest, my own limpness, thrown back and forth, as helpless as one of those stuffed crash dummies catapulted to and fro in slow motion.

A moment later, utter silence. Life was suspended. Traffic stopped. A high-pitched screeching inside my ears blotted out the living world. The dead world too.

I asked one of the paramedics, 'Is she alright?' My voice was a croak.

'Don't worry, flower. She's fine.'

Their hands were thick and strong and worked briskly over my body, checking, assessing, easing me out, lying me flat on a stretcher. Above, the arc of a streetlight against low cloud as I was carried away from the wreckage. I wondered at it. A perfect curve. So graceful. The bending arm of a dancer.

They thought I was asking about Gracie, still ominously silent in the back. They lied, of course. She was anything but fine. That horror was still to come. But at that moment, in the madness of

the accident, when the world was still spinning and I barely knew who I was, where I was, I actually meant *her*, that girl whose face was lodged in my head, that complete stranger.

Later, Richard told me.

'It was instant,' he said. 'That's what the doctors said. She didn't suffer.'

What did they know? They didn't see her eyes. The horror in them.

'Don't think about her.'

How could I do anything else? I couldn't help it. I had to keep asking. All the time the doctor was examining me. How old was she? What was her name? I needed a name.

'Don't, Ella.' Richard looked desolate. 'Stop it. There's nothing you can do.'

He was finally forced to tell me about Gracie when he put me in the taxi outside the hospital. He was all apologies, flustered as he handed the driver a bundle of notes to get me safely home. Sorry he couldn't come with me. So sorry. He ought to be looking after me. He knew that. But Gracie – well, it wasn't looking good. They weren't sure she'd make it. His eyes were red.

He bent low to kiss me before he closed the taxi door.

'You'll be alright?'

I didn't answer. I felt sick. Little Gracie. What if she died? Dear God, what if?

'It's not your fault, Ella.' He read the wretchedness on my face. 'You do know that?'

Wasn't it?

There's a tree outside the bedroom window. Its bare branches are sharp and scrawny, a scribble of black lines on white sky. A few more months and the buds will come again, leaves will clothe it. Sunshine and nests and greenery and she, that girl – they say

her name was Vanessa – she won't see any of it. All the plans she made, whatever they were, will never happen now.

Downstairs, the bang of the front door. I lie very still and listen. He goes into the kitchen and the fridge opens with a soft suck. The click and fizz of a can opening. Beer, probably. Or Coke. I wait.

His tread is steady on the stairs. When he comes in, I close my eyes and pretend to be asleep. Why? I want so much for him to hold me. I want to cry on him and tell him it's me, it's all my fault, if Gracie dies, it's because of me. I want to let it out and be comforted but I can't. Instead, I build a wall. It's what I do.

He stops moving and, in the silence, I feel him watching me from the doorway, wondering if I'm awake, unsure what to do. I hold my breath. Inside, I'm screaming: *come to me, hold me, my love, please.* The silence stretches, taut as skin.

Then it tears and he turns away, retreating, and it was my own doing; I'm pushing him away, and I shake, lonely for him. Why shouldn't I hurt? What right have I to be safe and whole when Gracie struggles for life and that girl, Vanessa, is already cold?

Later, much later, the mattress shifts as he lies beside me. A warm arm threads itself round my waist and I shudder and sigh. He kisses the skin between my shoulder blades. Not a sexual kiss, just tender. Just kind. *I don't blame you,* the kiss says. *It's not your fault.*

Gradually, his muscles relax and become heavy and I wonder how he can sleep, after all that's happened, knowing Gracie may not be alive in the morning.

He has come home to me but she will be there in the hospital, that dreadful woman. Sitting at her daughter's bedside. White-faced and frantic and making a martyr of herself. She will blame me. I feel it already. It's just one more reason to hate me. To wish I were the one who died.

I lie very still. My neck throbs. Richard breathes steadily against my skin, warming it. I am afraid to sleep and I keep

myself awake for a long time, reading the shapes in the shadows. I don't understand. How is it possible that, just this morning, a girl called Vanessa was alive and now she is not?

It terrifies me. Not the dying itself but the darkness, the oblivion that waits for us all. After all that's happened, after all I've suffered, how could it not?

Was she afraid of it too? Did she have any premonition that death was stalking her? When she put on her lipstick, slid into the seat of her car and switched on the engine, did she have the slightest sense that she was starting an endless drive headlong into nothingness?

CHAPTER 4

Jennifer

That night, I half-sat, half-sprawled across the chairs in the waiting area, opposite the peeling Minnie Mouse, close to the nurses' station. Time shimmered and blurred.

When I closed my eyes, strange images swam in and out. You, my love, lying so small and still in the hospital bed, surrounded by machines. Richard's drawn face and the fear in it. The supermarket with its bright, hard music as my hand reached in my pocket for the ringing phone.

I lost track of time. The only sounds were the slap of plastic doors and the soft hum of the overhead lights. Occasionally, shoes squeaked to and fro between rooms. The nurse, sitting over a book in a cone of artificial light, cleared her throat or shuffled her feet. The ward was infused with the smells of disinfectant. It brought back a sudden memory of my father when I was a child, of his lab coat, strange with the scent of the hospital where he'd worked.

I closed my eyes and leaned my head back against the wall.

The nurse shook me. I must have dozed. I was slumped against the hard arm of the chair and my back ached, my head throbbed, as I struggled to sit up quickly. My mouth was dry and tasted sour. The nurse handed me a cup of milky coffee.

'I thought you might want this.'

I stared at her blankly. There was movement behind her. Life was returning to the ward as cleaners and nurses pushed trolleys at the start of a fresh shift, a new day. The wall clock read five to six.

'How is she?'

'Doing well. A doctor will come and see you in a while.' She paused, watching me. She seemed to be deciding how much to say. 'He'll explain. But Gracie's doing well. You should have a wash. Drink that first. You look done in.'

In the cramped toilets, I splashed cold water on my face and dried it with a rough paper towel. My eyes were bloodshot, my hair straggly. As I watched, my eyes filled with tears and I blinked, rubbing them away. *Please God. Please. Make her well. I'll do whatever you want. Anything.*

I sat stiffly by the nurse's station, waiting for the doctor, jumping at every fresh footstep. Seven o'clock came. The kind overnight nurse said goodbye and good luck and went home. She was replaced by another, younger but brisker. At seven twenty, I got to my feet and went to the nurses' station.

'I'm waiting to see the doctor.'

The nurse had her back to me. She spoke over her shoulder. 'If you'd just take a seat.'

I leaned forward over the desk. 'I've waited all night. It's my daughter, Gracie. They said there might be news.'

'I've told you.' She turned round, impatient. 'He'll be with you as soon as he can.'

At eight o'clock, the doors to the ward swung open. A man's tread. I twisted to look. He had his back to me as he negotiated the doors, his arms burdened, but the shock of dark hair, the smart coat and the shining shoes were familiar.

I jumped to my feet as he approached me.

'Is it you? The doctor?'

He gave a rueful smile. 'Not exactly. I'm in paediatrics, not IC.'

My shoulders sagged.

'I just came by to see if you were still here.' He set down a takeaway cup of tea and a paper bag. 'Thought you might need breakfast.' He opened the paper bag to show a croissant inside.

'Thank you.' I didn't move to touch it. 'The nurse said she was doing well. I'm waiting to see a doctor.'

He looked so compassionate that I bit my cheek to stop myself from bursting into tears.

'A nurse wouldn't say that unless it were true. Look, I know it's hard but it won't be much longer.' He checked his watch. 'The day shift's just coming in.'

My legs buckled and I sat down with a bump.

He watched me, his face concerned. 'Try to eat something.'

He disappeared down the ward. I hunched forward, looked at the croissant but didn't move to touch it.

A moment later, he came back, his step brisk, and he leaned over me. The nurse watched us with a frown.

'I've had a word.' He kept his voice low. 'As soon as they're briefed, they'll be out to see you. OK? It won't be long.'

I nodded. I wanted so much to thank him but my mouth wouldn't work.

He looked at his watch. I imagined his own ward, his own patients, waiting.

'I've got to go but I'll try to look in again later, OK? And please, try to eat.'

He turned abruptly and left the ward again. The croissant was warm. I broke off an end, scattering flakes of pastry.

At eight-forty, a new doctor introduced himself and led me along the corridor to another small side-room. He had an American accent. He pointed me to a low chair with wooden arms, then perched on the edge of the desk in front of me, one ankle crossed over the other. His short white coat hung open and a stethoscope dangled from his neck. He looked barely forty.

'I'm cautiously optimistic,' he said. 'We're not out of the woods yet, but a few hours ago, Gracie showed signs of renewed brain activity in the frontal lobes. Where she had the bleed.'

'Is that good?'

He scratched his nose. 'It's early days. The overnight team reduced the medication. If she responds well, we may be able to start bringing her out of the coma by the end of the day.'

I stared, trying to follow. 'And?'

'So far all the indications are good.' He studied his bitten nails. 'I've just spoken to your, er, to Gracie's father. He's on his way. But if you'd like to see her?'

I was on my feet at once.

'Don't expect too much. She's still unconscious. We won't know the extent of the tissue damage for some time.'

He may have said more. I can't remember. All I heard was that you were making progress and I could see you and that was all that mattered.

The blinds in your room are drawn. The only signs of morning are the sharp lines of light along the edges. You seem so small beside the banks of machinery, so very vulnerable. Pale and silent.

The nurse leaves us alone together and I slip off my shoes and climb up onto the hard hospital bed alongside you, deep into your metal cage, thread my arms through the spaghetti tubes from your face, your arm, the pads taped to your temples, and lift your shoulders gently from the pillow until you're lying to one side with your head resting on the pad of my shoulder and I pull that stupid damp mask off my face so I can put my lips to your cool skin and whisper to you: 'Gracie, my love. It's Mummy. Mummy's here.'

I start to sing 'You are my Sunshine' very softly – it's one of our favourites – and as I sing, I see you twirling in the sitting room with your arms outstretched, your eyes widening as you spin and become dizzy, saying in your high voice as you start to wobble: 'That's lovely dancing, Gracie,' to prompt me to say it myself.

Time stops as I lie there with you and stroke your cheek and the only sounds in the world are the low whirrs and clicks of the

machines and your soft breathing and it's all that exists, all that matters, you and me, little Gracie, you and me together, keeping each other safe, hidden away from the rest of the world.

CHAPTER 5

Richard looked terrible. His chin was dark with stubble and his eyes bloodshot. He came hurrying in through the slapping doors and stopped, adjusted to the stillness, the quietness on the ward. He shrugged off his coat to show a baggy sweater and jeans and sat heavily beside me.

'Have you seen her?'

I nodded. I didn't trust myself to speak.

His knees bounced with jumpiness. 'They phoned me earlier. Doctor Anderson.'

I shrugged.

'He sounded very positive. She's responding well, he said.'

He leaned in, looked at me more closely.

'You alright?'

My mouth twisted and I sat forward, hiding my face in my hands, and crumpled into tears. I hadn't expected to… hadn't wanted to; he couldn't cope with crying.

'I'm sorry.' I sobbed like a child, snotty and hot. 'It's just – I keep thinking…'

His arm reached round my shoulders and he drew me to him, clumsily patted my hair. His body was tense but I didn't care, I just folded into him, collapsed, wet-faced, into his chest.

'I know. I know.'

You don't, I thought. *You have no idea.* He loves you, Gracie, he does. But not the way I do. He was never overwhelmed by it. He didn't suffer with love for you. That was one of our many differences.

And he left us both, left us for her. Don't forget that. He isn't the one putting you to bed alone every night, then sitting in a silent house with a glass of wine for company, worrying about money and childcare and wondering where it all went wrong.

'It's going to be alright.' He let me cry on until the front of his jumper was damp, then pulled a huge handkerchief from his trouser pocket. He shook it open and handed it to me. It smelt of fresh ironing. 'It's going to be OK.'

How many times had he said that to me, over the years? I blew my nose, pulled away from him and dabbed at his jumper. All the promises he made to me, to us, he broke. How could I trust him now?

I pulled away from him and he took his arm back from my shoulders and fixed his eyes on the opposite wall while I recovered and we settled there, side by side, exhausted, watching the wall and waiting, waiting, waiting.

I was young when I met your father. Too young. I'd just moved down to London after university and everything felt unsettled. I was on a graduate scheme with a telecoms company and already deciding I was more interested in HR than the accounts department I'd joined. I had a small room in a flat, sharing with two other girls. They were nice enough but older and both had steady boyfriends and I found myself staying out as much as possible, keeping out of the way.

It was a barbeque. A friend of someone from work. I didn't know many people and I wandered out of the kitchen to the garden, a drink in my hands, and there he was, a lean young man in a chef's apron, bent low, blowing on smoky coals.

'I'm guessing it's going to be a while.'

He didn't turn to look at me straight away but I saw his smile. 'One of the ten rules of life. Always eat before a barbeque.'

I thought about that. 'What are the other nine?'

He twisted at last to look me in the eye. He was thin-faced and handsome in those days and you know that smile.

'I refer you to rule number one,' he said. 'Never reveal the other nine.' Then he clapped his hand to his face in mock dismay. 'Doh! Now you know two.'

He was just shy. I know that now. That was why he was standing all alone in the garden, pretending to be busy. That was why he spoke in riddles. But at the time, I was intrigued. He was three years older than me and had his own car and was training to be a solicitor and he seemed mature and safe.

I became his helper, carrying out raw burgers and sausages and pepper and mushroom kebabs from the kitchen, and watching as he sprayed oil and turned them. The irony is, that was probably the first and only time he cooked for me in all those years.

At the end of the evening, he gave me a lift home and listened, and I found myself telling him about work and my boss and the girls in the flat and how strange it was to get up at seven o'clock every morning and go to work on the Tube after all that time studying and how I missed it, sometimes – the freedom to lie about all day and read and think, but of course I was grateful too; I was lucky, I knew that, to have a job at all.

When I finished, it went very quiet in the car. He focused on the road and it gave me the chance to look at him. He had a strong profile. A straight nose.

'I'm going to the South Bank tomorrow,' he said. 'To see what's on at the Festival Hall. You could come, if you like?'

And that's how it started.

CHAPTER 6

Ella

She thinks she can use this against me, their shared anguish about Gracie. A new weapon. She knows so little about me.

She's a fool, and from the start she got me all wrong. I was never the enemy. Not in the way she thought. And especially not now. For once, we're actually on the same side. She could use me.

If I had the strength, I'd be there in the hospital at Richard's side, making myself unpopular with the doctors and nurses by demanding everything on earth for Gracie, anything to give her the best possible chance. Like me or hate me, I don't give a damn. I'm beyond caring.

But I can't. I can barely lift my head from the pillow. Every nerve in my neck, in my shoulders is pinched and throbbing. My brain is a big, black ache.

So I lie here, sick with misery, thinking about Gracie and about *her* and remembering how it once was.

I wanted Richard as soon as I saw him. It was just one of those things.

We were at a gallery launch and he was the most awkward person there, wearing an old-fashioned suit, standing with his back to the smart crowd and staring for too long at each picture as if he were counting to a hundred before moving on. Knowing him now, perhaps he was.

There was an old-fashioned kindness about him. But he was also unhappy. I smell that on people. Misery is musty like mould.

He looked dazed when I appeared at his side and stood closer to him than necessary.

'Let me guess now.' I looked at the pencil drawing of a fox's head in front of us. 'Either you have a thing about foxes. Or you've found yourself trapped in the wrong party and don't know how to escape.'

He smiled, rueful. 'Is it that obvious?'

'Yes, my friend.'

His suit was a sober navy but his socks were sky-blue. I liked that. He struck me as a man who needed rescuing from his life, at least for an evening.

'Are you here with anyone?'

He shook his head. I drank off my glass of Prosecco, then took his from his hand and drank that too.

'Follow me.'

He wasn't the first strange man I'd taken home. People react to hurt in all sorts of ways. I'd reacted by hurling myself back into the world and pretending to be tougher than I was. But even then, at the beginning, I think I sensed, deep down, that he was different. Something about Richard's quiet sadness made me want to take him in my arms and hold him close and never let go.

I told myself that it didn't matter if I took him home because it clearly wouldn't go anywhere. He had 'married' written all over him. Worse than that, he wasn't even duplicitous enough to take off his wedding ring. And besides, I was far too damaged to fall in love again. It was the last thing I needed. A real, caring relationship? Never again.

He was uneasy in my flat. I fed him drinks and pretended to be drunker than I was and watched him out of the corner of my eye. He couldn't sit still. He kept a distance from me, which in that flat wasn't easy, and scrutinised every picture, every photograph,

every ornament, batting back my questions as if engaging me in conversation was itself an act of infidelity. I couldn't help but like him.

Richard. Married for three years but they'd been together for ten. He shrugged when he talked about it and I noted the heaviness in his voice. He had nearly backed out, when they were engaged, but it was too late. He couldn't do that to her. The invitations had been sent and the hotel was booked and everything.

'It's never too late.'

He turned, gave me a sharp look. 'Jen's lovely. I'd never hurt her.'

I raised an eyebrow. 'So where's the lovely Jen tonight?'

He blushed, looked down into his whisky glass. 'She's not well.'

I sat back and waited. 'What sort of not well?'

He opened his mouth to speak, then looked cross. 'Are you always like this?'

'Always,' I shot back at once. 'Are you?'

He took a seat wearily in a chair on the far side of the room. I was playing a part, acting the femme fatale who took married men home for no-strings sex and forgot them in the morning. It was an act, of course. When I think back to that time, I taste loneliness. He wasn't the only one going round smelling like mould.

And he hadn't come for sex, anyway. He'd come for companionship. Which is a much more dangerous act of infidelity.

'So what sort of not well?' I said again. 'Depressed?'

'No, nothing like that.' He answered too quickly. That was yes, then. 'She's pregnant. She's... I mean, we're expecting our first child.'

He said it as if he still didn't quite believe it.

'Ah.' Complicated. 'So now you're thinking: holy shit, it really is too late.'

He drank off his whisky, put his glass down with a bang.

'Look, I never said that. I'm sorry. I shouldn't be here.'

'Of course you shouldn't.' I leaned forward, poured him another whisky. 'But you are, aren't you?'

He was the sort of man who made love, rather than had sex. Afterwards, he tried to cuddle and I had to fend him off and protect myself from all that tenderness, all that potential to get hurt.

'You haven't done this before, have you?'

'Had sex?' He smiled.

'Cheated on the lovely Jen.'

His face clouded. He looked past me to the clock. Still only ten past nine. He could still make it home and pretend nothing had happened. He could rub this out and start again.

'Out you go.'

He looked surprised. He didn't know me yet. I liked to stay a step ahead.

At the door, I did my best to act nonchalant.

'Well, Mr Richard. You know where I live. Same time next week?'

It wasn't a good idea to see him again. I tried to pretend it was all a joke but we weren't the type for games, neither of us. Not really.

I found myself staying in the following Tuesday night, against my better judgement, and bought a fresh bottle of whisky. Just in case. I had a long shower and, when the bell rang, I went to the door in my underwear and a silky dressing gown.

He stared. Nervous. Clutching a bunch of flowers and a shop-bought cheesecake.

'I didn't think you'd come.'

He swallowed. 'Neither did I.'

But I think we were both lying. We both knew.

CHAPTER 7

Jennifer

Richard went home that evening, leaving me to spend a second night at the hospital. I knew there was nothing I could do. I just needed to be as close to you as possible.

The late-shift nurse handed me a packet of wet wipes when she came on duty and I wondered if I was starting to smell. She pulled a woolly hat off and her coat was damp across the shoulders. She made some remark about the rain as she hung it up in the cupboard behind the desk and I realised I had no idea what was happening in the outside world and I didn't really care.

The hospital settled into sleep. I was learning its rhythms. The bustle of early morning with its rumbling trolley wheels. The coming and going during the day. Red-eyed parents, clutching hands. Endless coffees. Waiting. I recognised the look. Dazed and disbelieving. None of us expected to find ourselves here.

They let me see you, just for ten minutes, to say goodnight.

I put my head on the pillow, my cheek against yours. You had a special ritual for settling your toys – your children, you called them. Kitty cat, the glove puppet, on one end. Then puppy, wrapped round in a piece of white cloth. Then the battered rabbit you'd had since you were a baby. Finally, your bear. We kissed each of their noses before I kissed yours.

You weren't allowed to have them in hospital, for fear of infection. But I talked you through the ritual just the same and pretended they were there and finally kissed the tip of your nose.

'I love you, little Gracie. Goodnight. Mummy's right here.'

Your eyes were closed. The drip, feeding liquid into your hand, clicked and whirred.

When my time was up, I trailed down to the café and sat in the same seat with a dreary sandwich and a cup of tea. The corridor was quiet. Another hour and the café would close. I picked at the ham in the sandwich and stared at the tabletop, thinking about you and wondering how long it would be until I could take you home.

'Is that all you're having?'

I looked up. Matt, smiling as he strode towards me, his coat unbuttoned.

'Hi.'

'I thought I might find you here.'

I shook myself. 'How was your day?'

He shrugged. 'Long. How about you? How's Gracie?'

'I'm not sure.' I paused. 'They keep saying there's progress. But she doesn't look any different.'

He nodded. 'It's a slow process.' He hesitated, looking again at my dry sandwich. 'Look, there's an Indian round the corner. I'm going for a curry before I head home. Come and eat some proper food.'

I shook my head. 'That's nice of you but—'

'Come on.' He reached for the sandwich and pushed it back into the packet. 'Keep this for later. They'll call you if there's any change.'

I frowned. I didn't like the idea of leaving you. Just coming off the ward felt hard. And I certainly wasn't interested in being sociable. But I was exhausted and frightened and very alone and he seemed kind.

'It's only a few doors down.'

I'd imagined something cheap and cheerful but the Indian was a proper restaurant with linen tablecloths and low lighting.

Matt had an easy manner with the waiter, ordering us a bottle of wine and a few dishes.

I unfolded my napkin on my knee and stared at the candle on the table. It struck me how unreal this all felt, having dinner with this doctor, a stranger, while you, my love, fought for life in a nearby hospital bed.

'You're doing so well.' His voice was gentle. 'You must be shattered.'

I bit my lip. 'She means the world to me. Gracie.'

'Of course she does.' He hesitated. I felt his eyes on my face as I focused on the tiny flame. 'Is there anyone you can call? Who can stay with you?'

The flame bent and flailed as I sighed. There wasn't anyone. No brothers or sisters. My father had died when I was a teenager. My mother was frail now and increasingly forgetful. I hadn't even told her about the accident. I hoped I wouldn't have to. She was still angry with Richard for leaving us.

'Not really.' I didn't want to talk about it. 'Her father, Richard, was here earlier. It was his partner, Ella, who was driving.'

I lifted my eyes to look at him, wondering how much he knew about us. How much doctors talked.

'Keep positive. Gracie's doing well. And at this age, they can rally very quickly. You'd be surprised.'

I didn't answer. The waiter brought the wine and poured us both a glass. A strong red. The taste of it was overwhelming. Matt reached forward and steadied my hand, guiding the glass back to the table.

'Eat first. You're running on empty.'

When the food arrived, he took my plate and served me, as if I were a child. I let him. It was a long time since anyone had taken care of me and, God knows, I needed it. My shoulders sagged. Just lifting my knife and fork seemed a monumental effort of will.

While we ate, he chatted lightly about the film he'd seen at the weekend, the thriller he'd just finished reading. I was grateful

for the distraction. His voice was low and thoughtful and as the wine slowly spread its warmth, my body started to relax, just a little, and my eyes to close.

He insisted on paying, waving the waiter away with his credit card before I could protest. He walked me back to the hospital's broad revolving doors.

'There's a chapel, you know. On the third floor. If you want somewhere quiet.'

I looked at my feet. 'I'm not really, I mean, I haven't been to church for—'

He lifted his hand. 'Sure. I just meant, a safe space, that's all. Somewhere a bit more private where you can sit and think.' He paused. 'It's usually empty.'

I don't know how it happened but I turned away to go back inside, then turned back and stepped wordlessly into his arms and he enveloped me in a strong, warm hug and for a few moments I felt safe and protected, for the first time in a long time.

The chapel was hidden away down a long corridor. It was a modern room, hushed and carpeted, with two high, round windows decorated with shards of stained glass. Printed notices at the back declared it a place of sanctuary for those of all faiths and those of none. Laminated prayer cards were piled beside copies of the Bible and the Quran.

A plain wooden cross stood on a table at the front, which was covered with a freshly laundered cream cloth. An aisle led the way towards it, between rows of soft-seated chairs.

I sat at the front and focused my eyes on the cross and tried to calm down. My thoughts ran everywhere. To the church I'd attended with my mother as a child, a draughty stone building that had smelt of damp. The priest had been elderly and given endless, rambling sermons. I'd stopped going as soon as I could.

I bent my head forward over clasped hands and tried to remember how to pray.

'Please, God. Please don't take her. She's too young. I need her.'

My knuckles whitened. I didn't know whether to beg God or to rail against Him for putting you through this. What was He thinking, letting this happen to a three-year-old?

My chest heaved as I started to sob.

'Please don't take her. She's all I've got now. You know that.'

My voice sounded hysterical. I barely knew what I was saying.

'Don't take Gracie. Don't. I'll do anything.'

I sobbed for a long time, desolate, trying to strike a bargain with a God I wasn't even sure I believed in.

Finally, I wiped off my face, went miserably back to the ward and slumped there, facing the wall, keeping watch as best I could until morning came.

At some time in the small hours, I must have fallen asleep. I woke with a start just after seven, aware of the ward once again stirring into life.

A warm coffee in a takeaway cup and a croissant sat in front of me on the table. 'Try to eat' was scrawled across the paper bag.

The day nurse was already on duty.

'Any news?'

'They'll tell you if there's any change.' She looked at me pitifully. Her hair was neatly pinned and she smelt of soap. I felt the contrast with my own wrecked, crumpled self and wondered how much longer I could keep this up.

I rubbed a wet wipe over my face and sipped the coffee.

At eight o'clock, they let me see you. I lie beside you on the bed, one arm across your chest, the other slipped under your head, resting it on my shoulder.

'Good morning, my love.'

Your cheek is smooth and cool. The early morning sun filters in through the blinds and paints stripes across the floor. I think of the chapel with its round stained-glass windows and the coloured light that must be streaming there.

'I love you, Gracie. Mummy's here.'

I keep my voice low and whisper into your ear, willing you to hear me.

'It's the start of another day, sweetheart. And you know what day it is today? It's the day you're going to start to get better. Much better.'

I sigh and my breath stirs strands of your hair. I lie quietly, utterly exhausted, feeling your small body in my arms, staring at the blank wall beyond the bed. As I look, scenes from the last four years play there in that small, sterile room, running in slow motion on the painted wall like a soundless black and white cine film from decades ago.

Your blotchy scrunched-up face the day we carried you home from hospital, holding you as fearfully as if you were glass. Richard, sitting on the settee and cradling you, your tiny head resting in the crook of his arm, gazing at you with so much tenderness that it stopped my breath. Your first wobbly steps in the garden, pushing a toy buggy piled with furry bears and rabbits.

A wall of such sadness rises up and knocks the breath from my body that I start to shake, my legs juddering on the bed.

I whisper to you, trying not to cry: 'Don't leave me, Gracie. Please. Stay with me. You're my whole world, my love. Please. Don't you know how much I love you?'

Then I see it. Your eyelids flutter and the tip of your tongue pokes out between your lips and a flicker of life, real life, comes back into your face. I pull away from you, jumping off the bed, and lean on the red emergency button and, at the same moment, the machine on the far side of the bed starts to bleep.

Footsteps slap hurriedly down the corridor and voices come with them and a tall, dark-haired nurse runs in, one I haven't seen

before. She takes one look at you and calls back over her shoulder to someone else and rushes to the bed, snatching up the clipboard from its base and scribbling some readings from the screens. Even as she does so, another nurse appears with the American doctor and someone else takes me forcefully by the shoulders and moves me back, away from the bed, to give them all room.

Not long afterwards, Richard appears in the doorway, his face tense. A nurse, understanding nothing about us, propels me towards him and he opens his arms and holds me, looking over my shoulder at you as you lie motionless in bed, and at the frantically working, rushing medics suddenly filling the room with their movements, their short, sharp, urgent exchanges.

I'm crying now, weeping into your father's collar, bathing in the old familiar smell of his skin. I press my face into his neck and the crying veers in and out of wild laughter and he pats my back awkwardly and murmurs: 'Hush, Jen. Calm down.'

I don't care. I know what's happened. The doctors do their best but they only know so much. You were lost in a place where even they couldn't reach you and somehow, even there, you felt me and heard me and came back to me, back to this troubled world just to be with me. I don't know how that's possible but it is. It really is.

CHAPTER 8

You progressed rapidly after that, moving first out of intensive care and soon, in a matter of days, there was talk of your coming home. All the tests came back clear. The bleed dispersed, the swelling subsided and your brain function was normal. The doctors spoke, some more robustly than others, of a full recovery.

I agreed, at last, to leave you for a few hours each day and for much of the night to go home to shower and change my clothes and sleep. It was during one of those brief returns to the house that a pair of police officers turned up and began asking questions about the accident.

'So the driver, Ella Hicks, I understand she's your ex-husband's partner? Did she often have sole charge of your daughter?'

The police officer speaking was middle-aged, her torso further thickened by body armour and an arsenal of equipment. Something in her manner made me anxious.

'Not often.' I shook my head, vehement. 'If I'd known she'd take Gracie out on her own, I wouldn't have agreed. I thought she'd be with her father all weekend.'

The police officer narrowed her eyes. 'Why wouldn't you have agreed?'

'Well, she has no business. I mean, Gracie's not hers.'

They both scrutinised me. A young Asian policeman sitting beside me, his hat on the carpet at our feet and his leather gloves inside it, made a note. He kept quiet, the more junior of the two.

'I understand that.' The policewoman leaned forward, probing. 'But why would you have objected to her looking after your daughter? Was there anything about her driving specifically that gave rise to concern?'

I searched my mind, trying to think of something.

'Not really.' I thought of Ella, confident behind the wheel, risking your life. 'But I don't trust her.'

'You don't trust her?'

'No. And I'm right not to. She nearly killed Gracie.'

The policewoman's eyes bore into me, appraising.

'You seem to blame Ms Hicks for the collision. I wonder why?'

I felt myself flush. *Because I don't like Ms Hicks. Because she broke up my marriage and stole my husband. Because she'd do anything she could to hurt me.*

I shrugged. 'She was the one driving.'

Her eyes stayed on my face. Beside her, the Asian police officer was alert, his pen poised.

I reached for the mug of tea on the coffee table in front of me and drank a little. My hands shook and the china juddered against my teeth. I used both hands to put it down again.

'There'll be a coroner's inquest, of course. But it should be straightforward.'

'An inquest?' I shook my head. 'Does that mean she'll face charges?'

'It's standard procedure, ma'am. When there's a fatality. We need to establish the cause of the accident.'

The young Asian flipped his notebook closed and reached for his gloves, his hat.

'I'm sorry. I know it's a difficult time.' The senior officer put a business card on the table beside my mug as she heaved herself to her feet.

'Who was she?' I asked. 'The other driver.'

'Vanessa Parkes. Twenty years old.'

'Twenty?' It shocked me. She was so young. 'A student?'

'An estate agent.'

I couldn't answer. I thought of her mother. Of the call from the police, breaking the news.

'We'll see ourselves out.'

I sat very still, following the creak of the floorboards in the hall, the heavy sound of their footsteps, the squeeze of the latch as they closed the door behind them and went down the path to merge with the early evening darkness gathering there.

At once, the house was too silent. I sat on the settee, my legs trembling, unable to move. Neither of them had touched their tea and I wondered why they'd asked for it, if there were some hidden trickery in keeping me busy in the kitchen while they lingered, unobserved, in here.

Finally, I forced my legs to take me upstairs to wash and change before I headed back to the hospital. Your room was hollow with emptiness. I sat for a while in the battered old armchair in the corner and simply looked. Then I made up your bed with clean sheets and arranged the mess of soft toys at the bottom of your bed – kitty cat, puppy, rabbit, bear – all waiting for you to bring them back to life.

CHAPTER 9

You came home but life stayed far from normal.

For some time, although I was exhausted, I struggled to sleep. My world became a dull blur of night and day. Footsteps in the street woke me, night after night, and I stood at the window, drawing the edge of the curtain round my body, looking out at the dark road and the soft stripes of lamplight along the pavement. Sometimes I thought I saw a figure there in the shadows, looking across the street to our house, and I imagined it was Richard, coming home again too, coming back to us.

When I went back to bed, my body shook as if the mattress were vibrating beneath me. The hard outlines of the wardrobe, the chest of drawers, the bedside table, melted and swayed as I watched.

During the day, I tried to stay calm, for your sake. I delivered you to nursery each morning, collected you each lunchtime, took you to soft play and to the library and to parties. But wherever I went, a shadow hung behind me, just out of sight. I never saw it. I felt it. A feeling or a phantom? I didn't know. All I knew was that when I turned to catch it, to look it in the eye, there was nothing but empty air.

Inside, I felt as if the physical laws of the universe, which all my life had formed the solid edges of my world, warped and gave way around me. When I think back to that time, my memories are a swirling snowstorm of static with occasional moments of horrible clarity.

Richard sensed something. He was the one who urged me to see a doctor. That in itself gave me hope that he still cared about me, at least a little. In the early days, when we first met, he made me feel so cherished. A beautiful word. He still cherishes you, Gracie. You must believe that. He carried on loving you long after his love for me died.

Do you remember the days before he left us for that awful woman? You slept so badly as a baby and he sat with you in his arms for hours on end, stroking the soft line of your back with tenderness. I'd wake with a start and reach for him across the bed only to find a rumpled absence and then pad through, bleary-eyed, to your room to find him in the armchair, a dark shape in the half-light, patiently caressing you back into sleep.

The doctor said I was experiencing post-traumatic shock. She prescribed tablets to help my nerves, as she put it. I don't know what was in them but I did take them each night for a while, mostly to please Richard, and gradually the wardrobe and chest of drawers settled back into place and let me sleep a little.

On the surface, we began to return to our old life, you and I, but it was a lie. We had both changed.

All I wanted now was to be with you. The bank agreed to let me take a leave of absence. Unpaid, of course, but I calculated that, if I was careful, we could manage on savings and the money from Richard. It would only be short-term, just until September when you'd start school and pull away from me, into your own world.

So in the afternoons, when you came out of nursery, we spent time together, living simply, just enjoying ourselves. You so nearly left me, my love, and suddenly nothing seemed more precious than being with you. I thought of the last few years and the hours I'd spent in offices, chairing meetings, running training programmes and suddenly I didn't want to miss another minute of your life.

We read stories and crayoned and, if it was dry enough, we wrapped up warmly and went to the park, with its bouncy animals

and seesaws and roundabouts and a brightly coloured train with an engine and carriages to sit inside where we shouted 'Tickets, please!' and 'All aboard for Toyland!', and imagined chuffing off on adventures.

Life seemed simpler. I realised, for the first time, that most things didn't matter. If you wouldn't put your coat on and wanted another story instead, why not? If you threw your spaghetti Bolognese on the floor or smeared finger paint on your clothes, who cared about the mess? You were alive and well and I was so grateful I sometimes felt I couldn't breathe.

You were different too. It took me a while to realise. I assumed at first that you were quieter because you were still convalescing but it was more than that.

Your drawings changed. You always loved to crayon – well, scribble in multi-colours the way small children do – announcing, if I asked what you were drawing: 'I'm not drawing, Mummy, I'm *writing*.'

When you first started, at the age of about two and a half, you only used black. Whole pages of princesses and rabbits and fairies were devastated by thick dark lines, etched with deep concentration by a small scrunched fist. That wasn't long after Richard had finally packed his bags and, after more than a year of rows and threats and time apart and struggles to reconcile, he'd left for good. I remember worrying that you were prematurely traumatised, that you were becoming the world's first toddler Goth.

Now, though, you went to the other extreme. You wore the yellow crayon to a blunt stump. You drew with the tip of your tongue sticking out between your lips, lost in your work as deeply as any Michelangelo. I sat at the table with you, colouring neatly and evenly inside the lines by way of example, and watched your passion as you made strong strokes of brightness across the paper, then sat back to consider them, then dipped again back into work.

'That's lovely, Gracie.' I pointed at the streaks across the paper. 'Look at all that yellow. It's like sunshine…'

You barely acknowledged me. You were too intent, too serious. You were nearly four years old and you knew your own mind. When a picture was done, ended as abruptly as it began, you pushed it away from you, dropped your crayon and slipped from the chair, running through to the sitting room with the same intense focus with which you did everything, to find something else to do.

And then you started to make extraordinary claims, saying you'd seen things so bizarre I didn't know what to make of them.

CHAPTER 10

The first time, it was a cool, bright day and we'd spent the afternoon in the park on the far side of the river. I had more time to spend with you but little money – at least, until I went back to work again – and we often hung about in the park, one of our many sources of free entertainment.

You played on the swings for a while, then rode your scooter up and down the paths, looking like an astronaut in your bulky pink helmet. Finally, we stood together on the embankment and threw bread down to the ducks that waddled far below on the stony shore revealed by low tide.

We had just hurled the last crust and shaken a final rain of crumbs out from the corners of our plastic bag. The mallards and large Canadian geese turned and waddled back towards the water and, one by one, launched themselves into the current, starting to disperse. I reached for you with one hand and, with the other, stuffed the empty bag in my coat pocket.

You tilted your face to the low, white cloud over the river, thoughtful.

'Mummy, do angels live in the sky?'

I blinked, then stooped to hear you better. 'Angels?'

Your face was solemn. 'Can they see us right now? If we wave?'

Below, the remaining geese squawked and pecked round each other's feet. You swung my hand in yours, pulling me forward.

'No, my love,' I said. 'Angels aren't real like that. Not like us.'

'Yes, they are.' You looked cross. 'I met one.'

I steadied my breath. You had been known to tell tall stories. You didn't mean to lie. You were still working out the difference between what was real and what was imagined. I remember finding a page torn out of a book and saying sternly: 'Did you do this, Gracie?' and you looked me right in the eye and said: 'No, Mummy, Bear did.'

But this seemed different. I steered you to one of the wrought-iron benches on the other side of the path and sat you down beside me.

'What do you mean, Gracie?'

'You made him laugh.' You looked thoughtful, remembering. 'In the hospital. Sticking mouse's ear back on the wall.'

My breath stopped in my throat. 'In the hospital?'

You smiled, gave an emphatic, exaggerated nod. 'Typical Mummy. That's what he said. Always trying to put things right.'

The lorries and double-decker buses made dark silhouettes against the sky as they followed the rounded arc of the bridge. I thought of the peeling picture of Minnie Mouse and the way I'd stood on the table to press it back. How did you know? Did someone else see and tell you? That was the only way I could explain it.

I slowed myself down, choosing my words with care.

'Gracie, do you remember when you were in the play at nursery? Angels are a lovely part of Christmas. But we don't actually meet them. Not nowadays.'

You frowned, squirmed, looked at your tangled fingers.

'But I did.'

I sighed. 'Maybe you had a very special dream, Gracie. When you were in the car.'

You shook your head and pushed out your lower lip. 'It wasn't a dream. It was real.'

You looked away from me, out over the water where seagulls were swooping.

I steadied myself, trying not to get cross. 'Sometimes I have dreams that feel very real.'

'No!' You screwed up your mouth.

I reached out and put my hand on your back and stroked you between your hunched shoulders. You shrugged me off, annoyed.

'OK. Tell me about it then.'

You glanced at me, judging whether it was worth saying more. A young woman in a tracksuit jogged past, listening to music. A moment later, a dog nosed round our feet, sniffing, and you drew up your legs, frightened of being licked.

When the dog's owner passed, calling the dog after him, I tried again.

'So where did you see him?'

You hesitated. 'Remember when we had the accident?'

'Of course.'

You hesitated, searching for the words. 'Well, in the car, I had a funny feeling in my head.'

'A funny feeling?'

'In here.' You pointed to your forehead, then hesitated. 'I was all floaty and I could see myself in the car seat and the car was all crumpled like paper and there were big men shouting and using knives to cut off the doors and get in.'

'You remember that?'

You nodded, your eyes clear. 'They put something round my neck like a dog and put me on a bed and we went in the ambulance. One of the men called me petal but that's silly, I'm not a flower. And suddenly I left them all behind and started to fly.'

'To fly?'

'One minute, I was looking down on them, rushing, rushing, and the next I went whoosh through a dark tunnel and there was a bright, bright light at the other end and he was standing there with his arms open, stretched really wide like this, waiting for me.'

You looked sideways to see how I was taking this. I tried to keep my face impassive.

'What makes you think he was an angel?'

'He was tall and he had light shining.'

I hesitated, thinking about the pictures of angels we'd coloured at Christmas, complete with wings and halos.

'He gave me a big cuddle and he was so happy to see me and I was happy too and he took my hand and started to lead me away.' You smiled. 'It was amazing.'

I bit my lip. You seemed lost in the memory.

'Then what happened?'

'We talked for a bit and then he asked me if I wanted to go with him or if I wanted to go back. When I looked round, I saw Daddy outside the hospital and when they lifted me out of the ambulance, he came running, shouting, and he was crying.' She paused. 'I've never seen Daddy cry before.'

'He cried the day you were born,' I said. 'But that was because he was happy.'

'Then I saw myself on a trolley and they put a needle in my arm and a mask on my face and pushed the trolley into a big lift and a nurse pressed the button with a four on it. When we were in there, the ambulance man put his hands on my chest like this and leaned on me and Daddy was shouting.'

I didn't know what to say. I just kept quiet and let you talk.

'Daddy was sad and I knew you would be too so I told the man: I think I'll go back please. And then I was there again, in my body on the trolley, and my head hurt and I felt sick and my ears were full of noises and when I opened my eyes, lights in the ceiling were rushing past me and I thought they were hardly lights at all, compared to the light I'd just seen, but Daddy's face hung over me and the doctor's and that man said "Stay with us, petal, stay with us", and then I fell asleep.'

You seemed tired when you finished and I reached an arm round you and hugged you to me, stroking hair from your forehead.

'Do you believe me, Mummy?'

I didn't want to tell you that I didn't believe you – it seemed to feel true to you and it is a terrible thing not to be believed by people you love. So I just said: 'I'm very glad you came back, Gracie. You don't know how glad. I love you very much.'

A chill wind blew along the river and clouds thickened overhead. You were starting to get cold. I stood up and you jumped to your feet and we walked back towards the bridge, hand in hand. I clutched you very tightly. I wanted to be normal with you but my head throbbed with the effort of understanding the implications of what you'd said.

'Please will you tell me,' I said, trying to sound matter of fact, 'if you remember anything else?'

'OK.' Your voice was chirpy.

A moment later, you let my hand fall and started to skip, jumping sideways on and off the edge of the path, your hair flying as if you'd forgotten about the whole thing.

That evening, after we'd read a story and I sang you to sleep, I sat on in your room, gazing down at your face in the shadows. Just you and me, in the silence.

You were sleeping on your knees, hunched forward over your bear, one arm flung out, your head lolling to one side, hair splayed across the sheet. You were so still that I kneeled down beside you and lowered my face to yours to catch the soft, barely audible suck of your breathing. You didn't stir when I put my lips to your cheek and stroked the hair from your eyes. Your skin smelt of lemons.

You stirred and I retreated at once and settled in the lumpy armchair and sat, my legs curled under me, my cheek against the rough fabric, thinking about you and how blessed I was to have you back again, here, alive. And thinking about that poor young woman, Vanessa, the estate agent, and her desperate mother, somewhere out in the darkness, who had lost her daughter forever.

CHAPTER 11

The following morning, you went to nursery and, as I shopped and cooked and did the laundry, I thought constantly about the strange story you'd told. All I could imagine was that you were experiencing your own form of post-traumatic shock, processing in some way all that had happened and reliving it in the only form you knew: a story.

By the time I collected you from nursery, I'd decided to take you with me to do something that had been in my mind for a while. To go and see the scene of the accident for myself. Perhaps, I thought, it would help us both.

I bought flowers. It was an overpriced winter bouquet and as I paid for them, I hesitated, wondering what on earth I was doing, busting my budget for someone I'd never even met. I seemed to hear my beloved father's voice, always the pragmatist. He laughed in my ear. *Nineteen ninety-nine? Really? And you're going to tie them to a lamp post and leave them there? Oh please, Jen, please.*

You clung tightly to my hand as we jumped off the big step of the bus onto the pavement and I looked round, trying to make out the landmarks. A dry cleaner's. A chemist's. A convenience store. A coffee shop.

I looked warily at the surface of the road. No dark patches that might be the remnants of spilt blood. No shattered glass. Nothing at all. Just the endless rumble of fast-moving cars and buses and lorries and a hard, damp chill in the air.

You helped me to find the end of the roll of brown tape and pick it free. We wrapped it round and round the flowers and the

lamp post behind. The stems stood upright, the heads leaning forward. I thought of witches, tied to the stake, waiting to be burned. I blinked, stuck the card on the front in its plastic sleeve. For Vanessa.

I drew you in front of me and stood there for a moment, my hands gripping your shoulders. A religious person would say a prayer. We were not religious people. You twisted round, expectant, trying to look at me.

'Did you know her?' A stout woman, full in the door of the coffee shop. Her hands were across her bosom, holding thickly padded upper arms, warding off the cold.

'Not really. I mean, no. I know the woman driving the other car.'

'Oh.' Her hand flew to her mouth. 'Is she...?'

'She's fine. Barely a scratch.'

'I saw it happen. I was stood right here.' She nodded at the doorway that framed her. 'That poor girl's car went out of control, swerved right across the road. Bang. Head on.'

I nodded. I wanted her to say more, to tell me what I knew in my heart, that whatever the other woman did wrong, the accident was partly Ella's fault too. Despite what the police said.

'And that poor kiddie in the back.'

My eyes travelled down to you and hers followed.

'Hello, darling. What's your name?'

You didn't answer, twisted back to me for guidance.

'Gracie,' I said. 'She's three. Well, nearly four.'

'Nearly four! What a big girl!' Her eyes rose again to mine and read my expression. 'Was it her, then, in the back?'

I nodded.

She looked you over. 'Come into the warm. You like marshmallows, Gracie?'

The coffee shop was almost deserted. We slid into chairs in the window and I ordered drinks and a toasted sandwich. You

faced the interior and watched with round eyes as the woman worked behind the counter.

I looked out at the street. The table juddered each time a heavy lorry rumbled past. The flowers hung unhappily on the lamp post. They blurred as rain spattered the glass. It was a sad offering, already desolate.

'I didn't know what else to do.'

'Of course you didn't.' She seemed to understand at once. She was bustling now, hissing steam and pulling levers as she made you a hot chocolate and stuffed the tiny cup with pink and white marshmallows, then made me a cappuccino and shook chocolate shavings over the foam. 'It's a lovely gesture. Two plates with the toastie?'

She waved me away when I reached for my wallet and came to sit beside me, facing the window. She jerked her head towards you and mouthed: 'Is she alright?'

I nodded. She considered us both, then pulled herself back onto her feet and returned with a tin of worn crayons and a printed colouring sheet and put them in front of you.

'Could you tell me a bit more, please?' I kept my voice low, watching you pick out a crayon and start to scribble, hoping you were too absorbed in your colouring to listen. 'What happened, exactly?'

She blew out her cheeks. 'I was stood right here. It was quiet, you see. I like to get some air.' She made a discreet smoking gesture over your head. 'See what's going on.'

You scribbled hard, the tip of your tongue sticking out between your lips as you concentrated. Yellow. Every now and then, your small fingers reached for a marshmallow and you bit into it, your brow tight as you chewed.

'Who was she talking to?' the woman asked. 'Do you know?'

I shook my head. 'Who?'

'Your friend. Didn't she say?' She nodded. 'On her mobile.' She put her splayed fingers to her cheek to demonstrate. 'Shouting.

Right old ding-dong. Don't know what she said but I heard her through the window, just before, you know. That's what made me look up. And then, bang.' She made the sign of the cross on her breast.

I set down my cup, spilling coffee in the saucer and out across the plastic tabletop. For a moment, my chest was so tight that I could barely breathe. I was right. I knew it from the start. Ella was to blame. She was shouting down the phone, distracted, when the accident happened. Not paying proper attention. With you, my love, in her care. You could have died.

The woman looked embarrassed. 'I'm sorry. I didn't mean—'

I swallowed hard, pressed the flat of my wrists to my eyes to stop myself crying. She filled the silence by reaching for a serviette and mopping at the splashes of coffee.

'And to think, that little one in the back. And she's alright, you say? Well.'

I couldn't speak. My hands, at my face, shook.

She looked away. You, oblivious, crayoned furiously.

'They took forever getting her out. Put one of those things on, round her neck. Poor little mite.' She raised her eyes to check on me. 'And she was your friend?'

My *friend*? Ella? I didn't reply.

Something seemed to occur to her and she got to her feet, dropped the sodden serviettes in the bin and went behind the counter, rummaging there. You lifted your head and watched. When she came back, she carried something small inside a folded carrier bag.

'I was going to take it to the police, you know, but I didn't know where to go. There used to be a police station just down there, along Flyfield Road, but they closed it. Turned it into a kebab shop. And I didn't want to get her into bother. Anyway, take it. You can give it to her now, can't you?'

I opened up the bag. A phone in a red leather case.

She pointed towards the listing flowers. 'It was just there, in the gutter. I thought I'd better pick it up before someone nicked it.'

You looked too. 'Is that Auntie Ella's?'

The woman gave you an indulgent smile. 'Well, aren't you the cat with nine lives? Bet you gave your mummy a scare, didn't you?' She looked back at me and lowered her voice again. 'I tell you, I didn't think she'd made it. When I saw her out there in this bad light, I thought for a minute I'd seen a ghost.'

CHAPTER 12

A day or two later, as we walked home from nursery, I had the sense that we were being watched. You chatted away about a story the teacher had read but I only half-listened. I stopped, there in the bustle of the high street, and feigned interest in a powder-blue dress and jacket in a shop window. Beside me, you flattened the tip of your nose and your lips against the glass. A tall figure, a man in a cashmere coat, his hair neat, grew in the reflection as he came towards us. His shoes shone with polish.

I turned to greet Matt as he reached us.

'Jen!' He smiled down at me and, although I felt awkward, I found myself smiling back. 'How are you?' He crouched down to your level. 'And this is Gracie? Wow! High five!'

He held up his hand and you slapped it.

'I'm a doctor, Gracie. At the hospital. Do you remember when you were there? You were such a brave girl. I've got a present for you, if that's OK with Mummy. To say well done.'

He opened his shoulder bag and pulled out a small chocolate bear, wrapped in gold foil.

'A bear!' You danced with excitement. I was conscious of living off my savings, so treats were rare.

He raised his eyes to me. 'Is that OK?'

You looked from him to me, waiting for my decision. I nodded. What else could I do? You took it and ripped off the foil at once, stuffed it into your mouth.

'What do you say?'

'Thank you.'

'You're welcome.'

'That's very kind. Really.'

'I always have a bear or two about my person.' His eyes were bright and amused. 'I'm so glad I caught you. I thought I saw you back there—' he pointed vaguely back towards the river '—at the traffic lights. But I wasn't certain.'

You tugged at my hand, feet still dancing. 'I want to go home now.'

'So how are things?' His look, intense and concerned, reminded me of those wretched days in the hospital. Of his kindness. Of the food he bought me, the coffees and croissants, the curry.

'I meant to call you. I'm sorry. To say thank you.'

'No need.' He broke into a grin. 'I mean, no need for thanks. Not no need to call me.'

A woman with a double buggy powered past, filling the pavement and forcing us against the side of the shop.

'Mummy!' You began to fret at my side, pulling me. 'Let's go home.'

'I should probably…' I hesitated.

He must have sensed that you were restless but he didn't take the cue to leave.

'Do you live round here? I go to the dentist off the high street.' He pointed. 'Not exactly convenient but a friend of the family.' He paused. 'I was just going to get a coffee, actually. Don't suppose—'

'Mum-my!' You twisted and tugged, getting cross now, pulling me away.

He looked at you, then back to me. 'Don't worry. Another time.'

'Look, we only live round the corner.' I didn't really want to invite him but he looked so disappointed that it just came out. 'Come for a coffee at our place, if you like?'

'Really?' His eyes lit up. 'Well, only if you're sure. I'm on lates today.'

I led the way across the high street and turned into our road. You ran ahead, racing to be first. By the time we got there, you were swinging backwards and forwards on the rusty gate.

I warmed some milk for you and left you to play, then went to put the kettle on. Matt leant back against the cupboards, large and solid in our small kitchen. He looked very much at ease, his expensive coat already draped over the back of a kitchen chair.

'Nice place.'

'Thanks.' I turned my back to him and began to put the shopping away.

He peered through the connecting door to the sitting room where you were busy rummaging through your toys. 'Been here a long time?'

'Six or seven years. Richard chose it. He wanted a bit of garden.' I shrugged, remembering. 'And now, of course, it's just Gracie and me.'

Matt broke into a grin. 'I'm so pleased to see you. I've thought a lot about you, Jen. Wondered how you were.'

I didn't answer. I turned my back to him, hiding my face, suddenly awkward. A mechanical tune rang out from the sitting room as you pressed buttons on a toy laptop. I concentrated on unpacking the shopping, wondering how long he planned to stay, whether I'd need to offer him lunch. He moved to the fridge and studied your drawings and paintings displayed there, bunched together with magnets.

'Does she like drawing?' He considered one closely. 'She's good.'

Your bear sat squarely in the middle of the kitchen table, propped against the fruit bowl from where he'd watched us eat breakfast. I moved him to the sideboard alongside placemats and colouring books and old shoeboxes of felt-tip pens, paintbrushes and crayons.

'Have a seat.'

His physical presence dominated the space. He pulled out a chair and sat a little away from the edge of the table, his long legs crossed. He was wearing black jeans, a smart pair, with a jacket and tie. They suited him. When Richard wore jeans, he always looked as if he were trying too hard.

I finished tidying and reached for mugs. His eyes followed me as I moved.

'It's only instant coffee, I'm afraid. Or builder's tea. Milk? Sugar?'

I made him a mug of tea and sat on the far side of the table, conscious of toast crumbs and traces of jam on the surface.

I had a clear view through to the sitting room where you'd settled on the settee with a book on your lap, your lips moving as you told yourself the story. I recognised the book from here. *Beauty and the Beast.* You couldn't read; you just had it by heart.

'So you're doing OK?' His voice was gentle.

His fingers, wrapped round one of Richard's old mugs, were long and delicate. His chest was broad. He smelled fresh, a pungent scent of apples. It was so odd to see him sitting here, at the kitchen table. I didn't really see friends nowadays, not since Richard left. It was just you and me. And in the evenings, just me.

'Yep, think so.' I nodded. 'I've taken some time off work. They've been very good. Just until Gracie starts school in September.'

'The days are long but the years are short.' He smiled. 'So what sort of work aren't you doing?'

'I run a training and development unit at a German investment bank. Not corporate training but personal development, one-on-one mostly.'

Richard always zoned out when I talked about work. I stopped bothering long ago. But Matt's eyes stayed attentive.

'It's all about helping people work towards what they really want to do. It's very rewarding. Well, most of the time.'

He considered. 'Do people know what they want?'

'That's half the battle. Helping them find out. Then we break it down into steps and work out how to get there.' I paused. I didn't know why I was telling him all this. I didn't really know why he was here at all. 'It can mean leaving banking, for some people. And that's OK too.'

I lifted my eyes, looked through to the sitting room. Your head was bent low over the story. I watched you for a moment and the sight of you, so engrossed, made me smile. I realised he was looking at me and turned. His eyes, on my face, were kind.

'Gracie's doing so well. I was frightened to death. You can imagine.' I stopped. I still found it difficult to talk about without crying. 'But she's completely fine. Just as bright and lively as she always was.' I nodded towards the open door. 'Well, see for yourself.'

He kept his eyes on me. 'And what about you?'

'What about me?'

'You've really been through it, haven't you?'

I shrugged, then bit my lip.

'I thought you were amazing.' He lowered his voice. 'What you did for her. The way you stayed there night and day. I was worried about you.'

I shifted my weight, feeling awkward.

'Well, all over now. Thank God.' I hesitated. I wasn't used to sympathy. 'Thanks.'

He changed the subject and started chatting about the book he was reading, a novel set in Peru or Bolivia or somewhere. I only half-listened. I studied my hands, thinking how engaged he seemed with the world and how isolated I'd become and wondering what he made of me. How had I turned into such a hermit – such a sad and lonely recluse that it felt like a major event to have someone round for a cup of tea?

Later, he said: 'You and Gracie seem so close.' He paused. 'How long has it been just the two of you?'

I considered. 'She wasn't quite two when Richard left. Now she's nearly four.'

'What a fool.'

He said it with such quiet intensity that he caught me off guard. I lifted my tea and the rim of the cup juddered against my teeth.

'That's what I said.' I tried to force a laugh. 'Well, it's one of many things I called him.'

He didn't smile. He sipped his tea and the silence stretched.

'Maybe I was the fool,' I said at last. 'I didn't have a clue, you see. Turned out he'd been seeing this woman – the one who was driving that day. He'd been seeing her for years.'

It felt easier, somehow, to discuss it with a stranger. As if I were talking about something that happened to someone else. I'd spoken about it so little, in the last two years. There was no one really to tell. My mother wasn't well enough to understand. Friends were busy with their own lives. Besides, there was only so much they wanted to hear.

He didn't flinch, just said quietly: 'Even before Gracie came along?'

'Seems so.' I swallowed, still feeling stupid. 'I had no idea.'

I never had made sense of it. Not really. How could anyone not know their husband was having an affair? But it's amazing what you don't see. Richard often worked late. Always had. And besides, I trusted him.

'I'm sorry.' Simple but the most sensible thing anyone had said about the whole sad mess.

I shrugged. 'Gracie wasn't an easy baby. I was shattered all the time. I focused on her. He must have wondered what the hell he was hanging around for. I see that now.'

'What did he expect? It's hard, being a new parent. You just have to get on with it, don't you?'

I thought about that for a moment. 'Do you have children?'

He twisted to look out through the window, at the flagstones, rimmed with weeds and set round by overgrown bushes. Richard was the gardener, not me.

'A daughter.' He shrugged. 'Her mother and I… well, let's just say it's a similar story. She moved on. Only in my case, she took our daughter with her.'

For a moment, he looked so hurt that I nearly reached out to touch his hand, the way he'd touched mine in the hospital. I turned and looked through to you, your head bent over your book, and tried to imagine Ella taking you away from me, after taking Richard. I'm not sure I'd survive that.

'What's your daughter's name?'

'Katy.' He looked up at me again and smiled and I found myself smiling back.

'Great name. Solid as a rock.'

'It was my grandmother's.' He hesitated, his face suddenly shy. 'Jenny's lovely too.'

I studied my hands for a moment, then pushed back my chair and went to the sink to wash up my mug.

He got to his feet at once. 'I'm intruding.' He reached for his coat. 'I'm sorry.'

'Not at all.'

On the doorstep, he hesitated and turned back to me.

'You're doing so well,' he said and nodded. It was a professional voice now, the doctor in him. It confused me, as if we'd just slipped seamlessly from friends to a home visit.

When I closed the door, I leaned against it for a moment and stood there in the quietness, trying to make sense of him and wondering what had just happened.

I went through to the kitchen, put bread in the toaster and rummaged in the fridge for lunch. As I stirred the pan of baked beans, you wandered through. You climbed onto a chair, reached for your bear and sat with it in your arms, watching me.

'You hungry?'

You didn't answer. I broke off a breadstick and gave it to you to eat while you waited.

'Did you like that man? He's a doctor. One of the doctors in the hospital who made you better.'

You munched the breadstick, spraying crumbs. Your eyes were thoughtful.

I thought you'd moved on but when I ladled the beans onto your plate and added the warmed-up sausages and set it in front of you with your miniature, coloured knife and fork, you said: 'It was a lady doctor, in the hospital.'

I sat beside you with my own plate.

'There was a lady, that's right. But there were men doctors too.'

You shrugged, looked down without enthusiasm at your lunch.

I pointed. 'Do you want me to cut the sausages?'

You shook your head. 'It's hot,' you said. 'I'm waiting for it to warm down.'

I looked out at the overgrown patch of garden and had a sudden vision of Matt, stripped to the waist, wielding a pair of shears. A man, a kind, capable man, bringing companionship. Making me feel less alone. I blinked it away.

'Good idea, Gracie.' I reached over and moved your hair out of your face, tucked it behind your ear. 'Good girl.'

CHAPTER 13

The next day, I came back from nursery to find a card on the mat. Hand-delivered. Firm, ragged handwriting in black ink. I stood there in my coat, looking at the envelope, reluctant to open it and be disappointed. It could be anything.

I carried it through to the kitchen and put it on the counter while I unpacked the shopping, put the kettle on. I forced myself to wait until I'd made a cup of tea and settled at the kitchen table before I opened it. There was a plain, cream-coloured card inside. Thick card. And just a few simple lines scrawled across the centre.

'Hi Jenny, I wondered if you were free for dinner one evening? Give me a call. Matt.' His mobile phone number was written underneath, just to make quite sure I had it. I sat very still and listened to the blood in my ears, to my heart. I was acting like a schoolgirl. All needy and excited. Just for a moment, I pretended to myself that I might not call him. I looked out at the messy kitchen, at the toys littered across the sitting room floor, waiting to be tidied away. I'd thought it was just you and me from now on. Just silence in the evenings and early nights. Maybe that was best, after all.

I remembered the warmth of his chest when I pressed myself suddenly against him, there at the hospital. His gentleness and kindness. The wounded look on his face when he talked about his daughter, Katy, and his ex-wife. My heart raced. Because I knew that I would say yes, that we would have dinner and that perhaps, just perhaps, it might lead somewhere.

I rushed to get my phone.

*

That evening, I was settling you down in bed after our story, arranging kitty cat and puppy and rabbit and bear in a little nest for you, the way my father did for me when I was your age, when you said:

'Mummy, are you going to die?'

I reached out and pulled you towards me, kissing your mess of soft, sweet-smelling hair. 'Everyone has to die someday, my love. But I'm planning to stay around for a very long time.'

Your forehead tightened. 'I don't want you to die.'

I hesitated. I didn't want to die either. Death never seemed real until it nearly took you away from me. Now it did. And when it came, however old I was, I knew I wouldn't want to leave you. I tried to remember what my own mother used to say when I was a child.

'By the time I die, you'll be grown-up, Gracie. You'll be married. You'll probably have your own children.'

Your lips quivered. 'But I don't want you to die.'

'Well, when people get very old, they get tired and they just want to go to sleep and rest. That's what happens. Dying is just like a very long sleep.'

You bowed your head and I couldn't see your face. After a few moments, you quietly asked, 'Was that lady very old?'

'Which lady?'

'The lady in the car. She died, didn't she, Mummy?'

I sighed. 'Yes, my love. I'm afraid she did. And you're right, she wasn't very old.'

You looked confused. 'So why did she die?'

'I don't know, my love. There are some things even mummies don't know. It's just what happened. It was very, very unusual.' I bent down and stroked your cheek with my finger. 'Now cuddle up to that bear and go to sleep.'

When you finally settled, I felt weighed down by an over-whelming exhaustion. I didn't have the energy to cook myself something to eat. I just sank into an armchair and sat alone in the quiet of the sitting room.

Outside, the rain had become heavy. Passing cars slushed on the wet road. Their headlights threw shifting shadows across the far wall. I imagined the noises rising in the high street, just a few minutes' walk away. They were the sounds of the old life before you came along, of bars and restaurants, cinemas and theatre, youngsters in huddles in doorways and bursts of raucous chat as heavy doors opened and closed.

During the day, I didn't let myself stop and think very much. You kept me moving. You lived so lightly, so intensely in the present. Now, without you here, the sitting room seemed dull and heavy. I sat very still, listening to the clock ticking on the mantelpiece, the low hum of the lights and the muffled splashes of the world outside.

You nearly died, my love. I nearly lost you. And she, that woman who took your father from us, she nearly took you too – shouting on the phone when she should have been watching the road. And no one seemed to realise, to blame her, except me. My hands came to my face and I rocked, hurting, trying to hold myself together.

Finally, restless, I got to my feet and stood at the mantelpiece, looking at the items there as if they belonged to a stranger. A framed photograph of you and me, one of the few Richard had taken. You were just a few weeks old, your eyes tightly closed. I looked haggard with tiredness but happy, really happy. I picked it up and studied it. It seemed a long time ago.

Further along, a pile of cards and postcards and old photos, stuffed behind the clock. I pulled them out and looked them over. A few postcards from last summer from friends in Cannes and Dubai, a photo-card from Disneyland of a friend's child hugging

Mickey Mouse, a Mother's Day card you'd made at nursery, your green crayon scribbled inside over an adult's steady writing: *I love you, Mummy, from Gracie.*

I sat in the chair with your card in my hand, thinking about you. Why were you so determined you'd flown down a tunnel of light and seen a man? Was it your brain playing tricks on you while you were in the coma? But why call him an angel? We never went to church, you and I. We never talked about God or Heaven and the only angels in your life so far had been the ones wearing wire-framed wings in the Christmas play and the plastic one on top of the tree. It made no sense. I looked at the card in my hands, traced the scribble with my eyes.

I shook my head. You'd described the accident so vividly. All that detail about the neck brace and the man calling you petal and Richard running to meet you at the hospital. And how had you known about Minnie Mouse and that ear peeling off the wall? Did someone see me do that?

I looked through to the empty, shadowy kitchen, to the table, outlined against the conservatory doors, where you and I liked to sit, side by side, eating cereal and toast. I narrowed my eyes, trying to understand and finding nothing but the quiet of my own loneliness.

Finally, I pulled myself to my feet and went through to the kitchen to get the phone and call Richard. We hadn't spoken for a while. His manner towards me had changed since those first days after the accident when he'd seemed so solicitous. Now he was back to off-hand, even brusque. Her influence.

'Jennifer.' He only called me that when he was annoyed. 'This isn't a great time, actually.'

'Can I just ask you something?'

He tutted. That would be for her benefit. He was making the point that he was the unwilling victim of my phone call, not a collaborator. I could almost see the pained look on his face. He

used to do the same with me years ago when his mother phoned just as I was putting our dinner out and I rolled my eyes, gestured to him to hang up, call back later. He never did. He was too polite.

Anyway, it was after eight. Surely they'd eaten by now.

'It won't take a minute. It's important.'

A sigh. 'What?'

'What happened when Gracie arrived at the hospital? Do you remember?'

He spluttered. 'What happened? What do you think? She was unconscious. They rushed her straight to intensive care. I phoned you as soon as I could, as soon as they got her stable.'

Now he sounded defensive.

'I know. It's not that.' I paced up and down the kitchen with the phone. 'But what exactly happened? I mean. Were you actually there when they lifted her out of the ambulance?'

'Yes. Right there.' He reverted to that new tone of voice that had emerged recently in our few conversations, patient and long-suffering, as if he were dealing with a mad woman who might also be dangerous. 'OK?'

'Did you shout?'

'Of course I bloody shouted. What do you think?' He paused, started again. 'Yes, I shouted. I don't know: "Oh my God" probably, and "That's my daughter". Something along those lines. OK? Can I go now?'

'You know how they said that she needed resuscitating?'

He hesitated. 'Yes…'

'Who did it? A doctor?'

'The ambulance guy.' I could hear him struggling to remember. 'Honeyman. Chris Honeyman. Looked about twelve. Maybe you didn't meet him. Anyway, he did CPR and she gave a sort of gulp and by the time we reached the ward, her breathing had settled again.'

'Where was it?'

He made an elaborate show of calling to Ella, like a ham actor calling offstage. 'Coming! On my way.' Then to me: 'Look, I've got to go.'

'Was it in the lift?' I raised my voice. 'Did Honeyballs give CPR in the lift?'

'Honey*man*.' He sounded cold. 'It might have been in the sodding lift. Maybe it was in the corridor. What does it matter, Jennifer? It's past. It's history. Don't you get it? I don't want to talk about it. OK?'

The phone went down. *Now he's feeling guilty*, I thought. He always did that. He'd try so hard to be patient and then he'd snap and blow it and feel bad about it for hours. *I've become his mother*, I thought. *And Ella has become me*. How strange life is.

I put the phone back and opened the fridge to search for something to eat. I had forgotten to ask him if he'd cried. I'd meant to. But the rest of it, the rest checked out.

I found an old yoghurt, a week past its sell-by date, on the bottom shelf. It had separated and I stirred it back to life with a teaspoon, took it through to the sitting room. You must have been conscious. It was the only explanation. At some level, you must have been aware of what was happening.

I settled on the settee, switched on the television and watched, blankly, some programme about a couple looking for their ideal home.

I wanted so much to believe you. To believe you went flying off to meet your angel and found him peaceful and smiling. However irrational, it would be a comfort. I shook my head.

The programme stuttered on. I scraped out the yoghurt pot without tasting it, letting my eyes glaze as I stared, barely seeing, at the television. However much I pushed it away, the thought wouldn't leave me: what if you were right? You seemed so matter of fact in discussing it, so sure about what you'd seen. What if it were possible, for you, with all your innocence, if not for me?

What if, in some way I couldn't yet fathom, something of us survived death and lived on?

I opened a bottle of wine, sank back into the cushions and let the chatter from the television wash over me. Finally, I found the will to rouse myself and start the weekly ritual of tidying up, sorting out toys and dropping them into plastic tubs and boxes. Next, I started on the pile of junk that always collected on the dining room table.

Underneath the old newspapers lay a crumpled carrier bag. I remembered it at once. It was the one the woman in the café had handed me, with Ella's phone inside. I went to find a charger and plugged it in, then poured myself another glass of wine and watched the screen flash as it came back to life. I clicked into her text messages and started to scroll through them, looking for Richard's name. My hands shook as I read her texts to him:

See you in 5.

On my way.

Running late – see you at the restaurant. Love u. x

Somehow the fact they were so boring made it worse. It showed how intimate they were. I recovered and carried on reading, picking through the rest of her messages. I don't know what I was looking for. Some sign of an affair, perhaps, that I could brandish in Richard's face. But there was nothing incriminating at all.

I sat in silence for some moments, looking at the screen, thinking about Ella's life. I had a piece of her right here in my hand and I should have been triumphant but all I felt was emptiness.

I remembered what the woman at the café said about Ella being distracted by an angry phone call just before the crash, clicked out of messages and went to look at the call log. The last call she'd received was at three eighteen in the afternoon, on the day of the accident. I narrowed my eyes. It could fit. That must have been roughly the same time. I bit my lip. It came from an unlisted number: No Caller ID.

CHAPTER 14

Ella

She has no idea how lucky she is.

I am sorry she and Richard weren't right together. Heaven knows, he tried. It was painful to watch. He contorted every bone in his body in the effort to change shape and fit into that marriage and be happy with her and he just couldn't do it.

And I never tried to prise him away. She needs to think that. I understand. But it's simply not true. I lost count of the number of times we made ourselves miserable by breaking up. We could never stay apart for long. He adores Gracie but suffocating in an unhappy marriage was never going to work. He's a better father for being happy with me.

She has Gracie. That's the point. She's the mother of a gorgeous, funny, bright, kind little girl. And if that isn't enough, heaven help her. However much I love Richard, and I do, I'd swap places in a heartbeat.

Hurt isn't clean. It's putrid. It makes strangers out of everyone you ever thought loved you. Once it touches you, you're on your own.

All that stuff about emotional damage bringing people together? Forget it. Hurt surrounds you with such a powerful force field of misery that no one else can enter. I know. I've been there.

All those so-called friends? Nowhere. They came the first time with their solemn faces and shuffled on their seats, trying not to

look at the clock, while I cried. They didn't come back. And I don't blame them. Who would?

I've been there too. It took a while but I got it into my thick skull in the end. No one else was going to help me. No one else wanted to know. So I learned to shut up and paint a face on and say I was fine and where's the party? Stupid loud music. Stupid loud clothes. Stupid loud men. And pretty soon, rooms stopped falling silent when I walked into them. People stopped ducking into shops to avoid me on the street. *Thank God*, they thought. *She's over it.*

You don't get over it. If you're doing well, you get used to it. You save it for silence. For darkness. For three o'clock in the morning. For the nights you're alone.

So that's the state I was in when I met Richard, with all his gentleness and kindness and decency. I lay next to him in bed as he slept, his arms wrapped round me, his breath warm and steady on my skin, and absorbed love from him like a dried-up sponge sucking in water.

I couldn't talk to him about what had happened to me. I didn't know how to put it into words. And I was frightened to try. In the early days, when I first realised I was falling in love with him, I was scared of spoiling it, of contaminating what we had and driving him away. He was sad enough. He didn't need more pain in his life.

And then the moment passed. It started to feel too late. So I just walled it off and lied when I had to and, right or wrong, it seemed best.

It's my hurt. Maybe it's better it stays secret, even from him.

CHAPTER 15

Jennifer

We were coming back from the shops that afternoon when you pulled free from me and ran.

'Gracie!'

You caught me by surprise. You never ran off. You were an obedient child but also you had more sense than most children your age about traffic and waiting for the green man and the danger of getting lost in crowds.

'Gracie! Stop!'

You weaved through the shoppers like a weasel. I felt a lumbering fool, chasing after you, laden with carrier bags. My handbag, strapped over my chest, banged on my ribs. You were wearing your mauve padded anorak, a hand-me-down from the family across the road, and by the time I got clear of a broad elderly woman with a shopping trolley on wheels and round the front of an on-coming buggy, it was rapidly disappearing round the corner, turning off the high street and down a small side road.

I ran after you, cursing under my breath. The side road was less crowded and I saw you clearly as you made a sharp left and disappeared just past the music shop. It was a road that was only ten minutes from home but one I had no reason, in normal circumstances, to go down.

There was a pub across the road with a hedged garden. You couldn't have gone that far, I'd have seen you cross the road. A

car park attached to a housing block. On this side, a café with chairs and tables outside, an overpriced delicatessen and the dingy music shop that had been there for as long as I could remember. I scanned both as I ran by. No sign of you.

I pressed on. *Here*, I thought, *just here. This must be where you'd disappeared.* I found myself at the entrance to a small parish church. I must have passed it a hundred times over the years and never really noticed.

It was a Victorian building, set back from the road. The metal gate and railings looked as if they'd seen better days. The front lawn was in the building's shadow and the bushes planted round its edge needed a trim. A noticeboard read: *Parish Church of Saint Michael, Anglican. All Welcome.* Underneath, a modern printed notice said: *Café* and listed the opening hours.

"Gracie!" I stood at the gate, heavy with bags, and looked in. No sign of you. Standing still, away from the distant rumble of traffic on the high street, all I could hear was the thump of blood in my ears. Panic made me shake. The gate stood open. I set off down the path and ran round the side of the church, looking for the entrance.

The plot extended much further than it looked from the road. It opened out into a narrow graveyard, set about with mature trees and bounded by a stone wall. We were so close to the modern rush of the high street and yet here I felt at once the sense of timelessness, of the passing of ages, of the unknown dead lying under the feet of the living.

'Gracie!'

Sunlight straggled through the foliage and made shifting patterns on the grass and its unkempt path and it stirred a memory of early childhood in me, some day when I must have played in such a place, in and out of shadows. I scanned the graveyard. No sign of you. Had you taken a different turning after all? My stomach clenched.

A modern, glass-walled annex rose along the far end of the church, invisible from the road. Inside, I could see the café and, through it, the entrance to the church. A movement drew my eye. A small figure in mauve, disappearing into the interior. I broke into a run again, frightened in case I was wrong, in case I was chasing a different child, pushed open the glass door with my shoulder and fell into the café.

Faces looked up. A cluster of elderly women, drinking tea together at a wooden table. A smartly dressed young man, sitting alone with a plate of bacon and eggs, his laptop open at one side. A care-worn couple, retired perhaps, sitting in silence, shoulders slumped. A young woman with swept-back hair stood behind a counter with a magazine open in front of her and, to her side, a display cabinet full of cakes and puddings and pots of salad.

I ran across. 'Did a little girl just come running in? She's three.'

My voice was loud and breathless in the quietness. Unlike every other café in town, there seemed to be no background music to hide behind. A display of cheaply printed leaflets about the history of the church, postcards and a stack of video cassettes in cellophane stood on the counter by the cash register.

The young woman lifted her eyes reluctantly from the magazine. She pointed towards the large wooden doors of the church, opened up to the public.

'She ran in there.'

I rushed after you into the dim interior of the church.

'Gracie!'

You were standing at the side of the altar, gazing up at the stained-glass windows. A matter of feet away, several votive candles burned on a metal stand. The building had the hushed dim mustiness of thick stone walls, high-leaded windows and centuries of prayer. The pews were solid wood and worn smooth by generations of worshippers. I crossed to you, conscious of the

click of my heels on the stone flags and the rustle of the shopping bags against my legs.

'What on earth—'

You looked up, smiling, pleased with yourself. I wanted to grab you by the arm and give you a lecture about the perils of running off but the silence of the building pressed in on me and its sense of holiness too and, besides, you seemed so delighted with what you'd found and I was weak with relief. *Sanctuary*, I thought. You'd picked the right place to hide.

You pointed up at the windows, craning your neck back to see.

'You know what this is?' I said. 'It's a church. It's a quiet place where people come to think. And it's very, very old.'

'I think that's him.'

'Who?'

I looked up at the section of stained glass. It gleamed red, blue and yellow with sunshine. The picture, high above us, showed a man with a beard and flowing white robes. His foot was on the head of a writhing serpent and he held a staff high above his head as he prepared to strike. He had large, bird-like wings and a halo. Straight out of an Old Testament picture book.

'That man.' You looked at me with joy. 'In the funny clothes.'

'What man?'

'When I was in the accident.' Your face was radiant, expectant, as if you'd proved your point. 'That must be why I wanted to come here. To find him again.'

I took a deep breath. 'It was just a dream, Gracie.'

Your face clouded. 'You don't believe me, do you, Mummy?'

I hesitated. 'I believe you think you saw him, my love. But that doesn't make it real. You see? You were asleep.'

You looked wounded. I set down my shopping bags and opened my arms to you but you turned away. I had disappointed you and it was unbearable but what else could I say?

'That isn't a real man.' I spoke in a whisper. 'Angels are—' I hesitated '—they're an idea. A lovely idea about goodness and the fact kind people are always more powerful than bad ones.'

You frowned. 'But I saw him.'

'I know.' It was cowardly of me but this wasn't the time. You were starting to get upset. 'I know you did.'

'You don't believe me.'

'I do.'

You gave me a sceptical look, clearly not convinced, and ran away into the deep shadows along the wall, touching your face and hands to the cool stone. I lowered myself onto a pew and sat too, shopping around my feet. It was a peaceful place. A place of prayer.

I sat quietly, thinking. The pews were worn and I imagined the grief, the despair, the loneliness people must have brought here over the years. It gave me a strange sense of connection, not with God but with all those other unknown women who had been before. Mothers who had lost daughters. Daughters who had lost mothers. I sighed. Even the stone flags under my feet were monuments to the dead and I turned my head to read the engraving nearest me.

Anne Elizabeth McIntyre, Beloved wife and mother, Gone to Join Our Lord, May 12, 1831. Aged 54. Death thou art but another birth.

'There are several McIntyres. Anne's daughters, Beatrice and Mary, are both buried in the churchyard. And there's a memorial stone over there to her son, James. He was lost at sea.'

I jumped. A woman of perhaps sixty had appeared beside me. She wore low-heeled soft shoes, shapeless black trousers and a baggy black top with a clerical collar. A large wooden cross hung round her neck. She smiled.

'Sorry, did I startle you?'

I reached towards my bags. Vicars make me nervous. I had refused point blank to go to church as soon as I became a teenager.

I don't see the point in discussing religion, especially with people who think they have all the answers, answers to unanswerable questions. It's never an honest conversation. All they want to do is prove that they're right and you, if you dare to disagree, are wrong.

She was still smiling. 'I've disturbed you.'

'Not at all. I just came in to get my daughter.' I looked over to see what you were doing. You had settled quietly on the end of a pew, your legs swinging, humming to yourself. The vicar lifted her eyes to watch you for a moment, her face serene.

I pointed up at the multi-coloured angel. 'May I ask you something? Who is that?'

She lowered herself heavily into the pew beside me. It creaked under her weight. 'That's Saint Michael, the archangel.'

I hesitated. I wanted to ask more but I didn't want to look ignorant.

'Is he slaying a snake?'

'The Devil himself.' She smiled. 'The Victorians were very literal. They liked drama. A different age.'

'And what are we now?'

'Now? Ah.' She looked thoughtful. 'Sceptical, certainly. And very metaphorical. Not many people nowadays believe in a Devil with a forked tail and horns. Do you?'

I shook my head.

'Exactly. Neither do I. We're generally a more—' she paused '—conceptual age.' She pointed back to the window. 'The striking part is the raised lance, isn't it? The eye is drawn to it. But look at his other hand. See what he's holding?'

I narrowed my eyes. She was right; I hadn't noticed his left hand before. Old-fashioned weighing scales on chains hung from it.

'For weighing sin?'

'Good and evil. A symbol of justice. It's the other side of power. Something we're still apt to forget even today, I fear.'

I smiled. Her manner put me at ease.

She held out her hand. 'Angela Barker.'

'Jennifer.' Her grasp was firm. 'And that's Gracie. My daughter.'

'Ah. God's favour.'

'Indeed.' I'd read up on your name once we finally chose it, although Richard seemed more inspired by Grace Kelly than by anything spiritual.

You came running over and stood beside me, looking into the vicar's face with open interest.

'This is Angela,' I said. 'She works here, in this church.'

You considered her. 'I like the windows.'

'They're special, aren't they?' Angela spoke to you evenly, as if to an equal. 'They're very old.'

'What's that?' You pointed to the cross round the vicar's neck.

'It's a cross. I always wear it.'

'Why?'

'Come on now, Gracie.' I reached for the shopping, embarrassed. 'Let's go home.'

Angela raised her hand. 'That's OK.' She leaned forward to you and spoke quietly. 'It reminds me of something important that happened many years ago, before any of us were born. Of a very special man with amazing powers.'

Your eyes gleamed. 'The angel?' You twisted round and pointed back at Saint Michael. 'I've met him. When I had my accident.'

'That's enough, Gracie.' My voice was sharp, eager to get you out of there. 'Come on.' I held out my hand for you to take and said to Angela: 'I am sorry. We'd better head home.'

She looked intrigued, her eyes on your face as I steered you away. She heaved herself to her feet and walked with us to the great stone archway separating the entrance to the church from the modern café beyond.

'Lovely to meet you, Gracie. God bless you.' She raised her eyes to me. 'Come and see us again soon.'

In the café, the young man was powering down his laptop and reaching for his coat. I crossed to the counter and picked up one of the leaflets about the church.

'How much are these?'

The young woman shrugged. 'They're free.'

I dug in my pocket, found a pound coin and dropped it into the tip pot.

As we left, the elderly ladies lifted their heads again and their eyes followed you out. I suspected you were the liveliest person to visit Saint Michael's for some time.

CHAPTER 16

'Do you know what we're going to do now, Gracie?'

I settled you down at the kitchen table with felt-tip pens and paper and a packet of multi-coloured tissue paper.

'You remember those coloured windows you saw in the church? Let's make our own.'

You set about working with me, watching as I drew a simple flower for you. I planned to cut the petals out of the paper and stick pieces of tissue paper across the holes. I'd done something similar one Christmas, years ago, when I was at primary school. It wasn't hard.

You crayoned with care the centre of the flower, the leaves and the stem, your brow puckered and the end of your tongue sticking out between your lips.

I opened the leaflet up on the table. 'That's the window, isn't it?'

You paused to look, considered. 'He has a beard. But it still looks like him. My angel.'

'He's called Saint Michael.' I tried to remember what I'd learned from my halting search on the Internet while you were eating your snack. 'People have been drawing pictures of him for hundreds of years. He was probably based on a real man but he lived so long ago, no one really knows what's true and what's just made up, just stories.'

You were crayoning again. 'I know. He's my friend.'

I didn't answer. I was trying hard to be patient but it was a growing struggle. I didn't know why the idea of an angel was

tangled up in your head with the trauma you'd suffered. You were an intelligent child. Perhaps you'd heard people talking about her death and were trying, in your own way, to get the measure of that?

But Saint Michael? A gaunt, bearded man in ancient robes, slaying the Devil? He had no place in your subconscious. None at all.

I looked at your head, bent forward over your picture. I was cutting green and red and blue tissue paper into petal shapes for you to stick on, once the colouring was finished. It was easier to talk when your hands were busy. That's why Richard and I had some of our most difficult conversations in the car when he was driving and neither of us could escape.

'It's not your fault, you know, Gracie. The accident. You do understand that, don't you?'

Red tissue paper, snip, snip. Out of the corner of my eye, I saw you look up, guarded, then turn back to your crayoning.

'Daddy and I were so worried about you, when you were in hospital.'

The crayoning slowed. A pause. 'Is that why Daddy cried?'

I took a deep breath. 'Of course.'

I picked up a sheet of blue tissue paper and started to cut that. You sounded worried but your face was low over your drawing and I couldn't see your expression.

'That's looking lovely, Gracie.' I couldn't even see, I just wanted to soothe you. 'That yellow is so cheerful.'

You didn't lift your head. I reached forward and scooped a clump of falling hair, tucked it behind your ear. Such soft, fine hair. Hairclips never stayed in place for long.

'I'll get some glue. When you've finished colouring, we'll cut out together and I'll show you how to stick tissue paper on the back so light shines through.'

I knew you. You would talk if you wanted to. You never responded well to questions. I rummaged in the back of the

kitchen drawer through blunt scissors and scattered paper clips and an unfolding ball of string until I found the glue.

You sat, eyes on my fingers, as I carefully cut out the paper panels and we started to stick on the tissue paper.

The window was almost finished when you suddenly said, in that way you had of launching a sudden remark from nowhere: 'Was the accident Auntie Ella's fault?'

The breath caught in my throat. 'Auntie Ella?'

You nodded. 'She was very cross, Mummy.'

My fingers fumbled the piece of tissue paper, stuck it crookedly.

'What makes you say that?'

Your eyes stayed on the petals.

'No, not red. Blue.' Your voice had a tremor as you pointed to the next petal, ready to fight me. I gave in at once. You could do it any way you wanted; what did I care? All I wanted was to keep you talking.

Once we'd glued the blue one into place, you said: 'She kept talking on the phone. She shouted. Screamy shouting. I heard.'

I stopped, looked at you. That's what the woman in the café said, that she'd been arguing on the phone. I hadn't considered that you must have heard too.

'Gracie. This is important. When did she shout?'

You looked petulant, annoyed by my sudden change of mood, by the fact I was interrupting you at a crucial creative moment.

'In the car.'

'But when?' My fingers trembled. 'Before the accident?'

You nodded.

'Auntie Ella shouted on the phone?'

'Yes, Mummy. I already said.'

I stared at you, imagining it. If she held the phone in one hand, she only had one hand on the wheel.

'You're spoiling it.'

You pointed at the tissue paper, crushed between my fingers. I set the picture on the table and you fell to smearing glue along the edges, ready for the final panel. A prick of sweat ran along my hairline as I watched you.

'Gracie, what did Auntie Ella say, do you remember?'

You didn't answer at first. Your face was tight with concentration. You held up the yellow tissue paper for me to cut.

'She said: "Go away. Stop it. Leave me alone." Like that.' You finally tore your eyes from the picture and looked up. Your eyes were mischievous. 'That's not very polite, is it? She should have said please.'

'Yes, she should have said please.' My head span. 'Even silly grown-ups forget sometimes, when they get cross.'

'Silly sausage.' You smiled to yourself. 'Silly banana.'

I wrapped my arms round your small body and squeezed you tightly, even as you struggled to pull away. I whispered into your neck. 'I love you, Gracie.'

You battled to extract yourself from me, brushed fallen hair from your cheeks, smoothed out the crumpled tissue paper and handed it to me. The sight of your sweet face, so serious, so intent, made my eyes swim. I blinked. I thought about what might have happened, about what so nearly did.

'I love you so much. You have no idea.'

If you heard, you gave no sign of it. You were here, fully focused on the present.

I left you to squeeze the glue on your own, getting it everywhere. I just couldn't help. My hands shook in my lap. I sat, trembling, watching you and thinking about the accident, wondering who had made Ella shout down the phone that day. I knew now with absolute certainty that Ella was every bit as responsible for that crash as that poor girl.

CHAPTER 17

That night, you cried out in your sleep. I stumbled through to you. Your eyes were screwed closed but your face was contorted, your arms flailing.

I sat on the floor by your bed and stroked the hair from your hot face, whispered: 'It's alright, Gracie. Mummy's here.'

Wherever you were, lost in some dream, I couldn't reach you there. What business did a girl have with nightmares when she wasn't yet four years old? After a few minutes, when you still didn't settle, I sat you up. You reached out, still half asleep, arms wide, to be lifted and I carried you through, your bear pressed between our chests, to my room. You lay in the middle of the bed, your compact body kicking and elbowing me as you made the space your own.

You opened your eyes, looked round at the shadows and smiled, pleased.

'Mummy and Daddy's bed.'

Just Mummy's bed now. I stroked your hair and you curled yourself round your bear, your head on his back, and dropped again into sleep.

I looped an arm round your firm body and put my face against your neck. Your hair was soft and fine and smelt fresh. You should always sleep here with me. Why did you have your own bed now, anyway? What did it matter? I lay quietly in the darkness, listening to your slow, soft breathing beside me, feeling your warmth.

We argued about this too, Richard and I, when you were a baby. One of many arguments. I never thought, when I was pregnant with you, so full of joy, of hope, hands protective on my swollen stomach, relishing the sight of it, everything an expectant mother is supposed to be, that he'd have so many dogmatic opinions about childcare. I thought he'd leave all that to me; wasn't that what men were supposed to do? But he was a passionate father, determined to do everything right and someone else filled him with ideas, I was sure of it. Ella, perhaps. She was in the background all along; I know that now.

I reached out and stroked your cheek with my fingertips, wondering if you could sense me, even through sleep. He was fiercely opposed to 'co-sleeping', as he called it. He said it was dangerous; we might smother you. We needed to set boundaries.

He wasn't the one breastfeeding every few hours. After you fed, you fell asleep against me, cuddled in the crook of my arm, your face against my warm skin, listening to my heartbeat. What could be more natural? It was the comfort and warmth all animals needed.

He ended up sleeping in the spare bedroom and moved his clothes into the wardrobe there so he could creep out to work early without disturbing us. I was glad. It put an end to the argument. There was no one to sigh and raise himself on an elbow and grimace when I brought you into bed to feed and kept you there. Was that very wrong? I went over and over it afterwards, once it was all too late and he'd left and news broke of the wonderful Ella, glamorous, amazing Ella with her pert breasts and tight stomach, who wanted him in her bed all night, every night.

You were my daughter. Of course I was besotted with you. Of course you were my life. I thought he'd understand that. I thought he'd feel the same.

I was clasping you too tightly. You twisted and bucked in your sleep and kicked away from me to settle again in the empty ocean

of the bed. I shifted my weight to move a little closer to you again. I didn't want to let you go. I wanted to feel the heat rising from your body through the Dalmatian pyjamas you loved so much.

I lifted a finger and ran it gently over your hair. Ella, you said, screaming down the phone, just when she most needed her mind on the road. The thought of it, of your anxiety as you listened from the back seat, made me physically sick. *I should have been there. I should have protected you.*

I closed my eyes. An image swam up of your tiny pale body, stretched out on the hospital bed, pierced by tubes and needles. I sat up, shook it out of my head and looked down at you now, sleeping beside me, your eyelids flickering as you dreamed.

CHAPTER 18

My mental image of the inside of police stations came from watching television dramas. Old-fashioned ones, mostly, full of dingy corridors leading to dark offices with shields mounted on the walls and heavy wooden desks with swivel chairs. And in some bright communal area, a large incident board, pinned with photographs of suspects, linked by pins and string and dotted with yellow sticky notes.

Our local police station wasn't like that. I'd walked past it a thousand times and never really noticed it until now. A 1980s multi-storey office building with tall glass doors, all chrome and concrete. The young man on the ground floor reception desk looked dubiously at the business card.

'Is she expecting you?'

I stood my ground. 'She told me to get in touch. Is she in?'

He narrowed his eyes, then hit a button on the phone box. His headset bobbed round his cheek.

He lowered his voice as he spoke into it. 'There's a Jennifer Walker, ma'am. Yes, ma'am. Right away.'

The police officer stood there in the lift lobby, waiting, as I emerged on the fourth floor.

'Mrs Walker. How's Gracie?'

'Fully recovered. Thank goodness.' I laughed nervously.

Her handshake was hard and her pace brisk as she led me past broad windows that showed an open-plan office beyond, two banks of desks crammed with people. It looked as soulless as a call centre.

She ushered me into a small, bare room with a plastic-topped table and four metal-framed chairs and gestured to me to sit. The walls were beige and the only object on them was a metallic clock with black numerals. Five past eleven.

She pulled a second chair up to mine and sat, her feet flat on the ground and her legs apart. She was no taller than me but her brusque manner and her uniform made her thick-set and masculine and, although she made an attempt at a smile, the overall effect was intimidating.

'So, how can I help you?'

The window behind her faced down the high street. Everything looked different from this angle. The three-storey rows of shops were low and poky. The red roof of a double-decker bus slid to a halt as the lights directly below changed to red and the small figures of pedestrians, two mothers pushing buggies, a stout middle-aged man, a willowy youth, an old lady walking with a stick, pressed forward from the edge of pavement. It was the ragtag, anonymous public of which I was part, which she was here to protect.

'It's about the accident.' I hesitated, feeling my way. 'I've got new information. I thought you ought to know.'

'OK.' She nodded, her expression non-committal. 'What's the information?'

I took out Ella's mobile phone and handed it to her. She looked it over, then raised her eyes, waited for me to say more.

'It's hers. See? Ella's.'

I couldn't tell what she was thinking, but it was clear she didn't understand how significant this was. 'It's Ms Hicks's phone? Had she lost it?'

'Yes,' I stuttered. She made me nervous. 'I mean, she probably didn't tell you, did she? That she'd lost it?'

She shook her head. 'No, I don't believe she did. Should she have?' She seemed at a loss. 'Was it stolen?'

'No!' My words were thick with emotion as I struggled to make her understand. 'It was at the scene of the accident.'

She gave a slight sigh. 'I'm sorry, Mrs Walker. I'm not sure I understand.'

I leaned forward, earnest. 'It's evidence. Of what happened. I just thought, if there's an investigation, you might need it. It's evidence *against Ella*.'

My voice sounded thin and insubstantial in the echoing acoustic of the small room.

Her eyes never left my face. 'Evidence of what, exactly?'

'Of what really happened.' I sat forward, my voice rising with my frustration. 'It was left at the scene of the accident. A woman picked it up. She saw everything and she gave it to me.'

'Why didn't she bring it to us, if she thought it was evidence?'

'I don't know.' I looked down at my hands, clasped in my lap. 'I don't think she realised how important it is. It shows, you see, that Ella was on the phone at the time of the crash. The call's logged.' I pointed to the phone, willing her to take me seriously and to look for herself. 'That proves it.'

She didn't even blink. 'Proves what?'

'That she was responsible too. For the accident. Yes, OK, that poor young woman veered across the road. But why didn't Ella react? Swerve to avoid her? Because she was on the phone. She was preoccupied. That's dangerous driving, right there.'

Below, in the street, the lights changed a second time and the traffic slowed, stopped. A ragged line of pedestrians hurried across.

'Is that why you've come to see me?'

'Ella was shouting at someone. Angry. Telling them to leave her alone. Clearly she wasn't watching the road properly. The accident – that girl's death – Ella is to blame too.'

She didn't answer. She just waited.

'That woman heard her. She's a witness. And so did Gracie, my daughter. She was right there. She saw everything.'

She got to her feet. 'I'm afraid I've got a lot of work to do.'

I jumped up. 'But you need to do something. If she was distracted—'

The police officer raised a hand to silence me. 'These are very serious allegations. You should be careful.'

'Me?' I blew out my cheeks. 'She's the one who—'

'Mrs Walker. The coroner has already given a verdict. Accidental death. The case is closed.' She handed the phone back to me. 'You might want to return this to Ms Hicks as soon as possible, if it's her property.'

I shook my head. 'But two people heard—'

'Listen. Firstly, even if this were a continuing investigation – which it is not – testimony from a traumatised three-year-old would not be reliable. Secondly, even if the timing of the call had matched the exact time of the accident, no coroner would have found Ms Hicks responsible.' She leaned in closer to me. 'The post-mortem found that Ms Parkes had excessive levels of alcohol in her blood at the time of the collision. She had a history of similar offences.'

I stared at her, my cheeks hot. 'So you're not going to do anything?'

Her face was hard. 'Such as?'

'I don't know. You're the police officer, not me. Prosecute her for dangerous driving. If Ella hadn't been distracted that young woman might still be alive today. Think of her family.'

She turned away from me towards the window and her shoulders rose and fell as she breathed deeply. I waited, my legs juddering. When she turned back to me, her features were stony.

'Mrs Walker, I understand you've been through a lot.'

'She had my daughter in the back. She nearly died too. What if I'd lost her? Then what?'

'That's enough, Mrs Walker.' Her tone was icy.

'She wasn't watching the road. She was on the phone, shouting. How's it not her fault, at least—'

The police officer raised her hand and the look on her face silenced me. She shook her head, crossed the room and opened the door for me to leave.

At the lift, she said: 'I'm very sorry. But as far as the police are concerned, this is now over. Take my advice. Leave Ms Hicks alone. Leave everyone alone. You have a lovely daughter. Go home and look after her.'

The lift doors opened and I stepped inside. She reached in to press the button for the ground floor. By the time the doors slid shut, she had already turned back towards the soulless office.

Downstairs, I walked straight out into the street and stood at the crossing, waiting for the lights to change, wondering which unseen people might be watching me from above and trying hard not to cry.

CHAPTER 19

Ella

It's early evening and the drone of a male voice, leaking through from the sitting room, tells me Richard is watching the evening news while I cook pasta. My neck and shoulders still hurt from the accident and I move round the kitchen with stiff robot arms, laboriously turning my whole upper body to reach for things, instead of bending naturally.

Then the doorbell rings. I go. I assume it's that young offender who keeps trying to sell me tea towels and oven gloves or one of those charity workers who come door-to-door just when we're about to eat and opens with cheesy lines like: 'Do you care about sick children?' If Richard goes, we'll never sit down to dinner.

So I open the door with a scowl on my face, to find two police officers standing there, the same pair who interviewed me in hospital.

'Ms Hicks?' The female officer. Hatchet-faced. 'May we come in?'

I hesitate for just a moment, wondering if I have a choice. I decide that, as Richard would say, non-compliance might not be in the best interests of the client.

They loom large in the sitting room, looking round, taking it all in. Richard jumps up to switch off the television and straightens the newspapers into a pile as if untidiness might be used in evidence.

'Good evening.' He goes into solicitor mode, all eager to please. 'How can we help?'

The female officer sits down without being asked and turns to me. Her sidekick, the young Asian man, takes out a notebook and pencil.

'Ms Hicks, we wondered if we could ask you a few more questions?'

I incline my head. In the kitchen, the pasta is no doubt turning to mulch but no isn't really an option. 'About the accident?'

'Yes.' She gives nothing away. 'At the time of the accident, were you having a conversation on your mobile phone?'

No beating about the bush, just straight out with it.

I stall, feigning surprise: 'Mobile phone?'

She isn't fooled. 'We've interviewed a witness who says she heard you. She says you sounded angry.'

'Ah.' I make a big show of remembering. 'I was cross with Gracie. That must be it. She was being a monkey in the back and I told her off.'

The young man writes furiously in his notebook.

Her eyes are on mine. They narrow. 'Just to clarify, you're saying you didn't take a phone call? Are you quite certain of that?'

I bite my lip a bit and try to look thoughtful. 'I may have had a call earlier. Work stuff. But not then.' I pause. 'I'd have remembered.'

I'm a damn good liar. There are two vital ingredients. Consistency. In other words, stick to your story. And keep your cool.

Her eyes bore right through me and I see in an instant that we understand each other perfectly. She knows I'm lying and she knows I know she knows. The question is: what's she going to do about it?

'It's a very serious matter, Ms Hicks.' Her tone is dry. 'A young woman is dead.'

I look pained. 'I know. Awful. I can't stop thinking about her.'

Richard, always a soft touch, reaches for my hand and squeezes it. The police officer's eyes are still on mine.

'If necessary, would you testify to that effect?' she says. 'Under oath.'

I nod. 'Of course. Anything.'

Richard shows them out. When he comes back, he puts his arm round me.

'Alright?'

I don't answer.

'Thank God you weren't on the phone,' he says. 'That could've been really serious. Imagine.'

The next day, Richard makes some calls and finds out that the inquest has already taken place. A verdict of accidental death. He seems puzzled. Why would the police come round and talk about testifying when the inquest is already over? I see at once. I know a warning when I see one. *We know exactly what happened, Ms Hicks. Too late this time but watch your step.*

So that's it. I'm safe, after all. It wasn't fear of punishment that kept me awake at night. It was fear that, if all this came out, Richard would discover who it was who called me. And why.

CHAPTER 20

Jennifer

I opened the door to the babysitter and went upstairs to say goodbye to you. You smelled the guilt as soon as I walked in. I never went anywhere in the evenings. I hated leaving you with anyone else, now more than ever.

'Mummy!' You sat up in bed, your arms round your bear. Kitty and puppy and the rest of the menagerie were lined along the wall. A story book lay open across your knees. You pointed. 'Read this.'

'Sweetheart, I've got to go. Dianne's here. Remember?'

You looked cross. 'Why?'

'Because I'm going out for dinner.'

'Why?'

'Because mummies have play dates too, sometimes.'

You narrowed your eyes. 'But I don't want you to.'

I wavered for a moment, seeing you there, then thought how ridiculous I would sound if I tried to explain to Dianne, now settling herself in the sitting room, that I didn't have the willpower to leave you for a few hours.

'I'll ask Dianne if she'll come up and read you a story. Would you like that?'

No answer.

I kissed each of your toys and then you. 'I love you, little Gracie. See you later.'

You wrinkled your nose. 'I'm not little.'

As I reached the door, you added: 'I don't like Dianne.'

I sighed. 'Gracie.'

'What if she touches my railway?'

'I'll make sure she doesn't.'

'Or my books?'

'Or your books.'

'But you won't be here.'

'Go to sleep.' I inched out of the bedroom door. 'Tell that bear all the things you did today.'

I brushed my hair, pulled on a dress and sprayed a little perfume. My hands trembled as I closed the front door, and my stomach churned. I wasn't sure if the nerves were about leaving you or meeting Matt.

As I got off the Tube and walked from the station to the restaurant, I started to feel sick. I tried to remember what I really knew about Matt. Not much. I hadn't had a date since Richard left. I just hadn't been interested, hadn't met anyone. My evenings were all TV dinners and early nights.

I hesitated in the street, scared of the bustle around me, of the women in high heels and short skirts who looked so fashionable and confident. My own dress, years old, seemed dowdy. I clutched my handbag and breathed heavily, in and out. After all this time, the rules must have changed. Maybe he'd expect sex if he bought me dinner. I wasn't ready for all that.

I stopped. It wasn't too late. I'd call him and make an excuse. Say you weren't well.

'Jenny!'

Matt, emerging from the restaurant a few doors down, had spotted me. He was wearing a well-cut blazer, his shirt open at the collar. That flop of fringe was pushed to one side. His eyes were amused.

'Are you OK?' He reached me, took my arm, led me forward into the tapas bar, which was teeming with music, with chatter.

'It's a bit noisy down here.' He leaned close to make himself heard and his aftershave came too. 'I've got a table upstairs. Come on.'

As I walked ahead of him, his hand hovered at the small of my back, guiding me through the crowd. Warm and strong.

He had chosen well. A corner table tucked into the broad windows, which gave onto the street below. A bottle of claret sat open beside wine glasses the size of goldfish bowls. Richard hated glasses like that. He said they were designed to make people drink too much. Up here, the clamour of the bar below was muted.

'I kept popping down to look for you,' he said. 'It's not the easiest place to find.'

'You've been here before?' I was fishing, of course, angling for little pieces of his life so I could fit them together and understand him better. Always, with Matt, it felt as if there were pieces missing.

'It's my local.' He smiled. 'My flat's down the road, near the Tube. Small but central.'

He poured us both wine and we clinked glasses. I tried to cross my legs, then uncrossed them, shuffled on my chair. I took a sip of wine, then another.

The claret was full-bodied and spread itself through my chest, down into my stomach, my legs. I let my shoulders fall an inch. The lights were low and a candle burned steadily in a glass holder. All around us, people chattered, ate, laughed. This was it then, being out. I had the sense of setting down a heavy burden, of emerging, lighter, from a cocoon. I was having dinner with a man who wasn't Richard. A man called Matt.

'So,' he said, leaning across the table, 'tell me something about yourself. Something about Jenny the person, not Jenny the mum.'

I hesitated, trying to remember. It had been a long time since anyone asked about her.

Matt was a good listener and when I finally faltered, he picked up the conversation with ease, chatting about a film he'd seen at

the weekend and the writers he enjoyed. We ordered half a dozen types of tapas to share but the restaurant seemed overwhelmed. The waitress brought us all sorts of things in a complete muddle, some we'd ordered and some we hadn't.

As time passed and the claret flowed, we gave up trying to sort it out with her and ate whatever arrived, making a game of guessing what it was. He made me laugh. I noticed too the way the waitress flirted with him as he teased her about the chaos and thought how attractive he was, how charming and wondered why on earth he was bothering with me.

Later, as we waited for coffee, the conversation slowed. My head was thick with wine and my fingers clumsy. Downstairs, the bar was still raucous but the upstairs diners were more subdued.

'How's Gracie doing?'

I considered, pleating my napkin absently in my lap. 'She's different.'

'What do you mean? Tired? Clingy? She's probably still healing, even if it doesn't show.'

'Not that.' I paused. 'She's said some bizarre things.'

He looked surprised. 'Like what?'

'Technically, Gracie died in the accident. I mean, they had to revive her.' I steadied myself, struggling to explain. 'Well, she says she went on a journey and there was a man waiting for her. An angel.'

Matt didn't move a muscle; he just looked at me.

'I know it's weird.' I swallowed. 'The thing is, Gracie's adamant. I've tried talking to her about the fact angels don't really exist and she just gets upset.'

Matt didn't reply. His eyes slid away from me, down to his hands.

'What?'

'What do you think?' he asked carefully.

I shrugged. 'I'm not sure.' I hesitated. 'I think she really believes it's true. That it really happened and there are angels with halos and wings in the sky.'

Matt looked out at the darkness. His reflection hung in the glass.

Finally he said: 'It might be chemical.'

'Chemical?'

He turned to face me. 'Her body was in shock. The brain bleed was extensive. It may have caused a vivid hallucination.' He paused, trying to gauge my reaction. 'It's just a theory.'

I considered. His voice was matter of fact and made it sound so plausible.

'It seems very real to her.' I thought of your happiness when you saw the stained-glass window. 'She talks about the angel as if he's her friend.'

Matt pursed his lips. 'Damage to brain tissue is complex. And it takes time to repair. It's possible, that when she's in a state of deep relaxation and her brain is processing information—' he shrugged '—well, it's perfectly possible she might have a secondary reaction.'

'Really?' I shook my head.

A faint shadow of embarrassment crossed his face. 'I mean, do you mind my asking, are you religious? Because I didn't mean to—'

'Not really.' I said it too quickly. 'I mean, I was christened so I suppose if I was filling in a form, I might put Church of England, you know, but I haven't been to church for a long time. A very long time.' I gave a quick nervous laugh. 'And I never took it literally, Heaven up there and eternal hellfire down below and all that.'

The coffee arrived and we sat in silence while the waitress set out our cups and milk and the cafetière. She tried to catch Matt's eye but he didn't notice her and she withdrew.

Matt poured the coffee and stirred in milk. I did the same. I was preoccupied, uncertain what I did believe.

'They're not uncommon, you know,' he said.

'What aren't?'

'Out-of-body experiences. I've heard of them before from patients who've been clinically dead and then resuscitated.'

I blinked. 'What do they say?'

'There's a classic pattern. Tunnels, bright lights, a sense of detachment, then hurtling back into a rush of sensory experience, of bodily pain.'

I stared. 'That's what she said. She flew down a tunnel and the angel was there at the other end, waiting for her. In bright light.'

He nodded. 'There you are then.'

I narrowed my eyes. My senses were befuddled with the wine and rich food. 'So what are you saying, that people imagine it?'

'Not imagine it, exactly. I'm not saying they make it up. They may experience those sensations, those images, as brain function is compromised.' He pulled a face. 'I'm just saying, Gracie's far from the first to describe something like that.'

I tutted. 'I take it you're not religious.'

'I'm a doctor. I treat the body.' He hesitated. 'But I try to respect what other people believe. When someone dies on the ward, a lot of nurses like to open the window so the soul can depart. Some of the doctors stop them. I don't.'

I stared. 'They think the soul flies out of the window?'

'Something like that.' He shrugged. 'People deal with death in their own way. There's no right or wrong about it. They do what they need to do.'

I twisted in my chair to look out at the lights in the street below. The beams of brightness from passing cars. The pools spilling out from shop windows and bars. The dark mass of people, shuffling and jostling, shouting and laughing, down the crowded pavement. I lifted my eyes and had a fleeting image of Gracie's soul flying in a streak of light through the night sky.

'What are you thinking?'

His voice drew me back into the warmth.

'I don't know. I've been thinking about it such a lot. About why Gracie would say that if it isn't true. Where do people go when they die? My father. He died years ago. I don't believe in Heaven, in pearly gates. It makes no sense. But if I try to imagine him as dust, as not being, not existing and, well, that doesn't make sense either. He was such a strong personality. He knew so much.' I paused. 'I don't understand where he went.'

He reached over and put his hand over mine. It was kind and comforting and I stroked his long fingers.

'Were you very close to your father?'

No one had asked me about him for years. I opened my handbag and pulled out my wallet, opened it. There were two clear plastic pockets inside for photographs. On one side was a picture of you, my love, all bunches and a beaming smile. On the other there was a washed-out old Polaroid from decades ago. I'd found it in Mum's house when I was sorting through papers.

I looked about your age, three or four. We were posing by the Royal Pavilion at Brighton. I was in a cotton summer dress and strappy sandals. Mum and Dad stood together behind me, their hands protective on my shoulders. Their faces looked impossibly happy. Mum must have been barely thirty then, younger than I was now.

'He worked in a hospital too. Not a doctor though. A technician.'

'He looks kind.' He nodded, smiled. 'And that's your mum?'

'She's still around.' I paused. 'Well, just about. Dementia.'

He shook his head. 'I'm sorry,' he said simply.

Afterwards, we set off together for the Tube, threading our way through the groups cascading onto the pavement from pubs and bars. He took my hand. I felt awkward at first, then relaxed into the warmth of his fingers, their firmness. It felt safe.

I had an acute sense of his body, now loosely attached to mine, of his breathing, of the muscles in his arms, his shoulders. I sensed the tension in my own body as it imagined being touched.

My mind raced ahead. He'd said his flat was close by. If he asked to come home with me, I'd say no. I rehearsed the words in my head: *I've had a wonderful evening, Matt, but it's a bit soon. I don't think I'm ready. And Gracie—*

'There's something I wanted to say, Jenny.' He slowed his steps and I kept pace with him, my eyes on our moving feet. 'Look, I can see things haven't been easy. What with Gracie being ill. And Richard and everything.'

My cheeks grew hot. My hand felt heavy in his.

'I really like you. This isn't just about Gracie. I want to get to know you properly, you know? If you like.'

He seemed bashful. A different man from the confident doctor who strode down hospital corridors and swept me off for curry that night. I smiled in the darkness.

'It's been a while.' I hesitated. 'I nearly bottled out tonight, you know.'

'I know.' He looked round and we grinned at each other like fools for no good reason. 'If I hadn't grabbed hold of you, you'd have run screaming the other way.'

We'd almost reached the Tube. A bright cone of light flooded out into the street from the concourse. We both slowed our pace as we approached it.

'So where's the flat?' I paused to look.

On the far side of the road, just beyond the Tube station, a large square stretched into the darkness, bordered by railings. The trees rose tall and black against the night sky. It was surrounded by grand Georgian mansions.

He pointed down a much narrower street beyond the square. 'Just down there. Second block on the left. Flat twenty-two.'

'Handy.'

'Not bad, as long as you don't want to swing any cats.'

I wanted to see it. You learnt a lot about someone from their home. But it also felt too much, too intimate, to suggest.

'Well,' he said.

I opened my mouth, ready to give my prepared speech about not wanting to rush things, to take my time. I didn't need it.

'Thanks, Jenny. It's been a lovely evening.'

'Thank you.' I tried to sound casual. 'It has.'

He smiled down at me. 'I bet we've both got an early start in the morning. Can I call you?'

I nodded. A moment later, he drew me to one side, out of the flow of passengers and into the shadows, cupped my chin with his hand and touched his lips to mine, so softly I felt almost cheated. His cashmere coat brushed against my legs as he moved to walk away.

It was only then that I remembered something I'd meant to ask him.

'Matt!'

He turned back.

'Intensive care at Queen Mary's. What floor is it on?'

He looked surprised. 'Paediatric ICU, where Gracie was? Five. Why?'

'Five.' I nodded. 'Thanks. I just couldn't remember.'

He hesitated, considering, then added: 'But Paediatric A&E is on four. She'll have gone there first.'

He disappeared into the crowd. I went through the turnstiles and started down the escalator to the platform.

Four. That's exactly what you'd said.

CHAPTER 21

'Gracie! Stop it!'

You pulled at my hand like a dog straining on a lead.

'Please, Mummy.'

We were coming back from the park and I was laden with shopping. My feet ached. I wanted to go home and have a cup of tea but you persisted, trying to drag me sideways off the High Street towards the church.

'Please, Mummy. I want to see Mr Michael.'

'Saint Michael.' I wished I'd never told you his name. 'He's not a real person, Gracie. You know that. He's pretend.'

You understood the difference between real and pretend. Heaven knows, your small life was already filled with animals in books and cartoons who talked and rode bicycles and went to multi-species playgroups, with dolls who had tea parties and a stuffed bear who was your best friend. You believed in them but you also knew, at a different level, that it was play.

But now you frowned. 'He isn't pretend.'

I sighed. I knew you. You were tired and if I tried to force you home, you might just tantrum.

'Quickly then. Just for a minute.'

You dashed off joyfully at once, darting ahead of me down to the railings and through the gate into the churchyard. I shook my head and plodded after you. It was a church. You were three. Whatever the reason for it, surely this fascination wouldn't last long?

The church was heady with the smell of flowers. Arrangements of lilies and roses bloomed alongside the altar and at the back of the church. The afterglow of a wedding, perhaps.

You went running to the front, the lights on the heels of your shoes flashing as they hit the stone flags. You stood for a moment beside the metal stand of votary candles, mesmerised by the three burning flames. Then you tipped back your head and looked up at the stained glass, at the robed man from another time and the vanquished serpent at his feet.

'Hello, Mr Michael.' Your voice was high and chirpy and full of warmth. I slipped into a pew close to the front where I could watch you.

When I was your age, it was Sunday School every week. Nothing too heavy. Pictures of angels with wings and God in Glory on clouds and the usual Bible stories in which Noah's Ark and the Good Samaritan dominated every year and there was a lot of colouring and sticking to fill in time before Communion when we could rejoin our parents.

I resented the older girls from school who were allowed to stay with the adults during the service. They lorded it over the rest of us because they were invited to take the bread and wine while we just lowered our heads for a blessing.

One by one, girls ahead of me got their white confirmation dresses and floated around in them, showing off the frills. At the altar, they placed their palms together in prayer, a far-away holiness in their eyes, glorying in their big moment. Later, the dresses were dyed red and worn to the school disco.

I didn't stay long enough to earn mine. I kicked up such a fuss about Sunday School that our family attendance dropped to a trickle, then finally stopped.

Now, I got to my feet and wandered through the empty church to the Lady Chapel off to the side. It was more intimate than the main body of the church, a miniature space with two short rows

of pews and a simple crucifix on the altar. Vases of white lilies stood on either side. I sat for a moment and thought about your angel. He was there in the hospital, you said, watching. He saw me sticking back Minnie Mouse's ear. Trying to put things right.

I closed my eyes and tried to sense him. The chapel smelled of polish and I wondered who cleaned it. My mother used to rub down the woodwork at home every Saturday morning with a yellow duster and white wine vinegar. I used to make fun of her, said the house smelt like a fish and chip shop.

I thought of my father, how gentle he was. And humorous. Spending all day in a hospital lab looking at germs. My mother starched his long, white lab coats every Saturday and ironed them on Sundays with my school blouses, hanging them all in a row along the back of the kitchen door. I was only thirteen when he went to work one morning, no sign of a weak heart, and never came home again.

I ran into the house from school that day, bursting with excitement because I'd been picked for the hockey team and stopped short in the kitchen, stunned by the sight of my mother, slumped at the kitchen table, her face red and swollen, a wet handkerchief balled in her hand.

A neighbour, Mrs Tebbit, sat next to her. The teapot was on the table and they were using the wrong mugs.

'Now, Jennifer,' Mrs Tebbit said. 'Mummy needs you to be a very brave girl.'

'Why?' my mother said, and I felt she was asking me. 'He was in a hospital. Why didn't they save him?'

Now, in the stillness of the church, a door banged. The door to the café, perhaps. I looked round to check on you. You were crouched on a flagstone, tracing the engraved letters with your finger and murmuring to yourself.

A prayer board hung at the back of the chapel and I stopped to read the cards. Poorly written, most of them, with spelling mistakes. *Thank you for many blessings. Please guide Gregory at*

this difficult time. God give Harry strength in his ill health. Prayers for Amy and Keith and family for God's help to bear their loss. A child's loopy writing: *Please get Daddy a new job.*

On impulse, I took a card from the pile and wrote in neat block letters: *Please look after my dad.* I looked at what I'd written, felt ridiculous, crushed the card and pushed it into my pocket. If he could see, he'd be laughing his head off.

I was just about to round you up and leave when the vicar, Angela, came into the church. She padded soundlessly on low, soft shoes.

'Hello again.'

I nodded to her. You were sitting on a pew, swinging your legs and looking through a sheaf of notices. You seemed in a world of your own.

She pointed me to a pew and sat beside me, looking forwards but talking sideways. Her voice was low, not quite a whisper but never loud enough to disturb the dusty silence of the building.

'How are you?'

For a moment, I wondered if she mistook me for someone else. 'Very well, thank you.'

A silence. 'Have you lost someone?'

I started and she gave me a sudden quick look.

'That's what brings most people here. Loss of one sort or another. You looked so deep in thought.'

'Did I?' I felt myself flush. 'Well, my father, a long time ago. I was thinking about him.'

'I'm so sorry.' The big feet in their soft black shoes shuffled a little on the stone. 'Shall we say a prayer?'

I could hardly say no. I was, after all, in her church. I couldn't explain that you'd dragged me there against my better judgement.

'What's your father's name?'

I hesitated. Again, I sensed that if he were watching – which I doubted – he would be scoffing. *Honestly, Jen. Look at yourself.*

'John. John Walker.'

I put my hands together in my lap and bowed my head and willed her to get it over with. I hardly listened as she murmured a short prayer. I was too busy wondering if you'd noticed what was happening, if you could hear, and how to explain it to you afterwards.

'Were you very close?'

'I don't know.' Images of my father crowded into my mind. Coming home in his lab coat, smelling of chemicals. Pottering at weekends in leather slippers. The back of his neck as he drove, towering over my mother at his side. His ruddy arms, sleeves rolled up, as he gardened. 'I think so. He died when I was a child.'

I expected her to come out with some comforting Bible verse or some chat about God working in mysterious ways. She didn't. She just sat quietly. The low hum of lorry and bus engines rose and fell between us.

'I keep thinking about him,' I said. 'Gracie had an accident, you see. She was in hospital. It's brought it all back.' I swallowed. 'I miss him.'

'When my grandpa died,' Angela said, 'I tried to phone him in Heaven. Not from home. I thought it would cost too much. I saved up my pocket money and went to the phone box at the end of the street and dialled a random number. I thought God would guide my finger and put me through.'

I turned to look at her, trying to imagine her as a child. 'What happened?'

She smiled. 'A man answered and I put the money in and of course it wasn't Grandpa at all; it was a complete stranger and he was very kind but I was so disappointed. I didn't forgive God for a long time.'

You jumped down from the pew, glanced over at us, then wandered to the edge of the altar and plopped down onto a stray hassock there.

She too turned to look at you. 'How's Gracie now?'

'OK.' I hesitated. 'She worries about dying. I mean, she asks me impossible questions, like whether I'll die. I don't know what to say.'

'That's a tricky one.' She turned to face me. 'What do you tell her?'

I considered. 'I flannel. I mean, of course I'll die. I can't say I won't. But I don't want to frighten her either.'

'Ah.'

In the café, someone called goodbye and a door slapped shut.

'I never lie to children,' she said. 'Sometimes it's surprising how much they understand.'

I paused. 'So what do you tell them?'

In Sunday School, they used to talk about God in white robes, sitting on a throne in Heaven with angels at his side. *Think of the most wonderful place you've ever been*, they used to say, *and it's even better than that, all the time.*

'I try not to be specific.' She paused. 'They need space to work it out for themselves. It's like explaining how big God is or how He can be everywhere at once.'

I hadn't meant to talk so much, but she was such a good listener and the church felt a safe place and the words just came.

'My daughter was in a car crash. The other driver died. A young woman. Gracie nearly died too. Well, technically she did for a while. She's fine now. But she's convinced that she saw an angel after she died and—' I hesitated, looking up at the stained-glass window and the stiff, medieval figure of the saint with glowing halo, doing battle with a serpent '—and she thinks he looked like Saint Michael. That's why she keeps wanting to come back here.'

Angela sat very still at my side. 'And what do you think?'

I exhaled, blowing breath noisily out of my cheeks. 'My friend says it's chemical. Something to do with the way the brain heals.'

She didn't reply.

'But one or two things she said… I don't know. Little things. Odd things. Things she couldn't have known.'

It was a relief to talk, to talk to a stranger, to admit how confused I felt.

'I've never thought much about Heaven.' I gave her a quick look. Her face was calm. 'But it's bothering me, the way she talks about what happened. I don't understand it.'

'Maybe you don't have to understand.' She sounded thoughtful. 'Maybe that's OK.'

I lifted my head. 'Really?'

'We only find answers when we're ready to hear them.'

You jumped on and off the low altar step, glancing across at us from time to time. When I got to my feet, you came running over.

You climbed onto the pew and knelt next to Angela, looking her directly in the face.

'Hello.'

'Hello, Gracie.'

The two of you shared a smile. I sensed how comfortable she made you feel and felt a pang of exclusion.

'Come on, my love.' I gathered together my bags. 'Time to go.'

I expected Angela to get up too, to make room for me to leave. She didn't.

'We have a small group here once a month.' She hesitated, reading my face. 'Older people mostly, but some younger ones too. Tea and cake and a chat. A lot of them have lost someone. You should come along.'

'Oh, I couldn't, I mean, I don't think –' I stuttered, trying to not to show how horrified I felt.

'It's very informal.' She reached out a hand to pat my arm. 'Do pop in. Even if you don't stay. It's eleven o'clock on Friday, in the café. The next one's on the eighteenth.' Her expression suggested we'd somehow reached an agreement.

I blinked, feeling wrong-footed.

'Bless you, Jennifer. You won't regret it.' She smiled. 'For one thing, it's jolly good cake.'

She pulled herself to her feet at last and moved sideways into the aisle to let me out.

As I moved on, she said: 'See you on the eighteenth. Don't forget, will you?' Then, as we drew away from her, your hand now grasping mine, she said: 'God sent you both here for a reason, Jennifer. I know He did.'

I didn't answer. I just wanted to get the two of us out of there as quickly as possible.

CHAPTER 22

You were crayoning. Another one of your shining drawings, all yellow swirls. Your concentration was so fierce that you didn't look up when I came to sit beside you at the kitchen table.

'That's very bright.' I pointed to the tiny stick figure in the middle of the sun-storm. 'Who's that?'

You frowned. 'I can't do it.'

I patted your shoulder. 'Of course you can. You can do anything.'

'I can't.' Your voice rose in a wail. You grabbed the paper and screwed it into a ball, threw it across the table.

'That's a shame.' I picked it up, smoothed it out on the tabletop. 'I like it. It has a lot of energy.'

'No!' You were annoyed now. 'I can't get it. The crayons aren't right.'

I hesitated, not understanding. 'Can't get what?'

'That place.' You were beside yourself. 'Where Mr Michael lives. I *told you*.'

I didn't know what to say. All those drawings, the worn-down yellow crayon, suddenly swam into focus. 'That's what you're trying to draw?'

You gave me a look of contempt and climbed down from your chair, ran out into the sitting room. A moment later, a furious banging as you hit your toy bin with a stick. I sat quietly, looking at the scrunched drawing on the table and the deep scores in the paper from your furious strokes, your attempt to reproduce an atomic burst of light.

I left you for a while and waited until the banging subsided. Then I came through with a plastic pot of raisins and a beaker of milk and sat on the carpet with them. You came over to join me. Your movements were weary. You looked miserable.

You sat on my lap and I stroked your hair from your face. I handed you the milk and you drank without enthusiasm, painting a thin white moustache on your upper lip, then reached for the pot of raisins.

'Are you sad, sweetheart?' I sat with my arms round yours as you steadily munched. 'Because of the accident?'

I hesitated, wondering if I was reading you correctly. You seemed restless and distressed, as if your emotions were too powerful for you to handle.

'It's OK, if you are. It was sad, what happened.'

You were quiet for a little while. You were facing forward, away from me, and when you did finally speak, I didn't catch the words.

I leaned forward. 'What was that?'

'Can we go to Venice?'

Your voice was a mumble and I strained to hear.

'Venice?'

'Is it a long way?'

You were making no sense. 'Why do you want to go to Venice?'

You raised your head, your chin defiant. 'Mr Michael told me. That's where Catherine came from.'

I shook my head. 'Catherine?' I searched my mind for a girl called Catherine at nursery, in a story, in a television programme.

You twisted round to look up at me, your eyes solemn. 'Auntie Ella's little girl.' You hesitated as if you were working something out. 'Why don't she and Daddy ask me for sleepovers any more? Are they cross with me?'

I tightened my arms round you. 'Oh no, Gracie. You mustn't think that. Daddy does want you to have sleepovers.' I hesitated,

thinking of Richard. 'He wants that very much. It's just that I love having you here with me.'

You reached the end of the raisins and spent a moment using the tip of your finger to hook the last one from a corner of the pot. I sat quietly, puzzled, wondering where this story about Catherine had come from. Ella couldn't have children. Richard had made a point of explaining that to me when he first broke the news that he was leaving. He seemed to expect me to feel sorry for her, as if it were only fair that if I had you, she should be allowed to take him.

'She really liked me, Mummy. I cuddled her.' You made a cradle with your arms. 'Like this. She's teeny-weeny.'

My mind raced. I thought of the neat stick figure, set in an explosion of light.

'And Auntie Ella's her mummy?'

You nodded. 'So we're sort of sisters, aren't we?'

'But Auntie Ella hasn't got any children, Gracie. You know that.'

You shrugged. 'Mr Michael says Ella sent her to him to look after because... because something bad happened so she couldn't stay with her mummy. He looks after lots of children.'

I turned you round on my lap to face me, your legs astride mine and held your arms, trying to force you to look at me.

'Gracie, my love, do you think this was another dream?'

'Stop it.' You squirmed and lashed out at me, struggling to get free. 'I met her! I did.'

I tried to think of books with girls called Catherine that might have given you the idea. 'What did she look like?'

You twisted away. 'Red hair and a nice face and stripy trousers.' You considered this. 'I said I wanted to take her home with me but Mr Michael said I couldn't. But he said maybe I could see her in Venice. So can we go? Please?'

You looked relieved once you'd finished speaking, as if you'd transferred a weight from your shoulders to mine. You ran across

to your books and began to pull them out and pore over them, picking through the pages.

I went through to the kitchen to make myself a cup of tea. I stood, dazed, leaning against the counter as the kettle boiled, watching you through the doorway. Catherine? I didn't know a child with that name. Neither did you. And why Venice?

Wherever this strange story had come from, you seemed instantly happier now you'd shared it. By the time I poured the tea, you were sitting by the toy bin, rifling through an assortment of hand puppets and a threadbare woolly sheep, chatting to yourself, lost already in your own world.

CHAPTER 23

'Daddy!'

You bounced on the bed, eyes shining, giddy with excitement.

Richard fell to his hands and knees on the carpet and crept over to you, starting your old game together. He'd called the following day, asking to come round after work and you were as pleased to see him as I was. You ran to jump on his back, clung on as he bucked and twisted and neighed.

The towel I was folding, still damp from your bath, hung limp in my hands as I watched. The two of you rolled about on the floor, Richard's shirt rising, showing the rounded flesh of his stomach above the waistband. Your eyes were joyful as you wrestled, as he swung you, ending with a bear hug.

You wriggled out of his arms.

'Take them off, Daddy!' You pointed at his shoes. 'Take them off!'

'You sure about that?' Richard looked amused as he prised them off, brandished his feet. 'Stinky smelly socks.'

I knew what you were thinking. Shoes meant he was about to leave. You wanted him to stay.

Richard read the bedtime story. The two of you cuddled up in the lumpy armchair, his broad, strong body curled round your smaller one. You rested your head against his arm, drowsy but safe. This was how it was meant to be, the three of us, cosy here in this home we bought together, made together. Richard looked happy as he held you, giving his all to the story. The strain eased from

his face. He was never a handsome man. Not to other people. But he was kind and loving. And loyal, I'd thought.

Afterwards, once we'd settled you with your bear and kitty cat and rabbit and the rest of the menagerie, his mood stayed thoughtful and a little sad. I watched as he kissed you goodnight, stroked your hair from your face. Maybe he did miss us. Maybe the accident had forced him to think how much he loved you and what he'd lost. Maybe visits like this reminded him of how happy we once were.

He followed me through to the kitchen, chewing the corner of his lips. He pulled on his jacket and I reached out and put a hand on the top of his arm, smiled.

'She's thrilled to see you.'

He turned away, embarrassed.

'She loves you, Richard.'

I had the sudden urge to say much more. To open up to him all over again. To say: *when I see you with her, I feel as if I still love you too, you do know that? Maybe it's not too late, after all. If you've realised what a mistake you've made. If you want to ask my forgiveness and ask if we can start again...*

He mumbled: 'I love her too.'

I turned to the bottle of red wine, open on the counter from the previous night, and poured two glasses, handed him one. He came through to the sitting room with me, his wine in one hand and his shoes bunched in the other, and perched on the edge of the settee.

'So.' His eyes strayed to the vase of roses on the mantelpiece. Matt had sent them, to say thank you for our date. I'd made sure they were prominently displayed; I couldn't help it. 'How are things?'

I shrugged, settled into an armchair across from him. 'OK. You know.'

'Not missing work?'

'Not really.' I bent down to pick up a stray piece of Lego on the carpet. I wasn't going to admit to him that I worried about money. I'd be earning again soon enough. 'Gracie keeps me busy. She seemed to need me more now. Since the accident.'

He bent over and started to loosen his shoelaces, push on his heavy shoes. 'She'll be off to school soon.'

'She will.' The house would be so quiet all day without her. So tidy. 'I'll miss her terribly.'

He finished with his shoes and sat stiffly, sipping his wine. His awkwardness was all the sadder because he was once so at ease here.

'Has she ever talked to you about Venice?'

He didn't look as if he were listening.

'She says she wants to go. I just wondered where it came from.'

Richard shrugged. 'A story?'

'We've never read a story about Venice. Don't you think it's odd?' I went to the table at the far end of the room where clutter gathered and picked up one of your pictures to show him.

'Look.' I held it out. It was one of your yellow light drawings, small dark figures set in a landscape of brilliance. 'She keeps drawing these. She says it's where she went when she had the accident.'

Richard glanced at it. 'She's always liked colouring.'

'It's more than that.' I paused. 'It's weird. She seems to... know things. And she keeps talking about death and what happens when people die. Maybe she ought to see someone. Like a child psychologist.'

He looked tired. His cheeks were soft pouches and the flesh below his chin was slack round the bone. When we first met, he was a lean young man, hungry in every sense, keen to make his mark on the world. That was a long time ago.

I put the picture down. 'I just thought you'd be interested.'

Richard leaned forward, cradling his glass. 'I think she's fine, Jen. Really. Let her be.'

'*Let her be?*' I looked up, stung.

He shook his head. 'I just mean—' He looked as if he wished he hadn't spoken. 'Maybe she needs her own space. Don't over-analyse everything.'

We sat awkwardly for a few moments, Richard staring into his wine.

'What's that supposed to mean?'

He sighed. 'Forget it, Jen. Really.'

He got to his feet, set down the glass. For a moment, he looked about to leave, then he crossed to stand at the window, looking out into the darkness. His reflection in the glass was ghostly.

'I want to see Gracie more often.'

His tone was suddenly formal. I steadied myself.

'Not just here. Not just a story at bedtime and the odd day out.' He paused. 'I want to take her properly again. For weekends. Maybe on holiday.'

He turned to face me. He spoke quickly but gently, as if he'd already practised the words, as if he was relieved to get them out.

'I know you've been through a lot. We all have. You've wanted to cling to Gracie since, you know, the accident. But she's my daughter too. You need to let go a bit, Jen.'

My pulse quickened. 'It's her, isn't it? Ella.'

'What is?' He sounded cross. 'Why I want access to my own daughter? It's nothing to do with her.'

It was everything to do with her. I didn't trust her. I took a deep breath.

'The accident was partly her fault too, you know. Ella was on the phone when the car swerved. Did you know that? Shouting. She was distracted.'

He made a guttural sound. 'God help me.'

'It's true. Gracie told me.'

'You should hear yourself.'

He moved away from me, towards the door.

'Gracie's your daughter. You can see her.' I got to my feet, grabbed at his arm. 'But not *her*.'

'That's ridiculous.' He shook his head. 'She adores Gracie. And Gracie loves her. You should see them together. Honestly—'

'Oh please.' I bit my lip, steadied myself. 'I don't want her anywhere near Gracie. I don't like her. I don't trust her.'

'She told me not to come.' He prised my fingers off his jacket. Our faces were close and for a second, I thought he was going to kiss me. Then he pulled away.

'I'm filing for divorce, Jen. I'm sorry. Ella and I want to get married. You understand?' He paused, reading my face. 'She's going to be part of Gracie's life from now on. Whether you like it or not.'

He disappeared into the hall. I wanted to follow him but I couldn't move. The sitting room seemed suddenly very cold. I found the edge of the armchair and sat on the arm with a bump.

Richard strode back in, buttoning his coat. His face was tight.

'I'm trying to do this the nice way, Jen. But if you make this difficult, I'll go to court. I'll have no choice. Don't make me.'

I couldn't answer.

A moment later, the front door banged as he let himself out. I sat quietly, perched there on the edge of the chair, my feet juddering on the carpet, listening to his footsteps fade in the street. I reached for my glass, drank off a gulp of wine.

It was over. He was going to marry her. She was taking Richard from me and she wanted you too. My stomach tightened. I bent over, one arm clutching my front. A dribble of wine slipped out from the bowl of the tilted glass and ran down my leg. The smell rose at once, rich and lush. I shook my head, thinking of you asleep upstairs. I'd nearly lost you once, my love. I wasn't going to lose you again.

CHAPTER 24

Ella

There's something about me that Richard struggles to understand. I'm not even sure I understand it myself.

He's kind, you see. And fundamentally, he's happy. And I'm not sure that I ever can be.

I'm in love with him. That's not an issue. Before I met him, I didn't think this battered old heart of mine was capable of it, but it's proved me wrong. But it's precisely *because* I love him so much that I'm afraid of being with him. That's the part he can't grasp. I'm afraid of corrupting him, you see. Like a virus.

My mother used to say that some people were born to be happy and some weren't and if you were one of the unlucky ones, there wasn't a whole lot you could do about it. It went through me like a knife when she said that.

I was eight years old and we had just walked past our local crazy man in the street. I don't know what his name was, but everyone knew him by sight. He stamped along the pavements and waved his arms about and muttered expletives to himself and shouted in shops for no reason. We all knew to steer clear. And here was my mother saying that a life of happiness or unhappiness was determined at birth. That frightened me to death. I knew which she was and I didn't want to be the same.

My mother didn't have a bad life, but something deep inside her was broken and whatever I did, however hard I tried, I couldn't fix her.

One of my clearest memories of childhood, perhaps my first, is of my mother sitting at the bottom of the stairs and crying, her face buried in her hands, her shoulders shaking. Silent, like an old film. I must have been three or four. I was terrified and the worst of all was that there was absolutely nothing I could do.

I sat beside her and wrapped my arms round her leg and tried to give her a cuddle but she didn't seem to notice me. After a while, she pulled away and disappeared into the kitchen and I sat there a few moments longer, miserable, listening to her blow her nose, then light the gas and fill a pan with water, carrying on like the martyr she always was.

The hall was poky and there was no fitted carpet, just a shabby rug. Cold air came up from the cellar between the floorboards and made me shiver. But I stuck it out for a while. It was an instinctive offering, a bargain with God. I made a lot of deals with God as a child. *I'll suffer this cold if you sort out my mum.* He couldn't. She was born to be unhappy. *What if I'm the same?*

It took a while for me to feel strong again, after the car accident. The physical aches, of course, but also the shock. I love little Gracie, how could anyone not? If she hadn't come through... well, it doesn't bear thinking about. I don't know how I'd have lived with myself. I'm tough, but I am human, whatever her crazy mother thinks.

Then, one Saturday morning, I was leaving my yoga class when Richard called me on my new phone. It was a relief to have a new number, believe me. Well worth the hassle. Suddenly, for the first time in a long time, the only calls I was getting were from Richard or close friends. Calls I actually wanted.

'Where are you?' Richard sounded stressed. 'Fancy a drink in the park?'

A bit odd, but why not?

We sat huddled together on a bench and he produced sangria in a screw-top bottle. He'd mixed it himself at home and brought

proper glasses and everything. I should have realised something was up. One of my favourite love songs is about a couple drinking sangria in the park, just hanging out, happy together. Richard is so thoughtful, it's overwhelming.

So we drank the sangria and watched the ducks on the pond. And the kids. A small girl with wild eyes wobbled as she struggled to ride her bike. Her father ran along behind, steadying the frame, cheering when she finally pedalled off on her own. A toddler, still unsteady on her feet, tried to throw bread to the ducks but dropped most of it. I looked away.

Richard's cheeks were flushed. The sangria had gone to his head. He got to his feet, packed away the bottle and wrapped the glasses carefully in kitchen towel. That care, that attention to detail, made me smile.

'Right,' he said, straightening up. 'Lunch. Shall we try the Chinese over there?'

I smiled. 'You hate Chinese food. You always say it's greasy.'

'You like it.' He shrugged. 'They do dim sum. Come on. I'll be fine.'

He'd planned the whole thing. I only found that out afterwards when, halfway through the meal, the waiter brought a single spring roll on a plate and Richard started fussing, pushed it towards me.

'That's yours.'

'I didn't order spring rolls.' I stared at it. One spring roll? What kind of order was that? I picked up the plate and handed it back to the waiter. 'Sorry. Wrong table.'

The guy shrugged, looked across at Richard.

'Leave it. Thanks.'

I pulled a face. 'Richard, it's not mine. I didn't—'

'Please. Ella. I ordered it. For you.'

I stared at him as he reached forward, picked up the spring roll with his chopsticks and held the end to my mouth.

'Try it.'

I steadied his hand – he was never very good with chopsticks – and bit into the end, humouring him. My teeth touched metal and I sprang back.

'What the – Richard, there's something in it.'

I was thinking: a bolt or a screw or who knew what. Then I saw his face. Excited, anxious, beseeching. I felt sudden panic as light dawned.

'It isn't…?'

He gave a sheepish smile, pulled open the doughy wrapper and lifted out a ring. A damn great solitaire, sticky with sauce. Before I could stop him, he'd scraped back his chair and was down on one knee, right there in the middle of the restaurant.

'Ella. I love you so much. Please. Will you do me the honour of marrying me?'

The whole restaurant was looking. I couldn't speak. His eyes were so full of love, of hope, I couldn't bear it.

'Get up.'

'Ella?' He looked uncertain. 'You haven't given me an answer.'

'Of course I will!' My heart thudded, blood surged in my ears. I don't know what I felt. Overwhelmed, for sure. Embarrassed. And panicked. 'Now get up.'

He beamed, shuffled forward and pressed the warm, wet ring onto my finger, then kissed me lightly on the lips, a discreet, public kiss. When he sat back on his chair, the waiters, watching in a huddle from the service area, gave a ragged round of applause.

I shook my head. 'I can't believe you just did that.'

Richard reached for my shaking hand. The ring slid, unfamiliar, down my finger.

'It's an auspicious date today.' The tension which had hung about him all morning was gone. He looked happy. 'They helped me choose it. The eighth, super-lucky, apparently.'

'Really?' I didn't know what more to say. I thought of Richard in a jeweller's shop, picking out the ring. Coming to the restaurant

and planning the spring roll surprise. I thought I knew everything about him but I didn't. I couldn't look him in the eye.

Later, as we lay together in bed, the ring, washed now, sparkled on my bedside table.

'Richard, are you sure about this?' I asked him. 'I mean, really?'

'Totally, absolutely, one hundred per cent.' He tightened his arms round me. 'I love you, Ella. I want to make you happy,'

That's what chilled me. It brought back that memory of my mother, crying at the bottom of the stairs, and my three- or four-year-old self, chilled to the bone, striking a bargain with God that He never kept and the terror, which had never left me since, that maybe I was the same as her and the same as the crazy man who yelled in shops, and that maybe there were people like Richard who were born to be happy in this world and I was simply not one of them.

CHAPTER 25

Jennifer

As well as sending flowers, Matt phoned every night that week. Sometimes he was at work and we only managed a quick chat. Other nights, we talked for an hour or more. He discussed articles he'd read in the paper and the new film he wanted to see and told me about the homeless man, Barney, who sat on the pavement near the hospital holding a cardboard sign reading 'Smile!'. Matt picked up a cappuccino for him on his way in, when he bought his own coffee. Barney was very exact: skinny cappuccino, two sugars.

And when Matt wasn't talking, he listened. I wasn't used to anyone showing interest in me, in my day, in my opinions. It took me a while to get used to it. He teased me when I hesitated before answering or asked him: 'Really? Do you really want to know?'

We arranged to go out again that weekend, for a quick dinner and then a film. I was still nervous but excited too. I counted down to it. Planning what to say, what to wear. And then, that afternoon, Dianne called – my one and only decent babysitter – and said she was so sorry, she had flu.

I texted Matt to cancel. *V sorry. Another night?*

He texted straight back. *Tonite! Can I cook at yrs?*

I stared at the screen. I was flattered, I admit it. He seemed determined to see me. But I couldn't imagine him cooking in my kitchen.

Another text appeared. *I'll bring it all. OK?*

He arrived just after seven, earlier than I expected. The spillage from your egg on toast was congealing on the front of my blouse, my hair was in clumps and I was only halfway through reading you a bedtime story.

He carried a bulging gym bag into the kitchen and swung it onto a chair. The zip was open at one end, showing groceries.

I hesitated. I wasn't sure I wanted to leave him alone in the kitchen, in our home.

'I'm not quite ready.'

He nodded. 'That's OK. There's just a few things I need.'

He ran through a list: weighing scales, cheese grater, knives, saucepan, wooden spoon. He looked over each item as I rooted it out of a cupboard or drawer, then lined them up in a neat row along the back of the kitchen worktop. He bent over to peer at the cooker, trying the ignition button to check that the hobs lit.

'Fine. Leave me to it.' He looked directly at me for the first time since he'd come in, gave me one of his disarming smiles, then turned away again, opened his bag and drew out ingredients with his long fingers. A packet of Gruyère cheese. Parmesan. Roquefort. Fresh pasta. He placed everything on the counter with precision.

He saw me watching and said: 'I hope you like cheese.'

'Mummy!' Your voice, from upstairs, was shrill.

Black pepper. Double cream. A bottle of mineral water, then a bottle of red wine. Valpolicella. He really had brought everything.

'I'm fine,' he said. 'Really.'

You were sitting up in bed, your arms round your bear. Other cuddly toys jumbled along the wall. A pile of picture books sprawled across your knees. You handed me the one we'd been reading.

'Where were we?'

'Has he come? Is he downstairs?'

'If you mean Matt, yes, he is. He's going to cook Mummy's dinner.'

You looked thoughtful. 'Why?'

I shrugged, opened the book. 'Because Mummy's hungry. Now, let's see what happens, shall we?'

I curled on the bed beside you and put my arm round your shoulders and you leaned in, your head against the soft pad of my arm. I started to read.

'Is he a doctor?'

I broke off, looked down at you. 'Matt? Yes. In the hospital. Remember?'

I went back to the book. Your expression was preoccupied for a while, as if you were thinking this over. Finally, your attention returned to the story.

When we reached the end, you cuddled down with your bear and I tucked you in.

'Goodnight, my love.'

A faint clatter of pans from downstairs. The rising smell of garlic.

'Where's Grandpa, Mummy?'

'Grandpa?' I reached out and stroked your soft hair. 'I don't really know. I think he's having a long sleep.'

You hesitated, considering. 'If I go to sleep, will I see him?'

'You might. If you dream.'

You lifted your head from your bear, your face creased. 'What if it's a bad dream?'

'Then shout out and I'll come upstairs and chase it away.'

You smiled, pulled your bear close again and put your head on its stomach.

I got up. As I crept away towards the door, you said: 'Matt won't play with my railway, will he?'

'I'll make sure he doesn't.'

'Promise?'

'I promise. Now go to sleep.'

I gave myself ten minutes to brush my hair, change my blouse, spray a little perfume.

Downstairs, Matt was in full swing. He'd taken my apron from its hook on the back of the door. It was so short on him that it barely covered his groin, slightly absurd where it strained round his waist and yet endearing. He was standing at the stove, tossing spaghetti in sauce with the wooden spoon in one hand and a salad server in the other. The tiles at the back of the cooker were splattered. The kitchen was warm with steam, rich with cheese, with garlic, with homeliness.

He looked round, used his forearm to brush his mop of a fringe out of his eyes.

'Glass of wine?' He gestured to the worktop.

The Valpolicella was open, breathing. Two wine glasses sat beside it. He must have found them in the end cupboard, a dumping ground for things I didn't use. They had broad rims and coloured green stems. A Christmas present, years ago, when Richard and I were still a couple and people bought everything in pairs.

'I'd pour you one but I'm just—' Matt's hands rose and fell as he tossed the spaghetti on the hob. Whatever he was doing, it looked complicated. I poured us both an inch of wine and hovered there, warming it in my hands. He'd rolled back his sleeves and the muscles in his forearms bulged as he worked. I leaned back against the counter, admiring them. He looked like a TV chef, all confidence and quick, competent movements.

'I'm nearly done. Five more minutes and it goes in the oven.' He nodded to one of my casserole dishes, greased and ready beside him. 'You go and sit down. I'll be through in a minute.'

I sat on the settee and crossed my legs, then, self-conscious, got up again and moved to one of the armchairs instead. I sipped the wine, looked through to the kitchen. Matt bent over the casserole, spooning the pasta, then tipping up the pan and scraping out what was left.

The wine tasted rich and full. The oven door closed. The kitchen tap ran in a furious stream. *My God, he even washed up.*

I sat very still. It had been so long since someone had cooked for me, I could barely remember how it felt. It was a relief to have someone else take control.

'Everything OK?'

He stood in the doorway, wiping his hands on the apron. I opened my mouth to ask him to use a towel, then closed it again.

'I think so. All quiet upstairs.'

He pulled off my apron, came through with his glass. 'You read a good story.'

I must have looked baffled because he pointed to the monitor. Of course. I'd forgotten. He must have heard every word.

'One of life's joys,' I said to the mantelpiece. 'Reading stories.'

He perched on the arm of the settee with the air of a man who had his mind on the oven. 'I heard her ask about her grandpa.'

'My dad. She asks about him sometimes. Wonders where he is.'

'Ah.'

'It's not easy, being three. Life, death, what happens to people. She's got a lot to figure out at the moment.' I hesitated. 'And it'll be divorce, next.'

'Divorce?'

A long pause. 'Richard's putting pressure on. We're not actually divorced, you see, just separated. I suppose I always thought maybe—' I felt my mouth twist and stopped, studied the carpet, then took a few breaths. 'He and…' I couldn't say her name out loud. 'Anyway, he says he wants to marry her.'

My breathing sounded loud in the room.

Finally, Matt said: 'How does that feel?'

'Not great.' I looked into my glass, my stomach tight. 'But, you know, what can I do? If that's what he wants.'

After a while, I dared to raise my eyes and found him watching me. His expression was gentle.

'You really try, don't you? To do the right thing.'

'I try.' I lifted the glass to my mouth but didn't drink, lowered it again. 'I don't seem to manage very well.'

A piece of green Lego lay under the table. A scrap of torn paper. A raisin.

The alarm on Matt's watch went off and he fiddled with it.

'Saved by the bell.'

'Not at all.' He gestured towards the kitchen, got to his feet. 'I'll be five minutes.'

I sat in silence and thought how strange all this was, how little I knew this man and yet how much I felt understood by him. Noises drifted through from the kitchen as he bustled about in there. It was peculiar to hear another person clattering my dishes, opening and closing my cupboards and drawers.

Finally, he appeared in the doorway and called me through. I entered the kitchen and stopped in my tracks. It looked like someone else's kitchen, a happier one, full of life and warmth.

The kitchen table, usually so grubby, was covered with a fresh white linen cloth. He'd set it for two with the Royal Derby crockery. It was a wedding present from Richard's mother and kept in the cupboard for special occasions, which meant it hadn't been used for years. Linen serviettes, pleated restaurant-style, stood upright on the side plates.

'Have I done the wrong thing?' His hands were in my oven gloves. He stood, poised, by the oven door, his eyes on my face. 'I hope I haven't—'

I shook my head. 'No, it's just—' He'd made such an effort. For a moment, I thought I might cry.

'Come on. My cooking's not that bad.'

I crossed to the table, set down my empty glass and sat, my hands clumsy and large in my lap. He bustled round me, serving his pasta with a flourish. The top was crusty with baked cheese.

'It smells wonderful.'

He reached over and re-filled my glass.

'I love cooking,' he said. 'Well, I love eating. Maybe that's it.'

He wound spaghetti in the bowl of his spoon like a pro. 'Anyway, I didn't want to miss seeing you this evening. I was looking forward to it too much.'

I concentrated on eating, my eyes on my plate.

'I thought we could still watch a film later, if you like? I brought some videos…'

I shook my head in disbelief. 'You think of everything, don't you?'

He looked pleased. 'Maybe not everything.'

He started to talk about an experimental play at The National. He'd seen it at the weekend, he said. Very Ionesco. It was a name I remembered from my English degree but hadn't thought of since. The only theatre Richard liked was Noël Coward.

Matt sat back in his chair, inhabiting the space as if it were his own kitchen, his own home. His hands drew pictures in the air as he talked. I wondered who'd been to the theatre with him or if he'd gone alone. He didn't say.

The sight of him, here in my kitchen, was a wonder to me. When he leaned back, he almost touched the fridge, which was empty apart from Diet Coke and TV dinners and plastic containers of pre-schooler food. It was decorated on the outside with crayoned pictures fastened in clumps by magnets showing faraway places. Places I had dreamt of visiting before you came along, before I married Richard.

When he got to his feet to offer seconds, I suddenly said: 'It must seem dull to you.'

He looked round, eyebrows raised: 'What must?'

'All this.' I hesitated, embarrassed. 'Living with a three-year-old and never going out.'

He shook his head, brought the hot dish back to the table to spoon out more.

'You do go out.'

'Not much. I used to.' The rising steam made the kitchen shimmer. 'I used to go to the theatre, to the cinema. I used to have friends, you know. I was a normal human being. But then—'

'I know. I get it, Jen.' He dropped a spoon of pasta onto my plate and smiled. 'I think you're amazing. You adore Gracie. Of course you do. Of course she comes first. And anyway, it won't be forever.'

'What won't?'

'Just—' he hesitated '—the way things are at the moment.'

'What do you mean?' I just wanted Matt to keep talking, to find out what he thought about me.

He twisted his fork in the spaghetti and started to eat again.

'You do what you have to do. That's all. I take the long view.' He waved his fork in a sweep of the kitchen. 'It's a privilege to be here. Don't you see? We'll go to the cinema another day.'

He sounded as if he'd really thought about it. His tone was so gentle, so thoughtful, that my eyes moistened and I had to bite down on my lip.

I stared down at my plate. 'OK, but I do wonder why you're bothering.'

'Then I can't explain.' He sat beside me at the table. 'Now, make me happy. Finish your pasta.'

Later, he produced dessert. Two slices of chocolate cake, the upmarket type that you buy by the slice in a patisserie.

As we ate it, I asked him more about his work. He seemed more comfortable talking about the shift system and the quirks of his colleagues than about actual cases.

'It must be hard,' I said. 'Working with sick children.'

I thought of you, such a tiny scrap of a person, lying on that hospital bed, all tubes and machines. I didn't know how anyone could bear that, day in, day out.

'You just have to be professional.' His tone was sad. 'It has its rewards.' He paused and seemed to retreat into a memory. 'Some children respond dramatically once you hit on the right treatment.

It seems miraculous, sometimes. And the look on their parents' faces when that happens…' He smiled to himself.

'They must adore you.'

He gave me a sideways look. 'Let's just say, I get a lot of whisky at Christmas.'

'And single mums eager to meet after hours?'

'One or two.' He raised his eyebrows. 'Even dads, once in a while.'

I laughed. 'I've been meaning to ask you something. Why can't I find you on the Internet? Haven't you written any cutting-edge research papers or anything?'

He pulled a face. 'You've been looking? I'm flattered.'

I tutted. 'Don't tell me you've never searched for me.'

He spread his hands. 'Of course. But what did I find? Just some stuff you'd written about personal development and setting goals. No scandal at all.'

'I could have told you that.' I narrowed my eyes. 'The hospital website's useless – everything is password-protected.'

'You tried?'

'Of course. I wanted to read up about you.'

He laughed. 'They've got a terrible photo of me up there. Doesn't do me justice at all.'

'Still, I'd like to see it.'

He shrugged. 'The hospital worries about giving out information about doctors. And they're probably right. It's better to keep a low profile.'

He was looking past me, towards the darkness of the garden. 'Why?'

'Some cases are very painful. You know?' He finished his dinner and set down his knife and fork.

I sat back in my chair, watching him, waiting.

'There was a little girl last year. Bernadette. Bernie, they called her. She was perfect – blonde curly hair, long eyelashes, you can imagine.' He paused.

'What was wrong with her?'

'Meningitis. I had her transferred to ICU in a matter of hours but she deteriorated so rapidly, there wasn't much we could do.'

'How awful.'

He got to his feet, gathered up our plates and clattered them as he stacked the dishwasher.

'Anyway, let's move on.' When he turned back to me, his face was resolutely cheerful. 'Time for a film?'

I made coffee and carried it through to the sitting room. He handed me the films to look through.

I was still reading the covers when Matt leaned over and touched the corner of my mouth with his finger, lifting a stray flake of chocolate. He held it to my lips to eat and, without thinking about it, I took the tip of his finger in my mouth too and drew on it. He froze. I sensed the tension in him, the tremble in his muscles. I shivered and reached again with my mouth for his finger and drew on it a little more firmly, teasing the tip by making a warm circle with my tongue.

He lifted the videos from my hands and set them on the coffee table, then opened his arms to me. His mouth was firm and moist and tasted of chocolate and, as it closed on mine, I was the one grabbing at him, reaching my arms round his broad back to clutch at the folds of his shirt, hurrying him along even as he tried to steady me. He eased me backwards onto the settee and lifted my shirt, put his strong hands on my hips and kissed his way slowly between them. I arched my back and sucked in my stomach.

He lifted his head. 'Just relax.' He looked more closely, arrested by something in my expression. 'Is it too soon?' He hesitated. 'Should we stop?'

Stop? He had to be joking. Suddenly, lulled by wine and good food, my problem wasn't uncertainty; it was frustration. It had been a long time. Richard and I hardly bothered with sex after you

were born. With the new lumpen look of my pouched stomach and fallen breasts, I didn't think I could ever feel desirable again.

Matt was studying me, his eyes intense. 'I want to look after you, Jenny. You know that?'

'Do you?' I blinked.

'We're two of a kind,' he whispered, 'you and I. You feel it too, don't you? We're good together.'

He turned his face back to my stomach and I felt the warmth of his tongue on my skin. After a few minutes, he unbuttoned my jeans, slipped them down to my knees and, pinning me there, pressed his mouth between my legs.

I sank back into the settee and groaned. Images rose and fell through the alcohol in my head – the sensible black pants I'd put on that morning and which he was now peeling away, the rough wool of the rug in my parents' house where my first serious boyfriend, Jimmy Brent, had taken my virginity when I was eighteen, and you, my love, lying on this same settee on my chest, downy haired and smelling of milk and the most perfect, beautiful creature I had ever imagined.

When I couldn't bear it any longer, I pushed him off and scrambled to unbuckle his belt, tug at his jeans. He lifted himself on top of me and we rocked together, creaking the settee springs. The clock chimed on the mantelpiece and I counted with it as far as three and then gave up.

I clung to Matt's shoulders, his back, as if I were pulling myself out of a pit, out of hellfire itself, and when I came, I heard myself cry out 'God in Heaven!', and then struggled through the fog to remember who had said that, close in my ear, whose voice was it, before remembering it was Richard, there in the hospital, when you came back to me in a rush of life and I fell into his arms, surrounded by rushing doctors and beeping machines. My God in Heaven.

'Are you alright?' Matt's voice was breathy in my ear.

His weight, collapsed on top of me now, pressed the air from my chest and it was a relief to be crushed. I didn't have the power to answer him. I lay with my face in his neck, shuddering, sloppy with crying, coming back to myself from whatever place he'd taken me, limp and ready to sink into sleep against him.

He raised himself on his arms to look down at me. Cool air flooded in.

'Are you OK?'

I nodded, wiped a hand across my eyes and settled him beside me, lying tightly together on the settee, arms wrapped round each other to stop ourselves rolling off onto the floor and buried my face in the sour-sweet smell of his neck as my breathing slowly slackened.

CHAPTER 26

I woke up in darkness with a stiff neck and a dry mouth. Your blanket, which usually lay across the back of the armchair, had been unfolded and spread over my waist. The settee creaked as I moved and remembered where I was, what had happened. I was alone on the settee and lay still for a moment, listening.

A rustle of movement. I lifted my head. No sign of Matt. The kitchen was dark. The noise came again. A creaking sound, coming from the monitor, from your bedroom.

I pulled myself to my feet, and put on the pants and jeans that still lay in a heap on the carpet. Matt's clothes had gone. I peered at the clock. Twenty-past twelve. It felt later. The road outside was silent. I knew every rickety floorboard, every creaking joint in that house. Heaven knows, I'd spent enough hours creeping round it in darkness, first when I was pregnant and restless at night, sneaking down for bowls of cereal at two in the morning, then, once you came to join us, the blur of day and night as you fed and cried at all hours.

The only sound as I made my way with care up the stairs and across the landing to your bedroom was the pump of blood in my ears. I always kept the door ajar so I could easily check on you. I slid through the doorway and stood for a moment, adjusting to the deeper darkness of your bedroom with its heavy curtains and blackout blind.

My hand flew to my mouth. The black shape of a figure, a man, was solid in the armchair by your bed. Silent and still, hunched forwards in the shadows.

I whispered, without thinking: 'Richard?'

'It's me.' He rose to his feet, quietly crossed the room. 'Matt.'

I stared, then felt a sudden surge of anger. 'What the hell are you doing?'

He looked embarrassed. I pointed to the door and stood there, glaring at him as he left, then went to check on you. You were on your back, sound asleep, your arms sprawled above your head, your hair wild on the sheet. I stroked your cheek, my fingers trembling, tucked the duvet round you and headed back downstairs.

He was standing in the middle of the sitting room. He strode across as I entered, put his hands on my shoulders. His eyes were apologetic.

'I'm so sorry. I was looking for the bathroom. I saw the door ajar and I went in to check on her.' His eyes, on mine, were anxious. 'I didn't mean to intrude. I'm sorry.'

I was still shaking. I thought of him, sitting silently in the darkness beside you. 'How long were you there?'

'Not long.' He hesitated. 'Ten minutes, maybe. I didn't mean any harm.'

He hung his head and looked down into the lattice of his fingers. A long silence. The clock chimed half-past.

'I miss Katy.' His voice was quiet.

'Your daughter?' I sat down in the armchair across from him, my eyes on his face. My hands were tense and I folded them in my lap. He didn't look threatening. He looked defeated.

'She's seven now.'

I sat on in the silence, waiting, willing him to explain.

'It didn't end well. She – Katy's mother – she was very depressed after the birth and started taking antidepressants. They weren't good for her. She had a—' he hesitated '—a sort of breakdown.'

'What happened?'

He looked exhausted. 'She became really paranoid. I could see it was the medication but she wouldn't believe it, she wouldn't

listen to me. She imagined all kinds of things. That I was undermining her all the time. Once someone says that, it's hard to carry on. Her parents were sympathetic, they could see what was happening, but it was hard for them too.'

I went to sit beside him, put my arm round his shoulders. 'That's awful.'

He leaned in towards me and let out a deep sigh.

'Well, anyway, she ended up leaving and taking Katy with her. She was four at the time, not much older than Gracie is now.'

'Was there someone else?'

'No.' He shrugged. 'Not that I know of. She just said she wasn't happy. You know, the usual stuff. She wanted her space, thought she'd be better off alone.'

'And what about Katy?'

'She doesn't let me see her.'

I frowned. 'She can't stop you, can she?'

He blew out his cheeks. I thought how gentle he was with you, how he made you laugh. He'd be a devoted father, I could tell.

'You're her father. You have rights too.'

'Through the courts?' He sighed, shook his head. 'Not easy. She was never diagnosed with anything, just baby blues. And family courts, well, they tend to side with mothers, not fathers. My brother, Geoff, is a policeman, a detective. He talked to a few people. A lot would come down to her word against mine.'

He hesitated, his face tight. 'I just don't think I could face it.'

'So you don't see her at all?'

He shook his head, ran his hands over his face.

'I get snippets of news about Katy. She's learning the violin. Doing well at school. She would, she's bright. Our mothers speak to each other, once in a while. They're Katy's grandmas, after all. But that's it.'

I stared at the shadows on the wall, the reflections through the curtains from the streetlights. He was such a caring man, so

kind. I thought of the way he'd comforted me when you were so ill, helped me to pick myself up again.

'Is that what brings you here? Because Gracie reminds you of her, of Katy?'

He shook his head. 'You bring me here. The way you are, the way you love Gracie. My ex was never like that. Never like you.'

He turned to me, opened his arms and drew me to him. His breath was warm in my hair. 'I'm sorry. I wanted to talk about it earlier. I suppose, if I've seemed a bit cautious... well, the timing never seemed right.'

I nodded. It had felt as if a piece were missing. Now I had it.

'You must miss her terribly.'

'Not my ex. I hated her for a while. Not any more. But Katy—' He paused. 'It's hard. Hard for me. Of course I miss her. It tears me apart. But I try to tell myself not to be selfish. If I went into battle with her mum, kicked up a fuss, what would that do to her? Kids can't cope with all that. It's confusing.'

He paused. He turned away from me as if he were wrestling with himself and didn't want me to see.

'But I try to keep some sort of contact. I send her presents, you know, for Christmas and her birthday. But I don't know what she has, what she likes. I don't even know if she gets them.' He paused. 'Or if she even remembers me.'

'That's terrible.'

His jaw was clamped shut and I saw his struggle to collect himself before he could speak again. 'Perhaps that's why I under-stand a little bit of what you're going through. You can't bear the thought of anything happening to Gracie. I see that. I suppose I can't bear the fact I lost Katy, in a different way.'

I hesitated, tried to imagine it. 'Maybe, one day.'

'Maybe.' He nodded but his face was without hope. 'I think that, sometimes.'

'I'm so sorry. I don't know what to say.' I reached out and stroked his cheek. 'And I'm sorry I was angry. It was just—'

'You were right to be. I should have explained.'

He gathered his clothes and shrugged on his coat.

'I should go. Get some proper sleep.'

In the hall, we kissed and it was a new kiss, less electric and a little sadder, as if we knew each other differently as a result not just of the sex we'd shared but because of what he'd told me.

Before I crawled into bed, I came into your room and sat there in the armchair. My eyes slowly adjusted to the darkness. I tried to see it all though his eyes. The framed pictures on the walls, old-fashioned scenes from nursery rhymes: Humpty Dumpty tottering on a wall, a fine lady on a white horse, the princess and the little nut tree. The shelves of stuffed toys and storybooks. The creams and wipes and thermometer and bottles of medicine lined up on the top shelf, out of your reach.

You were curled round now, your arms clutching your bear. I leaned forward until I could hear your soft breathing, so close that I could smell your hair, your skin.

I tried to imagine it. To imagine Richard taking Gracie away from me and never being allowed to see her, to hold her. I thought of Matt going alone into toy shops twice a year, into department stores, struggling to choose presents for a little girl he no longer knew. Not knowing if she opened them.

He was right. I couldn't bear to lose you. You weren't just what made life worth living. You were my life.

CHAPTER 27

The next couple of weeks were pleasantly warm and we spent our afternoons at the park. I pushed you on the swing or bounced up and down at the other end of the seesaw or played hide and seek in the bushes.

You were far more fun to be with than the other mothers and nannies who sat with hunched shoulders on the benches, gossiping and drinking their takeaway coffees. As I listened to your giggle and looked at your lovely, laughing face, for the first time in a long time, I felt truly happy.

I still worried about you. Some nights, I lay awake in bed until late, watching the shadows of passing cars swing across the walls and worrying about everything you'd said. About Mr Michael. About Catherine, your imaginary friend with stripy trousers and red hair. But at other times, during the day, my breathing eased. You were my life and now, tangled up with us both, there was Matt too.

He had made himself a regular fixture. We went out often – to dinner, to the theatre, to the cinema. Once or twice, to cut back on babysitting, he came round to cook. The days varied to match his rota but that didn't matter to me. I was always here.

We found ourselves in that mad, heady phase of falling in love when we couldn't get enough of each other, couldn't stop talking, could barely tear ourselves away each evening. Was it like this with Richard, at the beginning? It must have been but I couldn't remember it.

Slowly, Matt began a battle to win you over too. At the weekend, he sometimes took us both out. For an afternoon on a steam railway, run by volunteers. To a fun fair with a mini-carousel and dodgems. To a new petting zoo. He always had a surprise in his bag when we met up: a chocolate bear or a packet of sweets or a small toy. You seemed to love him as much as I did.

Some evenings, you specifically asked, as I tucked you up with your bear and kissed you goodnight: 'Are you seeing Uncle Matt?' Your voice was excited, as if you were pleased for me.

I didn't push it. I wasn't sure how you'd feel if he stayed all night and was still here at breakfast. Besides, I quite enjoyed the fact that we parted like teenagers in the small hours, sexed up and crumpled, sleepily kissing goodnight at the door. Somehow it was more romantic than waking up side by side in the morning with bad breath and messy hair. The time for that would come soon enough.

But through it all, the memories of the strange things you'd said just wouldn't go away.

'Can I talk to you about something? It's bothering me.'

We were lying on the sitting room floor in each other's arms, post-dinner, post-sex, under a throw. Matt's body was strong and warm and smelt pleasantly of fresh sweat.

He tipped back his head to look at me. 'What?'

'This is going to sound mad. OK?'

'OK.'

'Gracie says she met a little girl, that time she went off and saw an angel. Mr Michael.'

'When she was—' he hesitated '—unconscious?'

'Yes.' I swallowed. 'She calls her Catherine. Says she's got ginger hair. Anyway, she said she was Ella's daughter, you know, Richard's girlfriend? I thought that was odd because she can't have children. Richard told me.'

Matt tensed. 'Does Gracie know that?'

'I think so. She does now.' I paused. 'And there's something else. She said Ella sent Catherine to Saint Michael.'

Matt gave me a sharp look. 'What's that supposed to mean?'

'I don't know.' I paused. 'Gracie's very intuitive. I wonder if she's picked up on something. Maybe a sense that Ella doesn't like children. Doesn't like her around. And this is her way of telling me.' I considered. 'After all, what sort of mother wouldn't do anything to hang on to her own child?'

'Not one like you.' He lifted his hand and stroked the line of my chin. 'You're an amazing mum.'

'I don't know about that.' I kissed his fingers. 'Weird though, isn't it?'

'Very.'

'Why would she say that?'

He lifted himself onto his elbow and looked down at me. His chin was dark with stubble. 'How much do you know about Ella?'

'Not much. Not really.' I swallowed, tried to put my sense of foreboding into words. 'I keep thinking… maybe this is Gracie's way of warning me.'

He studied my expression. 'Warning you about what?'

'That she doesn't feel Ella wants her. Maybe doesn't even feel safe with her.'

He nodded. 'You're really worried, aren't you?'

'Maybe I'm being stupid.' I hesitated. 'But why would Gracie make it up? What if she's right? If Ella does resent her being around? How can I let her spend weekends with them if I'm not sure?'

He kissed the tip of my nose. 'Richard's her father. He might not be a very good one, I mean, given what happened between you two. But he's good with Gracie, isn't he?'

I nodded, thinking of them horsing around, having fun.

'So he's got a right to see her, hasn't he?' His voice was gentle. I thought of his situation, denied access to his daughter. It was cruel.

'He has.' I paused. 'But she hasn't.'

His eyes were on mine, watching me. I saw my face reflected there, pinched and anxious.

'I don't trust her. What if she's unkind to Gracie, as a way of getting back at me?'

He hesitated. 'Why would she want to do that?'

I shrugged. There was hatred between Ella and me, there always had been, but I didn't know how to put it into words. 'I just don't trust her.'

He sat up. 'You really feel threatened by her, don't you?'

I nodded miserably.

'But you know what Gracie's saying makes no sense. If Ella can't have children.'

I sat up beside him, thinking. 'Is there any way of finding out?'

'If she's infertile?' He looked baffled.

'Not that exactly. If she's had a child. If Catherine could possibly be real.'

He widened his eyes. I reached out, put my hand on his shoulder and stroked it. 'You're a doctor. Can't you get access to birth records or hospital records or something?'

He frowned, looked away. I sensed his unease.

'Please? Just to put my mind at rest.'

He didn't answer for a moment, then turned back and kissed me lightly on the lips. 'It's not exactly ethical. But if it means that much to you, I suppose I could try.'

He wrapped his arms round me and pulled me close to him. When he spoke, his breath was warm on my neck. 'I'd do anything for you, Jen. You must know that by now. Anything.'

He got to his feet, padded through to the kitchen and came back with a pen and a piece of paper.

'Write down what you know about Ella and I'll check the NHS database. And I'll ask Geoff too. He owes me a favour.'

'Your brother?' The police officer.

'Keep it to yourself, won't you?' He gave me a sharp look. 'He shouldn't really.' He paused. 'Well, neither should I.'

He pushed the paper into his pocket, kneeled on the floor in front of me and stroked his hand down my thigh. I felt better already, less alone.

'Try not to think about it,' he said. 'Until we know a bit more. Can you?'

Later, as he gathered together his clothes and got ready to leave, he said: 'I was thinking. Maybe we could go away somewhere fun for a weekend. The three of us.'

I hesitated, trying to imagine it. 'Where?'

He shrugged. 'What do you think? Euro Disney?'

'Gracie really wants to go to Venice.' I thought of your eager face, asking where it was. 'Something about meeting this imaginary girl again.'

He laughed. 'Is that what she said? Love it.' He was still smiling. 'Hate to break it to you but it sounds to me as if she's having you on.'

I frowned. 'You think so?'

He nodded. 'Not in a bad way. Kids do that. She's a smart girl. She picks up on things. Maybe she's heard about Venice somewhere and thinks that's her best chance of getting you to take her.'

I wasn't convinced. You always struck me as such an honest child. 'Maybe.'

'Gracie'd love Euro Disney. She hasn't been, has she? Well, then. We could take the Eurostar, stay a couple of nights.'

He smiled down at me and I tried to smile back. I wasn't convinced. Once you got an idea in your head, there was no moving you.

'Or a posh hotel here, if you like? A country house with an indoor pool for Gracie and open countryside.'

I couldn't answer. He drew me closer and kissed the top of my head, rocked me for a moment in his arms. Suddenly, he pulled away and looked me in the face.

'You really want to take her to Venice, don't you?'

I nodded. I was embarrassed. It felt ungrateful, but I really did. I thought it might settle you, lay all this to rest.

'Well, it is a great city.' He hesitated, looking down at me. 'If it'll make you happy, then sure. Let's go.'

'Really?' I buried my face into the warm, musky creases of his neck and hugged him. 'Thank you.' Here was a man willing to love me and Gracie too. As if she were his own.

'She'll love it.' He drew back. Our faces were almost touching. 'All those boat trips. The world's best pizza. Ice cream. No cars.'

When I kissed him, his lips smelled of coffee and red wine.

At the door, as he pulled on his coat, he said: 'Let's do it. I'm serious. Not this weekend – I'm on call – but the one after that.'

'About the cost… I mean, is Venice expensive?'

He put his hands on my shoulders, kissed me lightly on the lips. 'My treat. Doctor's orders. OK?'

He was gone before I had the chance to argue, leaving me standing there, heavy with wine and food and sex.

In the kitchen, I cleared away and stacked the cutlery, the plates, mugs and wine glasses in the dishwasher. My movements were slow. My body still carried the feel of his fingers, his mouth. I saw my reflection in the dark window and lifted a hand to rake through my dishevelled hair. My cheeks were flushed and my eyes looked wide and brighter than they had for a long time. Since Richard left and I thought I was finished with all this.

I leaned over to sling the empty wine bottle in the recycling and, as I moved, I saw a sudden streak of light behind me, reflected in the dark glass. I span round. Nothing but a shadowy, empty kitchen.

I gripped the edge of the sink and leaned into it to catch my breath. I closed my eyes. I was tired, that was all. It was nothing.

It must have been a shaft of light that bounced off the curve of the bottle.

But as I steadied myself, my fingers trembled with a more visceral feeling. A feeling that something of my father was there in the quietness with me, watching as I bowed my head and gathered my strength.

Venice, he seemed to say. *Beware, my child. Beware what you may find.*

CHAPTER 28

Ella

Richard's buoyant this evening. He comes rushing home to drop news at my feet, a dog bringing a stick to its master, tail wagging, eyes imploring, desperate to be stroked. He starts before he even takes off his coat.

'Guess what? She's seeing someone.'

No need to say her name. She haunts us like Banquo.

I pull a languid face, acting cynical. I try to make him laugh, when he talks about her. There's no point in discussing her any other way. Richard knows full well what I think. He should toughen up, not let her manipulate him, the way she does.

'Whoopity-doo. Some desperate single parent she met at nursery? I can just see him. Paunchy, balding, his wife died and he's all sad and lonely. Don't tell me: his little Ermentrude and Gracie are best friends?'

Richard smiles, shakes his head. 'Someone she met at the hospital. And it sounds serious. He's taking her to Venice next weekend. Gracie too.'

I start, putting my hand to my stomach, feeling suddenly sick. He doesn't see. He's too busy unbuttoning his coat, hanging it in the hall, heading through to the kitchen to fix us both gin and tonic.

'What's for dinner?'

He lifts the lid of the pan on the stove and smells the Bolognese sauce, sticks a spoon into it and turns to me as he tastes. I am leaning against the doorway. My face says too much.

'You alright?'

'What's his name?'

'She did say…' He frowns, trying to remember. 'Why?'

I can't answer. He moves round the cupboards, pulling out glasses, adding ice, pouring gin. The new bottle of tonic cascades in a fizzing plume over his hands when he opens it and he swears, dashes to the sink, looks down, cross, at the spray across his trousers.

When he's mopped them with a tea towel, he comes over, hands me a drink. I gulp it.

'Mark? Mike?' Already he's heading past me towards the sitting room and the lure of the television news. Over his shoulder, he adds: 'Good luck to him, I say. I hope they're very happy. Now maybe she'll leave us alone.' He considers. 'Just as long as Gracie likes him.' Then, his tone slightly wounded as he settles on the settee: 'Anyway, thought you'd be pleased.'

I don't know how I get through dinner. I can barely eat, but he doesn't seem to notice, he's too focused on the crisis in the Middle East or Sudan or wherever the hell it is. I don't care.

All I can think is: *it's him. It must be. And she has no idea.*

Later, I run a long bath and take the radio into the bathroom with me. I turn it up loud and lie flat and low in the landscape of bursting bubbles, my hair floating in tendrils round my head, the oval mask of my face just protruding above the water.

My breathing is shallow and quick. I try to press myself down into the smooth, hard plastic of the bath, to hide myself away. I'm afraid to close my eyes. I'm afraid of the darkness that waits for me there, that draws me always back to Venice and the dreadful days there I've struggled so hard to forget.

CHAPTER 29

Jennifer

'It's amazing, Matt.' I stand in a daze at the long windows. 'It's unreal.'

The louvred shutters are fastened back, revealing the broad sweep of the Grand Canal in Venice. The sunlight glimmers and gleams in streaks across the moving water below, stirred into life by a dozen boats of all sizes, passing at all speeds. A low breeze carries the tang of brine. Voices call, distant, soft with lilting Italian. On the far side, the fabric of the tall, thin buildings that face ours is crumbling with age.

Matt, coming up behind me, slips his arms round my waist and kisses the top of my head.

'See that big dome, there on the left?' He lifts a hand to point. 'On that spit of land, sticking out into the water. That's Santa Maria della Salute. One of the plague churches. Sixteen something.'

I crane to see. 'Plague churches?'

His breath is warm in my hair. 'It came on the ships. Decimated the population. Anyone who showed signs of it was shipped out to an isolated island, out there in the Lagoon. Rather a brutal sort of quarantine but it worked. When it was over, the survivors built churches to thank God. That's one of them.'

I twist round to him. 'How do you know all this stuff?'

He smiles and lowers his face, touching the tip of his nose to mine.

You run in from the adjoining room, eyes shining and throw yourself between us.

'Mummy, come on!' You tug at my hand, pull me after you into the small second bedroom. Bear sits on the pillow, propped up by pink satin cushions. An oil painting, an old-fashioned scene of a regatta on the Grand Canal, with the Rialto in the background, hangs grandly over the bed. Your shoes, already kicked off, lie on a sheepskin rug. Your coat is abandoned on an antique chair with a plush red seat and gilded wooden back.

I smile to myself. 'Do you like Venice?'

You nod, jump onto the bed and bounce there. 'It's springy.'

I wonder how much of this you'll even remember.

'We must say a big thank you to Uncle Matt. Remember? This is his treat.'

I look round at the antique furniture. The walnut wardrobes with ornately carved doors and gold handles. The polished side tables with spindly legs. The mirrors with massive frames, which bounce reflections of the sunshine from one to another across the room. Heaven knows what it all cost. Matt just waved me away when I offered to pay our share.

'Can we go out?' You're on your feet again, manic with excitement. 'Can we?'

I nod. 'Let's go and explore.'

That first afternoon, Matt takes us to a café in St Mark's Square and we sit right there at the edge of the Piazza, gazing out across the vastness of the square towards the Basilica. A string quartet plays behind us, fighting against the noise of declaiming tour guides and the chatter of tourists. Matt orders drinks in Italian from a waiter.

When the glasses arrive, you point past your cloudy lemonade to our glasses, your forehead crumpled with interest.

'Fizzy orange.' You look at me. 'Is that yours?'

'They're spritzers.' Matt lifts his glass to show you. Light pours through the glass, turning the colour to fire. 'They're for grown-ups. Don't think you'd like them.'

I take a sip. Sparkling white wine and water, ice cold. And another taste too within that, something bitter.

'What's the orange?'

'Ah. A secret ingredient, known only to Venetians.' He leans closer as if he's confiding a great truth. 'Aperol.'

We share a smile, just from the pleasure of being there, together. The sun throws shards from the marble surfaces around us, bouncing off the expanse of paving stones. I fumble in my bag, find my sunglasses and put them on.

You watch, then ask: 'Are we on holiday?'

'Yes, my love. We certainly are.'

You look out across the square. Small children totter there, reaching for pigeons. Older ones, closer to your age, chase them, sending them scattering into the air in a flurry of feathers, only to settle again a little further away. Here and there, hawkers sell snacks and ice creams and cold drinks. Distantly, their cries drift across: *Panini! Gelati! Bibite!* To the right, at the foot of the Campanile, tour groups cluster, waiting for guides who hold aloft flags or furled umbrellas.

You break in: 'Can I go and play?'

I look at Matt, unsure.

'Of course.' He points. 'Just stay in this big square, OK? Where we can see you.'

'OK.' You slip down from your chair and set off, a tiny figure running out into the vastness of the Piazza, as countless small children have done before you and will do in years to come.

'She'll be fine. No traffic.' Matt reaches for my hand, there on the table, and covers it with his own. 'Happy?'

I nod. 'It's amazing, Matt. I can't believe it.'

'It's special, isn't it?' He looks grave. 'I love this place. It's either a miracle of faith or a miracle of engineering, depending on your point of view.'

'What do you mean?'

'Look at it. Look at what they built on a swamp. All this, here where we're sitting, it's resting on a bed of nails. Tree trunks, thousands of them, driven into the lagoon. That's all that's holding us up.'

I laugh. 'Really?'

'The Venetians are a pragmatic lot.' He grins. 'Smart and self-sufficient. They have a saying here: "Venetian first, Italian second." They stick together. That's how they've survived this long.'

A hawker skirts the café tables, showing off the tourist souvenirs crammed onto his cart. Postcards. Glossy brochures of Venice in half a dozen languages. A string of brightly coloured plastic masks with curved beaks and streaks of glitter down the cheeks. We watch him pass.

'We should come next year,' Matt said. 'For the carnival. *Carnivale*. It's all about masks. Disguise.' He draws his fingers across his eyes, play-acting. 'Here you can be anyone you like. Do anything you like.'

I raise my eyebrows. He leans forward and kisses me. His mouth is soft and the kiss makes my body ache for him. Tonight will be our first proper night together. The first time we share a bed like a normal couple. Fall asleep together and wake in the morning in each other's arms.

He says in a low voice: 'Thank you for saying yes – for agreeing to come.'

'I'm the one to say thank you.' I wave at the Piazza, at the drinks. 'All this.'

He shrugs. 'If we're going to do it, might as well do it properly.'

Out on the square, you've befriended another child and the two of you run in wild circles in the sunshine, chasing each other,

lacing an invisible thread back and forth through the crowd. Even from here, I feel your excitement, your sense of freedom.

I pause, wondering if it was the right time for an awkward question. I sip the spritzer.

'You said you'd been before?'

He looks away into middle distance, slow to answer.

My stomach contracts. I can't leave it there. 'Holiday?'

Finally, he turns back to me, lifts my hand from the tabletop and encases it in his own. *Here it comes.* I have a sudden urge to lean back, to pull my hand away.

'I came here several times but ages ago. A good friend at medical school, she was Venetian. Maria-Eletta. There aren't many of them left, true Venetians. They've all moved out. She came from a very old family, been here for centuries. Very proud.'

He twists and makes a vague gesture back towards our hotel and the Grand Canal.

'They have an amazing old house on the Grand Canal, further down than us. Been in the family for generations. All high ceilings and antiques and sweeping staircases. The bedrooms had tiny wrought-iron balconies over the water. We used to sit there for hours and drink coffee or these—' he points at the drinks '—and just let the world slide by. You know what it's like when you're young. You think you're immortal.'

I don't answer. He seems lost in the memory of it. Of her.

'The house had a particular smell. I don't know if I can describe it.' He hesitates. 'Our hotel's got it too. A sort of worn, fusty smell of age and salt-water and crumbling walls.'

I sit quietly, absorbing this, thinking of the old houses opposite our hotel with their decaying brickwork and imagining Maria-Eletta. A lover, presumably. A brilliant young doctor with the romantic soul of a true Venetian. I wonder again, for the hundredth time, why he's bothering with me.

'What happened to her?'

He pulls a face. 'She came back. We lost touch.'

He lifts my hand to his lips and kisses the tips of my fingers, one by one. His lips are cold from the spritzer. 'Anyway. Long time ago now.'

'Amazing.'

He catches the tone of my voice and smiles. 'Venice is amazing. She wasn't.'

That evening, after we put you to bed, we order room service and sit late over dinner. Matt orders a bottle of our favourite, Valpolicella. My head thickens with the rich food and wine. We leave the shutters thrown open and cool salt air blows in from the water below. Neither of us speaks very much. I'm preoccupied, thinking of the night ahead. Perhaps he is too.

Later, we stand together at the open window, looking out at the Grand Canal. The buildings across the water gleam with falling light, chopped into stripes by half-closed shutters. The reflections dance on the choppy surface of the canal. The water beneath is black and deep.

The breeze reaches in to us, carrying the tinny strains of music and raucous voices. A few moments later, a tourist boat glides past. The deck is strung with coloured lights. People stand along the rail and some wave, giving a general drunken salute to Venice, as they pass.

Matt holds me in front of him, pressing my back and buttocks close against his chest, his stomach, his groin. His arms reach round my body and his hands, warm where the breeze is cooling me, touch my breasts. He trembles against me and bows his head. His lips kiss their way along my neck, my ear. His fingers unzip the back of my dress and pull it loose from my shoulders and it falls to my feet and pools there. He unclasps my bra, reaches round to cup my breasts.

He turns me to face him and puts my hand on his groin. The salt air chills our skin, exposed now to the night, and we press

together, craving each other's warmth. He slips off my pants and presses me against the open shutter. The panels clatter shut behind me.

He goes down on his knees and his lips move to my stomach and I stand leaning back against the smooth wood with one hand caressing his hair, the other on his shoulder. I have at once a glimpse back into the room behind him, now dense with shadow, and, if I shift my head only slightly, a view out into the night, straight down the open mouth of the Grand Canal, past the grand, ornate dome of Santa Maria della Salute and far beyond to the open Lagoon itself.

It's a scene as rich and beautiful as a painting and I imprint it on my memory, even as my legs start to buckle under me and he reaches for me and guides me to the floor.

Across the canal, the double-doors to a broad balcony are flung open and, in a rush, a crowd spills out, loud with drinking.

I whisper: 'They'll see us.'

'Let them,' he says in my ear, and his voice is hoarse, and I realise I don't care either; I'm flushed and free and already revived by Venice, this eternal city, finding again here my younger, undamaged self, reckless and joyful, the self I feared forever lost.

Later, when we are both heavy with tiredness, he lifts me onto the soft double bed and pulls the counterpane over us. He holds me close, warm against his chest, my head on the muscle of his arm, and lulls me to sleep.

CHAPTER 30

Something tugs my arm. A hand, pulling, a low voice whispering. My head is thick and dull and I struggle to come round. Cool air on my skin and the taste of salt.

'Mummy.'

I open my eyes. Your face hangs beside me, level with the edge of the bed, pale and eerie in the half-light. Memory floods in. Venice. We're in Venice. And Matt is there in bed beside me, breathing deeply.

I put out a hand and stroke your hair. 'It's night-time, Gracie. We need to go back to bed.'

'But Mummy…' Your voice is high and thrilled.

'Sssh. Very quiet.'

I manage to slide my feet to the floor, then ease out the rest of my body and straighten up, pointed across to the connecting door.

You stare. 'You haven't got any clothes on.'

I put my fingers to my lips. The gilded edges of the chairs and wardrobe gleam. The breeze blowing in from the Lagoon is chilling. I steer you back to your own room and climb into the narrow bed, make room for you beside me. You put your cold feet on my legs to warm them and reach for your bear.

'Did you have a bad dream?'

You shake your head. 'She's here.' Your eyes are gleaming. 'I can feel her.'

My stomach clenches. 'Who?'

'Catherine!' You shake with excitement.

I stiffen. 'What are you talking about?'

You still look pleased. 'Catherine, silly Mummy. If Auntie Ella is her mummy, is she my sister?'

'Auntie Ella hasn't had children. You know that. Now go to sleep.'

I try to rest your head on my shoulder but you struggle, sit up. My tone has become cross and you look indignant.

'But why?'

'Why what?'

'Why are you saying that? I dreamed about her and then I woke up and I heard her. She's here, Mummy. In Venice. Like she said.' You stop, read my expression more closely. 'What?'

'I'm just tired, Gracie. You've been dreaming. That's all. A dream. Now settle down and let's go to sleep.'

'But—'

'Hush, Gracie. That's enough.'

Your lip trembles and for a moment you look about to cry but you swallow it back and just frown. I wrap my arms more tightly round you and hold you against me, trying to calm my breathing. Your skin is hot. Maybe you're going down with something. You lie still for a moment.

'Mummy, will you miss me when you die?'

'Gracie.' I twist round and try to make out your face. 'What kind of question's that?' Your eyes are anxious. I sigh. 'I'm not going to die. Not for a long time.'

'Not until you're very old?'

'Not until I'm very old. You'll be grown up then.'

Your eyes fill. 'I don't want you to die.'

'I'm not going to die.' I hold you close, rock you in my arms, press my face against the top of your head and breathe in the clean scent of your hair. 'It's all right, Gracie. Mummy's here. Go to sleep.'

Your limbs slacken and your breathing slowly deepens. I lie in the silence, trying to understand you. Waves of light, reflections

from the stirring water down below, ripple across the shadowy ceiling.

As I finally fall backwards into sleep, I'm gripped by a strange sense of timelessness, of confusion, as if the solid lines that usually contain us are warping and shifting, leaving us drifting, any age and all ages, in a world without form.

CHAPTER 31

We start the next day with a lazy breakfast of coffee and hot brioches on the hotel terrace, overlooking the Grand Canal. You kneel nearby on a low wall and hang your arms over the rail, watching the passing boats and waving at the tourists inside. You say nothing more about Catherine and I don't mention it to Matt.

Matt places his chair close to mine, his hand reaching often to stroke my hand or the back of my neck as we sit, lazy. The air is fresh on our faces.

'I thought we could take the *vaporetto*,' he says. 'Out to the islands. They have glass-blowing workshops on Murano. Gracie might like that. Plenty of room for her to run around. Or there's Torcello.'

I nod, only half-listening. He seems happy to take charge and it's a relief to sit back and let someone else organise.

'And this afternoon, do you think Gracie would cope with the Palazzo Ducale, the Doge's Palace? It's stunning. You can't come all the way to Venice and not see it. We needn't stay long. The artwork is fabulous. Just the ceilings alone.'

I try to imagine you staring at painted ceilings. You'll probably last about five minutes. But Matt seems so earnest and if we give you a busy morning, you might be worn out by then.

I smile. 'It sounds great, Matt. All of it.'

*

The clouds are low and dull and it's still too early in the year for most tourists. The first *vaporetti* we see look almost deserted as they glide past. We take a boat that's heading straight out into the Lagoon and sit huddled together on a wooden seat at the bow, overlooked by the crew in their elevated glass cabin.

Your nose wrinkles as you face into the salt breeze, your hair flowing out behind you. You're excited and your eyes gleam. It's the same fervour I saw in you last night when you talked about Catherine. I should be excited too but, watching you, I feel cold with foreboding. I tighten my grip on Matt's hand and press closer to him.

We pull steadily away from St Mark's and the mouth of the Grand Canal and head out into the open swamp. A low mist rolls across the water, veiling everything from sight. The horizon slowly vanishes as water and sky meld together in a formless smudge of white. I have a sense of floating, of becoming untethered, unleashed from the land, from the city, from the modern world.

As the mists thicken, the crew quietens the engine to a purr. It's the only sound in the muffled air. We creep slowly forward as if we're explorers, navigating the unknown. One by one, wooden stakes, hammered into the water to mark channels of safe passage, emerge from the banks of cloud. Each seems a relief, a blessing, handing us forward from one to another through the invisible dangers on all sides.

Now we are far out, in open water. The wind whips low and stings my eyes. Matt rubs my arms and reaches to put his jacket round my shoulders. You delight in it. You jump down from the seat and stand forward against the rail, leaning over, trying to reach the dark water far below with your trailing hand.

'Be careful, Gracie.'

'Relax.' Matt smiles and reaches sideways to kiss the tip of my nose. 'She's fine.'

The men running the boat, dark-skinned Italians, call to you as they work and laugh amongst themselves.

Matt has taught you to say 'thank you' in Italian – '*grazie*' – and you consider it your own special word because it's so like your name. Now you say it endlessly, to everyone. One of the men, younger than the rest and thick-set, feeds you sticky red sweets in shiny paper and you're so delighted that I don't have the heart to stop you eating them.

Eventually, when I'm stiff with cold, the solid outline of a dock appears and the crew, gathered now on the small deck, set about the business of coming alongside. Matt takes your hand as we bump to a halt and the two of you jump off together onto solid ground.

A boatman, a young Italian inked with tattoos, gallantly takes my hand and straddles the gap to help me disembark. The water sucks and laps as the boat knocks against the wooden platform.

'*Attenta, signora.*' The boatman nods to me, smiles. He is young and sure to break foreign hearts when the tourists arrive in earnest. For now, he makes do with charming me. His voice is a song of Venice, drawing out the vowels as if they were operatic. '*Benvenuta a Torcello.*'

You run on ahead down the long, straight path alongside a canal. The island seems tiny, a narrow, largely featureless strip of land that offers little choice but to go forwards. I fall into step beside you and you reach for my hand.

'Where's this again?' What I really mean is why are we here.

'Torcello.' He looks happy and I think how at home he seems here. 'This is where it all began.'

I look round doubtfully as we walk on past deserted cafés, restaurants and small shops selling canned drinks and postcards and guidebooks. The strains of a solitary radio drift through the air, playing a jaunty Italian folksong.

'Does anyone even live here?'

'Hardly anyone. They've all moved out.'

Away from the water, the air becomes heavier and more humid. A fly buzzes in my face and swerves away. Insects buzz at our feet in the scrubby marsh grass. Overhead, birds swoop in from across the water and cry.

We approach a small, shabby square. It has an air of neglect, of abandonment.

'There.'

Matt nods towards two buildings that stand side by side across from us, dominating the piazza. Their walls are made of worn, dull bricks that suggest great age, and the facades are marked out by prominent crosses. The nearest has a colonnade with a low roof, covered with curved terracotta tiles.

A square bell tower rises from the far end of the other, higher building. It soars above everything else on the island.

'That's what we've come to see. *Cattedrale di Santa Maria Assunta.*'

His pronunciation is slightly Anglicised but, like the boatman, his tongue lingers over the music of the Italian. I squeeze his hand.

You're already there before us, a tiny figure waiting outside the arched entrance, tilting back your head to crane up at the walls.

'This was the first church ever built here in the Lagoon when settlers first came, all those centuries ago.' Matt turns to check my expression and hesitates. 'I know it doesn't look much but come and see inside.'

Matt buys entrance tickets and we head into the gloom. The mood changes instantly. The sounds of life outside, of the birds, the insects, fall away to silence. The salt air is replaced by the fug of an ancient, crumbling building and the cloying smell of spent candles and incense. The church has only just opened for the day and we seem to be alone.

I lean in to Matt as he joins me, dropping my voice to a whisper.

'How old is it?'

Matt shrugs. 'It goes back to the seventh century, to the start of Venice. I'm not sure which bits are original.' He looks round. 'The mosaics are ten-something.'

He steers me forward down a narrow aisle. It ends in a high dome, encrusted with gold mosaics. In the centre, a towering figure of the Virgin Mary in flowing blue robes gazes down at me. The infant Jesus sits in her arms, a chubby hand raised as if in blessing.

Matt whispers: 'This is what Venetians were busy making while we were being invaded by Normans.'

I don't answer. I can't. I stand, enthralled, staring up into the vast sweeping curve of the dome. The Virgin Mary's tall, slim figure dominates the entire space, isolated in a sea of shining gold. Her face is gentle and her hands, cradling her child, are full of love. I bite my lip.

'It's beautiful, isn't it?' he says quietly. 'I knew you'd feel the same.'

When I can finally tear myself away, I turn to find you. It isn't a vast church but it's dark with shadow and hidden spaces. Matt, sensing my sudden anxiety, turns to look too. He touches my shoulder.

'You stay here a bit longer. I'll find her. She wouldn't leave without us.'

He strides off at once down the aisle and I turn back to the mosaic, tracing the shapes with my eyes and trying to fix it in my memory. I can't concentrate. Whatever Matt says, I'm worrying. I need to know where you are.

I skirt the main body of the church, hoping to cover different ground from Matt. The windows here are high and small and the columns of dusty light finding their way through the plain glass barely penetrate the darkness. I walk on, peering behind sculptures and ornate thrones, reluctant to call out to you and disturb the silence.

Then I hear it. A giggle. Ahead, in the shadows. Low and stifled.

I creep forward, craning to see. 'Gracie?'

Silence. Then the light, high-pitched giggle again. I follow the sound, sensing the barely audible shuffle of a small body creeping to find a new place to hide.

'Gracie, come out.'

I find myself at the bottom of wide steps. It's the entrance to the bell tower. A notice, giving basic information and the price in four languages, is tattered. A man sits beside it on a wooden stool. He's elderly and unshaven.

I hesitate. 'Excuse me, did a little girl just go up there?'

'*Campanile*,' he says, pointing up the steps with a nicotine-stained finger.

I hold out my hand to show your height. '*Bambina*. Girl.'

He shrugs. I don't know if he understands me or not but he gestures with an open palm for me to pass, to go and see for myself. The thought of you running up there to hide and possibly falling sends me rushing forward.

The stone path is broad and rises gently, falling to steps at the corners. I climb at speed. Blood pumps in my ears and within a few minutes, my breathing is hard. Here, away from the body of the church, I dare to call out.

'Gracie!'

The high giggle bounces down along the curve of the wall.

'Gracie, it's not funny.'

I press on, determined to catch up with you but you seem always ahead. Fitter than me and more nimble. After a while, I stop for breath and strain to listen. Silence. Then the whisper of quick, shallow breathing drifts down to me from somewhere above. I race on.

I'm tired and cross now. *It's not funny, Gracie. It's naughty and it's dangerous. What have I told you about running away? You're old enough to know better.*

Just when the aching in my chest is becoming unbearable, I make a sudden turn and all at once the steps give way to the brightness of daylight and the outside world. Fresh salt air hits my face. I spill out onto the top of the tower and stand, leaning heavily against the wall, blinded by speckled patterns of light as my blood races. I struggle to breathe. Then I turn, scanning the corners of the tower, baffled. I'm alone. It's deserted.

I walk back and forth across the stone floor. The perimeter is enclosed by wire. There's nowhere to hide. You are nowhere to be seen. But I heard you. I sensed you. I followed you.

I am only dimly aware of the spectacular view out across the Lagoon, stretching into the mist, of the breeze cooling my flushed face and lifting my hair from it. I stand at the tower wall and peer down, narrowing my eyes, frightened of seeing what I know is impossible. Perhaps you've somehow climbed, penetrated the mesh and fallen. Could that be possible? But there's no tiny broken body far below. Nothing. My legs, exhausted now, give way and I sit on the cold stone, exhausted and suddenly afraid.

I find you both in a café on the far side of the piazza. You are sitting together at an outside table, keeping watch for me. Matt lifts his hand in a broad arc of a wave as soon as I step out of the cathedral and back into the light.

You don't look up. Your head is bowed over a sundae and you are busily scooping up chocolate and vanilla ice cream. I see as I approach that it's nearly gone. You must have been here all along.

'You OK?' Matt gets to his feet as I join you. His face creases with concern.

I shake my head, sitting down.

'I'm sorry.' Matt looks confused, guilty. 'I thought you wanted some time to yourself. Gracie had had enough so I thought we might as well…' He hesitates, uncertain, says again: 'Sorry.'

'OK.' I let out a long breath, not knowing how to explain what happened, what I heard. The giggles. The child's quick breathing.

'I thought she'd gone up the tower. I went up after her.'

He lifts his eyes to the tower, square and dark against the sky, and he frowns. For a moment, he looks so troubled that I reach at once for his hand and grasp it, eager to pull him back to the present and to me.

CHAPTER 32

It's the middle of the afternoon by the time we return to Piazza San Marco and go to queue at the entrance to the Palazzo. We're all tired. You whinge, pulling on my hand and saying as we inch our way forward towards the entrance: 'I don't want to see it, Mummy. I'm tired. I want to go home.'

I'm starting to get a dull headache, brought on by the humidity and a glass of wine at lunchtime and I'm inclined to agree with you but Matt seems determined to take us round it.

Inside, you trail up the marble steps without enthusiasm, a dead weight dragging on my hand. You fuss and twist and run away down echoing corridors every time Matt tries to point something out. I run after you, apologising to Japanese and German and every other sort of tourist as we barge past, interrupting them in their quiet contemplation of Venetian paintings and sculptures.

My head throbs and I can feel myself getting short-tempered with you and cross too with Matt for dragging us in here and with myself for letting him. After all, it isn't really a palace; it's an art history museum and you're not even four.

Finally, I decide to call a halt and tell Matt that I'm sorry but you're too tired and I'm taking you straight back to the hotel. He's somewhere ahead of us and I take you firmly by the hand and urge you forward to find him, even as you struggle and protest. We plough on, you dangerously close to a tantrum, when you suddenly shake me off and stop in your tracks. I feel your mood change in an instant. You stand, stock still, just staring.

'Look, Mummy.' Your voice falls to a whisper. 'Look.'

The painting is striking. I stand close beside you and gaze.

It's in muted colours and clearly centuries old. The bottom two-thirds show naked, long-limbed figures against a dark background. Their bodies contort as they gaze in reverence backwards and upwards, guided and encouraged by others, suspended around them, who are robed and winged.

But it's the top third of the painting to which the eye is drawn, the object of the figures' gaze. It shows a whirling vortex of light, growing in brilliance as it twists in a cone towards pure white at the far end. A tunnel of brightness.

I crouch down beside you, putting myself at your level. You can't take your eyes from it, just reach a hand sideways to find mine.

'That's it.' Your voice is hushed. 'What I saw.' A long pause until finally, almost to yourself and in wonder: 'How did he know?'

Your face is radiant. I look again at the painting, dramatic with fifteenth-century religious fervour, then again at your ecstatic expression.

'That's what you saw?'

'I went down that tunnel.' You lift your free hand and point at the light. 'That's where Mr Michael is. And Catherine. Don't you see? Down there.' You turn to me and break suddenly into a broad smile. 'The man who did this painting,' you whisper in my ear, as if you've stumbled at last upon a great truth, 'he must have gone there too.'

CHAPTER 33

That evening, Matt announces that he wants to see if he can find a little family hotel-restaurant he remembers, off the beaten track. If it's still there, he says, it has the most amazing pizzas. He seems suddenly obsessed with finding this place, as if it really matters to him, and I'm afraid to ask why.

We set off with a map. We're venturing far from Piazza San Marco and we soon leave behind the main tourist routes and find ourselves twisting and turning through a maze of increasingly narrow side streets. At times, these give way without warning to hidden squares, built round modest churches with low lights.

We enter a series of paths along the edges of minor canals that are so gloomy that I call you back and make you hold my hand. The water here smells stagnant and forbidding, its surface barely visible in the darkness. I draw you away from the edge, frightened that if we fell in, we'd simply disappear into nothingness.

There are few streetlights in this forgotten stretch and the buildings look decayed and deserted. Arches and doorways are toothless with missing bricks and bowed by the weight of history. Matt walks on with purpose but his map is useless in the darkness.

Finally we emerge, as if by miracle, into a small piazza. A typical Venetian campo, Matt says, looking round as he gets his bearings. He's clearly delighted and leads the way with renewed confidence to a tall, narrow house on its edge. It's barely identifiable as a hotel. It looks dilapidated and cramped but full of character.

Downstairs, restaurant tables spill out onto the pavement. A middle-aged woman, prematurely thick around the waist, sits smoking at a corner table, reading a newspaper. Matt leaves us and crosses to greet her.

She raises her eyes with little interest at first, then feeling floods into her face and she jumps up, kisses him on both cheeks and embarks on an animated flow of Italian. Her eyes shine but her expression becomes wistful as she talks.

After a while, he gestures towards us and she looks over fleetingly at me, then more closely at you, pressed against my side. Her eyes are curious but I see none of the warmth in them with which she greeted Matt.

He comes back to claim us and steer us to a table.

'Sorry,' he says, smiling. '*La patrona*. I wondered if she'd still be here.'

I think of his student friend, Maria-Eletta, and wonder if there's a connection here that he's politely omitting to mention.

'She certainly remembered you.'

He is already leaning over the pizza menu. The woman has picked up her newspaper and retreated inside, leaving us alone. A much younger woman takes our order.

Matt is suddenly subdued and I sit quietly beside him, wondering why. The pharmacy on the corner is still open and every now and then a bell jangles as the door closes on customers. Dusk deepens around us. A wrought-iron streetlight, holding three ornate lanterns, casts lengthy shadows across the paving stones.

You sit with us while we all eat, folding the edges of your pizza slices into curves, delighting in being allowed to eat with your hands.

When you've had enough, you jump down from your chair and, while Matt and I linger over our wine, you make your own game of hopping and skipping across the campo's flagstones. You buzz with life and, as I watch you, a lithe figure in your

buttoned-up coat, I think back to the painting we saw together, to its twisting tunnel of light and the naked figures reaching for the perfect brightness ahead.

Matt leans closer and reaches an arm round me. 'I'm sorry. I've been lousy company tonight.'

I take his hand between my own. 'Are you OK?'

He nods and draws me closer to him. His body is firm and warm against mine and I'm comforted by it but still uneasy. Something about this place, about talking with that woman, dampened his mood and I don't understand why.

'You were upset, weren't you, this afternoon?'

I hesitate. His tone is sympathetic and I want to respond to it, to talk about you and your strange reaction to the painting but I'm also reluctant to change the subject and move on.

'She was so struck by that painting,' I say, remembering the emotion in your face. 'Maybe she's right. Maybe the artist did go through something similar.'

'Maybe he did.' Matt shrugs. 'Experiences like that, however you explain them, must have been around for centuries. We might call them near-death experiences. Maybe they just called them visions.'

'When did you say it was painted?'

He pauses. 'About fifteen ten. A superstitious age. They all painted religious stuff.'

I don't answer. Your light, high voice drifts across the campo on the breeze. You're chattering to yourself, lost in your own world. Your hair flies round your head as you leap in and out of the shafts of light thrown across the paving stones by the lanterns, jumping between light and darkness, light and darkness. I have a strange sense of you jumping also in time, back and forth through the thin, shifting veil between past and present, between this world and the next.

Mist is gathering along the far side of the campo, rising from the canal, creeping in from the Lagoon. It blurs the edges of buildings there and swallows the shops beyond the canal.

You run back to me. Your eyes shine with the excitement of being outside so late.

'Is it night-time, Mummy?'

'It's very late, my love.'

'It's dark!'

I just nod, reach out a hand and tickle the back of your neck. You have a habit of stating the obvious sometimes, as if you just enjoy the pleasure of making conversation.

'Soon,' I say, 'we'll go back to the hotel and then it's straight to bed.'

You skip off again. This time you head towards a narrow hump-backed bridge over the canal in the far corner of the campo. It is already becoming engulfed by swirling mist. I narrow my eyes and struggle to keep you in sight.

Your voice drifts clearly through the still air. *One. Two. Three.* You count the stone steps up one side of the bridge, run back and forth across the top, then come back again, springing off the bottom step with a bound.

'This time tomorrow,' I say, 'we'll be back in London.' It seems impossible.

Matt pulls me closer. When I encircle him with my arms, his back is broad and strong.

He kisses my cheek. 'I don't want it to end.'

You start to climb the steps again, this time hopping with your feet together. I hold my breath as you reach the top of the bridge and, for a second or two, disappear into the hanging fog, only to reappear again.

An Italian couple, strolling by, call out to friends and stop to talk. The song of their voices, the lilting music of their words, washes over us.

Matt lowers his voice. 'It works, Jen. You and me. Don't you think? And Gracie too.'

I nod. It's been a happy weekend. For the first time, I've had glimpses of the three of us as a unit. As a family.

He clears his throat. 'I know it hasn't been very long.'

Part of me wants him to stop there, to leave things as they are and not risk spoiling them. Another part wants him to carry on.

'I love you, Jen. You know that, don't you? We belong together, you and me. I sensed it the first time we met.'

He cups my chin with his hand and turns my face away from you to him. His lips close for a moment on mine, stopping my breath.

'I don't want to rush you.' His eyes loom large, streaked with low light. 'But I want to take things a step further. Will you think about it? I want to look after you. You and Gracie. I want to wake up with you every morning, not creep out of the house at night as if we don't really belong to each other.'

I pull a little apart from him.

'Jen? What is it?' His voice is gentle. 'Is it too soon?'

I shake my head. 'It should be,' I say. 'How long have we known each other? A matter of weeks. That's no time at all.' I hesitate. 'But that's not how it feels.'

'How does it feel?'

'Like a dream,' I say, in a low voice. 'If you'd told me a few months ago that I'd be sitting here in Venice with a doctor, talking about being together—' I broke off.

'Think about it. Please.'

He moves in and kisses me.

'I love you so much, Jen. I don't know how I'd carry on without you.'

I close my eyes.

When I open them again and look round, you're standing on the curved back of the bridge, barely visible in the thickening mist: a slight, shadowy figure leaning forward over the wall and peering down into the canal.

I look more closely, then pull away from Matt and sit up straight.

'Is there—'

The fog swims round you, at times obscuring you, at others giving you back to me. I get to my feet. My heart pounds. It may be no more than streaks of light shimmering in the mist but it seems to me, as I gaze, that there's something or someone beside you, a presence even slighter than your own, there at your side. I blink, straining forward to get a better look.

'Is that someone with her?'

Matt doesn't seem to hear me at first. Then he understands and says: 'With Gracie?' He too sits straighter, cranes forward. 'I can't tell.'

'Can't you?'

I push past the table and stride towards you. I am suddenly afraid, gripped by the same fear that chilled me this morning on the boat and again as I stood high on the bell tower, looking out across the vast expanse of the Lagoon, and thought you gone.

I quicken my pace. The fog deepens and you are lost for a moment. Then I hear it. A stifled giggle drifts across the campo towards me. It is followed a moment later by the soft, light breathing of a child. The same sounds I heard so clearly as I raced up the bell tower.

The mists sway and thin in the breeze and you emerge again, leaning away from me now, over the far wall of the bridge. I shiver and run towards you. As I draw near, I catch the low murmur of voices.

'Gracie?'

You look up, alarmed, and shout at once: 'No, Mummy. Go away!'

You stand squarely on the narrow bridge, guarding it from me. I try to peer past you, into the darkness.

'Come away now. It's late.'

You stamp your foot, furious. 'No! You're spoiling everything.'

'What?' I've almost reached you now, my arms open, but as I move to embrace you, you pull away. 'What's wrong?'

'You made her go away.' You hit out at me, arms flailing. 'Why, Mummy? Why did you do that?'

'Calm down, Gracie!' I try again to hold you but you lash out and struggle, barely able to contain your rage. 'It's alright.'

'It's not alright.' Your face crumples, close to tears. 'She was here and you've frightened her away.'

'Who?'

'Catherine.'

'Gracie.' I shake my head. As I look past you, all I see is a wall of dense fog, streaked with light bouncing off the fast-moving water below. 'It's very late.'

You lean over, peer down at the black stream gliding through the darkness. Your pale face, reflected there, shimmers.

'We need to go.' I hold out my hand for you to take. 'Come on.'

You burst into sobs, fall to the ground and bang your fists, your feet.

I stand, helpless, watching you.

'Gracie. Sweetheart. Get up.'

I lean over you, lifting your shoulders even as you struggle against me, trying to pull you to your feet.

'No, Mummy. You don't understand. She's gone again. It's your fault. Why did you come? Why?'

I can't answer. I manage to hoist you up into my arms, battling to contain you as you scream and kick and shout: 'No! No!'

I carry you down off the bridge, away from the water and back onto solid ground. As we cross the campo towards him, Matt stands motionless, watching us approach, his face pale.

CHAPTER 34

'Have you got bear?'

You opened your bag to check, nodded. Your face was solemn.

Richard held up your coat, trying to push your arm into the first sleeve.

'Daddy will look after you. But if you need me, you know you can phone. Alright, my love? Any time at all, day or night.'

Richard said into the coat: 'Maybe not night.' Your second arm found its sleeve and he reached round you, zipped up the front. 'We'll be fine, won't we, sausage? We'll be too busy having fun.'

'She's got two lots of pyjamas, just in case. And make sure she cleans her teeth properly, won't you? Not just the front ones.'

Richard didn't answer. I knelt down to you and opened my arms, squeezed you tightly for as long as I could until you wriggled free. 'Don't forget how much I love you.'

You didn't answer. You were busy with your gloves, finding the right holes for each finger.

'All the way to the moon and back,' I whispered into your soft hair. 'And a bit more.'

'Come on.' Richard put his hand on your shoulders, reached to open the front door and steered you out. I stood there on the threshold, sick to my stomach, watching as you climbed into the back of his car and he fastened you into your seat. Ella, resplendent in the front, twisted back to talk to you.

I waved as he pulled away and eased into the road but you didn't even look. When I shut the front door, the house was unbearably silent.

It felt strange, setting out alone that evening. As I got on the train, I expected the other passengers to stare. I missed you so much, my love. Such a physical sense of your absence. I sat quietly on my own, without your small, fidgety body on the seat beside me, climbing back and forth over my knees, craning to look out of the window. I had to remind myself not to point out the power station, the police car flashing alongside the railway, the horses in a dark field.

I got out my phone and texted Richard. *All OK?*

No answer.

Matt had chosen the restaurant, a little Italian bistro in town, hidden away down a side street, close to Waterloo. I left myself plenty of time to find it but even though I arrived early, he was already waiting.

My heart skipped when I looked round the restaurant and saw him there. Handsome and kind. He'd taken a cosy table in semi-darkness at the back. A tea light candle burned in a glass holder. The tablecloth was starched linen. Heavy doors swished as the waiters, stout Italian men in old-fashioned uniforms, strode to and from the kitchen, releasing smells of basil and tomato and the rich aroma of simmering meat.

'Darling.' He kissed me on the lips, pulled out a chair and settled me beside him. He was already drinking from a bottle of Valpolicella and a waiter leaned forward to pour for me. I lifted my glass to touch his.

'Memories of Venice,' he said. 'And many more holidays to come.'

I looked round. The walls were crowded with heavy black and white photographs. Italian piazzas and villages on hilltops. Pictures of small town celebrities: boxers and politicians and actors. I thought back to the first time we went out to dinner

properly together, in that noisy, crowded restaurant. It wasn't very long ago and yet it felt it. I was so nervous then and knew him so little. Now we were already a couple.

The waiter handed me a menu and I opened it. The names of the dishes were all in Italian and I smiled, trying to remember what he'd taught me in Venice.

'Well!' He smiled across at me. 'Here we are again.' He reached for my hand.

A moment later, the waiter interrupted to announce the specials and Matt ordered for us both. I asked him about work and he started telling me about his patients that week – a little boy with a heart condition and a ten-year-old just diagnosed with leukaemia. His eyes grew intense as he described their cases, giving more medical detail than I could understand.

I sat quietly as we ate and drank more than my share of the wine and let Matt do the talking. He seemed more at ease with me since Venice. More willing to trust me, to confide in me about his work. It was clear, just from hearing him, how much he cared about his patients. I let the wine loosen my limbs and gazed at him. Despite all my worries about you, about what you were doing, what Ella had given you to eat, if you were missing me, I was happy to be here with this extraordinary, loving man who doted on me.

The waiter cleared away our plates. Matt leaned forward and took my hand.

'I missed you this week.' He stroked my fingers. 'How are you doing?'

I shrugged, feeling embarrassed that he had so much to tell me and I had so little.

He looked thoughtful. 'You're worrying about Gracie, aren't you?'

I tried to smile. 'Is it so obvious?'

'It must be hard.' He pulled back as the waiter set dessert in front of us. A rich chocolate mousse, one to share. 'She needs time with her father.'

I nodded. Ella was the one I didn't trust. We picked up our spoons.

'Look.' He pointed his spoon at me. 'Of course you'll worry. You're an amazing mother. But it'll do you both good. She needs time with Richard. And you, madam—' he leaned forward and kissed the tip of my nose '—you need time with me.'

When he disappeared to the toilets, I checked my phone. Nothing. I started another text to Richard – *All OK?* – then deleted it.

We were almost at the end of a second bottle of wine. I was flustered that evening, anxious about you, self-conscious about being out at all, and I barely remembered drinking it. The waiter leaned in, a linen napkin on his arm, and poured the last of the bottle into my glass. My fingers fumbled the glass as I lifted it and I spilt some, then mopped at the mess with my napkin, making it worse.

Matt reappeared. 'Paid.' He wafted away my thanks with his hand. 'My treat.'

When I got to my feet, the table swayed. The waiter steadied my elbow as I headed towards the door. Outside, the air was cool and fresh. I stood still for a moment, feeling it on my cheeks, thinking of home and sleep.

'Let's not rush back.' Matt seemed suddenly full of energy. 'Come on. Do you know DDs?'

I shook my head. Matt, taking my arm, was already hailing a cab.

'How often do we get the chance, Jen, really? Come on.'

DDs was a double-fronted club just off Shaftesbury Avenue. Stylishly dressed couples, some of the girls barely out of their teens, queued inside a rope. A thick-set bouncer in a tux guarded the door.

Matt winked. 'Watch.'

He pulled out his wallet and flashed something at the bouncer, who unclipped the rope and lifted it aside for us. I hesitated before following him inside. The taxi ride had left me feeling queasy.

The club was all darkness, scored with criss-cross lines of coloured lasers. It pulsed with noise. The vibrations reached for me as soon as we entered and rose up through my legs to my stomach. Matt steered me up a short flight of steps to a low balcony and a young man in a torn T-shirt with the rippling chest and biceps of a body builder escorted us to a table with a red shaded lamp. Matt said something in his ear and he nodded and disappeared.

We settled side by side in cushioned seats and looked out across the dance floor. It was heaving with gyrating bodies. They swam in and out of the moving lights, arms high, faces sweaty, eyes stupid with alcohol or drugs or both, like some modern vision of Dante's Inferno.

I thought at first, *My God, I'm too old for this*, but as my eyes started to adjust to the dark, the faces became clearer and I saw how many of the people around us were actually middle-aged or older.

The young man came back with two glasses of champagne and Matt paid at our seat with a card. He raised his glass in a toast.

'To nights out!'

My head was already swimming with Valpolicella and I had to concentrate to wrap my clumsy fingers round the champagne flute and touch it to his without spilling it. The champagne was icy on my lips and in my throat. I took just a sip, then another, then turned back to the dance floor, focusing my eyes on a distant point as I tried to steady myself. The music throbbed inside my head.

Bubbles burst somewhere deep in my stomach and a sour trace of acid rose into my mouth. Sweat moistened my hairline. I peeled off my jacket and rolled my sleeves up. Matt drummed his fingers on the tabletop in time to the thudding music and the banging travelled along the surface and into my bones.

I tried to sit back. I wondered how soon I could ask to leave, how we could get home quickly. I thought of you. Maybe you'd woken up and were crying, calling for me, and I wouldn't even

know. Why had I had so much to drink? I shook my head and the lights flew so rapidly, I had to blink to stay upright. Perhaps it would be better if I moved, if I splashed water on my face.

I took hold of the rail that ran along the edge of the balcony and used it to hoist myself to my feet. Matt looked up and I managed a vague nod before turning and groping my way back along the narrow walkway to the entrance.

The lights in the ladies' were dazzling after the club interior, and I stood at the sink for some time, blinking, running cold water on my wrists and dousing my face. It was a relief to escape the worst of the crashing noise. I looked ghastly, my skin sallow and my eyes unfocused.

I swayed, gripped the edge of the washbasin to stop myself from falling. Time to head home. I'd go straight back to Matt and say I was really sorry, I just didn't feel well, it must be something I'd eaten. I nodded at my reflection and saw the pale face bob, then turned and went into a cubicle.

I sat inside with my head in my hands, trying to hold myself steady. My eyes throbbed. My hands came away slippery with sweat. I wanted the headache, the sickness, to go away and to be well again and to be with you, to hold you and see you settled in my arms, sleeping, as if you were a baby again. Safe and close.

My feet juddered on the tiled floor. I opened my eyes, braced myself against the seat and managed to get to my feet, stood for a second getting my balance before opening the door and stepping out.

CHAPTER 35

The lights were strobing. The club jumped and shifted in the jerky beams. I groped my way to a handrail and stood, gripping it tightly, trying to keep my balance in the thumping music and popping light. I stared across the gyrating bodies on the dance floor. Each moment was separated, frozen. A series of photographs of raised arms, grinding torsos, locked limbs.

One revealed Matt, in the background, on his feet. I focused, trying to piece together the set of jerking pictures. He was half-turned, leaning forward, talking intently to someone. To a young woman. His body obscured her face but I caught glimpses of her curves. Tall and slim and encased like a sausage in a tight, figure-hugging sheath. Sexy.

I felt my way along the handrail towards them. The floor was sticky with spilt drinks. Matt's body was tense as he leaned in to her. The strain showed in his hunched shoulders and the jabbing movement of his hand as he talked through the music.

I found my way across the edge of the seating. As I climbed the steps up to our seats, I lost sight of them behind a row of pillars. At the top, I turned, closer now, then stopped dead as I saw the woman's face. Her. The last woman on earth I wanted to see. Ella.

She shifted her gaze and saw me. For a moment, our eyes locked. She didn't have the grace to look embarrassed, just stared me down with a hostile, superior glare. I stared back and she turned away, all disdain, and began to stalk off on her high heels,

this woman who had wrecked my marriage, whose dangerous driving nearly killed my daughter.

Rage took me. I broke into a messy run, banging against the backs of the seats as I closed the gap between us, reached her, grabbed her arm to swing her round to face me.

'Why're you here?' I paused. 'You followed me, didn't you?'

Her eyes showed surprise, then became cold. She reached calmly down to prise my sweaty fingers off her sleeve, brushing away all trace of them.

'What were you saying to him? Leave us alone. Haven't you done enough?' I plunged on, my mouth out of control. 'You can't bear to see me happy, can you? Is that it?'

She made again to turn away from me. She simply pretended she couldn't hear me, that I didn't exist. The more composed she looked, the more she infuriated me. I barged into her.

I called through the blast of noise from the speakers. 'Who's Catherine?'

She stopped in her tracks and swung round. Beneath all that make-up, her cheeks turned grey. *You were right, my lovely girl. You were so right. Why did I ever doubt you?*

'So it's true. You had a child, didn't you?' Every word hit home now. Each one pierced her. She couldn't move. She stood there, rooted, and took the blows.

Matt stepped forward and put his hand on my arm. He tried to pull me away, but I threw him off. Someone else took possession of my tongue and I couldn't have stopped if I'd wanted to.

'Even Richard doesn't know that, does he?' I don't know where the words came from. They just tumbled out, fuelled by the wine and the hate I felt for her. She was capable of *anything*. I just knew it. 'What did you do to her? Did you hurt her, like you hurt Gracie? Too wrapped up in yourself to consider the safety of a poor, defenceless child?'

Her eyes were wide, staring. The emotion in them was raw but hard to read. Fear, perhaps. Or panic. Or just fury.

Her arm flashed out. She struck me hard in the chest and I tottered. The room tilted sideways and slid as I crashed, unguarded, to the floor. Pain stung the side of my face as it caught the hard edge of a chair. White shards flashed through my eyes and burst like fireworks. I groped blindly, stunned.

Matt moved quickly to stand between us, shielding me. He had his back to me but I saw her say something to him, her mouth twisted and tight. Then she bent over me. When she spoke, the words were hot against my ear.

'You're not fit to say her name.'

And she was gone.

Matt reached for my arm and heaved me to my feet. He looked pale. He picked up his jacket, held me upright against him and guided me slowly towards the exit.

In the taxi back home, I pressed close to him, feeling sick and grateful for the darkness. My head was spinning with alcohol and confusion. My ears still buzzed and whistled after the noise. My cheek throbbed.

'What did she say to you?'

'I don't know.' He shrugged. 'She was drunk.'

'Something about me?' My mind was whirling, trying to work out what had happened. She must have seen us come in and waited her chance to approach Matt. To cause trouble. 'What?'

'I couldn't even hear.' He stroked my hand. 'She didn't make much sense.' He paused. 'Anyway, we don't care, do we?'

I saw again the sheath dress, the heels. 'You do realise who she is?'

He nodded, avoiding my eyes. 'She said.'

I hesitated. 'What's she doing out anyway? Is Richard with her?' My voice was rising. 'Who's looking after Gracie?'

Matt shook his head. 'She was with a group of girls. Quite a rowdy crowd. A hen do, maybe.'

The taxi braked suddenly and I slipped forward, tumbled off the seat. Matt crouched down and lifted me up. His hands were strong and warm and his eyes kind.

'I'm sorry,' he said. 'It's my fault. You were right. We should have gone home after dinner.'

He settled me against him, his arm firmly round my shoulders. The streets were crowded with young people, drinking, jostling, chatting in jumbled clusters. I wondered if you'd fallen asleep quickly and if you'd wake in the night and call out for me and if Richard had remembered the monitor.

'Forget her. She doesn't matter, does she?' Matt whispered in my ear. His breath was hot. 'We're happy, aren't we? We've found each other. Nothing can spoil that.' His hand, resting on my arm, shifted until his fingertips stroked the curve of my breast. 'Let's enjoy every minute.' His lips closed on the soft skin of my neck.

CHAPTER 36

We spent Sunday morning in bed, then pottered to a local café for a fry-up. I kept my body as close to Matt's as I could, conjoined by sex and sleepiness and the laziness of a slowly dispersing hangover.

He finally left in the afternoon and I was just sorting out the washing and putting the house straight again when you arrived home. You came tearing into the house – bear under your arm – as I opened the front door. You were on fire with excitement.

'Mummy, Mummy, I've got bunk beds!'

'Bunk beds?' I looked back to Richard who was wiping his feet on the mat, his face turned to his shoes.

'She's always wanted them.'

'I know that.' I blinked, already cross. 'And we always said no because they're dangerous. What if she falls out in the middle of the night?'

'She won't.' Richard shrugged, avoiding looking at me.

You skipped round the kitchen, calling out to me: 'There's a hidey-hole underneath the stairs! Full of toys.'

'You should have talked to me about it first,' I said to Richard. 'I'm her mother.'

'And I'm her father.' He moved into the hall and set down your bag there. 'It's perfectly safe, OK? It's got proper carpeted stairs for climbing up and down and a big lip on the top bed. She couldn't fall out if she tried.'

We were talking in low voices and you came running back to find out what was going on.

'Mummy!' You stopped in your tracks, stared at my face. A red weal stretched across my cheek where I'd hit the edge of the chair. I thought I'd done a good job concealing it with make-up but you weren't fooled for a second. 'Was it a wolf?'

You lifted your hand and I stooped to let you touch it, tracing the lines with your finger.

'I had a bang, Gracie. That's all. Silly Mummy.'

You looked doubtful. 'Will it get better?'

'Of course it will. Now take your coat off. You can have a quick play and then it's bath time.' I held up my hand. 'Five minutes.'

You disappeared into the sitting room.

When I turned back to Richard, he narrowed his eyes, looking too at my bruised cheek.

'Your girlfriend gave me that. Did she tell you? She just happened to bump into us.' I drew sarcastic quote marks in the air around the words 'just happened'.

'My fiancée.'

'Oh, please.'

He hesitated, shuffled his feet. His brown lace-ups looked cheap compared to Matt's shoes. I thought of him in the evenings, sitting cross-legged on the kitchen floor, surrounded by brushes and tins of polish, one hand inside a shoe and the other patiently buffing the leather.

'Ella was very upset when she came home.'

'She was upset?'

'Look, I don't know what happened—'

I opened my mouth and he held up his hand to stop me.

'And I don't want to know. I said the same to Ella. I'm not interested. Leave her alone, Jen. Please. This isn't about us any more. It's about Gracie. You two need to get along, for her sake. Alright?'

I wanted to defend myself, to point out that Ella was the one who'd bothered us, who'd gone out of her way to cause trouble,

but I saw his face and swallowed it back. It wasn't worth it. He'd never believe me anyway. I took a deep breath.

'You told me she couldn't have children.'

He looked taken aback. 'What's that got to do with it?'

I hesitated. I knew Richard and he didn't look guilty or embarrassed. Quite the opposite, in fact. He looked indignant, as if I were the one being mean.

'Richard.' I didn't know how to tell him my suspicions. 'I think Ella had a daughter.'

'What're you talking about?'

'Ask Gracie. She says she's seen her. Ella's daughter.'

Richard looked cross. 'That's ridiculous.'

I pulled a face. 'But Gracie—'

'What? She's three, for god's sake. She wants to pretend she's got a sister. That's all.'

I opened my mouth and closed it again. How could I tell him about the look on Ella's face, her utter shock? About Venice and the strange giggling inside the bell tower. About the shadowy presence beside you in the mist.

He went into the sitting room to say goodbye to you, then pushed straight past me to the front door. He hesitated there and turned back.

'I'm sorry for what happened, Jen. Believe me. I never wanted to hurt you.' He hesitated. 'But I'm starting to wonder if I knew you at all. I never had you down as silly. Or cruel.'

Afterwards, I joined you on the sitting room floor where you had the bricks out and were building a multi-storey garage for your cars.

'So, sweetheart.' I tried to join in, to win you back. 'How was your sleepover? Did you have a nice time?'

You didn't answer, just scrabbled through the box of bricks looking for the piece you wanted. I moved in closer and added a few bricks of my own to your wall.

'How was Auntie Ella? Was she fun?'

You nodded without looking up.

I reached round you and kissed your hair, inhaled its fresh, lemony smell and tightened my arms in a hug.

'Don't, Mummy.' You fought me off, cross. 'I'm busy.'

CHAPTER 37

On Wednesday, the weather lifted. It was bright and typically English: warm in the sunshine, cool in the shade. When I picked you up from nursery, we headed straight to the park on the far side of the river, the sprawling one with ducks and rose gardens and zones for everyone, from the skateboarding youths you stopped to watch, eyes wide, to the dog walkers and the joggers in Lycra.

We spent an hour at the play area, on the Big Girl swings without backs, which you still tended to fall off, on the seesaw, and on your favourite, the roundabout. I ran round, turning it for you, getting dizzy and out of breath, as you beamed.

We ate ham and cream cheese sandwiches on a bench by the river and counted boats. Small racing yachts with white sails. Rowers, schoolboys mostly, wrenching their way in packs against the tide. The strains of the cox's voice, made monstrous by a megaphone, bounced across the water like skimmed stones. A police launch bounced at speed through them all and made waves that tipped and tossed the sailing boats, the rowers and made us laugh.

You pushed down from the bench after a while and took the remains of your last sandwich to the rail along the steep embankment to the river below. You threw bits of bread, aiming at the stray ducks below on the water but attracting a sudden swirl of seagulls who made a cloud round your head and frightened you into dropping the lot.

'London seagulls,' I said. 'Cheeky.'

I pulled out an apple, polished it on my trousers and bit into it. The gulls moved on and you wandered along the rail, a hand trailing on the bar, looking down at the river. You looked suddenly old in your cream coat, a proper child now, lost in your own thoughts. A girl, already growing away from me and getting ready for school. I tried to imagine dropping you off at the school gates and walking back to an empty house. I sucked juice from the apple and chewed. Richard was right. I'd be ready to go back to work by then. I needed to get earning again and, besides, I'd need to fill my days and not just count the hours until I could be there at the school gates, looking for you.

I closed my eyes and saw Richard there, standing so awkwardly in the sitting room we'd furnished together, as a couple, all those years ago. The same sitting room where we had fallen asleep, slumped against each other, a thousand times. Where I'd nursed you, stroking your downy head with the tip of a finger, utterly content, feeling as if I had at last joined the human race, joined the cycle of life. Matt was right. It was time to move on. Let him marry her, if that's what he wanted. He could find out the hard way what she really was.

Ella was brassy. I thought of her tarty dress at the club. She couldn't bear to see people happy. She was that kind of person. Destructive. She'd taken Richard from me. He was so naïve when it came to women. He couldn't understand why she and I hated each other. I knew what she was up to. She wanted to drive a wedge between me and Matt, if she could. Well, she couldn't.

I thought of Venice and the smell of the salt air from the Lagoon and the firmness of his body as he reached for me. I missed him, now, sitting here in the sunshine, more than ever. He'd done so much for me, for us. It was a miracle that he'd walked into our lives the way he did.

Someone passed, walking a panting dog, and blocked the sun for a moment. I opened my eyes, looked for you. The rail stretched

along the edge of the path, empty. I pushed the last sandwiches back into my bag and got to my feet. No sign of you, no flash of cream coat, of shoes with light-up heels.

I took a step to the rail, half-smiling at myself for worrying. Of course you were there. I'd see you any minute. You were testing me again, making a point about how grown-up you were, how independent. You never went far.

I stood at the rail, the peeling paint pricking my fingers, and scanned the river below, fearing you'd somehow climbed or fallen through. No cream coat. I started to walk down the path.

'Gracie!'

You liked hide-and-seek. Maybe that was it. I peered into the bushes along the verge, green and full-leaved now.

'Where are you?' I tried to make my voice a sing-song, to keep it a game. A bush stirred and I spun round, ready to smile, ready to see your face, laughing at me. A large dog, collar jangling, sniffing as it ran out onto the path.

I quickened my step, shouting every few steps: 'Gracie!' Reached the end of the path where it gave way to a mud trail towards the swings. My heart was loud in my ears, my breath short.

Beyond the final bushes, the grass opened out and gave a clearer view ahead. I narrowed my eyes, concentrated, searched the walkers, the dogs, the youths, the children, for your small figure in cream. The park looked empty. What if this was it? What if I never found you? My legs trembled and a cold sickness rose through my stomach into my chest.

'Gracie!'

I tried to tamp down the panic. You weren't a baby. You were nearly four. I was panicking. In a short time, any minute, I'd see you, I'd run to you, it would all be over and seem absurd, a story to tell people. It was only a matter of minutes, I'd say, but it seemed like forever. I could almost hear your voice in my head, saying: 'Silly Mummy!'

'Gracie!'

I turned, walked back to the section of rail opposite the bench where I'd last seen you. If you came running back to find me, it would be here. I climbed up on the bench and tried to see through the trees, the foliage. A middle-aged couple came past, Labradors at their heels, and gave me an odd look.

'My little girl,' I said. 'Have you seen her?'

The woman frowned.

'She's in a cream coat.'

The man shook his head and they walked on.

I climbed down and sat heavily on the bench. The strength drained from my legs. I looked down the path one way, then the other. Just vacancy, stretching on forever. I felt utterly lost. I must be sensible, keep calm, but for a moment, I lost all sense of what to do. Should I set off round the park, walking briskly, searching? It was a large park. How much did I cover? How far should I go?

Or should I sit here, half-hidden from the lawns by the bushes, and try to stay calm, trust you to find your way back to me?

My breathing was so shallow that my chest ached. I pulled out my phone. A mechanical voice told me that Matt's mobile was switched off.

I left a message: 'It's me. Sorry to bother you but could you call me back? Please.'

I already imagined myself feeling a fool when he called, later, and we were already together, crisis over. I'd laugh about it, about how flustered I'd been, honestly, what a hopeless mother.

I got to my feet again, paced back to the end of the path and this time headed out down the dry mud trail towards the swings. Of course. You'd be back on the roundabout, on the seesaw. I almost ran to the gate and into the playground. It was clouding over and the swings were quieter now. I scanned the equipment. Ran round the grassy mound to check the baby swings, to look inside the play train. Nothing.

I sank to the grass. It was cool and damp through my jeans. How long had it been now? Ten minutes? Twenty? I didn't know. I pulled my diary out of my bag and looked for the number of the hospital, then dialled it. My hands shook.

Switchboard. The woman who answered sounded mechanical. A foreign accent. East European.

'Doctor Matthew Aster, please.'

'Who?'

I stiffened. 'Matthew Aster. Paediatrics.'

A pause, then the call clicked onto music. I got to my feet, restless, and started walking round the edge of the playground, scanning the park.

The woman finally clicked back onto the line. 'No doctor with that name.'

'A-S-T-E-R.' I spelled it out with exaggerated care, trying not to lose my patience. 'Paediatrics. You know, children?'

'I know that.' She sounded shirty. Tap, tap as she checked. 'I can't help you.'

'Can you at least put me through to the department?'

'Are you a relative?'

'A relative?'

'Of the patient?'

I wanted to reach into the phone and shake her. 'I'm not trying to reach a patient! I'm trying to contact a doctor. Doctor Matthew Aster.'

'I'm sorry, there's no—'

I ended the call, pushed the phone back in my pocket. Stupid woman. Anyway, Matt might have picked up the mobile message by now, might be trying to call me back.

I left the playground, rushed back towards the riverside path. I was almost at the bench when I saw you, a daub of cream, crouched down low right at the far end of the path, close to the entrance to the park. You were bending forwards, your forehead

pressed against the bottom bar of the railings, peering at the river below.

I broke into a run. As I got close, you must have heard my thundering feet, my panting. You glanced round, unconcerned, saw me, then looked down again.

'Gracie!' I put my arms around you, tried to pull you to me in a hug. 'Where were you?'

You fought me off, annoyed at being interrupted. 'Look.'

You pointed down at the river. The fast-flowing water was brown with churned mud. A stick swirled past, followed by a piece of clear plastic, swollen, rising and falling in the current like a jellyfish.

'What?'

'Wait.' You stared down, transfixed. 'I saw her.'

I sucked in my breath, trying to be patient.

'Who?' I knew the answer before you spoke.

'Catherine. She waved to me.'

You seemed so separate from me. So calm.

'Don't be silly, Gracie. There's no one in the water.'

You weren't listening. Your mind was elsewhere. My heart thumped. The panic, the running and now this, your strange stillness.

'Gracie.' I crouched low, took hold of your arm. 'Don't ever run away like that again. You hear me?'

You ignored me, focused on the flowing water.

I reached more firmly for your shoulders and pulled you round to face me.

'Gracie, listen to me. Mummy was very worried. We've talked about getting lost, haven't we? It's dangerous. Very dangerous.'

You stared back, cross. 'I wasn't lost, Mummy. I was here.'

I put my arms round you and pulled you to me again, relishing the soft warmth of your body against mine in the few seconds before you struggled free.

About half an hour later, as we walked back home, hand in hand, my phone rang.

'Everything OK?' Matt.

'Fine.' I was exhausted. All I wanted just then was a cup of tea, a chance to sit down in the knowledge that you were there, safe, at home. 'Long story but we're fine now.'

'You're sure?' He sounded concerned. 'I'm sorry. I only just got your message. I was worried.'

'Me too.' I swung your hand in mine as we walked. 'I lost Gracie. That's all. But I found her again.'

He went very quiet. 'And you're OK?'

'I'm fine. I'll call you tonight.'

When I hung up, you said: 'I wasn't lost!'

'I couldn't find you, Gracie.' You seemed to have no sense of the fact you'd run off and how frightened I'd been. 'I was worried.'

'But I wasn't lost,' you said again, indignant now. 'I was right there.'

CHAPTER 38

That night, I came downstairs after reading you a story to see a dark shadow against the glass of the front door.

I went into the sitting room and peered out through the side window. Matt stood on the doorstep, with flowers in one hand and a bag of groceries in the other.

When I opened the door, he said: 'Hello, gorgeous. Surprise.' He handed me the flowers. The neck of a bottle of wine poked out of the shopping. 'I come bearing gifts.'

'You shouldn't have.' I moved out of the way to let him in. We stood close together in the hall and kissed. I thought of the TV dinner in the fridge. Much, much better to have Matt here.

'Missed you.' He pulled back and looked into my eyes. 'I was worried. You didn't sound yourself this afternoon.'

I nodded. 'It was a bit of a shock.'

In the kitchen, I sat on a chair and sipped wine and felt my shoulders relax. He tied my apron round his waist, pulled groceries from his shopping bags and set to work, washing and chopping mushrooms, yellow and red peppers.

I liked watching him work. It was the same pleasure as watching any devoted craftsman. He was so intent, so absorbed in his tasks, so quick with his hands. It was sexy as hell but in a soothingly lazy way, all the passion still to come, and it was comforting to be there with him in the light, in the warmth, watching those same capable hands which healed sick children.

It reminded me too of being a child, hanging around in the kitchen at home. My mother made terrific pies, with crunchy

crusts and fluted edges and – from about your age, about three – she used to give me pastry off-cuts to roll out and cut. The bottoms for jam tarts and pastry people with currants for eyes and waistcoat buttons.

'Earth to Jen.' He paused to look at me, his knife poised. 'You're miles away.'

'Sorry.' I nodded, smiled. 'How was your day?'

He shrugged. 'Intense.'

I'd guessed that from the vehemence of his chopping. Some days his cooking seemed a kind of frantic therapy. Those days, we had a lot of diced vegetables.

'Tough case?'

He shifted his floppy fringe from his eyes with the top of his arm. 'A three-year-old boy. Pneumonia. I think we caught it in time but only just.' He sighed, set his knife on the board and pushed the pile of chopped mushrooms off, into a bowl. 'He was critically deoxygenated on admission.'

I nodded, tried to look wise. 'What did you do?'

'Gave him oxygen, basically. He's a strong chap though. Responded well.' He looked round, suddenly self-conscious. 'Sorry.'

I shrugged, sipped my wine. 'Don't be.'

He sliced open a pepper, started to de-seed.

I swallowed, watching his hands. 'When I called the switch-board, they couldn't find you.'

'Really?' He was bent over the chopping board. 'Did they page me?'

'I don't know. I don't think she got that far.' My memory was obscured by a fog of cold panic. 'She wouldn't put me through to paediatrics. I remember that.'

'Natasha, probably.' He looked round. 'Did she sound Bulgarian?'

I considered. 'Something like that.'

'And a bit chippy?'

'Definitely.'

'That's Natasha.' He laughed. 'People are always complaining but they won't get rid of her. She's ruthlessly efficient, well, most of the time.' He fell to dicing peppers at speed. 'She seems to think it's her job to stop people bothering us. Not ideal. Especially if people are upset to start with.'

I wandered over to the worktop. 'What's the recipe tonight?'

'Ratatouille and pork casserole, a la Matt.'

'Ah.' I bent low and kissed the backs of his hands. 'My favourite kind.'

'Anyway—' he turned, kissed me quickly on the lips, not ready yet to be distracted from his cooking '—if you need me, mobile's best.'

CHAPTER 39

When Friday the eighteenth came round, I dropped you off at nursery, as usual, went to the shops and then found myself heading across to St Michael's. I wasn't sure until I walked in that I'd really go. It was just something about Angela. I didn't want to let her down.

I arrived early and sat for a while in the stillness of the church. The morning light streamed through the stained glass. Multi-coloured columns splashed onto the gravestones set amongst the flags that made up the floor. Saint Michael, locked in his eternal battle with the serpent, gazed down at me as I said my own quiet hello.

Just before eleven, I went back into the bright, living world of the café. Angela looked up as I appeared and smiled at me. She was dragging tables together to make a long central spine down the room and scraping the chairs as she arranged them round it.

A queue of elderly women stood at the counter, ordering cups of tea, scones and pieces of cake from the young woman there. I went to help Angela. By the time we'd finished, the elderly ladies were settling into their seats, ten or eleven of them altogether and one solitary man. No sign of any younger people.

Angela went up to the counter and gestured to me to join her at the table. When she returned, she set a cup of tea in front of me and a piece of coffee and walnut cake.

'On the house.' She looked flushed with pleasure. I wondered if she'd really expected me to come.

'Now, everyone.' She tapped her teacup with her spoon to call for silence.

The rows of lined, thickly powdered faces turned.

'We have a newcomer today.' She indicated me with her hand. 'This is Jennifer. I hope you'll make her welcome.'

The ladies exchanged whispers, looked at me with interest. One of those closest to me nodded and smiled.

They bowed their heads as Angela said a prayer.

'Bless us, Lord, as we gather here in your name and feel your presence.'

I lowered my head, embarrassed. I couldn't imagine what Matt would say if he knew I were here.

'Help us to understand your purpose in taking home to your kingdom those we love and miss here on Earth.'

I stared down at my teacup, at the untouched cake, wondering how soon I could escape.

'Help us to trust your promise of eternal life and to remember your triumph over death. O death, where is thy sting? O grave, where is thy victory? Amen.'

When she finished, the women dissolved into chatter. My knuckles whitened as my hands gripped each other in my lap.

The lady beside me said, rather loudly: 'It takes a bit of getting used to, doesn't it?'

I hesitated, not sure what she meant.

'Bernard and I were married for forty-one years. There isn't an hour goes by that I don't think of him. It's been thirteen years now but, do you know, every night, I set two places at the table. One for him and one for me.' She smiled, showing crooked teeth. 'Silly, isn't it? I know he's gone. But it's a comfort.'

'I'm sorry.' I didn't know what else to say. I reached for my fork and took a mouthful of cake. It was sweet and light, home-made, and reminded me of my mother's baking.

The lady watched me for a few moments as I ate. She leaned towards me, bringing with her the scent of talcum powder and a flowery perfume.

'So what's your story, dear?'

I blinked. My confusion must have shown in my face.

She prompted: 'Have you lost someone?'

'Well, my father.' My hand shook and I set down the fork. 'But that was a long time ago.'

'Awful.' She tutted sympathetically. 'You poor thing.'

She reached out and patted my hand. Her knuckles were swollen with arthritis.

'Well, you're very welcome here, dear. We've all got a cross to bear, haven't we? No one's spared.'

I didn't answer and, a moment later, she turned to reply to a question from someone on her other side. I sat quietly for some time, letting the sounds of conversation wash over me and focusing on my tea and cake.

After a while, Angela turned to speak to me.

'All these ladies have lost loved ones. Husbands. Brothers and sisters. Even children. It does help to talk about it.'

I didn't know what to say. I turned, looked out, beyond the end of the table, into the darkness of the church. I could almost see you there, a shifting shadow, a small, fragile figure, kneeling on a hassock and stretching forward, running your fingers over the stone flags, reading the engravings as if they were Braille.

'I worry about Gracie.' I thought of the women gathered here, burdened by their losses, their grief. 'I keep thinking how close I came to losing her.' I hesitated. 'I don't feel I can keep her safe any more.'

'When you talk about Gracie, your whole face changes. Do you feel it?' She gave me a thoughtful look. 'I see God there.'

My cheeks felt hot. I shifted my weight on the chair.

She considered me. 'If I say love, is that an easier word?'

I swallowed. 'My father adored my mother and when he was feeling sentimental, he'd say: *I love that woman more than life itself.* Tears in his eyes. I was only a child. I thought it was just a figure of speech. But now I understand.'

Something inside me loosened and words started to come.

'You know that myth about the goddess whose daughter was abducted and taken down to Hell and she grieved so hard that she brought winter on the world?'

'Persephone,' Angela said. 'And Demeter.'

'Exactly. I'd do that. If I had to.'

She smiled. 'I doubt you'd find her in Hell.'

I took a deep breath. 'I do struggle to believe in Heaven. Literal Heaven. Somewhere with radiant light where you meet God and people who've already died.' I shook my head. 'So how do I deal with my own little girl saying she's been there, telling me things she couldn't possibly know?'

We sat in silence for a moment, an island in the general hubbub of conversation.

One or two ladies pushed back their chairs, hauled themselves to their feet and tottered away. Several leaned heavily on sticks as they disappeared towards the toilets. Others gathered at the counter to order a fresh cup of tea. Those who were left continued to chat.

'There's probably a rational explanation,' Angela said. 'She might have overheard something. Or absorbed information without even realising. She's a perceptive child.'

I nodded. 'I suppose so.'

'That's one theory.' She carried on talking to me as she nodded across to ladies who were starting now to disperse, to say their goodbyes. 'Or you stop trying to rationalise. You let go. That's the thing about faith. It isn't about proof. It's about making a choice. Choosing to believe.

'From all you've told me,' she went on, 'I believe your daughter did go to Heaven, that she really did meet Saint Michael and was blessed by him. Maybe you think of that as an actual place, a place where God is. Or, if that makes you uncomfortable, think of it as love. As the universal love which is all around us, which survives us.'

Chairs scraped. A voice rose in thin, elderly laughter. She leaned in closer to me.

'That love your father felt for your mother, that you feel for your daughter… I don't think it ends with death. There's more than just nothingness.' She paused, considering. 'That's what I choose to believe. But what you choose is up to you.'

I sat very still. Something hard inside me shifted and my mouth trembled. I couldn't answer. I looked through to the church again but all I could see was darkness and weak shafts of coloured light.

'You know, perhaps Gracie came back to you because it wasn't her time. Or perhaps your love for her was so strong, so overwhelming, that God showed mercy to you both by sending her back.'

An animated woman interrupted by tapping Angela on the shoulder and she turned away to talk to her.

On the far side of the table, the elderly man shuffled to his feet and started, with slow, deliberate movements, to thread his arms into the sleeves of his coat. The young woman from behind the counter came out into the café and started to separate the tables again, re-ordering the café as if our meeting had never been.

CHAPTER 40

By the time I headed to nursery to collect you, the skies had clouded over and the clouds looked heavy with rain. I was thinking about lunch and what to feed you when my phone rang.

'Jen. I need to see you.'

'Matt?' My heart thumped. Since the accident, unexpected calls frightened me and he sounded anxious. 'Are you OK?'

'Fine.'

Traffic thundered past on the main road and I strained to hear him. 'What?'

'I said, what about this afternoon?'

I frowned, struggling to understand what was so urgent. We'd already planned to meet up over the weekend. 'I'm on my way to get Gracie.'

'Please, Jen.' His tone was sharp. My stomach contracted. 'There's something you need to know.'

We arranged to meet in a soft play centre at three o'clock, just a ten-minute walk from the house. We hadn't been for a while and you were delighted. You ran in, shedding your coat on the ground behind you, as soon as we entered through the turnstile. You were always bursting with energy, even after a morning at nursery. My biggest challenge each day was finding new ways to exhaust it.

By the time Matt arrived, you'd pulled off your shoes and were tumbling on the miniature bouncy castle. Your hair was wild with static as you threw yourself back and forth. It was an effort for me

not to interfere, not to caution: 'Be careful, Gracie! Mind your head!' I saw so many dangers unravelling. You were so perfect, so precious, I found it hard not to imagine we were only one clumsy landing, one twisted neck from catastrophe. Perhaps all mothers are the same. Perhaps, after all we'd been through, I was worse.

It was term time and just before the end of the school day and the centre was quiet. The air was punctuated by the tinny notes of a children's television programme, the mechanical beeps and squawks of ride-on cars and trains and the occasional burst of wailing from a young child. It was a woman's world of babies and toddlers.

I waited for him in the café corner, drinking a black Americano. It was almost deserted. Just a few huddles of women who shared gossip and advice and roused themselves every now and again to change nappies or wipe noses.

The only other man on the premises was the youth behind the counter in reception. Matt, with his broad shoulders and bohemian hair, looked as if he'd come striding into the wrong building. The mothers and nannies watched him as he picked his way through the chaos to buy himself a coffee. He sat opposite me at the grey, plastic-topped table. It was gritty with spilt sugar.

You were busy now on the jungle climbing frame, heaving yourself up staircases of padded blocks, running back and forth across a rope net like a mad monkey and sliding down a tube, only to jump out and run round to do it all over again. As Matt settled with his coffee, you looked across at us and took in the fact of his arrival with a solid, steady gaze.

'How are you doing?'

His face was set and it worried me. He looked down into his cappuccino and stirred it. Chocolate powder melted into smudges in the froth.

The other women seemed suddenly quiet. I leaned forward and lowered my voice.

'Whatever it is, please. Just tell me.'

He sighed. 'I've heard from Geoff.'

My stomach tensed. 'Your brother?'

I'd almost forgotten Matt's promise to look into Ella, to ask Geoff to do the same.

'You can't repeat this. To anyone.' He bent forward to me. 'I only did this because I love you so much, Jen. I'd do anything for you. I leaned on Geoff to do this as a favour to me. You understand? If anyone found out—'

'I get it.'

Cartoon music burst out of one of the rides as it rocked into motion.

Matt was hesitant. 'It may not be the same person. I mean, there could be more than one Ella Hicks.' He spoke carefully, weighing each word. 'She did have a baby. A girl. Found dead in her cot.'

I couldn't breathe. Teeny-weeny. You were right.

'What happened?'

His eyes were on mine. 'Febrile convulsions.'

'What does that mean?'

He shrugged. 'Seizures. They're not often fatal but they can be.'

Auntie Ella sent her to Mr Michael because something bad happened so she couldn't stay with her mummy. That's what you said.

'Was it her?' I swallowed. 'Was it something she did?'

Matt hesitated. He seemed too reluctant to answer.

'I don't know,' he said at last. 'The coroner's report wasn't conclusive.' He paused. 'But convulsions can be the result of injury. Of being shaken.'

The air swam and I closed my eyes, grasped at the edge of the table. He reached for my hand at once and encased it in his own as if he were trying to protect me.

I saw you, a newborn, with your scrunched-up face and perfect, tiny hands. How could anyone hurt a baby? And a mother, what mother harmed her own child? It was obscene.

'Are you OK?' Matt's voice was close and warm.

I nodded, pulled my hand free and wiped my eyes with my fingers. 'I'm sorry.'

When I opened my eyes, he looked anxious. 'I'd never hurt you, Jen. You know that, don't you? You mean the world to me. You and Gracie.' He paused. 'I just thought you needed to know.'

'Of course.' I reached in my sleeve for a tissue. 'I do.'

My body was heavy on the seat. Exhausted. *How did you know, my love? How?* I didn't understand. How could she do such a thing? I shook my head. And what about your safety? How could I ever leave you with her again? 'What did they do to her? I mean, was she charged or anything?'

His eyes stayed on my face. 'The police interviewed her. It's all there, on record. But they couldn't prove anything. In the end, the coroner gave a verdict of death by natural causes. That was it.'

I almost didn't bother with the next question. I knew the answer. 'What was the baby's name?'

He paused. 'Catherine.'

'Catherine.'

You were right, my love, all the time.

A toddler, barely walking, stumbled over to our table and stood there, staring up at me with unblinking eyes. A voice called: 'Holly!' and she turned, considered her mother's outstretched arms, teetered back to her.

I felt a sudden physical need to hold you and looked over, trying to search you out in the cloud of moving children. There you were, hanging upside down from bent knees, your legs hooked over a metal bar, your hair streaming to the ground like water. My love, where did you go, in those awful moments of lifelessness, as the paramedics rushed you to intensive care? How could you know these strange unknowable things?

'Jen?' Matt came around to my side of the table and sat next to me on the cushioned seat, so close that his thigh pressed against

mine. I put my hand on his leg and he wrapped his fingers round mine. 'Jen, darling, are you OK?'

'What do I do?'

'Do?'

I thought about Richard. He was a kind man. A gentle one. That woman had manipulated him from the start.

'What if they have a baby together? She might do it again.' I breathed deeply. 'And what about Gracie? She might hurt her.'

He squeezed my hand, shook his head. 'You can't do anything, Jen. You know what? I think you're right. I think she *did* kill her baby. But medically that's so hard to prove. The evidence just isn't conclusive.'

I sat very still, trying to take it all in. My feet, under the table, juddered against the hard, shiny floor.

His hand, round mine, tensed. 'You know now. You know what she is. Let's forget about them. Leave them alone. Focus on our own life together.'

'Richard needs to know.'

'Really?' He pulled away from me. 'What are you going to say? You know Ella killed her daughter because an angel told Gracie when she was in Heaven? Do you know how crazy that sounds?'

I couldn't answer. He was right. It sounded absurd.

He raked his hand through his hair. 'I'm sorry, Jen. I didn't mean—'

He reached an arm round me and drew me closer against his chest. We sat like that for a while. The children's cries, the grating mechanical music filled the silence.

Finally, he said: 'Richard's a lawyer, isn't he?'

'Solicitor.'

'See this through his eyes.' He paused. 'So much of what we know is hearsay. Things Gracie has told you. Maternal instinct. A question of faith. None of that's evidence.'

'Yes, but even so—'

He winced, awkward. 'From what you've told me, he already seems to doubt you, to think you're—' he hesitated, feeling his way '—over-wrought. That you've got a grudge against Ella.'

I sighed. He was right, of course. I did hate Ella. And Richard was already exasperated with me.

'I know that's not true,' Matt went on. 'I'm just saying. You can't tell Richard. Or anyone else. They'd never believe you.'

I shrugged. 'So what do I do?'

He looked at me closely. 'Why do you have to do anything?'

I swallowed. 'For the baby. Catherine. She deserves justice.'

'In a court of law?'

'Yes.'

He sighed. 'You're not listening to me.' He shook his head. 'You have no evidence she did anything wrong. The coroner already gave a verdict. OK?'

I looked at the scratches along the surface of the plastic tabletop. A knife, maybe. A metal toy.

'I just think—' I broke off, trying to find the words. 'Richard's making a life with this woman. He needs to know what she is.'

'He's in love with her.'

I frowned, turned away. You ran across to the dressing-up baskets and rifled through the capes, hats, aprons there.

'And you can't mention Geoff. You give me your word? He doesn't even know I'm telling you.'

'He'd get into trouble?'

'Trouble? He'd lose his job.'

We drank our coffees. The centre started to get busier. A small boy astride a pink plastic car banged into our table, reversed, struggled to get clear.

We tried to be normal for a while, chatting without enthusiasm about nothing much. You and our plans for the rest of the day. His late shift at work.

When we finished our coffees, I said: 'You should probably make tracks.'

He put his hands on my shoulders and turned me to face him, right there on the bench.

'I love you, Jen. You do know that, don't you? I adore you.' He spoke in a low voice. He was so close that his breath, coffee-scented, was warm against my cheek. 'I want to spend the rest of my life looking after you. You see? You and Gracie. My two gorgeous girls.'

I nodded, moved in closer to touch my lips to his, conscious of the mothers and nannies all around.

'I love you too.' I mumbled the words into his neck.

You were in the toddler area, building towers out of coloured foam blocks, then knocking them down again. Now, as Matt reached to hold me, you stopped and lifted your eyes to watch. Your expression was knowing.

His voice was in my ear. 'I want to be with you always, Jen. I know it's a lot to take in. Just think about this.' He paused. 'I want to us to be a proper family.'

I didn't move.

'My place is great for me. But it's tiny. Far too small for three. Why don't I move in with you? We were made for each other. I know we were and I think you do too, don't you?' He kissed me chastely on the top of the head, pulled away. 'Let's do it. Soon.'

Your eyes hadn't left us. Across the play centre, even with the cries, the beeps, the noise, you seemed to know exactly what we were discussing, to hear and understand every word. I blinked, my eyes on yours. How could you be so wise? How could you know about Catherine and be privy to these strange secrets from the past? Unless of course everything you'd told me from the start, however incredible, was actually true.

CHAPTER 41

That night, at bath time, you said, from nowhere: 'Do you like him as much as you like Daddy?'

I had just lifted you into the bubbles and was drawing shapes on your back with my finger. It was a guessing game, my mother did the same with us when we were children, but at this age, there wasn't a lot of guesswork. Half the time, you told me what to draw before I started.

I carried on, pretended not to hear.

'It's got a big body and four legs like this and a large head with big flapping ears.'

You didn't move.

'And a very, very long trunk.'

You twisted round, delighted. 'An elephant!'

I tried to look amazed. 'How did you know?'

'Another one. Do a bunny.'

I dipped my finger in the bubbles again.

'This one is really hard.'

You tensed, eyes forward towards the taps, bracing your back as you concentrated.

'So. This one is small with long floppy ears. One. Two. And big feet. And a small round tail called a scut.'

'A bunny!'

'Yes!'

You beamed.

Later, we snuggled together in the armchair by your bed. You were wrapped up in a big, warm towel, then wrapped again in my

arms. Your pyjamas, your favourite ones with the Dalmatians, lay across the back of the chair, waiting until we'd finished our cuddle.

'I love you, little Gracie.'

The ends of your hair were still damp and I rubbed them dry in the folds of the towel. You wriggled, twisted sideways to lie across my lap like a baby. Sometimes you liked to play babies when we were alone. I rocked you, put my lips to your cheek, your hair. You smelt clean, of lavender soap and scented bubble bath. You kicked as you settled and your tiny pink feet came free from the towel.

'What story do you want? Have you chosen?'

You turned your face up to mine and that look came in your eyes, a knowing look, older than your years. 'Is he downstairs?'

'Who?'

You didn't answer, just looked at me, as if to say: *you know exactly who I mean.*

'If you mean Uncle Matt, no, he isn't here tonight. Just Mummy.'

'If you marry him, will he be my daddy?'

I hesitated, tried to find the right words. 'Daddy will always be your real daddy, Gracie. Uncle Matt is Mummy's special friend. He's been very kind to us, hasn't he?'

'In Venice?' You squirmed until you were sitting upright again, reached for your pyjamas and began to put them on. I fought back my urge to help you. It only caused an argument.

'Yes, in Venice. And when he takes us out and buys us treats.'

You considered. 'Daddy buys me treats too.'

'He does. Daddy loves you very much, Gracie. He always will. Whatever happens with Uncle Matt.'

'So I'll have two daddies?'

'In a way.'

'And two mummies. You and Auntie Ella?'

'Possibly.' I struggled to keep my face neutral. 'Into bed now.'

You finally let me tuck you up and I lay beside you while we read a couple of stories together. I switched off the light and sat in the armchair. You lay on your stomach, hunched forward with your forehead buried in your bear, your legs drawn up under you.

'Shush.' I made the word a long, steady sigh, which formed a wave of white noise through the quiet room. Gradually, as my eyes adjusted to the semi-darkness, familiar objects grew. The nursery rhyme pictures. The shelf of medicines, of stuffed animals and dolls, of books.

We moved you in here when you were just six months old. I didn't want to. I wanted your cot to stay in our room, by my side of the bed, but Richard was adamant. He nearly broke his back, carrying the armchair up from the sitting room. If we're going to spend half the night in here, he said, we may as well be comfortable. He didn't know, then, how much of the time you'd end up sleeping in our bed, curled up with me.

You sigh, turn onto your back, bear abandoned, arm sprawled above your head. I lean forward for a closer look.

You look so beautiful, my love, you always do. I sit there for some time, listening to the rise and fall of your breathing and marvelling at you. Your skin shines clear and fresh. Your fair hair is splayed on the sheet. Your eyelids flicker as you dream and I wonder where you've gone to, what you're seeing and feeling in sleep.

I try to imagine a baby girl called Catherine with ginger hair. Ella must have sat beside her as she slept and kept watch, as I'm keeping watch over you. She must have nursed her and changed her and stumbled out of bed, night after night, more asleep than awake, to lift her out of her cot when she cried and rock her back to sleep. How could she not adore her, protect her? I shake my head. Was it really possible that she'd lost her temper and shaken her so hard that she'd hurt her? How could any mother do that?

When I climbed in beside you in your hospital bed, amid the wires and drips, to hold you as tightly as I dared, to bring

you back, you felt so frail, so lost. You had the bones of a bird. I blinked, remembering, then lowered my face to yours until I was so close that I could hear the puff of your breath.

I love you, little Gracie. If anyone tries to hurt you, ever, I don't know what I'll do. I close my eyes, wrap my arms round myself and shudder. I'll do anything to save you. I know I will. Anything it takes.

CHAPTER 42

For days after that, all I could think about was Ella and that poor baby, Catherine, and what she did to her. It was unbearable. It made me shiver each time I thought about how much you'd known, so long before I did, and the innocent way you'd described your new friend with ginger hair.

Richard suggested dates for a holiday in July. He wanted to book, he said, to take you away to Spain. The three of them. Sea and sand and buckets and spades. You'd love it.

When I tried to stall, to say I wasn't sure, I needed to think about it, his tone turned cold. *There's nothing to think about, Jen. You took her to Venice with your boyfriend. What's the difference?*

How could I explain? How could I tell him that if Ella was capable of doing such a monstrous thing to her own child, she might hurt you too? I couldn't sleep for worrying.

Matt was right. I knew it. If I wanted to stop her, I needed evidence. And finally, my chance came.

The following weekend, Richard invited you for another sleepover. This time, instead of letting him collect you, I insisted on taking you to their house myself. It was your idea, I lied. You were desperate to show me the bunk beds. You'd talked of nothing else.

Richard sounded hesitant. I knew why. She didn't like me visiting their house. But I insisted and he didn't have much choice.

I played one of your CDs in the car and while you sang along in the back, your voice high and off-key, I tried to relax, to steady

my breathing and think through what I needed to do. The car stuttered and jolted through heavy traffic.

When Richard first left, he moved into Ella's flat. I picked up bits and pieces from little things he said, from the background noises when we talked on the phone. It was a tiny flat in the heart of the city, throbbing at night with live bands and rowdy drunks outside.

You were only just walking then but even at that age, you seemed fascinated by Ella, with her tight clothes and glittery shoes. It led to petty battles. Sour notes from me when you returned one day with your thumbnails painted red and, another day, with the temporary tattoo of a winged horse on your thigh.

It was a second-floor flat with steep stairs. A nail salon on the first floor. Two men above who worked nights in a bar. It made me laugh at the time. Bitterly, of course. It was hard to imagine a place less like Richard — my dear, stay-at-home, prematurely middle-aged husband. But then he wasn't any more, was he?

Eventually, the two of them took the next step and moved into a small Victorian terraced house in the suburbs, closer to us. A big lifestyle change for Ella. I assume Richard persuaded her. They needed more space and a second bedroom for you. He tried, I give him that. I'd seen it from the outside once or twice when I dropped you off but she'd never invited me in.

Now I turned off the main road, with its parades of grocery shops, newsagents and dry cleaners, the streets became residential and quiet. A smart young woman, earphones in her ears, pushed a buggy. A traffic warden passed, strolling, watchful, punching registration numbers into a hand-held device. Further down the road, there was a clatter of metal as builders unloaded poles from the back of a truck.

The blood banged in my ears as I approached number forty-two and found somewhere to park. When we got out, I paused at the hedge for a moment, looking it over. The gate

was latched. The lid of the bin was pushed up by a bulging bag inside. Upstairs, the bedroom curtains were drawn back but the windows were dark.

Richard answered the door. You ran in past him, your bear under your arm, shouting hello to the quietness. A moment later, you shed your coat, leaving it on the floor, and went clomping up the stairs as fast as you could.

Richard and I looked at each other. His face was strained.

I managed to smile. 'What about these bunk beds? Can I have a look?'

'I told you.' He shrugged, stood aside to let me squeeze past. 'They're perfectly safe.'

I crossed the bare-wood floor of the hall, wondering if I was supposed to take off my shoes. The door to the left stood open and I paused for a glimpse inside at a large, open-plan sitting room. The walls and carpet were cream, the furniture all glass and metal. It was sparse and modern, a stark contrast with our home, which was a clutter of tired wooden furniture inherited from family over the years or picked up second-hand. Our interiors weren't designed, they just evolved.

I looked at the pristine surfaces and imagined you crayoning on the walls or running over the carpets in muddy shoes and thought what pleasure it would give me if you did.

'No Ella?'

'She's popped out.'

I bet she has. Waiting until the coast's clear. He didn't offer me a drink, just pointed the way up the stairs after you, as if he wanted this over and done with as soon as possible.

There was a small first landing with a bathroom and a closed door. I carried on to the next level, following the sound of your voice as you called to me.

There was no doubt which room was yours. You'd already kicked off your shoes and were crouched on a fluffy pink rug

in the shape of a bear, playing with a patchwork elephant. The walls were cream, decorated with framed pictures of fairies and princesses. Behind you, against the wall, were the new bunk beds with their carpeted stairs. The duvet hung over the edge of the top bunk. The cover showed rainbows and unicorns.

The lower bunk was piled with stuffed animals. A spotted horse. A family of rabbits in dresses, with patchwork ears. A teddy with a pink bow. Everything looked brand new. I set your overnight bag down in the corner and went to sit beside you.

'Look, Mummy!' You scrambled to your feet and crawled across the lower bunk to disappear into the hidey-hole under the stairs. Your voice came out: 'Where am I?'

'I don't know,' I said, playing along. 'Where's Gracie gone, Daddy?'

Richard stood awkwardly in the doorway, his shoulders hunched. He didn't answer. He looked embarrassed. The expense, perhaps. Your room here was so much more extravagant than I could give you at home. The liberal splashes of pink were tacky but you were three; of course you loved it. I knew exactly who was behind it all. It was another weapon in her battle to seduce you, to win you over.

I smiled at him. 'Do you mind if I play with her for a bit? I won't stay long.' I lowered my voice to a whisper to add: 'She's been so keen to show me.'

'If you want.' He didn't look pleased but he gave in and turned away. I listened to his heavy footsteps on the stairs, heading back to the ground floor.

As soon as he'd gone, I whispered to you: 'Gracie, I need you to be very good. Can you do that? Mummy's got to go and do something.'

You poked your head out, uncertain. I kissed your nose.

'You play quietly here with elephant and horse and teddy,' I said. 'Until I come back. OK?'

I left you chattering to your toys while I crept across this second landing to the main bedroom at the front of the house. I faltered on the threshold and steadied my breath.

My eyes went at once to the bed. A king-size, unmade, the duvet thrown back, as if someone had just climbed out. The sheets crumpled. I crossed to it, found my feet caught up in a furry bedside rug. Hers. Not Richard's style. I rubbed the edge of the sheet between my fingers. Cool and crisp. Good quality cotton. Our sheets at home were soft with over-washing.

There were fitted wardrobes down one wall. I opened them quietly, door by door, and looked inside, checking the floor space for boxes, for files.

His suits hadn't changed much but he wore pure silk ties now in brighter colours and bolder designs. Pale pink and blue shirts hung alongside the white. That was her influence.

Her wardrobe had slinky cocktail dresses. At least six. Two long evening dresses, shrouded in dry cleaner's bags. Waterfall cardigans in cashmere. An angora wrap. Crisp shirts and blouses in all shades. Beneath, neatly arranged on a chrome rack, about a dozen pairs of evening shoes. Long spiked heels and spaghetti straps.

I closed the wardrobe doors and got on my hands and knees to check under the bed. A noise, just outside the house. The click of the front gate. I scrambled to the window to look, standing back against the curtain to peer down. The postman's red trolley stood on the pavement.

Downstairs, the letter box clanged, then a smack as post hit the mat. A moment later, the postman went back down the path and wheeled his trolley forward a few paces to next-door's gate.

My stomach was tight, my skin hot. I stood still, listening. Richard's tread on the wooden floor as he crossed the hall to pick up the letters. My heart thumped. The footsteps faded again, back to another part of the ground floor. I needed to be quick.

The bedroom was unnaturally bare, so unlike my own. I had a whole suitcase full of your baby things. Then there were my old diaries, boxes of school reports, photographs. I even had a box under the bed with souvenirs from our wedding, right down to the ribbon from the cake.

I crossed to the chest of drawers and rummaged through the drawers. Tights and stockings in packets. Richard's cotton boxer shorts and boxes of cuff links.

Then a drawer of her silky underwear. I tried not to imagine her wearing it. Not to imagine Richard taking it off. I reached a bottom drawer when my fingers felt something different, something cool and hard. I crouched down and pulled out the drawer as far as it would go. It was her overflow space, filled with suspender belts, jewellery boxes, handkerchiefs and purses. I lifted them out in handfuls. Right at the back was a slim, clear plastic folder.

I first at thought that the photographs, in plain cardboard mounts, like old-fashioned school portraits, were remnants from another generation. The pictures were black and white but seemed muted. There was also a stillness about them, a timelessness. I sat there on the carpet, gazing at them.

They were Ella's features but transformed by such tenderness that I barely recognised her as the woman I knew. Her shoulders were covered by the lacy sleeves of a nightdress or bed jacket. Her hair was loose round her neck.

In one, she gazed with wonder at the baby in her arms. The scrunched face of a newborn with closed eyes. Another picture showed the baby's tiny hand curled round her manicured finger. The final image was of the baby, clothed in a sleep-suit and a delicate lace-edged bonnet, fast asleep in a Moses basket. A printed slip inside the frame read: Celebrating the birth of Catherine Louise. The date was eight years ago. The final item in the folder was wrapped in tissue paper. A tiny lock of ginger hair.

I tore the paper label off the back, with the name, address and telephone number of the photographer, and shoved it inside my pocket. The intensity of feeling in Ella's eyes made me physically sick. It was impossible to reconcile that love with the knowledge of what she did to her, so soon after these pictures were taken. I shook my head. The photographer who framed those artistic portraits would be just as shocked.

'Richard?'

Her voice, calling, down in the hall. The slam of the front door behind her. I stuffed the pictures, the hastily re-bundled hair and tissue paper, back into the plastic folder, threw the handkerchiefs and jewellery boxes on top and closed the drawer. It shut with a bang that sounded deafening in the quiet.

A creak from the stairs. I bolted across the landing, back to your room.

'Where were you, Mummy?' You looked cross. You didn't like being on your own.

I picked up the first stuffed toy I saw and started to talk to it, pretending we were in the middle of a game.

'Yes, Mr Elephant,' I said, 'of course you can have tea too. Do you take milk?'

My breath was short and the words came out in gasps. You narrowed your eyes.

'What, Mummy? What are you doing?' Then you looked past me, and smiled. 'Auntie Ella!'

She stood there, in the doorway. Watching me. Her eyes were cold.

You jumped up and ran to hug her, and her eyes softened as she folded her arms round you and hugged you back.

I felt my cheeks flush. The stolen label from the back of the pictures burned inside my pocket. I was afraid to move quickly in case it fell out. I thought of the plastic folder, shoved back so quickly, and the belongings heaped on top, left in disarray.

The silence stretched. She waited, her forehead tightened as she looked down at me. Finally, she said: 'I think it's time you left. Don't you?'

CHAPTER 43

When I reached home, I copied out the name and address of the photographer from the sticky label and hid the paper in a drawer. I didn't want to risk losing it. Then I made myself a cup of tea and sat alone in the emptiness of the kitchen, considering the label.

It was true then. You and Matt were right. Ella did have a daughter, Catherine Louise. A baby with a shock of ginger hair. This woman, Stella, had documented it. I sipped my tea, thinking. This was the evidence I'd wanted that Ella really did have a child. But how could I prove what she'd done to her?

I fingered the label. These pictures were taken years ago. Stella, whoever she was, might have closed down by now or moved away. Perhaps she would have forgotten Ella, just one of hundreds of clients over the years. Or have nothing to tell me anyway. It was all possible, I knew that. But I had to try. My hands shook as I picked up the phone and dialled the number.

It rang out and I was about to give up when a young woman answered. Her tone was a bored sing-song.

'Stella's Photography, how can I help you?'

I took a deep breath. 'I'd like to make an appointment please. To see Stella. As soon as possible.'

A rustle of paper as she turned the pages of a diary or appointments book.

'I'm afraid she's fully booked today.' Pause. 'She's in tomorrow. After lunch. Perhaps around three?'

Later, I took the bus into central London to meet Matt.

I gazed out of the window, distracted by the vibrancy of the outside world. I missed you. You had such a capacity for living in the present, for being excited by the smallest, everyday things: the stripes of a zebra crossing, a cat sunning itself on a flat roof, a small boy on a scooter.

Matt stood at the entrance to the shopping mall, waiting for me. His hands were deep in the pockets of his coat. His chin was dark with twenty-four hours of stubble. My pulse quickened at the sight of him.

'Darling.' He opened his arms to me and I disappeared into a hug. He held me so tightly I could barely breathe. When he finally loosened his embrace, he kissed me.

'Missed you so much.' He lowered his head and kissed me again, this time for even longer. 'Thank you for doing this.' He took my free hand and tucked it away in his pocket inside his own. His fingers, warm and strong, enveloped mine. 'Toy shop?'

'Lead on.'

I stood ahead of him on the escalator and he wrapped his arms round my waist as if he couldn't bear to be parted from me for a minute.

It was large, brightly coloured toy shop with animated displays in glass cases. Small children stood with their noses pressed against one, watching trains whirr through tunnels and over bridges. Inside the next, there was a fairground made of play bricks. The roundabout, complete with small figures, was slowly turning, a set of swings rocking mechanically back and forth. A small girl looked lost in it.

Matt set off down an aisle, picking up boxes, looking at them briefly, then pushing them back on the shelf. His shoulders were tight and hunched. I watched, sad for him.

He wouldn't talk to me about Katy or his ex. There was so much I wanted to know about them both but I'd learned not to

ask any more. If I tried to, even the vaguest question, he frowned and his mood darkened. So I was very conscious, as I trailed after him, that I was setting out across thin ice.

I found him at the far end of the shop, frowning at a display of jigsaws.

'How old is she going to be? Eight?'

He nodded quickly, walked a little further away.

I tried to imagine you at eight. Tried to imagine missing all those years between now and then and the pain of choosing gifts without knowing what to send.

I caught up with him again and stood at his shoulder. He stared down at the picture of a little girl on a box, her blonde hair tied back in a ponytail, her face beaming as she played with a doll's tea set.

'Maybe a bit young?'

He didn't answer. He looked utterly miserable. I wondered how he'd managed to do this on his own, year after year.

'What about something to make?'

I walked on down the aisle, scanning the brightly coloured boxes, the shiny mass-produced plastic. Paints and felt tips and crayons. Stamps and moulds. I picked up a junior tapestry kit with a picture of a pair of kittens.

'I had one of these.' Mine had shown a cat sleeping in the doorway of a country cottage with roses round the door. A gift from an aunt and uncle. I smiled to myself. I hadn't thought of it for years. It kept me busy for a whole Easter holiday and we'd framed it afterwards. It must be in a box somewhere. 'I loved it.'

He came to look, turned it over, his voice doubtful. 'I don't know.'

I put it back, moved him on to sewing kits. Make a fabric doll. Sew a set of doll's clothes.

'What about this?' I turned it over. 'Age seven to ten.'

He frowned. 'I'm not sure.'

It wasn't like him to be so indecisive. He seemed frightened. Afraid to get it wrong. This was his only link to his daughter until Christmas, assuming she was even given these gifts. I wanted to help but I didn't know how. I had no idea what she might like and, from the way he was behaving, neither did he. I put my hand on his arm and gave it a squeeze.

'Let's keep looking.'

We moved on to the next aisle.

'A game?'

I tried to remember being eight. I played a lot of board games with my father. He was patient. I realised now that he must have been tired when he came home from the lab but he always had time for me. He spent a long time teaching me chess.

I reached up, past the stacks of draughts and chess and classic family games and lifted down a box. The glossy picture showed a family of actors, a beaming mum and dad and a perfect boy and girl sitting between them, all waving their hands and exclaiming in delight. It didn't look like any family I'd ever seen. His face, taking it all in, was dejected.

I pushed the box back, moved him on past more games and a bank of jigsaws and came finally to a small display of books.

'*The Hobbit*.' I took it down and handed it to him. 'Loved it. Didn't you?'

He thumbed through in silence.

'Just the right age for it too. Eight.'

He stopped, looked more closely at one of the old-fashioned line drawings. 'Maybe.' He didn't sound convinced.

'And you can write a message in the front with the date. She'll have it forever.'

He hesitated, thinking this over. 'She might already have it.'

Of course she might. He could say the same about any book I suggested. About any game we found. He closed the book.

'I don't think so.' He put it back. 'I'm being a bit useless, aren't I? I'm sorry.'

I reached up to him, kissed his cheek. His forehead was tight with worry. It was clear how desperately he wanted to get this right and I loved him for it.

'It's OK.'

We had almost exhausted the shop when he pulled out a box. Make your own charm bracelets. A girl smiled out, her chin cupped in her hands, her wrists resplendent with pink and white loops of plastic.

'What about this?'

I took it from him, read the blurb on the back. It was a mixture of beads and miniature charms. I had no idea whether she'd like it or not. It was a blind guessing game. I said: 'Well, there's a lot to it.'

He took it back, looked again at the picture, at the smiling girl.

'It's not too babyish?'

'I don't think so.'

He sighed. We chose a card and a sheet of Happy Birthday wrapping paper, decorated with pink cupcakes, and he finally queued to pay, weighed down by the burden of it all. His shoulders were hunched and he seemed so vulnerable, so fragile. It was a side of him I hadn't seen before and I felt a surge of affection for him, for this man who had appeared from nowhere and inserted himself in our lives, who tried so hard to look after me when he saw me struggle.

Afterwards, he found me at the door of the shop with his plastic bag in hand and we ventured together into the bustle of the shopping centre. He looked dazed. I threaded an arm round his waist and hugged him and his face, when he turned back to me, was sad.

'Thank you.' He kissed me on the tip of my nose. 'No one's ever done that with me before.'

'Let's get some lunch.'

'I've got padded envelopes at home.' I nodded down to his bag. 'You write the card and I'll sort the rest.'

'That's sweet.' He smiled. 'Thank you.'

That evening, I left Matt in the kitchen, where he was chopping and stirring and steaming, and went for a long, hot bath. I lay soaking, surrounded by bubbles, and thought how unfair life was. That Ella, blessed with a beautiful baby girl, could care for her so little and yet Matt, clearly besotted with his daughter, was so cruelly forced apart from her.

I picked up the set of ducks on the side of the bath and set them free to bob round the islands of my knees. I wondered if you were asleep in bed now, tucked up under your rainbows and unicorns with bear. I missed you, my love. Always. The house was never the same without you in it.

I read an article once about a mother with terminal cancer who bought and wrapped Christmas and birthday presents for her young children, all the way through to their twenty-first birthdays. I often thought about that.

First, about how anyone could bear to do such a heart-breaking thing. Then, about what I would choose for you, if I knew I were being taken away, leaving you to grow up without me. It struck me as a courageous act, that woman's desperate attempt to defeat time and to stay present in her children's lives for all those years into the future. And yet it was strangely melancholy too. What if the gifts were the wrong ones? If the children simply didn't grow into the people she expected them to be, without the tastes, the interests she imagined? Like Matt, she simply couldn't know.

'I was beginning to think you'd drowned.'

Matt was sitting at the kitchen table, looking over the newspaper. The air was rich with the smell of chicken and the strains of one of my old CDs.

'I didn't know you liked Springsteen.'

'I didn't know *you* did.' He raised his eyebrows. 'Saw him in concert three times. Amazing.'

I smiled, imagining him as a younger man. I remembered how desperately lonely the evenings were before he came along, the silence and the solitary glass of wine and the early nights. And how normal it seemed now, to have him here in my own kitchen.

He opened an arm to me and I perched on his knee, wrapped my hands round his neck and kissed him.

'You smell nice.' He murmured into my neck. 'You've been away far too long.'

'Sorry.' My body felt clean and relaxed in sloppy trousers and shirt and I shifted my weight as he ran a hand under my shirt and across my skin. 'What time's dinner?'

'Soon. If you stop distracting me.' He lifted me down, got to his feet and lit the gas under a pan. 'About ten minutes.'

I took scissors and tape from a drawer and went through to the sitting room to wrap the bracelets craft set, then sealed the present and birthday card in a padded envelope.

I called through: 'I can post Katy's present tomorrow for you, if you like?'

'That's OK.'

Before I went back into the kitchen to join him, I sat for a moment, looking at the parcel, trying to imagine the young girl who'd open it, what she'd feel as she tore off the paper, what she remembered, if anything, of the father who'd chosen it with such love and such pain.

CHAPTER 44

Matt was working a late shift on Sunday and left straight after lunch. I pottered around the house, stacking the dishwasher and putting a wash on. I made your bed and arranged your toys along the bottom. A few more hours and you'd be home again. Then I picked up the photographer's address and set off.

The bell jingled when I pushed the shop door open. The girl behind the counter didn't lift her head. She bent forward over a magazine, her nails painted vivid pink. Her hair was long and swept up in a ponytail, tied with a green ribbon.

The interior was shadowy after the bright sunshine of the street. I made a show of looking at the frames: wood, plastic, metal, multi-frames, singles.

I crossed to the display wall towards the back. Portraits by Stella. She offered several styles. Young children playing, dressed up as pirates or princesses. They laughed, open-mouthed and joyful as only a small child can be, looking up and slightly to one side, their attention caught by someone or something offstage. I wondered how many shots it took to get those perfect photographs and thought with a pang how gorgeous you'd look.

Others were more formal, portraits of families sitting together in posed groups, children with slightly strained faces, in the protective hoop of their parents' arms.

The final section was artistic. The face of a girl, about your age, on the far side of a bubble, just before it burst. A boy, a chubby toddler in a sailor suit, reaching for a falling balloon. It was hard to believe the images weren't faked.

'Can I help you?' The girl, finally. She spoke without moving.

'I've come to see Stella. Jen Walker.'

She blinked. 'Have you got an appointment?'

'I called yesterday. You told me to come around three.'

She frowned. 'You didn't speak to me.'

'Well, whoever it was, that's what they said. Is she in?'

She sighed, heaved herself down from her stool and padded to the back. Her heels echoed on the wooden floor as they clattered through.

Stella was about fifty, with long, unashamedly greying hair and no make-up. She strode out in baggy trousers, flat shoes and a loose, blouson top. Her eyes were quick and her handshake firm.

'You wanted to see me?'

'I was thinking of arranging a photo shoot as a present for a friend,' I said. 'Could I ask you about it?'

The back room had the feel of an artist's gallery. The walls were exposed London brick, the woodwork painted a brilliant white. The ceiling gave way to a long, strutted skylight down the centre, which flooded the whole area with light. Around the walls, individual framed pictures were picked out by spotlights on tracks.

Against one wall hung a screen: the pull-down, rolling type, which offered different coloured backgrounds. Next to it, there was a large wicker basket that overflowed with props and children's costumes.

'May I have a look round?'

'Feel free.' She settled at a long desk in one corner of the room, covered with mounts and prints, and bent over her work.

I walked round, past the wedding portraits, the family shots. They were standard colour prints, not the old-fashioned sepia of Ella's pictures. I hesitated, wondering if I'd got the right place. Perhaps it had kept the name but changed hands.

After a few minutes, I sensed her watching me and turned. She got to her feet and came to join me, handed me a brochure and price list.

'Was there something in particular?'

'My friend's having her first baby next month,' I said. 'I wanted something special for her. You did some striking pictures for another friend of ours, a few years ago. Of her newborn.' I hesitated, pretended to think about it. 'Well, seven or eight years ago, actually.'

She looked at me more closely. 'I don't really do newborns.'

'Really?' I opened the brochure, looked down the prices. They started at three figures. 'I'm sure she said Stella. They were such lovely shots. The baby only looks a few hours old. There's one of her in her mother's arms and another of their hands together, the baby's little fist curled round her mother's finger, you know? They were really evocative.'

She didn't speak for a moment. She just stood there, staring at me with an odd expression on her face. I turned away and studied the price list, feeling my face flush. I always was a terrible liar.

'Your friend, the one who's expecting a baby,' she said at last, 'is everything alright?'

'Yes, well, I think so.' I faltered.

Her face became stern. 'Are you a lawyer?'

'A lawyer?' I blinked. 'No.'

'I'm sorry.' She looked at me thoughtfully. 'I get them, sometimes. I don't want any part in all that. Good luck to people, if that's what they need to do. Personally, I don't think it helps.'

She stood for a moment, looking me over, then seemed to come to a decision. She crossed to a shelf and ran her finger along a bank of large albums there before lifting one down. It was ivory and tied with cream ribbon. She opened it on her desk, gestured me across to join her as she started to turn the pages.

'I don't put these out,' she said. 'Are these the ones you mean?'

I recognised the style at once from the pictures hidden away at the back of Ella's drawer. They all had the same timeless sepia tint, the same stillness in the features. Tiny babies, some of them impossibly small and fragile, some with blue veins bulging at their temples through marble skin, some wrapped round in fluffy white towels, other dressed in baby grows and bonnets, all with their eyes screwed closed.

'I don't charge for these,' she said. 'But I only take referrals from the hospital. The midwives know me.'

I didn't know what to say. I didn't understand.

'I went through it myself, you see, years ago,' she went on. 'There was nothing available then but a lot of people find it helps. It gives them something to remember. Otherwise, the whole experience, well, it can seem very unreal afterwards.'

She glanced at me. My eyes moved again to the photographs. Slowly she turned the pages, showing me family after family. I started to see the dreadful sameness in the pictures. How still the babies lay. Not one of them was crying. Not one had its eyes open.

'Your friend,' she said. 'The one whose baby I photographed. You didn't know her very well, did you?'

I shook my head.

'How did you see her pictures?'

'At her mother's house,' I stuttered. 'That's all. She had them on the wall.'

She narrowed her eyes and looked thoughtful. 'Did your friend suddenly drop you after the birth? Avoid you? Some women do that, you know. Don't take it personally. You can't imagine, until you go through it yourself. The pain of being the only woman on the maternity ward without a baby. Your breasts filling with milk, just as if your baby needed it. And all those well-meaning people, people who haven't heard, phoning you, texting, asking if it's a boy or a girl, wanting names, weights, pictures.' She closed the book. 'It's not an easy thing to talk about.'

She put the album back on the shelf. When she turned back, I was still in the same spot. My feet were rooted.

'Now you know why I don't do newborns,' she said, 'in the normal sense. Plenty of other studios do.' She paused. 'I'm sorry if there's been a misunderstanding.'

She turned and escorted me to the door.

At the entrance to the shop, she said: 'Born sleeping. That's what I like to say.' She paused. Again, the curious, appraising look. 'If you thought your friend's baby was really alive, well, I must be doing something right.'

CHAPTER 45

I barely remembered getting home. My body carried me along. The rest of me was numb. Ella's baby girl. Stillborn. God, how awful. The pavement, the passing traffic, swirled and blurred as I stumbled on.

I couldn't make sense of it. Was it true then, after all? Was there really some medical problem, a reason she couldn't have children? My palms sweated.

And I believed Stella. There was so reason for her to lie to me. *Stillborn.* How did she bear it?

I remembered the calmness in the baby's face. I'd thought she was just sleeping, but it was more than that. I saw it now. It was true. She was already at peace.

I thought again of the pictures. Of the tender look on Ella's face as she held her newborn baby, Catherine Louise. She knew, even as she looked down into that scrunched face, that she'd already lost her baby. That those tiny eyes would never open and fasten on hers. What courage it must have taken to hold back her grief, her anger and cradle her dead baby's body with such love. I kept walking, my hand on my stomach, trying to imagine it, oblivious to the world around me.

My thoughts were jumbled, confused. I thought of the strangeness in her eyes when she saw me teasing you, cuddling you. It was there too when you ran to her and hugged her. A hardness I always read as loathing. Evidence of her bitter hatred of us both. Now, knowing what she'd been through, what she'd lost, it seemed something else. Something far worse. Pain.

At home, I crawled into the crumpled, unmade bed and pulled the covers over my head, trying not to feel, trying only to hide. I shook for some time, my eyes screwed closed. Then a fresh blow hit me. I sat bolt upright, my hands to my cheeks.

What about the medical reports? The seizures? How could both things be true? I drew up my knees, wrapped my arms round them and hugged them to me. Had Matt's brother, Geoff, made a mistake, looked up details of the wrong case?

I stared at the wall, struggling to figure it out. *Was there more than one Ella Hicks?* It wasn't such an unusual name. I hesitated, forcing my brain to work. But both with babies called Catherine, born around the same time and both dying? I shook my head. It didn't add up. Someone was lying and I didn't think it was Stella.

I moaned, lay back on the bed and curled into a ball. I saw it all again. The club. Ella, there in front of me. Her face when I'd taunted her about Catherine. My body flushed hot with shame. *I didn't know, how could I? What had she thought of me?* She was very upset when she came home, Richard had said. His face was stern. *I didn't have you down as cruel.* I put my hands to my face, trying to scrape away the memory, too ashamed even to cry.

Later, when Richard dropped you home again, I couldn't look him in the face.

I waited until he left, then lifted you into my arms and pressed you against my chest, holding you tight even as you struggled, my wet face pressed into your hair. My own sweet girl, the day you were born was the most miraculous, the most wonderful day of my life. The thought of anyone losing their baby, just as their child's life was meant to begin, made me tremble and I clung to you as if you were the only solid creature in this sad, swirling world.

Before you went up to bed that evening, we crayoned together at the kitchen table. You were happy and full of stories about the weekend. You told me about the little boy you'd met in the park.

You'd grabbed his hand when he tried to run through the open gate and escape onto the road.

'He was so naughty, Mummy,' you said. 'I held his hand very tightly like this because he wanted to run away. What a silly banana.'

You shook your head, fondly despairing of a boy who sounded only about two. You sounded so adult that I had to look up to reassure myself that you were still only three years old, crayoning with passion, your hair spilling forward down your cheek. Your words sounded at times like a window on your future, as if time could fold and past and future merge right here in the kitchen and show me your much older self.

I crayoned slowly alongside you, struggling to concentrate. My chest was tight. I was weighed down by thoughts of Ella and baby Catherine and the sadness of what happened to them. Life seemed suddenly so fragile, so unpredictable, that I couldn't quite believe you had survived and were here with me now, and couldn't bear to think how barren my life would be without you.

All I wanted, as I made my careful strokes within the lines and let your chatter fill the silence, was to fold my arms round you and hold you close. I realised how angry I'd been. Angry with Richard for abandoning us and angry with Ella for stealing him away and frightened too that she wanted to take you next and then maybe even Matt. The people I loved most.

Now the anger fell away and I was left limp and exhausted and had to bite my lip to stop myself breaking down and sobbing in front of you. Ella had suffered, suffered much more than I had, suffered grief I couldn't imagine.

CHAPTER 46

Ella

I know exactly what she did. I heard her running across the landing, away from our room, as I came up the stairs. It was obvious the minute I saw her there beside Gracie, flushed with guilt, pretending they were calmly playing together, when her chest was still heaving. She's a terrible liar. An amateur.

I didn't bother talking to Richard about it. He'd never believe me. He doesn't have a prying, malicious cell in his body. But she and I are more alike than she cares to admit. Funny that, isn't it?

That drawer sticks. It's easy to open but there's a knack to closing it and it wasn't properly shut when I went to look. And inside, my mother's old handkerchiefs and her jewellery lay jumbled in a heap. I would never leave them like that. And Catherine's pictures shoved in their file in the wrong order. No one has the right to touch those. No one in the world, apart from me.

I know she hates me. I know she blames me for taking Richard from her. I understand that, however wrong she is. But she's gone beyond that now. She's become like him. Obsessive. Vengeful. He does that to people. Something terrible happens and they have to blame someone. To punish them. It's how they make sense of things, even if the truth is, it's no one's fault. The car crash? She *needs* it to be my fault, another reason to hate me.

And what happened to little Catherine? He always needed to lay that on me, heaping it on top of all the other hurt until I nearly suffocated. Now he's filled her mind with poison too.

Good luck to them both. All I ever wanted was for him to leave me alone, to take his grief out of my sight and leave me to deal with mine. I have dealt with it. I may not be whole but I'm still here. We're all just trying to survive at the end of the day.

I knew it was him. I knew as soon as Richard told me that she'd met a man at the hospital who was suddenly part of her life. Oh yes. I didn't need to hear the name.

I know what he does. I hear about it all the time from friends and from my mother who refuses to end her friendship with his. I know he asks about me obsessively. He asks about Richard. He stalks us both. He has so little in his life. He can't let go of mine.

So of course he found out at once about the accident, about poor little Gracie, about Jen, the wronged wife, suddenly vulnerable and alone at the hospital. She fell right into his lap.

That's why he was hanging around the ward, walking the corridors, looking for us all. That's why he just happened to bump into her and befriend the suffering, needy mum. And she lapped it up, just as he hoped.

And then I saw him at DDs. It's not the first time he's gone there looking for me on a Saturday night. He knows it's my favourite club. I took him there myself, once upon a time. And so he takes her there to find me, to show me what he's doing. Pathetic, really.

I've thought a lot over the years about what happened with us. I've wondered, in the middle of the night, what on earth attracted me to him in the first place. I think back to my mother and the black hole inside her that I tried endlessly to fill. Maybe I saw something of her in him, thought he was someone I could finally fix, if I only loved him enough. Maybe I even liked his neediness at first, his fragility. Maybe he made me feel wanted. I don't know.

I was a mess for a while. That wasn't all his fault. Grief plays strange tricks on people. It warps their hearts. You know that children's story about the magic mirror? The one that smashes into fragments which lodge in people's eyes, in people's hearts, so they see and feel only ugliness in the world, only evil in the people around them? That's how it felt. For a long time. Until Richard came along.

I forgive him most things. The craziness. The stalking. The endless phone calls, even that string of abusive calls on the day of the accident, the ones that nearly cost little Gracie her life. I take responsibility for that. He can't help who he is, not really, and I should never have let it go on like it did.

But there's one thing I struggle to forgive. Why he took her to Venice. That wasn't for her benefit, it was for mine. I felt it. A message to me. A new way to hurt me. A cruel way of trying to force me to remember. As if I could ever forget.

I was nearly eight months pregnant when we went. It was our last holiday before Catherine came and my very last chance to fly. We stayed in a small family hotel in the backstreets, all we could afford. Matt charmed *La Patrona* with his good looks and his smattering of Italian and she doted on me as only an Italian Mama can care for a woman about to give birth to her first child.

By dusk, once the tour groups headed back to their hotels, we had Venice to ourselves. One evening, we strolled through to Piazza San Marco in the fading light and treated ourselves to drinks in one of the over-priced cafés there, right on the Piazza. I sipped ice-cold freshly squeezed orange juice, one hand on my rounded stomach, and watched the lengthening shadows as Catherine stirred and kicked inside me. Matt was fussing beside me, warning me about the heat, the mosquitoes and who knew what other dangers he feared.

I didn't even care. The last fingers of sunlight set fire to the gilded façade of the Basilica and it was so magical, so serene, and I loved that little girl, teeming with life inside me, with such passion that I was filled with hope. Maybe it was possible. Maybe, despite everything, despite my mother and Matt and all their unhappiness, maybe *I* could be happy, after all.

The following day, we took the *vaporetto* out to the islands. We had lunch in Burano, with its multi-coloured houses and cafés and shops piled with lace. I bought a tiny lace-trimmed bonnet for Catherine. I still have it. It's the one she's wearing in the photograph, as she lies, so small and so still, in her Moses basket.

And then to Torcello. I'd read about the cathedral and the amazing view from the tower. He said it was too much for me, I'd be tired. I wouldn't listen. So I paid my extra lira and headed up there. It wasn't such a steep climb after all. And the view was stunning. It was a clear day and I could see right across the Lagoon. The great dome of Santa Maria della Salute. The Campanile in St Mark's.

There was a breeze up there and I stood against the wire mesh with my eyes closed, feeling its fingers cool and refreshing on my face after the stickiness of the walk below. It was timeless. Sometimes now, when I need to escape, I close my eyes and feel myself there again, the salty air on my cheeks, alone on the deserted tower, my beautiful baby girl safe and well inside me, high above the world.

It happened on the way down. I don't know how. I was about two-thirds of the way to the ground. My legs were tired and perhaps Catherine's weight unbalanced me too, pitched me forward. The sheer rounded bulk of my stomach made it impossible to see where I was placing my feet.

One moment I'm coming steadily down the steps. The next, I'm stumbling and falling forward into nothingness, my hands flung wide, scraping the smooth, curved walls as I pitch past, crashing and bouncing helplessly down towards the bottom. I

don't even have time to scream. I fall with such dreadful suspension – the moment stretching forever – and yet with such speed that I'm powerless to save myself. To save her.

He finds me close to the bottom of the steps, curled round in a heap. My hands and one leg are bloodied, my face bruised. When I finally hobble in to the hotel that evening, limping and half-carried by Matt, *La Patrona* makes the sign of the cross on her breast and kisses the crucifix round her neck.

She and Matt huddle in a corner and I know they're discussing me. The fact he wants to rush me to a local hospital and I won't go. It's something else he holds against me, later. I'm not bleeding. I'm not in pain. Whatever's happened, I don't see how they can help. I want rest, that's all. I want to believe there's still hope.

So I lie awake all night, my hands spread across my stomach, trying to protect her, to heal her with my love. *Please God, let her be alright. Please God. I'll do anything.* I don't feel a single kick.

We took the first flight back to London the following morning and went by taxi from the airport straight to the hospital. Nothing they could do. Too late. No heartbeat.

They gave me injections and we had a desperate, endless wait until the contractions started and by afternoon, I was in labour. I suffered all that pain to deliver a baby girl who was perfect in every way apart from one small detail. She was born sleeping.

She was beautiful, you see. My Catherine Louise. Even now, there isn't a day I don't think about her. Perhaps not even an hour. And every night, every single night, I go to sleep praying to have that dream.

The dream where I'm holding Catherine in my arms and she's so beautiful and she opens her tiny blue eyes and looks up at me and she's alive, she's breathing and it was all a mistake, a terrible mistake. I live for that dream. Even now.

Then I wake up and it's one more day without her. One more day alone, without my angel, sleeping in my arms.

CHAPTER 47

Jennifer

I hardly slept that night. The bed seemed to shift and pitch. Nothing made sense. I'd made terrible mistakes, I saw that now, but I was left adrift, confused about all that had happened and what to believe. All I could think was that Geoff had lied to Matt, fed him nonsense about Ella. I longed to see Matt, to feel him hold me and comfort me and talk all this through with me, so we could work out the truth together.

On Monday, I took you to nursery and then drove around, not sure where I was going. The day stretched ahead without purpose. When I tried to call Matt, his phone went to voicemail. He'd been on late shift the day before but he should be home by now, pottering and having a shower before he made up some sleep.

I pulled into a garage, filled up with petrol and bought a coffee. Afterwards, I parked at the edge of the forecourt, sipping it and trying to decide what to do.

My hands shook. All I wanted was to be with Matt, to be held so tightly that I felt safe from all this, from Ella's grief and your strange stories and my own sense of loneliness. I imagined him in his tiny flat, close to the Tube station, and had a longing to be there with him, to talk, to crawl into bed and hide away together. I finished my coffee and punched the name of the Tube station into the satnav.

He always made fun of his little flat in central London, about what a postage stamp it was and the fact that two of us would

have trouble squeezing inside at the same time. I didn't care. He'd turned up on my doorstep plenty of times without warning. I didn't see why I couldn't do the same.

I drove in to the city centre, guided by the satnav, and finally found the entrance to the Tube and the private, leafy square just across from it. It looked different in daylight. The restaurant where we'd first met for dinner was closed and silent. It all seemed a long time ago. A very different time.

I turned into the square. The pavements here were almost deserted. Many of the Georgian houses had brass plates on the doors, suggesting corporate offices or embassies. It was a warm day and I lowered the window as I crawled along, looking for somewhere to park. The outside air smelt of blossom and mown grass.

I finally found a metered space for the car and set off on foot towards the narrow side street he'd pointed out to me that night. I wasn't sure how I'd find the right block but in fact, there was only one contender, a grand Victorian mansion block, hidden just off a street crammed with bistros, sandwich shops and offices. The entrance was set in a horseshoe round an ornamental garden and a small, spouting fountain with a stone bowl.

I stood by the water and ran my eyes across the array of flats in the three-storey block. Flat number twenty-two, he'd said. Easy to remember because it was the same as your birthday. The windows were still and dark. Many were concealed by curtains or blinds. I felt a sudden chill, wondering where Matt was and how he'd react when I appeared at his door.

The stone doorway was secured by a glass door. I put my face to it and cupped my hands until I could make out, through the reflection, a dimly lit lobby. A bank of metal postal boxes covered a side wall, most of them leaking flyers. In the centre, there was a polished wooden table with a large display of dried flowers. Ahead, up several carpeted steps, the metal shine of two lifts. The whole block had a hushed, opulent look.

I tried to imagine Matt, in his expensive coat, crossing the lobby and smiled to myself. I had a sudden sense of him lying close to me, in fresh cotton sheets in a modern apartment, all glass and chrome. He would stumble to the door in a dressing gown, bed-warm and drowsy, his face prickly with overnight stubble and open his arms to me to go inside and join him.

One of the lift doors swished open and a young man stepped out. A city type in a dark suit, a mac in the crook of his arm. The young man paused to check his mailbox, then held open the door for me to go inside.

I crossed to the lifts, feeling like an intruder. The second-floor landing had the same deep pile carpet as the lobby. I counted down the brass numbers on the doors. The landing was empty. All the doors looked identical.

I lifted the brass knocker on number twenty-two. The clatter made me jump. My pulse beat in my ears as I waited, listening. I had the same anxious flutter I once felt as a teenager when I hung round the school stairwell, hoping to catch sight of Jimmy Brent and his friends. Silence.

Behind me, the lift purred as it slid down its shaft.

A key rattled in a neighbouring door, then, again, silence. I got out my phone, dialled Matt's number and stood close to the door in the hope of hearing it ring inside. Nothing. It clicked straight to voicemail.

I lifted the knocker, banged it again, a little harder. Waited. I was deflated, embarrassed. Perhaps he was still at work.

I was turning away when the door suddenly opened, just a matter of inches, held in place by a metal safety chain. A woman peered through the narrow gap, her eyes suspicious. She was in late middle age, her cheeks floury with powder, her lips an unfashionable red.

'Hello.' I straightened up, smiled. 'I've come to see Matt. I'm Jennifer.'

'No man. Please.' She had a strong foreign accent and made to shut the door in my face. I stopped it with my foot, wondering if she'd understood.

'Doctor Aster? He works at Queen Mary's Hospital.'

She shook her head. 'No hospital.'

I tried to peer past her into the flat. I'd envisaged a stark modern interior, all black and grey and cream with few home comforts. My stereotypical idea of a bachelor's pad. This hallway was hectic with polished wooden furniture and knick-knacks. A large ceramic pot against the wall bristled with walking sticks and umbrellas. The wall above was crammed with three rows of framed pictures of all sizes, watercolours and photographs competing for space. A walking frame stood, partially folded, underneath.

'Please—' I began.

'No. You please.' The woman kicked away my foot with unexpected force and the door slammed. I stood for a moment, stunned, my heart thumping.

I stood, staring at the closed door in disbelief. I was certain he'd said flat twenty-two, the same as the door in front of me. Was I in the wrong block? Or the wrong street? I didn't see how I could be.

I was just reaching home when my phone rang and I stopped at the side of the road.

Matt's voice was breathy. 'Are you OK?'

I shrugged, looking out at the traffic. 'Well, not really.'

'I'm so sorry. Only just got your messages. Had my phone switched off. Been a night and a half.'

He sounded tired. I felt a bit better, just hearing his voice.

'Where are you?' I wondered for a moment about turning round and driving back. I wanted so much to see him, to be held.

'Still at the hospital. Won't bore you but it's been non-stop. Going to grab a shower and then sleep here.'

I took a deep breath. 'Matt, is someone staying in your flat?'

A couple of teenage boys trundled past on skateboards, shouting to each other. Their wheels drummed on the cobbles, drowning out his reply.

'Didn't hear you.' He sounded distant, as if he'd moved away from the phone. 'In the flat? Hope not. Unless I've got squatters. Why?'

I opened my mouth to say more, then closed it again.

'Has something happened?' He sounded concerned.

I tried to picture him in the hospital accommodation block, crawling exhausted into bed in some anonymous bedroom on a shabby corridor.

'Yes. I mean—' I didn't know where to start. 'I really miss you.'

'I miss you too. Sorry. I'd come over but—' A crackle on the line. 'Love you.'

I hesitated. 'You too.'

The house was empty with you at nursery. I went into your room and sat in the armchair with your bear in my arms, looking at your bed, trying to calm myself. Downstairs, I put the kettle on and stood against the kitchen counter with a cup of tea I didn't really want, looking out at the sunlight falling in shafts across the overgrown yard.

My legs juddered. I couldn't keep still. I could feel my father there with me, quietly invisible in the background as he always liked to be. And Catherine too, a baby with ginger hair who never had the chance to grow. I paced up and down the kitchen, my hands trembling on my cup. I thought about Ella and the love in her face as she looked down at her little girl.

And I thought of Matt. Of the knowing look in his eyes as he leaned forward to me across that gritty table and told me what he'd discovered about Ella Hicks and his suspicions about her dead child. Of his vagueness that night in the taxi when I asked him what Ella said to him in the club.

You deserve each other, she had told me.

The parcel, now neatly addressed to Matt's daughter, lay there on the side. I grabbed it, reached again for my coat and car keys and headed for the door.

CHAPTER 48

The address on the parcel was in west London, a suburb about half an hour's drive away. As I drove closer, the streets looked increasingly depressed. The route took me down a main road, which was dotted with small parades of shops: kebab, pizza and burger chains, late night convenience stores, laundrettes, betting shops.

The ground was patched with scraps of litter. The walls that bordered the road were daubed with spray-can graffiti in bright colours. I stared out of the window, feeling a growing sense of unease.

As I entered the neighbourhood, I lost confidence and pulled into a burger place. It was soulless. The interior was designed not for comfort but to thwart vandals and drunks. The tables and benches were made from cheap plastic with rounded corners and were moulded to the ground. The floor was covered in scuffed tiles.

I bought some chips from a spotty Chinese youth in a paper hat and sat in the window to eat. The shiny table, designed to be indestructible, was scored with cigarette burns. I looked out through the grimy window at the scruffy people waiting at the bus stop across the road. A homeless man, over-dressed in woollen hat and miser mitts, sat in a corner of the shelter, bulging with carrier bags. I wondered what kind of home Matt's ex lived in and what sort of upbringing his daughter was getting.

The house was a little further on, a few minutes from the main road, set in a cul-de-sac on an estate. The properties were square and uniform. Nineteen-thirties, perhaps. They might have been council-owned until Margaret Thatcher put them up for grabs.

They reminded me of my childhood. Each had a short driveway and a curve of rounded bay windows across the front. The sort of rather poky house my mother would have described as a two-up, two-down.

I stopped just before number thirty-eight. The sitting room of number thirty-six was concealed by net modesty curtains. A vase with a cornflower blue posy, flanked by two neat rows of china dogs, decorated the sill. They were the kind of ornaments my grandmother used to own, before she moved into a home and most of her possessions went to the auction house.

The next house, clearly visible over the low fence, was the same design. A small garage sat beside the house, its paint peeling. The driveway was empty.

I hesitated. My thoughts had been focused on finding the house and learning what I could about it, with the pretext of delivering the parcel. Now I faltered, unsure quite why I was here. My legs faltered. The taste of chips was thick and greasy in my mouth. I didn't know if I really wanted to meet Matt's ex. Or his daughter.

A car slid past. It slowed, turned round at the far end of the cul-de-sac and came crawling back. I felt conspicuous. I thought of the police officers and their warning all that time ago. No more trouble.

I unfastened my seatbelt, reached for the parcel and climbed out of the car.

The house needed a fresh coat of paint. I marched up to the front door, eager now to get this over with and go home. Perhaps no one was at home and I could just leave the parcel on the doorstep.

The curtains were drawn back and I glanced through the windows as I approached. It was dark inside but light enough to show an old-fashioned and solidly conventional sitting room. It was dominated by a brushed cotton three-piece suite, set round a coffee table and angled towards a medium-sized television set

on a stand. A few magazines lay on the table in a neatly aligned pile. A mirror with a gilded frame hung over the fireplace. A pair of candlesticks stood at either end. A mantel clock with a dark wooden case sat plumply between them. It was exactly the sort of room my mother would like. *Tasteful*, she might say. *Unpretentious*. It might have waited, unchanged, for the last thirty years.

I blinked. For the second time in a day, I must have picked the wrong house, the wrong street. There was no trace of a child living here. No toys, no clutter, no books. This was not the house of a young woman, a Londoner of about my own age.

A shadow shifted. I started, jumped back. A figure there, to one side of the room, watching me. A stout woman. She disappeared. My palms made sweaty marks on the padded envelope. I turned, ready to bolt.

Before I could move, the door opened. The woman stood there in the doorway. She was smartly dressed, about seventy years old. She had short, permed hair. With one hand, she pulled together across her stomach the draping flaps of a cardigan. Her other hand held the door.

'Hello.' She looked thoughtful.

'I'm sorry,' I stuttered. 'I think I've got the wrong house.'

She reached out, lifted the parcel from my hands and studied the address, the handwriting, then, with the same appraising look, studied me. Her eyes were faded blue, as if time had slowly drained the colour from them. She looked familiar but I couldn't place her.

'You're Jennifer, aren't you?' she said calmly, reading me as if she understood everything. 'Won't you have a cup of tea?'

She opened the door wider and stood to one side to let me in.

'I thought you'd turn up, sooner or later.' She sounded resigned and rather sad. 'But I wasn't quite sure when.'

CHAPTER 49

I perched on the edge of an armchair in the hushed sitting room and followed her movements in the kitchen by sound. The whoosh of water as a kettle filled. The click of a cupboard, opening and closing. The soft suck of a fridge door.

I blinked. The parcel sat on the coffee table beside the women's magazines. Beneath, the carpet was hectic, with red and pink swirls. The cushions on the beige settee seemed carefully chosen to reflect the same shades. The wall-lights were semi-transparent glass, the bulbs held by pale-pink petals.

Jennifer. She'd greeted me by name before I had the chance to speak. Had she mistaken me for someone else? It made no sense. I wondered what Matt would think if he knew I'd come.

'Do you use a teapot?'

She came in carrying a laden tea-tray, lined with a lace-edged cloth, and began the methodical business of setting out the teapot, covered with a hand-knitted cosy, two cups and saucers, the milk jug, a sugar bowl and teaspoons. A plate of plain biscuits. Serviettes. She was entertaining, in the old-fashioned way. Making an effort.

'So many people have lost the ability to make a decent cup of tea. Don't you find? I went to New York once. A long time ago, when Harold was still alive. I asked for tea at breakfast and do you know what they brought me? A mug of lukewarm water, no saucer, with a rather dismal teabag floating in it.' She tutted. 'They may be the leaders of the free world but really, they have a lot to learn about tea.'

She spoke softly but efficiently as if she were used to being in command of her own ship. Her back was straight and firm as she sat forward to pour the milk, then placed a metal tea strainer over my cup and added the tea. It was strong. She struck me as the kind of woman it might be dangerous to underestimate.

'Do have a biscuit.' She set a plate in front of me and a serviette, folded into a triangle. 'I always use loose-leaf tea. Everyone seems to use teabags. But you know what they put in those bags? Sweepings from the floor.' She nodded. 'It's true. I read an article about it.'

She seemed perfectly at ease, crossing her legs neatly at the ankle and watching me with a half-smile as I sipped my tea. She was wearing light slip-on shoes, rather than slippers, and I wondered if I'd interrupted her as she was getting ready to go out.

I took a deep breath. 'I am sorry to disturb you. I was delivering a parcel, you see. For a little girl. It's her birthday in a few days and I didn't trust the post.'

She nodded as if she already knew. 'Katy.'

I stared. Katy's name wasn't written on the envelope, only her surname, Aster.

She smiled, watching me. Again, I had the sense that she understood far more than I did and was giving me time to catch up.

'Let's drink our tea and have a chat first. Then I'll explain about all that.'

She talked easily for a while, as if we were old friends. Inconsequential chat about the warm weather. The accelerating pace of life in London and the demise of good neighbours. The changes to the cul-de-sac since she and Harold moved there, more years ago than she cared to remember.

I listened for clues but her conversation was as carefully neutral as the three-piece suite. She clearly cherished the vanishing English art of small talk as dearly as she valued properly made tea.

Finally, as we reached the bottom of the pot, she set aside her cup and saucer, picked up the parcel and got to her feet.

'Come.'

CHAPTER 50

I followed her out of the room and up the stairs to a narrow landing. She opened the door to a box room. It was a little girl's bedroom, with cream walls and a small chest of drawers painted with stars and moons. A jewellery box rested on top. A clown doll, with a soft body and chipped china face, sat slumped against it.

A single bed, squeezed in against the far wall, was covered with a bobbled pink counterpane and a cushion with an appliqué dancing elephant. The elephant's tutu, a semi-circle of starched white net, stood proud from the fabric.

A row of soft toys sat along the length of the bed, their backs against the wall. Teddy bears with red ribbons, a knitted rabbit, a giraffe, felt dolls.

It was too still, too tidy. The sunshine streaming in through the small window danced with motes of dust.

She pointed, inviting me to step inside. There wasn't a lot of room. A low table sat behind the door. It was piled with brand-new toys.

Dolls in unopened packaging. Jigsaws, still in cellophane. A shiny box of building bricks. Packet of pristine crayons, paints, felt tip pens. Above it all, a framed drawing of a large, ornate letter 'K'. On the end of the table stood a bud vase with a single yellow rose, its petals already loose and starting to fall.

I turned back to her. She was watching my confusion, her expression sad.

'Katy's room?'

She nodded. She opened the padded envelope, tore off the wrapping paper I had taped with such care and placed the box on top of a jigsaw. The little girl, her wrists decorated with plastic bracelets, smiled up at us both. The room was lifeless.

'She doesn't live here, does she?'

'Not exactly.' She frowned. 'But we like to feel she's here.'

She ushered me out. The door directly across the landing was open, showing a second bedroom. That one was clearly occupied. I crossed to the threshold and peered in.

The walls were a neutral beige, the carpet and curtains dark blue. The jazzy duvet on the double bed was crumpled as if it had been pulled across in haste. The bedside table was piled with books and scraps of paper.

A pair of men's trousers hung across the back of a chair. Used socks and a pair of underpants were strewn on the seat. Across the bottom of the bed, an abandoned sweater. Matt's sweater.

She stepped past me and stooped to pick up the dirty washing, then dropped it with a low sigh into the canvas laundry basket by the door. It was an automatic gesture that suggested years of repetition, years of arguments.

I looked again at the line of her jaw, the shape of her eyes. 'You're his mother.'

Her forehead creased, worried. 'I am.'

I looked back towards the box room. 'Katy's grandma.'

She nodded.

I shook my head, looked again at the messy male room. 'He lives here?'

'He didn't tell you, did he?' She reached forward and patted my arm. 'He's a good boy. Don't be angry with him. He really cares for you. I'm his mother, you see. I know. He just hasn't been himself. Not since we lost Katy.'

I stepped further into his bedroom. Along the wall to my left, partly hidden by the door, hung a long cork noticeboard. Its surface

was covered with a mess of black and white pages, stuck with coloured pins. Grainy photographs, printed off from a computer. My stomach contracted. I went across to look more closely.

Pictures of me. Walking through the shopping centre. On the high street. Outside nursery. Standing in the park. Images of our home. Some taken from the far side of the road, shot through parked cars. Others from right outside the house, from the gate. They were scribbled with marker pen. Hearts drawn crudely round my face. A cartoon flower stuck in my hand, another in my hair.

Several were dark, taken at night. Dim close-ups of the shadowy front door. An image of my bedroom window, a line of light tracing the edges of the curtains. 'How dare he.' I turned back to her, angry now and slightly sick. A memory rose in me from those weeks just after your accident when I felt most vulnerable and had a sense of being watched, of being followed, of glimpsing a figure in the shadows, staring at the house through the darkness from across the road.

'He followed me, didn't he? Before we really knew each other. He spied on me.'

She spread her hands by way of apology and inclined her head.

'He didn't mean anything by it. He just wanted to protect you. He felt it was, well, his mission.' She hesitated. 'He'd never hurt you. You know that?'

I didn't answer. I didn't know anything any more.

She guided me back downstairs and into an armchair. She set a glass of water in front of me and I drank it off, my head spinning. All I wanted to do was to run out of that mummified house and go home, lock the front door and crawl into bed. To hide away from all the confusion, the hurt, the betrayal. My legs shook and she seemed to pin me there, with her politeness, with her kindness.

'You have to understand, it's an illness.' Her eyes never left my face. 'He can't help it. It's a tragedy, really. He could have done so

much more. He was always clever. Did well at university. And he almost qualified, you know, as a doctor.' She hesitated, reading my shock. 'Ah. That's what he told you, isn't it? A doctor?'

I stared, shaking with fury. I felt stupid. Tricked. Who was this man who had walked into our lives and lied to me? Who deceived me, abused me.

She went quietly on. 'Matthew works in a restaurant. The smart restaurant at the hospital, on the top floor. Have you tried it? A bit pricey but very nice food. It's not a bad job. He's very reliable and he cooks well, don't you think?'

Her look was almost sly as if she knew, as if she could see him there in my kitchen, my apron round his waist, his strong arms chopping and cutting, grating and stirring. As if I should have known.

'They didn't plan the baby. But once he got used to the idea, he wanted it desperately. You've no idea. He loves children. And then, when they lost her...' She trailed off, gazing past me at the wall, unseeing. 'It was devastating. And then she left him almost at once. It was cruel, really. It was more than he could cope with.'

I put my face in my hands. My temples throbbed. 'I should go.'

'He said you were different, Jennifer. That you might understand. He told me about all you've been through with your husband, with your little girl. We're both so sorry.' She hesitated, her eyes back on my face, beseeching now. '*We're two of a kind, Mother.* That's what he said. *Two of a kind.*'

'I went to his flat.' I thought of the stylish block and the contrast it made with this place. 'He doesn't have one, does he?'

'Oh dear.' She looked away. 'No, I'm afraid not.' She leaned forward, stacked the plates and cups on her tray.

I sat there, stupid with shock. She got quietly to her feet and carried out the tea things. I looked down at the swirling carpet and pictures seemed to form there. Matt, appearing from nowhere as I sat, alone and desperate, in the hospital café. Matt, appearing

on the high street as I walked you home from nursery. Matt in the kitchen, capable and confident as he cooked. Matt, sitting silently in your darkened bedroom, hunched forward, his eyes sad.

When she came back, she was carrying a large box. She seemed pleasantly surprised that I was still there. She set the box on the table between us.

'What about Geoff?' I said suddenly.

'Geoff?' She blinked.

'He doesn't have a brother, does he? A policeman. A detective.'

Her face seemed to crumple and she looked down, fiddled with the lid of the box.

'How could he tell so many lies?' I was on my feet, my hands balled at my sides. 'Everything. Everything he's told me!'

'Not everything, Jennifer,' she said very quietly. 'You mustn't think that. He does care for you.'

The room was unbearably oppressive. I strode through to the kitchen. Compact, neat, ordinary. The tray sat on the worktop. The cups and saucers, already washed, sat upside down on the draining board. I stood there at the sink, looking out at a small handkerchief of garden. The borders were planted with rows of white and yellow alyssum. The square of lawn in the middle was freshly cut. I imagined Matt, his sleeves rolled up, pushing a mower up and down the patch of grass, straightening the edges with shears while his mother, pottering in the kitchen, watched from the window.

I ran the cold-water tap, splashed my eyes, my face, trying to steady myself.

He was never a doctor at the hospital. He chopped vegetables and stirred soup for a living. All the stories he told me about difficult nights, about desperately ill children, they were all lies. What a fool I'd been.

I went back into the sitting room where she was steadily emptying the contents of her box onto the table.

'They didn't know anything was wrong,' she said. 'No one did. Matthew painted the nursery. They had everything ready, the sweetest little booties, dresses, bonnets, everything. Then they went on that silly holiday. I did advise against it but they wouldn't listen. They rushed to the hospital and it was too late.' She paused, remembering. 'Poor things. Imagine. Having to go through all that. To give birth to a child who's already passed away.' Her voice caught and she hesitated, collected herself. 'It doesn't bear thinking about, does it? Please try, Jennifer. Try to find pity in your heart for him.'

I turned to her to say goodbye. I thought of Matt and his sad little life, pictured him striding into this dim room in the evening, sitting with his mother, watching television. I shook my head. I never wanted to see this wretched house again.

'I'm sorry,' I said.

She pulled out a thin cardboard folder and opened it, held it up for me to see.

'This is Katy.'

I looked down at the photograph. I recognised it at once. A sepia study of a newborn with closed eyes, wearing a sleep-suit and a tiny hat with lace trim and lying in a Moses basket. A sticker on the mount said: Portraits by Stella. On the table, beside the box, nestled in tissue paper, lay a lock of ginger hair.

'Ella was his ex, wasn't she? It was his baby she lost.' I pointed, my voice sharp. 'Catherine Louise.'

She shrugged, smiled. '*She* preferred Catherine. But we always called her Katy. It was my mother's name too, you know. And besides, Catherine is such a formal name for a baby girl. Don't you think?'

CHAPTER 51

On the way home, my hands shook on the steering wheel. I bit down on my lip to stop myself from crying. When I stopped at traffic lights, the eyes in the driving mirror were frantic. I switched off my mobile and pushed it to the bottom of my bag.

I drove as fast as I dared but I was late collecting you from nursery. Your face was tight with hurt, the teachers cross.

As soon as we entered the house, I locked the door behind me and bolted it, then went through to the sitting room and closed the curtains. You watched, wary.

'What are you doing, Mummy?'

I swallowed hard. 'Let's watch television this afternoon. It'll be fun.'

A moment later, the phone started to ring in the kitchen. I couldn't move. We stood there, side by side, listening to the ring. Finally, it stopped.

After lunch, I got the box of videos out and let you watch as many cartoons as you liked. You were utterly absorbed. You clutched your bear to your chest, sometimes bouncing on the settee with excitement, sometimes chuckling, lost in the world of your programme.

As I watched with you, I could almost feel myself a child again, watching television in the afternoon, fresh from school, barely aware of the sounds that ran always beneath the soundtrack, the distant thud and crash of my mother as she moved about the kitchen, scraping and stirring and washing as she made my tea.

I took out my wallet and studied the picture of myself as a small girl, innocent in a summer dress and sandals. A scene from a world that was lost now. My parents close behind me, protecting me. Their faces so impossibly young.

I was still gazing at it when your video finished and you hung over my knee to reach for my wallet, to see what I was looking at.

'Mummy, what's that?'

I bent low and kissed your head, smelled your hair, your skin.

'That's an old picture.' I hesitated, letting you look before I explained. 'Guess who these people are?'

You peered more closely at the faces, then shouted. 'Mr Michael! Look!' Your eyes glowed with pleasure. 'It's him, Mummy. Look! Why did you say he was made up? He's real!'

I stared. I couldn't speak.

You grabbed my wallet with both hands, excited. 'He's got normal clothes!' You considered. 'Where is he? Who's that girl?'

'That's me, sweetheart,' I managed to say. 'When I was about your age. With my mummy and daddy. That's me.'

You hesitated, thinking.

I pointed. 'See? That's Grandma. Doesn't she look young?'

'Grandma?' You narrowed your eyes as if you were struggling to reconcile the young woman in the picture with the elderly one you knew. 'Why's she with Mr Michael?'

'That isn't Mr Michael. That's your grandpa.'

You shook your head. 'I don't have a grandpa.'

'You did. You just never saw him. He died a long time ago.'

'Silly Mummy.' You laughed. 'He isn't dead. He's looking after baby Catherine and the other girls and boys.'

I looked again at the young man, thinking of the father I remembered. Gentle and funny and strong and wonderful with small children.

'So you *do* know Mr Michael.' You sounded hurt now, considering. 'Why did you say he wasn't real?'

CHAPTER 52

The phone kept ringing all through that long afternoon of videos and snacks. In the end, I stopped it for good by unplugging it at the wall.

When your bedtime finally came, I wrapped my arms round you, hoisted you high and carried you up the stairs in my arms.

'Is Uncle Matt coming tonight?'

'No, my love.' My voice was tight.

You sensed that something was wrong but I didn't know how to explain and you didn't ask any more questions. In the bathroom, you perched, still and silent, on the linen basket as I ran a bubble bath for you. The cascade of running water shut out other noise. The rising steam in our small bathroom drew us together and hid us, kept us safe.

You sat, waist-deep in water, unnaturally withdrawn as I drew animals on your back with the bubbles, tried to make you laugh by tickling your toes.

When you were dry and warm in your pyjamas, smelling of lavender and argan oil, I drew the curtains on the outside world and let you climb into my bed, Mummy and Daddy's big bed. We cuddled together there, the duvet tucked round us, reading as many stories as you wanted. Slowly, despite yourself, you started to yawn and your eyes grew heavy.

You fell asleep there, lying on your side, your arms clinging to your bear and my arm tucked safely round your waist. I put my face between your shoulder blades and tried to slow my heart

to the soft rhythm of your breathing, to fill my senses with the smell of your skin, of your freshly washed body.

Later, I crept downstairs. The kitchen was full of shadows and I stood in the doorway, weary, letting my eyes adjust. Slowly, the shapes emerged. The kitchen table where Matt and I had so often sat together to eat. The worktop where he chopped and diced. The fridge. The silver gleam of the window over the sink.

I didn't put the light on. I was frightened of the darkness but I was even more afraid of being seen. I thought of the photographs pinned to his wall and the way he'd spied on us, day and night. He hadn't come across me by accident, that night in the hospital. I saw that now. He must have known about the accident soon after it happened. I imagined him tracking Ella at first, his ex, photographing her as crazily as he had me. Then extending his obsession to Richard, once they fell in love. And then to me and to you too, my love. He stalked us. He planned it all.

I opened a bottle of red wine and sat, curled in a corner of the settee in the darkness, cradling a glass. My body trembled.

I thought about Matt. About his focused pursuit right from the start. The chance meetings in the hospital, on the high street. I shivered. They looked different to me now, not accidental at all but deliberately engineered. The way he phoned me every evening to talk, turned up on my doorstep, invited or not, saying how desperately he missed me, promising to take care of me. Of the way he wouldn't take no for an answer when I tried to cancel. The way he constantly hurried the pace. *I love you so much, Jen. I don't think I could live without you. We belong together. I'd do anything for you.*

I'd seen it all as devotion, as proof of his love. I wanted to. I'd been so lonely. I let him into our lives. I trusted him.

I thought of him sitting in the darkness in your bedroom, silently watching you as you slept.

When I closed my eyes, I saw his poky bedroom with its tasteless beige, his mother stooping to pick up socks and

underpants. The thought of it made me nauseous. I drank off the glass of wine and then another and finally the edges of the room started to blur. After a third glass, I buried my face in the cushion and sobbed.

I must have dozed. When I woke, I groped my way across the kitchen and filled a glass from the tap, drank it off. My hands trembled. I stood in the silence for a moment, trying to steady my nerves.

A sound. I stiffened, strained to hear. The low groan of our gate on its hinges, barely audible. A ting as it closed. Footsteps. A pause. Then the bang of the knocker on the door.

'Jen! It's me, Matt.'

I leaned against the sink, afraid to move.

Crash. The knocker again, slammed with force now.

'Jen. I know you're in there. Come on. We need to talk.'

I didn't want to talk. I didn't want to see him. I crept across the kitchen and into the hall, feeling my way in the darkness. I made it to the bottom of the stairs, and took hold of the banister.

The clatter of the letter box rang out. His voice came again, clear now. I imagined him sitting or kneeling on the doorstep, his mouth against the metal, speaking into the darkness. I shrank into the wall.

'I know, Jen. I know how it looks. But let me in. I can explain.'

My breathing blew through the silence of the hall. He seemed to sense me there.

'All I ever wanted was to take care of you. You and Gracie. Don't you see? I love you so much. Come on, give me a break. Did I ever hurt you? Or Gracie? I would never do that.'

A pause. I held my breath, waiting.

'Don't do this. Let me in. We can sort this out. We can. We belong together. We're a family now.'

He broke off. A strangled noise. A sob.

'I love you, Jen! For God's sake. Please. Give me a chance to explain.'

The letter box clattered shut, then, a moment later, opened again, even wider. I sensed his eyes there, peering into the house, into the shadows, reaching for me.

'Come on, Jen. Open up. I know you're there.' His voice was thick. 'I'm begging you. Don't do this.'

I turned and ran up the stairs, climbed into bed beside you and drew the covers over us both, panting. I tightened my arms around you, your slight shoulders, your small body, pressed you to me and rocked.

You stirred, twisted onto your back, murmured: 'Mummy?'

'Hush, my love. Mummy's here.'

I buried my face in your hair. Your neck tasted salty.

From down below, footsteps crunched on the gravel as he retreated down the path. Then, again, silence. I sensed him out there in the dark night, his hands in his pockets, looking up at the house, at our bedroom window, keeping watch as he had so many times before.

I lay stiffly against you. My body shook the mattress. Your small, warm feet pedalled my leg as you made sure of me, even in your sleep.

I stroked your hair and managed to whisper: 'It's alright, Gracie. It's alright.'

CHAPTER 53

I woke early the next morning and lay, groping my way to consciousness, my eyes trying to focus on the blank spread of the ceiling.

As I hung, for a moment, between sleep and waking, life still seemed normal. Then the memory of the day before, of Matt and his mother and his unspeakable lies, came crashing in like a tidal wave, knocking the air from my chest. I felt sick. I lifted my head from the pillow, twisted to see you. You lay curled on your side, your breaths puffing through parted lips, deep in sleep.

I peered past you to the bedside clock. Already seven. I slid sideways out of bed as stealthily as I could, pulled my dressing gown from the back of the door. Your hair was flung out across the sheet and I bent to smell it, then to touch my lips to your forehead.

The kitchen floor gleamed with shafts of weak morning sunlight. The wine bottle, almost empty now, sat on the table with my dirty glass. I clicked on the kettle, reached for a mug and turned back with it. Screamed. Crash. The mug, slipping from my fingers, exploded like a grenade on the hard floor. Shards and splinters skimmed in all directions.

'Get out!' I didn't recognise my own voice. It was high. Scratched at the air. 'Get the hell out. How did you—'

'Jen.' He rose from the settee, there in the sitting room, arms out, hands extended as if he were calming a storm. 'Please.'

I put a hand out and grasped the edge of the sink.

'Any nearer, I'll call the police.'

'Really?' He shook his head. 'Don't be like that, Jen. Please. Hear me out.'

I pulled the folds of my dressing gown more firmly round my body, tightened the cord.

He blinked, his eyes heavy and red-rimmed. 'Let's talk, Jen. Work it out. Can't we do that?' His tone was wheedling. 'Please, darling. I love you. What else can I say? We're good together.'

I narrowed my eyes and looked past him to the sitting room windows. The curtain on the right hung crookedly and the lining billowed as a breeze stirred it.

'Forget about Richard. He and Ella – they aren't like us, Jen. They don't love deeply and forever. Not like we do.'

Beyond, out in the street, a car passed. The noise was too loud, too clear. The window was open. He'd forced it, lifted the sash high enough to climb in.

'What do you want?'

The kettle burbled, shuddered on its stand as it began to boil.

'I just want to talk. That's all.'

He came slowly towards me, his arms outstretched, his face pleading, crossing the threshold into the kitchen.

'Don't.' I flinched.

'For heaven's sake.' He stopped and stood there, running his hand through his hair. His skin was grey.

He must have sat down here all night. All the time I was holding you close upstairs, imagining I was keeping you safe, he was here, in our home. He could have come into the bedroom in the darkness. I started. Perhaps he had.

'I won't touch you, if you don't want me to. OK? Jen, please. Don't do this.'

As he advanced further into the kitchen, I took a step backwards and bumped up against the worktop.

He shuddered. 'This is ridiculous. Alright, I've got some explaining to do. Hands up. I admit it. But I'm the same person, Jen. I'm no different.' He hesitated, his face tense. 'I love you so much. You know that. And deep down, you know you feel the same about me.'

He pointed me to a chair. I sat on the far side of the table, putting a barrier between us. The kettle boiled and he took down mugs, made tea. His hands, usually so capable, shook as he poured the water onto the tea bags. I thought about his mother and her teapot, her strainer and knitted tea cosy. I opened my mouth to say something about her and where he really lived, then, uncertain, closed it again.

We sat opposite each other. He hunched forward over his cup, his chin moistened by rising steam. I stared at him, taking in the curve of his cheek, his jaw. I was seized by a strange sense of nothingness, of floating unanchored between two worlds, between reality and illusion. I knew this man, knew him intimately. And yet I didn't know him at all. All the times. All the times we'd sat at this table, dined on food he'd cooked. Talked through his difficult cases, the small children struggling against infections, against diseases. It was all lies.

'A doctor.' I couldn't stop myself. 'Why did you say that?'

'I'm almost a doctor. Alright, not a paediatrician, not at the hospital. I shouldn't have pretended. I just thought, well, would you have bothered with me if I'd told the truth.'

'All that stuff about seeing us in the street, wanting to know if we were OK—'

'I did want to know. I was concerned.'

'You followed me for weeks. Took photographs of me. Why? You didn't know anything about me.'

'Of course I did. I heard what happened. What Ella did to you. Her mother and mine still talk.' He spread his hands. 'We're two of a kind, you and I. She hurt me, just like she hurt you.

I admit, that's what it was about, in the beginning. I wanted to use you to get to her.' He shrugged, smiled. 'Then we fell in love. We couldn't help ourselves. I know you love me too, Jen. Don't fight it.'

I stared at him. 'Why didn't you tell me? Why didn't you say she was your ex? All that stuff about a mysterious girlfriend who took your daughter from you.'

He looked at me, his face calm now. 'She did.'

'Matt, I know what happened. She was stillborn, your baby. I'm sorry. That's awful. But you can't blame Ella for that.' I paused, remembering. 'You encouraged me to think she killed her own baby!'

He shrugged. 'She did, in a way.'

I thought of Catherine, her tiny eyes closed, lying in Ella's arms. 'How can you even say that?'

'You really want to know?'

I looked down into my cup and the tea swirling there. 'Not really.'

'She was reckless. Wild. I liked it when I met her. But then she had a baby to think of, our baby. I told her to calm down, to be careful. She just laughed in my face. I couldn't bear it. That poor little girl. She was my daughter and I couldn't protect her.' He paused, ran his hand down his cheek. 'Ella fell, you see. In Torcello. We had a fight about her going up that tower and she wouldn't listen. It was her fault. Her fault our baby died.'

I blinked, thinking of the winding stone slope, the giggling up ahead as I climbed.

'I don't believe you.'

He lifted his head, looked me in the eye. 'That's up to you.'

'Why did you take me there?'

'Why?' He looked incredulous. 'I didn't want to. You wanted to go so badly. You pushed me into it. Remember? All that nonsense about Gracie's angel. I went for you, Jen. To show you how much you mean to me.'

I lifted my tea. I didn't want to listen. I just wanted him to go. To leave us alone.

'And then she walked out on me, Jen. I told her how much I loved her. I said I'd take her back, despite what she did. But she wouldn't listen. I thought, for a long time, that she'd realise what we had and come back to me. I kept telling her I'd forgive her. We could start again. We were made for each other.'

I shook my head. 'That's what you said about us.'

His voice rose. 'I mean it, Jen. Ella doesn't matter to me any more. We've got each other now. You and me and Gracie. We're bound together. You can't leave. We love each other too much.'

He pushed back his chair and got to his feet, made to come round the table to embrace me, his eyes on my face.

'No, Matt…' I put my mug down on the table, sloshing tea in a dark ring round the base. 'I'm sorry. '

I got to my feet. Matt's eyes were brimming with tears and all I wanted was to go back upstairs, crawl into bed and wrap my arms round you. Lie there, lost in your smell and the slow, steady rhythm of your breaths, until you woke.

I took a deep breath. 'Please go.'

He bit down on his lip. 'Don't do this, Jen. *Please*. I love you.'

I didn't answer. We both stood there, a few feet from each other, tense. When he spoke again, his tone was sneering.

'All that stuff about Gracie going to Heaven and meeting the dear departed. I mean, really?' He shook his head. I thought again how little I knew him. 'I didn't argue. I kept my mouth shut. Did I tell you it was nonsense?'

'Maybe it isn't nonsense.' I swallowed. 'How do you know? None of us do.' I looked past him, through the house to the shadows in the sitting room. 'How could she know those things? About the accident. About Catherine.' *And about my father*, I thought. The quiet man still taking care of the children as he always did in life.

He shrugged. 'She heard things. She sensed them. She's bright. That's all.'

I hesitated, watching him. 'It was you, wasn't it? On the phone to Ella.'

His eyes flicked away from mine, just long enough for me to know I was right. I thought of what you'd said. *Auntie Ella had shouted down the phone. Go away. Stop it. Leave me alone.* The fury and frustration of a woman whose ex simply wouldn't stop calling, wouldn't stop stalking her.

'It was you.'

He didn't answer. And that night in the club when I'd come across them arguing so furiously. She hadn't followed us there at all. He'd gone looking for her.

'Go.' I didn't want to hear any more. I wanted to be rid of him. 'Go away. And don't come back. Ever. Don't phone. Don't follow me. If you do, I swear, I'll call the police.'

'You don't mean that.' A look of sudden panic crossed his face. 'We belong together, Jen. We do. I'll make it up to you. Just give me a chance.'

He reached across the table for my hand and I snatched it away.

'Leave me alone.' My legs, under the table, shook. 'Don't you understand? I don't want to see you again. I mean it. It's over.'

He didn't move. He sat, wordless, staring at me. Something in his eyes seemed to fold and crumple and I saw the pain there but couldn't respond, couldn't speak. His breathing was short and hard. I sat very still, holding myself separate from him, willing him to recover enough to leave. From above, the drone of an aeroplane's engine swelled, then faded as it crossed the sky.

Finally, he seemed to regain control of himself. He pulled his eyes from mine and looked down at his lap. His voice became quiet: 'So that's it.'

When he looked up again, his expression had changed. Where before his eyes seemed desperate, pleading, now they seemed cold. 'How very sad.'

'I'm sorry—' I stuttered '—but you need to go.'

He scraped back his chair. He stood for a moment, looking down, broader and stronger than me.

'Fine.' His voice was too calm. 'I need the bathroom, OK? Then I'll go.'

I sat there in the silent kitchen, pinned to my chair, listening to his heavy, familiar movements round the house. Up the stairs. The thud of the bathroom door. Later, the rush of the cistern as the toilet flushed, the creak of the banister as he came down again. I didn't look up, didn't go through to the hall to watch him go, just listened to the bang of the front door as he left.

CHAPTER 54

The silence in the house became intense. My head ached. I made my way slowly up the stairs, my legs shaking, exhausted by him, by his strange, intense emotions. I wondered if you were still asleep. I wanted to crawl back into bed beside you and stay there, cuddled round your body, for a little longer.

The door to my bedroom stood open. Morning sunshine reached round the curtains and sent weak streaks of light down the carpet. I walked in, already unfastening my dressing gown, moving round the edge of the door towards the bed. Stopped.

The bedclothes were tossed back. A rumbled sheet. A pillow, twisted to the side. You were gone.

I turned and ran blindly next door to your room. Your own bed was empty too, the sheets neat, unused.

'Gracie? Gracie!'

I rushed back to my room and fell to my knees, scanned under the bed. Your bear, arms crooked, abandoned. Wildly now, I pulled open the doors to the wardrobe, pushed the clothes aside. They screamed along the rail.

'Gracie!' Panic suffocated me.

I hurtled to the bathroom, nowhere there to hide, then stumbled downstairs, crossed the hall in a second and heaved at the front door. I ran into the street, my dressing gown flapping round my legs, my bare feet pricked by the gravel.

'Gracie!'

A man, passing. A steady, unhurried step. A middle-aged man in a sensible coat.

'Please. Help me!'

I ran to him, grabbed his arm. He stopped, looked down at my hand as if the sight of it on his sleeve worried him.

'Quick. He's taken her. Go after him.'

'What?' He frowned. His eyes travelled over my naked feet, the dressing gown cord unravelling at my waist.

I clutched at him, clawing at his coat even as he pushed me away.

'Please.' I started to sob, losing control. 'My little girl.'

My face was close to his, my breath sour with last night's wine. He grimaced, turned his head away.

He nodded past me to the house, the front door standing open. 'Call the police if you need help.'

CHAPTER 55

The policewoman was restless. She strode round the sitting room as I talked and looked things over, her eyes making professional judgements, of the windows, of the house, of me. Her radio kept spitting static and I strained to hear if there was news.

From the kitchen, the light slap of cupboard doors. The kettle rattled on its stand and boiled in a rush of steam. A few moments later, the young Asian officer came through with a cup of strong, sugary tea and set it in front of me. He gave me a meek smile.

'Forced entry?' The policewoman lifted back the curtain and studied the gaping sash. 'No locks?'

I shook my head. Time had stopped. I was hoarse. Dizzy. They kept asking meaningless questions. Exactly how much had I had to drink last night? What exactly was my relationship with Matthew Aster? Was there anything else I could tell them about him? Anything at all, however trivial?

I could barely think. All I could say was: 'Please. Hurry. Please find my daughter.'

My eyes were sore from crying. My arms ached with emptiness. He'd taken you. My beautiful daughter. I'd given them photographs of you. The portraits last term, taken by the photographer at nursery. They didn't do you justice but they were clear. They'd reproduce well, the young man said and he was trying to be kind, I could see, but the senior shot him a look. I thought about posters with your face pinned to noticeboards, stuck on trees: *Missing*. It set me crying all over again.

If I closed my eyes, I could almost feel you against me. Your small, hard body on my knee, your face against my shoulder, your warm breath on my neck.

'And this was, what time?'

I opened my eyes. Her words hung in the air.

'What?'

She spoke more slowly.

'At what time did he enter the property?'

I took a deep breath to stop myself from shouting at her. What did it matter?

'I don't know. Some time in the night. I came down at about seven and he was here, sitting right here.'

Scratch, scratch of the young officer's stubby pencil.

'Are you aware of any missing items?'

My voice trembled, hit a higher note. 'Just her, my daughter. I keep telling you. Why don't you find her?'

'There's no need to shout.' She looked down at me without expression. 'We're doing everything we can.'

The young officer, glancing from her to me, said in a low voice: 'I know you're upset. But just try to answer the questions. OK?'

I shook my head, feeling tears rise again.

He set down his notebook for a moment, lifted the mug of tea from the table and put it into my hands.

The police officer's radio squawked. She raised it with her thumb and forefinger, talked into her lapel.

She spoke across me to the young officer. 'Not at the property.'

'What property?' I said.

She sat beside me, rested her hands on her thighs. 'We sent a car to Mr Aster's home. To the address you gave us. He isn't present but officers are interviewing his mother.'

I thought of the dingy sitting room and of his mother, presiding over the teapot, dignified and endlessly polite. Of the officers,

bristling with kit, perched on the old-fashioned suite, helping themselves from a plate of biscuits or of buttered scones.

'So now what?'

'We've already extended the search. Believe me, we're doing all we can. We could have news any minute.' She hesitated, her eyes on my face. 'We've every reason to stay hopeful, at this stage.'

She and the young officer exchanged glances and drifted through to the hall together. Furtive whispering. Another blast of radio static and a short, sharp exchange on the walkie-talkie.

Something tightened in my chest. I tried to relax my shoulders, panicked now, and focused on breathing. In, out, in, out. Slowly, the pressure eased. My arms, my legs hung like weights. The room tipped, shivered, then righted itself. Your books stood in a row against the edge of the mantelpiece. The shiny purple cover of *Beauty and the Beast* stuck up above smaller books. The spine, weathered, curled up at the bottom.

When they came back in, the senior officer asked: 'Is there anyone who could come over? Anyone we can call to sit with you?'

I shook my head. 'Not really.'

'Any news at all, we'll let you know. OK?' She pointed to the windows. 'I'll send someone to fix those.'

As she left, the young man said gently: 'They're trying to get hold of the family support team. I can stay until someone comes, if you like?'

'No.' I got up. 'I can't just sit here. I want to look for her too.'

He looked worried. 'Please don't go far. In case we need to get hold of you.' He hesitated, then seemed to reach a decision, gave me a final nod and turned to leave.

The front door opened and slammed shut. His heavy boots slapped down the path. The gate clanged as it closed.

I thought of the bed upstairs, its sheets still crumpled. The clock said ten past nine. Two hours ago, we both lay there, you

and I, my body curled round you, keeping you safe from the world. Now you were gone.

I picked up my phone and dialled Matt's number for the twentieth time, my fingers trembling. Again, it clicked onto voicemail and I left another frantic message.

'Please, Matt. Bring her back. We can talk. But please don't hurt her.'

I ran to get dressed, trying to think where Matt might take you and where you might run to hide if you managed to get away from him.

CHAPTER 56

The church café had just opened. The young woman was unloading metal trays of scones and croissants and Danish pastries into the glass-fronted cabinet. She didn't look up as I ran through the door.

'Is she here?'

She frowned. 'Who?'

I scanned the café. Deserted.

'Gracie. My daughter.' *What was the matter with her?* 'You know. She's three. Nearly four. About this high.'

She shrugged. 'I've been in the back.' She gestured to the fresh food. 'Still setting up.' She went back to fiddling with her pastries, straightening them in their baskets.

My heart pounded. I ran through to the church. The morning light filtered softly through the stained glass. I crossed to St Michael's window and checked under the pews there, trying to think where a three-year-old might hide. Nothing. The Lady Chapel too was empty.

I stood beside the altar, looking back down the body of the church, breathing hard. I'd been driven by the sudden hope that she might be here, that she'd seek refuge here if she could. Now I was again at a loss, deflated by the silence, the emptiness. I didn't know where to go next. What to do. I checked my phone. Nothing.

The loss of you pressed down on my head and shoulders, a suffocating weight. I slid sideways into the nearest pew and leaned forward, rested my forehead against the worn wood.

I closed my eyes. I saw you again in the hospital, a frail, small figure, stabbed with wires. I remembered the commotion as machines sounded and nurses and doctors came rushing in. Richard smelled faintly of aftershave when I pressed against him, close in his arms. You were saved. I thanked God for it. Thanked him for sending you back to me.

'Are you alright?'

A shift in the light. I looked up. The vicar, Angela, looked down on me, a cardboard file in her hand. Her face was creased with concern.

'Oh.' Her expression altered as she saw who I was. 'Jennifer.'

She bent over me, put her hand on my shoulder. Her breath smelled of coffee.

'What is it? Do you want to talk?'

My thighs trembled on the wooden pew. I felt a stab of anguish, of fear, deep in my stomach. I needed so desperately to see you, to hold you. No one seemed to know how to help.

'It's Gracie.' I put my hands to my face. 'He's taken her. Matt. I don't know where she is.' I started to shake, then to sob, managing to blurt out: 'What if he hurts her?'

She slid in beside me on the pew, a warm, soft bulk of person.

'What do you mean, taken her? Should we call the police?'

'I have.' I raised my wet, running face to look at her solemn one. 'They're looking.' I pointed to my phone. 'They said they'd call me the minute they had news.' I paused, trying to explain. 'I just thought she might be here, you know. If she got away. She loves this church.'

She nodded. 'She does.'

I gulped, tried to stop crying, to stop the shudder in my breath. I looked past the pew to the swimming patterns of light on the stone.

'She likes to play up there, under the windows.' I could almost see you, sitting on a hassock with your knees drawn up, jumping up and swinging on the end of a pew.

She reached out and put her hand on mine. 'Wherever she is, Jennifer, she's in God's hands. That's what I believe. He's taking care of her.'

I thought of Matt's eyes, so desperate and full of pain.

'But what if he hurts her?'

She sighed but didn't answer. We walked together back towards the café. The young girl was unpacking a bundle of newspapers and setting them out on one of the long, wooden tables.

My legs buckled and I sat heavily. My hands shook so much that I fumbled my phone, scrabbled on the floor to pick it up again, dropped it on the table. The sharp lines of the counter, of the tables, started to blur. I hung my head and stared unseeingly across the café. Please God. Bring her home. Please. I was too exhausted now even to cry.

A low buzz. On the table, my phone rang. I snatched it up.

His voice. But different. Desperate. 'Jennifer …'

'Is she alright?'

He paused. I strained to listen to the noise in the background. The throb and rattle of traffic.

'You called the police, didn't you?'

'No.' My voice was wild. 'Where are you?'

'Don't lie to me.' His breath juddered as if it were close to breaking. 'They've been to my mother's house. Upsetting her. Why did you do that? What's she ever done to you?'

'Matt. Please.'

Angela, listening, came to stand beside me and put her hand on my arm.

'Just bring her back. Please.'

'What about me?' His voice rose in a wail. 'I love you, Jen! You can't leave me! Don't you understand?'

I felt sick, took a deep breath. 'Please. We can talk. Just tell me where you are.'

'Come on your own. Promise? No police.'

A few moments later, as I ran across the café to the door, Angela called after me: 'Is she alright? Was that the police?'

I didn't stop to answer.

CHAPTER 57

It was cool by the river. A low breeze blew across the water and stung my cheeks. I walked quickly, shoulders hunched, arms folded, down the path through the park, towards the embankment, scanning always for him, for you, sick with dread.

The concrete path running alongside the bank was quiet. I stood at the rail, looking down at the river far below. The tide was in and the brown, swirling water was fast-flowing, carrying sticks and duck feathers and scraps of water-logged plastic.

Off to the left, beyond the park, buses and cars roared across the curved stone bridge which straddled the river. It was edged by ornate Victorian streetlights, shaped like lanterns, which gleamed in the sunlight. I thought of Venice and the wrought-iron lights there, which made pools across the darkening campo and glistened on the canal. Another time, another world.

On the far side of the river, a battered Land Rover was parked just above the slipway. A crewing car. Teams of rowers, hearty public-school boys with floppy hair and branded gear, carried two boats, upturned on their shoulders, from a boathouse to the water's edge. Their calls to each other, jovial and mocking, flew on the breeze. Jeremy and Roland and Sebastian.

Mallards and Canadian geese scrabbled away from the bank as the boys lowered their boats into the water, making sudden waves. They waded out into the shallows and clambered inside and their oars slapped the water.

A middle-aged woman in a headscarf and sensible shoes strode past me, her eyes too scanning the river, the boys and their boats. Her dog, a wiry terrier, ran back and forth, nosing in the bushes. The air between us was thick with the scent of blossom and rising sap.

You used to scoot here, up and down this path. We played hide and seek in those bushes. It was just there, at the far end of the path, close to the rampart of the bridge, that you crouched and looked down into the water and said you saw Catherine in the depths of the river, waving to you. Saying, when I found you: *I wasn't lost, Mummy, I was right here.* I swallowed hard, wiped my hands across my eyes.

I paced back and forth, restless and afraid, then stood with my back to the railings, leaning back against the flaking metal, waiting.

I recognised him from a distance, as soon as he came down from the bridge and turned into the park. He had you by the hand and you ran at his side, uneven and stumbling as you struggled to keep pace with him.

His strides were loose and long and his coat flapped round his knees and I sensed the strength in his body, the lean muscle I once found so attractive and which now only frightened me. His hair stuck out in clumps as if he'd raked through it with his fingers and his chin was dark with stubble.

I lifted my hand. He saw me but didn't respond. He steered you instead to the far end of the path, some distance from me.

You twisted and strained, held tight by the wrist, and shouted: 'Mummy!'

When I started to walk towards you, he called: 'Stay there!' Then, to you: 'Be quiet, Gracie.'

He pushed you down, sitting you on the edge of the low wall that ran beneath the railings. I waved at you, trying to make a game of it.

'Hello, my love. Be a good girl. Do what Uncle Matt tells you.'

I was close enough now to see him properly. His eyes were red-rimmed and bright and he was agitated, shuffling his feet, brimming with anxious energy.

A blast of sound flew out from the river and he started, looked round.

He doesn't trust me, I thought. *He's afraid of what he's done, of the police.*

The current drew the schoolboys further into the river and they rowed, backs bending, muscles straining, searching for a common rhythm. Their coach, a young man in a speedboat, shoulders hunched in his windcheater, made loops against the tide and shouted instruction through a megaphone.

Matt swung his eyes back to me. You sat at his feet, your head low between your knees. You looked unhappy but resigned, studying your shoes, the path, waiting for this strange adult drama to play itself out and for normal life to resume.

'Why did you have to spoil it?' Matt's voice shook. 'Why? What's the matter with you?'

I took a quiet step towards you both. 'I'm sorry. It was just a shock, that's all. Maybe you're right. We need to talk. Maybe we can work it out.'

He shook his head. 'You don't mean it. You don't care about me.' His fingers made furrows through his hair. 'After everything I did for you. I looked after you, didn't I? What more could I do? I did everything on your terms. Don't you see? For what? You only care about yourself.'

I took another small step. 'That's not true. I do care.'

His face was pinched. 'Don't you know what it cost, that trip to Venice? I don't earn a lot. But I didn't complain. I wanted to make you happy. That was all.'

I nodded. 'It was wonderful, Matt. We were happy, weren't we? It was special.'

His face clouded. He seemed lost, vague, a different person from the calm, capable man I thought I knew.

'I thought you were special. But you're not, are you? You're just like her. You're all the same, in the end. You take and take and when there's nothing left, you walk away.'

His words came more thickly now, as if he almost forgot where he was, that we were there with him. 'I can't go on without you, Jen. Without you, what've I got left to live for?'

Blood throbbed in my ears. I took another step towards you, my eyes on your lowered head. You picked up a stub of stick and traced a pattern on the concrete.

'Maybe I was too hasty. Maybe we could give it another go. If you want to?'

He didn't seem aware that I was moving, closing the distance one slow step at a time.

I kept talking. 'Do you want to do that? Give it another try?'

I was only a few metres from you now. If we caught him by surprise, if you realised what I was doing and suddenly ran, I might snatch you up, save you from him. My body ached with longing to hold you. It was so intense, I could almost feel you in my arms, your hard, slim body pressed into my chest, the sweet, fresh smell of your hair, your skin warm and soft against my face.

A sudden blast of static. We all jumped.

Out on the river, the coach screamed: 'No, Justin! No!' A pair of mallards, startled by the noise, rose from the water, honking, and soared high through the air.

The megaphone split the quiet: 'One, two! One, two!'

Matt came back to the present, as if from a dream.

'I loved you so much, Jen. I adored you. I really thought—' He saw now, I read it in his eyes, how close I'd edged towards you both, that I was steadying myself, choosing my moment, ready to pounce.

He reached down in a single strong movement, grabbed you round the waist and hoisted you up, pinning you under his arm

even as you struggled, kicking, beating feebly on his chest with your fists.

'Gracie!' I screamed, transfixed.

He stepped in a single, fluid movement onto the low wall, swung a leg over the railing, then climbed over altogether, balancing on the far edge of the narrow wall, one hand on the rail, holding himself in place, the other locked round your waist.

His eyes were on mine, bright with self-pity.

'All I ever wanted was a family. A family of my own. Was that so wrong? Was it?'

He leaned away from the railing, suspended over the rushing river below, holding my gaze as if it were the one thread that held him steady, held him to life.

'Matt. Please.'

The sounds all around us, of the park, of the road, of the river, fell away to silence. The world held its breath, watched with me. He hung there, his eyes on mine, you clinging now in fear to his side, then with a sudden twist, he jumped, falling into nothingness, still clutching you.

Time stopped. You hung there, your eyes wide with shock. Your hair, caught by the rising breeze and shot through with sunshine, flew out from your head in a circle of perfect yellow. You were suspended there, for barely a second and forever. Then you fell, plummeting, and disappeared from sight.

I ran to the railing, clambered over and jumped.

CHAPTER 58

A smack, so hard it seems to shatter my bones, to break me in pieces. The shock of cold. Water filling my mouth, my ears, my eyes. Splashing, closing over me. White sky, high above, blurred by a wash of brown. Light flying in shards and specks on the surface, disappearing. Bubbles bursting in my ears, then the slow, dense whoosh of underwater quiet.

My mouth, opening, drawing in liquid. Peat and mud and filth. My feet kicking out, frantic, trying to stand, finding nothing, slipping, falling through emptiness.

My head breaks the surface. Water in my throat, then both air and water. Eyes, blinking, water-logged, struggling to clear. Air noise: wind, birds, shouts. A blur of greenery high above, bright sun, the bank already drawing away, the current catching me, sweeping me, into the depths.

Ahead of me, you rise and fall, arms flailing, eyes panicked, your mouth too full of water to scream. The surface churns to foam. I throw myself forward through the current, my lungs bursting, arms pumping, straining for you, Gracie, my love, my life, seeing you swept on always by the water.

The tide draws us both into the narrowing, sucking channel of the bridge, funnelling us together through one of the high Victorian arches. My fingers lock round your hair and I pull your head towards me, rest it on my chest, my hand cupping the curve of your jaw, willing you to stop struggling, to be still against me and let me hold you, keep you afloat, keep you here

in this precious world with its sun-flecked water and rushing noise. I hold you steady in the current, my body flat under yours, bearing your weight as water washes over my face. My eyes close.

Sudden lightness. All at once, the weight of my body falls away and I soar, rising clear of the river's dirty, snatching water. Below, I see my own body, gently rising and falling, arms limp, legs splayed, with you, lying on your back on top of me, your own human life-raft, your panicked face white and turned to the sky.

Coach in his speedboat, the motor racing, bounces like a skimming stone across the surface towards us. His face is grey with shock. He reaches over the side, tipping the boat, gropes for your billowing clothes, your arm and drags you up.

You hang there on the side, then flop, a caught fish, smack into the bottom of the boat. He, panting with exertion, pumps your arms, puts his mouth to your chill, dark lips in the kiss of life.

My body, inert now, moves rapidly away from him, lost in its own silent music, floating on downstream.

The boys watch from their boats. Chastened by the horror of it. Oars dangling. One, Jeremy or Roland perhaps, bends over the side and vomits noisily into the water and no one mocks him.

Far ahead, further downstream, Matt drifts ahead of me, face down, unseeing and unseen. His hair streaks in tendrils from his skull. His coat, bloated now by mud and water, spreads round him. A stream of blood trails from the gash where his head, driven forwards by the current, crashed against the rising stone arch of the bridge. The blood divides into streaks and finally disperses.

Now I am soaring, seeing the boats, the bridge, the river all shrink as I draw away from them, propelled with a great whoosh of energy into a swirling tunnel of darkness and, even as I fly down it, I think: *you told me*. This is what you said and I didn't believe you, *why did I never believe you, my love, when all you ever told me was the truth?*

A pinprick of light at the end of the spinning vortex grows like an exploding sun and we seem, both of us, the light and I, to rush always towards each other.

I hear nothing but I feel myself soaked in laughter. In peace. A figure then, emerging as a silhouette from the brightness, steps forward, arms open to embrace me. My father. A smile on his face, those kind features I've almost forgotten, his eyes gentle, his hair jet-black as if he were again young.

And even as I sense him, another figure emerges, smaller and more distant and I fly forward to greet you, weeping with joy, my arms reaching for you, my lovely girl, hearing your giggling and seeing your smile, your eyes on my face. Gracie, my love. Thank God. Don't leave me. Don't ever leave me again.

And you cling to me, your arms warm and tight round my waist and your hair soft and sweet-smelling and your eyes, when you tip back your head to look up at me, more radiant with love than I have ever seen on this earth.

'I can only visit, Mummy,' you say. 'I've got to go back.'

'Gracie.' It's all I can say. 'Please. Not yet.'

But even as I try to speak, to cling on to you, your words are lost and you fall backwards, away from me, out of the radiance and back into the darkness we call life.

EPILOGUE

Venice, eighteen years later

Something's changed. I sense it at once, as soon as you appear. You step with care up the worn stone steps from the *vaporetto* and emerge on the edge of the Piazza, your leather travel bag in hand. You are always beautiful, my love, but today your eyes are preoccupied, thoughtful, and I watch you from a distance, wondering why.

We meet often here in Venice, always at this time of year. In April, the city is still lazy with pleasure, relieved to have emerged once more from the chill and fog of winter but not yet hardened by the summer heat and the invading tourists.

It is still early in the day and the air blowing into Piazza San Marco from the Lagoon is fresh and salty. Waiters, crisp and self-important in formal dress, set out tables and metal chairs along its fringes. Shopkeepers clatter open their shutters. Street cleaners in green municipal coats sweep and sluice.

You walk slowly, your loose coat billowing, and send up swirling, wheeling arcs of pigeons. You are dwarfed by the great Basilica with its round arches and vast domes. Its gold façade glints in weak sunlight. You pass the foot of the red-brick Campanile, which shoots an eternal arrow to Heaven.

A waiter pulls a chair for you as you approach the café and his smile as you settle is part-chivalrous, part-flirtatious. You sit, your face lifted to the sun, looking back across the vast grandeur of

the Piazza. You seem a little lost. Your eyes stray to the waterfront where you've just disembarked and your expression is wistful.

You're waiting for someone, my love. I know you too well. Your thoughts are divided between me and this unknown someone, and at once I am both hopeful and afraid for you, as only a mother can be.

The waiter brings you a glass of ice-cold orange juice, freshly squeezed, and a brioche. You love them. You always did. No coffee though. That surprises me. You seldom start with the day without it.

You are more radiant today, my love, than I think I have ever seen you. Your skin glows. You are young and happy and very lovely. The waiter sees it too. He hovers, lingers too long when he returns to remove the empty plate, smiles as he asks if there's anything else you'd like.

When he leaves, you put on your sunglasses and tilt back your head, basking in the early sunshine. Waiting.

I am only here because you are thinking of me, of that strange, intense time we shared in Venice, all those years ago when you were a little girl. This place is special to you because you know you always find me here and now, I sense, you've brought someone else to share it.

I wait quietly with you, watching, grateful to be here again, to be with you.

I miss you. Sometimes it seems as if that is all I am now. An emotion. A depth of love for you that even death can't destroy. If I exist at all, it's only in these moments. Moments when you think of me. When you stop and pause in the midst of all your busyness, your helter-skelter of a life, and remember me and at once, here I am, right here, with you. Do you feel me now?

Richard gave you my jewellery when he cleared the house and for a long time, when you were a teenager and brim-full of feeling, you wore it and I was glad to be so often with you.

No one else can ever be your mother. Not even death can take that from me. And although no one else could ever replace Catherine, Ella loved you. She cared for you as if you really were her own. I'm grateful to her and to Richard too. The three of you learned to be happy and found joy in each other as a family, despite all the suffering that went before. Perhaps Angela was right. Perhaps you were always in God's hands. Perhaps He is taking care of you. Perhaps His universe is, after all, unfolding as it should. I still don't know.

And there he is. A man strides quickly across the Piazza, sending up clouds of scattered pigeons, hurrying as if he's late. A young man, perhaps three or four years older than you. He wears his hair long and his shirt and trousers need pressing but as he hurries across the stone flags towards you – as he catches sight of you there, languishing in the sun with your eyes closed – he smiles to himself and his eyes are so full of love that I forgive him the crumpled clothes and decide yes, this is a kind man, a good man and clearly he is in love with you, as any sensible young man should be.

He creeps round the table and approaches you stealthily from behind, cups his hands over your sunglasses and when you jump, he says: 'Guess who?'

And you laugh and say: 'The waiter?'

'What waiter?'

'The handsome one who's been keeping me company all this time. Where were you? I've almost finished.'

He pulls out a chair and sits beside you, leaning in to make his excuses, to kiss you and in the kiss everything is forgotten, everything is forgiven. I am still here with you, my love, but at a distance now. Which is exactly how it is supposed to be.

Later, when he finishes his coffee, he pulls back your chair and helps you to your feet with such care, such tenderness that my heart sings.

And then I see. Finally, I understand why you're so very lovely today. The soft swell is barely visible under your loose clothes but, as you walk, you touch a protective hand to your stomach and although it lasts only a moment, it's a gesture I recognise at once, from the time long ago that I was carrying you and so full of happiness I could barely contain it.

And that's when I realise that I have nothing to fear. I will not be erased by this man and your love for him. I will be remembered all over again, in your future child and your love for her and in the overwhelming joy she brings you, as powerful as the joy you gave me.

And you'll understand, finally, why I jumped without hesitation into the river that day and why, my love, you would too, to save your own daughter's life.

I don't know what happened to me when you were pulled alive from the river and I was not. I don't know what it meant. The flight into the light. The sense of peace and of finding my father.

I know what many people would say. And perhaps they're right. Perhaps it is just chemical. The fantasy of a desperate, fading mind as it fights to hold on to life. Perhaps I have now come to dust and exist nowhere but here, in your memory.

But today, as I follow the two of you across the Piazza and into the cool of the Basilica, into the gentle hush of this ancient, echoing building undulating with arches and domes, the sculptures and mosaics crafted by fingers that long ago ceased to move, where so many have worshipped who no longer have tongues to pray, I look into the dance of light across the stone flags and see the shadows shift and, just for a moment, I feel that all too familiar hope that something of us all is truly eternal, and that one day, when your time does come, you will fly, twisting and weightless, through a great swirling funnel of light and I will be waiting for you, my love, my own sweet child, my eyes radiant and my arms stretched wide in welcome.

A LETTER FROM JILL CHILDS

I want to say a huge thank you for choosing to read *Gracie's Secret*. If you enjoyed it, and want to keep up-to-date with all my latest releases, just sign up at the following link. Your email address will never be shared and you can unsubscribe at any time.

www.bookouture.com/jill-childs

I started writing this book when one of my twin girls – she was three at the time – started asking me tough questions. *Will you die, Mummy? If you do, will you miss me? Will I ever see you again?*

I always try to tell the girls the truth but in this case, I struggled. Yes, I will die – hopefully not for a long time. And what will become of me afterwards? Well, I'm really not sure. Not very reassuring answers for a small child.

But her questions also rekindled an idea I'd had years earlier. It was inspired by accounts of near-death experiences from young children. I found the stories fascinating. Sometimes children accurately described events taking place when they were clinically dead or described meeting people who'd long since died.

Was it possible they briefly visited another world, something like Heaven? Or did it all have a rational, medical explanation? I didn't know what to think. And I wondered how I'd cope if one of my children woke from a coma with an equally extraordinary tale to tell.

And, like many parents, I was caught off guard by how utterly overwhelming my love was for my children. Yes, I would run into

a burning building if they were inside. Or lift a truck so they could crawl free. I just would. So what else might a besotted mother be willing to do to protect or save her child? It was out of all this that *Gracie's Secret* was born.

I hope you loved *Gracie's Secret*. If you did, I would be very grateful if you could write a review. I'd love to hear what you think and it makes such a difference in helping new readers discover my books for the first time.

I love hearing from my readers. You can get in touch on my Facebook page or on Twitter. Thank you!

All best wishes to you and yours,
Jill Childs

 @author_jill

ACKNOWLEDGEMENTS

Thank you to my wonderful editor, Kathryn Taussig, and all the team at Bookouture.

Thank you to my brilliant agent, Judith Murdoch: the best in the business.

And thank you, as always, to Nick and the rest of my family for all your love and support.